Political Economy and the Rise of Capitalism

Political Economy and the Rise of Capitalism

A Reinterpretation

David McNally

University of California Press

Berkeley · Los Angeles · London

University of California Press
Berkeley and Los Angeles, California

University of California Press, Ltd.
London, England

© 1988 by
The Regents of the University of California

Library of Congress Cataloging-in-Publication Data

McNally, David.
    Political economy and the rise of capitalism: a
    reinterpretation
    David McNally.
      p.   cm.
    Originates from author's doctoral dissertation,
    completed in 1983.
    Bibliography: p.
    ISBN 0-520-06133-0 (alk. paper)
    1. Classical school of economics.   2.
    Capitalism.
        I.   Title.
HB94.M37   1988
330.12′2—dc19   88-3185
                                                   CIP

Printed in the United States of America

1 2 3 4 5 6 7 8 9

In memory of Kathy

Contents

Acknowledgments

Many people have shared in the labours through which this book came to be written. I would like to acknowledge the generous support of Louis Lefeber, Ellen Meiksins Wood, Nick Rogers, and Neal Wood during and since my work on the doctoral dissertation, completed in 1983, from which this book originates. I would like to thank James Moore and Robert Brenner for their comments on this work and their abiding interest in the larger body of research of which it is a part. Thanks are due also to the staffs of the library systems at York University, the University of Toronto, the Goldsmiths Reading Room at the University of London, and the Bibliothèque Nationale in Paris. Ruth Griffin of Glendon College typed parts of the manuscript with her customary efficiency and good humour. Financial support has been provided at various stages by the Social Sciences and Humanities Research Council of Canada. I wish also to acknowledge the assistance of Gina McIntosh with translations from French sources. All the members of my immediate and extended family must be thanked for their support over the years in which this project, in all its forms, was undertaken, but Adam and Joanne deserve special mention. Finally, this book is dedicated to the memory of my sister, Kathy. Those who knew her will know why.

Introduction

This book challenges the conventional wisdom about classical political economy and the rise of capitalism. It is written in the conviction that modern interpretations of political economy have suffered terribly from acceptance of the prevailing liberal view of the origins and development of capitalist society. By the liberal account, capitalism emerged out of the centuries-old competitive activities of merchants and manufacturers in rational pursuit of their individual economic self-interest. Over time, this account claims, the persistent activity of these classes developed new forms of wealth and productive resources and new intellectual and cultural habits, which eroded the existing structure of society. The rise of capitalism is thus explained in terms of the rise to prominence of the most productive, rational, and progressive social groups—merchants and manufacturers. Not surprisingly, classical political economy came to be seen as an intellectual reflection of the ascendence of merchants and manufacturers and as a theoretical justification of their interests and activities.

This book argues that capitalism was the product of an immense transformation in the social relationships of landed society and that this fact is crucial to understanding the development of classical political economy. Without a radical transformation of the agrarian economy, the activities of merchants and manufacturers would have remained strictly confined. By no inexorable logic of their own were mercantile and industrial activities capable of fundamentally transforming the essential relations of precapitalist society. Rather, the changes in agrarian economy, which drove rural producers from their land, forced them onto the labour market as wage labourers for their means of subsistence, and refashioned farming as an economic activity based upon the production of agricultural commodities for profit on the market, established the essential relations of modern capitalism. In what follows, these processes are described in terms of the emergence of *agrarian capitalism*.[1]

I further argue that the classical economists of the seventeenth and eighteenth centuries were generally aware of the crucial importance of agrarian social change, that such change figured centrally in their account of the emergence of modern society, and that they conceived of capitalist society in largely agrarian terms. Classical political economy thus represents a social and economic theory of agrarian capitalism. The greatest political economists of the period constructed a comprehensive theory of state and society in which the essential relations of economic life were those between landlords, capitalist employers, and wage labourers. Agricultural production was for them the most fundamental sphere of the emerging capitalist economy; they generally conceived commercial and industrial activity as subordinate (for economic, political, and moral reasons) to production on the land.

My argument thus challenges the traditional view that the classical political economists constructed an economic liberalism designed to justify the individualist and self-seeking activities of merchants and manufacturers in a market society. According to the traditional line of thought, political economy developed a theoretical defence of commercial and industrial capitalism which contained three interrelated elements. First, it conceived of the capitalist market as a mechanism which automatically harmonized the selfish actions of individuals without intervention by the state. Second, it saw an expansion of national wealth as the automatic result of a system of market exchange which harnessed selfish individual passions, created a network of economic interdependence (organized in a social division of labour), and rewarded industry and frugality. Third, it presented the self-seeking economic behaviour of merchants and manufacturers, through the wonder of competitive markets, as beneficial to society as a whole and as the most enlightened basis upon which to found the economic policies of the state. For all these reasons, the traditional line argued that classical political economy constituted an ideological defence of the modern system of industrial capitalism.

Adam Smith is widely identified as the dominant figure in the development of economic liberalism. In his writings more than those of any other political economist, the traditional view finds a sustained theoretical rationalization for industrial capitalism and its representatives. Harold Laski writes, for example, in *The Rise of European Liberalism* that

> With Adam Smith, the business man is given his letters of credit. Liberalism has now a fully analysed economic mission. Let the business man but free himself, and, thereby, he frees mankind. . . . With Adam Smith the practical maxims of business enterprise achieved the status of a theology.[2]

Consistent with this approach, another commentator has argued that the central achievement of Adam Smith was to "justify the activities of embryonic industrialists" through the elaboration of "an economic analysis of civil society."[3] Likewise, Eric Roll in *A History of Economic Thought* has claimed that Smith "gave theoretical expression to the essential interests of the business class"; he maintains that Smith was merely building upon an intellectual justification for industrial capitalism which had been in process of construction for nearly two centuries:

> In the eighteenth century the development of modern industrial capitalism was greatly accelerated. Its theory, embodied in the works of the classical economists, comes to maturity in the period of forty years that separates Smith's *Wealth of Nations* and Ricardo's *Principles*. But its roots reach back almost two centuries.[4]

According to this view, the development of economic liberalism, advanced most clearly by Adam Smith, was a theoretical expression of developments in the economic and social spheres—the rise of industrial captialism—and an intellectual justification for the activities and practices of that class most closely associated with this process, the industrial bourgeoisie. Indeed, one modern commentator has begun a study of Smith on the "axiomatic premise" that "capitalism is an embodiment of Smithian principles."[5]

The present study takes issue with this argument. In the chapters which follow I shall argue not only that classical political economy prior to Ricardo did not represent the interests of industrial capi-

talists but also that the classical political economists up to and including Smith were strongly critical of the values and practices associated with merchants and manufacturers.[6] Much as they may have
approved of certain important economic effects of division of labour
and market exchange, the greatest classical economists did not seek
to ground political life in the activities of self-seeking individuals.
Nor did they seek to advance a justification for industrial capitalism.
On the contrary, the pre-Ricardian economists betrayed a definite
bias in favour of the agrarian, not commercial or industrial, classes
and a profound fear that the "commercial spirit" of their age might
undermine the agrarian foundations of society and corrupt political
life by replacing the classical goal of a state operating according to
public interest and public virtue with a polity ravaged by the pursuit
of private interest.

On the basis of these concerns and of their analysis of those processes which were transforming traditional rural economy, the political economists examined in this study developed a theory of agrarian
capitalism. At one level, their investigations constituted important
attempts to comprehend the most significant social and economic
changes of their age. The industrial revolution was not a fact of life
before the publication of Smith's *Wealth of Nations*. The primary
focus for these writers was thus agrarian, not industrial, change. At
another level, their theories of agrarian capitalism contained an important element of prescription. Concerned to reap the beneficial
effects of economic growth while resisting moral and intellectual corruption and the decline of civic virtues, they looked forward to the
development of a capitalist agriculture which could sustain a state
uncontaminated by private interests. Their economic theory of agrarian capitalism thus served both a moral and political purpose—
which is to say that it was *political* economy in the fullest sense.

There were, however, profound differences between the conceptions of the relationship of the state and agrarian capitalism which
characterized British and French political economy. As I shall demonstrate, British political economy developed from the Commonwealth tradition of political thought, which conceived of the state
largely in terms of the self-government of landed gentlemen. By contrast, French political economists—especially the Physiocrats—
thought in terms of a centralized absolute monarchy constituted over
and above civil society as a bulwark against the influence of particu-

lar interests upon the state. These differences, as I shall show, correspond to the quite different paths of social and economic development taken by Britain and France in the early modern period.

Despite these differences with respect to the nature of the state, the British and French political economists alike advanced a theory of and program for agrarian capitalism. They sought to direct the processes of capitalist development to preserve the agrarian basis of society and, in so doing, prevent excessive influence upon economic development and political policy by commercial and industrial interests. For the Physiocrats, such an objective required that the state shape social and economic development. For Adam Smith, however, such development required merely that the state break the manipulative activities of merchants and manufacturers and guarantee an institutional order in which no section of society would have any form of monopoly power. But such a state could not be based upon commercial or industrial interests, since these were incompatible with those of the public; instead it would have to rest largely upon enlightened, public-spirited representatives of the landowning class.

Eighteenth-century Britain and France were—albeit with major divergences—societies in transition from feudalism to industrial capitalism. The characteristics of the transitional society of eighteenth-century Britain we will describe as agrarian capitalism. France, labouring under the creaking structures of feudal absolutism, had not experienced the breakthrough to agricultural improvement and economic growth which had occurred in England. Yet the frame of reference for her most important political economists was without doubt the system of agrarian capitalism which had emerged in Britain. No major thinker in Britain or France had yet grasped that economic development based on capitalist farming (which largely separated the direct producers from the land and transformed them into wage labourers) led in the direction of industrial capitalism. Subsequent attempts to depict these earlier theorists as prophets of nineteenth- and twentieth-century capitalism have seriously distorted our understanding of their theoretical efforts and of the society they attempted to understand and influence. As I shall show in the course of this work, the classical political economists of the seventeenth and eighteenth centuries developed an agrarian-based model of the emerging capitalist economy, adhered to values markedly different from those generally associated with industrial capi-

talism, and accorded priority to the formulation of just and benevolent policies which could guide civic-minded statesmen in the
pursuit of wealth, power, prosperity, and justice. I shall conclude by
arguing, however, that their acceptance of the basic social relations
of capitalism undermines any attempt to employ the work of these
theorists as the basis of a concrete and comprehensive critique of
modern industrial capitalism.

From Feudalism to Capitalism: The Historical Context of Classical Political Economy

Classical political economy, wrote Karl Marx, "begins at the end of the seventeenth century with Petty and Boisguillebert."[1] In making this statement, Marx not only identified the historical period of the emergence of classical political economy, he also implicitly identified the countries of its origin—England and France, the respective homes of Petty and Boisguilbert.[2] Classical political economy developed in England and France during the decisive phase of the "great transformation" of Europe which ushered in capitalist society. In one sense, classical political economy was an intellectual product of this transformation. In another sense, as we shall see, classical economics was also an active element in this historic transition; it represented in part an attempt to theorize the inner dynamics of these changes in order to shape and direct them.

Although a certain commonality of problems associated with the transition from feudal to capitalist society provoked the theoretical efforts of the classical political economists, the divergent paths of English and French development during the seventeenth and eighteenth centuries forced theorists in these two countries to conceive the problems of economic development in markedly different ways. In England, the emergence of agrarian capitalism during this period made analysis of agricultural production—and especially the problem of increasing the agricultural surplus—the central focus of British political economists. In France, however, the rise of the absolute monarchy (and its appropriation of a substantial share of the economic surplus) placed the issue of the relationship between state and society in the forefront of the concerns of French economic writers. Proposals to reform the rural social structure were often central to their analysis of state and society. But French agriculture failed to make the breakthrough to self-sustaining growth experienced by England; and this crucial fact largely accounts for the different emphases of French and English political economists. This chapter sketches the basic patterns of social development in England and France to illuminate the background for the theoretical efforts of English and French political economists in the seventeenth and eighteenth centuries.

THE CRISIS OF EUROPEAN FEUDALISM

The view that late medieval feudalism experienced a general social crisis appears to date from Marc Bloch's *French Rural History,* published in 1931. Since the 1950s, economic historians have generally identified the fourteenth century as a period of feudal crisis. Indeed, most would accept the view of Michael Postan that western Europe underwent an "agricultural crisis of the fourteenth and fifteenth centuries."[3] It is further agreed that this sustained crisis was preceded by a prolonged expansion of the feudal mode of production.

The basic historical sequence seems clear enough. After the year 800, European feudalism underwent a slow, sometimes sporadic, but nevertheless steady growth. In the middle of the eleventh century a sharp and qualitatively new upswing began. Bloch quite accurately described this period as the beginning of the "second feudal age."[4] At the heart of this process of growth was horizontal expansion—the reclamation of previously uncultivated land. The period from 1150 to 1240 in particular saw a major expansion of ancient villages and the creation of new ones. Reclamation appears to have begun as a growing population pressed against the available cultivated land. This movement of reclamation and colonization began to exhaust itself in the middle of the thirteenth century. Reclamation encouraged further population growth and extended onto increasingly marginal lands. The result was a classic case of diminishing returns: as decreasingly fertile land was brought under cultivation, productivity and per capita yields fell.[5] Eventually, the returns on the investment involved in reclamation could no longer be justified. Nonetheless, population continued to rise for a considerable period after declining productivity had put an end to reclamation. As a result, the land-labour ratio fell as productivity slumped. The inevitable result was a crisis of subsistence.

The fourteenth century experienced a catastrophic decline in the level of the European population. Famines were legion throughout the century. Moreover, an extended period of substandard diet probably increased the susceptibility of the population to contagious disease. Certainly the dimensions of the Black Death must have been influenced by the deterioration of dietary standards. So disastrous was the rise in mortality that the population of Europe appears to have been halved between 1315 and 1380. Moreover, this was a crisis which persisted. The evidence suggests that the European economy experienced two full centuries of stagnation and decline. Stagnation set in during the middle of the thirteenth century. The crisis and decline began in the first quarter of the fourteenth century. From then on, most of Europe experienced a downward spiral until the middle of the fifteenth century. In other words, during the period from 1240 to 1440 European feudalism knew little other than stagnation and decline; and for over a century (from 1320 to 1440) it underwent a major contraction.[6] Furthermore, so deep-rooted was this crisis of late medieval feudalism that it carried over in much of Europe into the seventeenth century (in some cases following a half century or so of recovery in the sixteenth century).

The feudal mode of production contained no self-correcting mechanisms for resolving this crisis because of the surplus-extractive relations which characterize feudalism. Feudal lords, as Robert Brenner has pointed out, did not have the option of increasing their incomes through capital investments that would raise the productivity of peasant labour and enable peasants to produce more output during their surplus labour time. Since feudal peasants possessed their own means of production, their economic reproduction was in a sense independent of the surplus-extractive demands of the lords. The production of a surplus product required extraeconomic compulsion over a labour process which the lords did not control or direct. To invest in improving the technical basis of this labour process would have been an extremely risky undertaking. Furthermore, because neither lords nor peasants depended upon access to the market for their subsistence (although they might well enter into market transactions by choice) they were under no direct economic pressure to produce competitively. As a result, the drive to innovate in order to raise productivity was absent as a general dynamic of feudal economy; the market did not impose this necessity upon peasants or lords, and the organization of the labour process was a disincentive to innovative investments by the lords.[7]

The pressure on seigneurial incomes created by crisis did not therefore lead to investment and development. On the contrary, the efforts of lords to raise their depressed incomes further exacerbated the crisis. They tried to increase their incomes by squeezing the living standards of their peasants, primarily through increased rents or labour services. Continual pressure from the lords tended, however, to prevent the peasants from accumulating a surplus, that is, an amount above their own subsistence needs which would be adequate to replenish the soil and maintain or improve its fertility. The response of lords to crisis thus led to a decline in the productive powers of the most basic means of production in the feudal economy—the land.

Under such circumstances the main avenue by which feudal lords could increase their incomes was *distributional* struggles. Since the feudal mode of production lacked a developmental dynamism of the sort which characterizes capitalism, lords did not generally have the option of raising their incomes by investments designed to increase the total social output. If a lord were to increase his distributive share, he had to do so at the expense of his peasants or of other lords (the latter redistribution of income requiring war). Crisis, which heightened the downward pressure on incomes, thus tended to unleash bitter class and intraclass struggles. As we shall see, it was the specific, historic outcome of those struggles which shaped the general direction of social and economic development in England and France. In England, the ability of a section of the peasantry to improve its situation was critical to the development of agrarian capitalism and in the long term to self-sustaining economic growth. In France, by contrast, the ability of the monarchy to build an absolutist state as the last line of defence of noble power imposed a system of surplus extraction which made sustained economic recovery virtually impossible.

ENGLAND: TOWARDS AGRARIAN CAPITALISM

Following the decimation of the labouring population during the Black Death, the English aristocracy launched an offensive to compensate for the fall in noble incomes brought about by the reduction in their workforce. One analyst has estimated that manorial income in the 1370s was only 10 percent below its level of the 1340s. Since the population had fallen by at least 30 percent, there must have been a substantial increase in the level of exploitation of the English peasantry. This increased exploitation stimulated widespread peasant resistance and led ultimately to the massive peasant uprising of 1381. The rebellion of 1381 was directed against the lords' attempts to increase money rents and to maintain village assessments for the poll tax despite the decline in population. Although the rebellion failed to achieve its objectives, on-going peasant resistance did win substantial economic concessions from the lords.[8] In these circumstances, the conditions of agricultural labourers improved markedly. In fact, farm labourers experienced a 50 percent rise in wages during the period 1380–1399 relative to the period 1340–1359. Overall, there was a shift of national income away from lords and towards peasants and labourers.[9]

Under these conditions, the situation of the peasantry improved substantially. Incomes rose, obligations were lightened, and a growing amount of land was let out to peasants on a copyhold basis, which was accepted increasingly as legal tenure under common law. As a result of the breakup and leasing out of the big demesnes, the size of manors contracted and on average peasant holdings grew. The fifteenth century, therefore, has correctly been called "the golden age of the English peasantry."[10] At the same time that they were obtaining increased security of tenure, English peasants were winning stable, long-term leases (often as long as ninety-nine years) and, moreover, prices for agricultural products were rising. Between 1500 and 1640, for example, food prices in England rose by 600 percent. With rising prices for their marketed produce and relatively stable money rents, many richer peasants began to accumulate a growing surplus above their own costs of production (including subsistence and rent). The drive to small-scale accumulation and expansion of holdings followed logically from the ever-present threat of contraction in bad years. Petty investment and accumulation insured against the future; a system of simple reproduction (where the basic drive is to maintain the peasant farm, not endlessly to expand it) does not reproduce itself evenly over the years but, rather, through a cycle of small-scale expansion and contraction which may always be halted by a profound secular crisis. In the unique economic circumstances of the fifteenth and sixteenth centuries, it was possible for petty accumulation to become a remarkably sustained process, at least for the better-off peasants. These peasants were able to buy up small pieces of land and invest in livestock (the most important source of fertilizer) and improved implements. While increased rents did take a share of the growing output, rents generally failed to keep pace with the level of increases in the prices of farm produce. Furthermore, the gap between agricultural and industrial prices also moved in favour of the agricultural producers, thus reducing their relative costs of production.[11] Thus, the richer peasants producing for the market were in a uniquely favourable situation—characterized by rising prices, falling relative costs of production, and stable or declining real rents—to use a share of their rising income for investments that would expand their base of production, raise the productivity of land, and increase the surplus product in their possession. In this way, the diversion of income from lords to peasants contributed to petty accumulation and a steady rise in agricultural productivity.

This expansion of petty commodity production enabled the richer peasants to emerge as independent commodity producers, increasing the productive resources at their disposal. Buying land from poor, indebted peasants, the top stratum of peasant society emerged as a group of petty commodity producers sometimes called *yeomen*.[12] The yeomanry has been described as "a group of ambitious, aggressive small capitalists."[13] The term "capitalists" must be used with enormous care since, as I have suggested, a cycle of petty accumulation could emerge within the logic of the feudal mode of production itself and need not presuppose a new, capitalist economic logic. Nevertheless, within an economic system reshaped by profound crisis and a changed balance of class relations, the yeomanry emerged as a small but dynamic rural middle stratum, exploiting its advantage throughout the fifteenth and sixteenth centuries to improve its social and economic position. Thus, it was among the yeomen that enclosure first began. The early enclosure movement involved the formation of compact fields out of fragmented strips of land, the redivision and reallotment of land, or what Tawney called "a spatial rearrangement of property."[14] The bulk of enclosure by peasants was by agreement. Sometimes it also involved a collective decision by the villagers to divide the commons; in other cases it involved simply the exchanging or buying of land.

Ironically, it was sections of the landlord class which reaped the greatest long-run benefits from the early enclosure movement and the rise of the yeomanry from the ranks of the English peasantry. One effect of the social differentiation of the peasantry was the dispossession of many small tenants and the creation of a new class of rural poor. By the early seventeenth century, both an indigenous gentry and an indigenous proletariat had emerged from the newly differentiated village community. Its traditional solidarity undermined, the village was now increasingly divided between rich and poor. As one historian has stated, "It was the consolidation of the yeoman oligarchies that decisively changed the realities of village life."[15] This transformation of the village community opened up opportunities for those gentry and noble lords who saw a gain to be made through enclosure on a large scale. As a result, it was these enclosing and improving landlords who were, in the long run, to be the main beneficiaries of those economic processes which enriched the upper section of the peasantry and sealed the fate of the traditional peasant village community.[16] And it was these members of the landed class who were the main agents in the emergence of a full-fledged system of agrarian capitalism.

From the late sixteenth century onwards, sections of the gentry took advantage of the weakened status of the village community to launch a sustained offensive against the rights of the small tenants. Increasing numbers of lords attacked peasant rights, trying to halt the decline in their incomes as their more or less stable revenues clashed with ever-rising prices. They attempted to break the grip of copyhold agreements and to turn them into forms of leasehold renewable only at the will of the lord. They drove up rents every year or every few years ("rack-renting"). They attempted to supplement income by increasing fines and enforcing obsolete obligations. And, most important, they undertook to enclose and reorganize lands—a path which tended to raise the productivity of the land by 50 percent on average. Contrary to older views which saw the eighteenth century as the great age of enclosure, modern research suggests that by 1700 three-quarters of all enclosure had already taken place. As a result of this multifaceted offensive, rents doubled during the half century from 1590 to 1640.[17]

The landlords' offensive often involved a shift to large-scale capitalist farming in the form of pasturage as well as new crops and rotation patterns which brought more land into productive use year in and year out.[18] At the same time, the farm was being transformed into an economic unit specializing in a limited number of productive activities (especially of foodstuffs) geared to the market. More and more, the market dictated the internal organization of the English farm: prices, profits, wages, and rents were increasingly determined by market conditions. Having enclosed and consolidated their estates, a growing number of landowners rented them out to prosperous tenant farmers who hired rural labourers, made substantial annual investments, and paid large rents. Thus emerged the classic capitalist structure of English farming characterized by the tripartite relationship of landlord, capitalist tenant, and wage labourer in which the farm became a specialized productive unit geared to the market. The landowner was now a new economic agent, one whose wealth depended upon the surplus product of capitalist agriculture. This transformed ruling class now sought to ensure that the property rights and political "liberties" of landowners would be protected by (and from) the state.

The processes described above occurred at a time when the landed classes were growing enormously—they tripled in size between 1536 and 1636—and in which there was a major shift of land into the hands of the gentry. In the century after the seizure of church lands by the Crown during the religious Reformation almost one-quarter of the land of England was sold on the market at a cost of six and one-half million pounds. At the same time, there appears also to have been a flow of land from the aristocracy to the gentry between 1559 and 1602.[19] The increasing social importance of the gentry was expressed in political terms. During the second half of the sixteenth century, the House of Commons grew from three hundred to five hundred members, while the gentry's component of the House increased from 50 to 75 percent.

Following the rise of faction and intraclass conflict that led to the virtual breakdown of government during the middle of the fifteenth century, Tudor governments encouraged the expansion of the power of the gentry, in order to undermine the local power of large nobles. A stable and—at least initially—self-sufficient monarchy was constructed by the early Tudors, who used increased parliamentary representation and low levels of taxation to win the gentry's support as an important counterbalance to the traditional power of the upper nobility. The Tudor monarchy, therefore, relied increasingly on new sources of landed wealth and political power in exchange for concessions to the gentry, such as low taxation and increased powers at the local level, particularly in the administration of justice. The result was a significant weakening of the independent powers of the Crown, a strengthening of the political power of the landed proprietors, and a departure from the absolutist path.[20] By the beginning of the seventeenth century, then, England was undergoing the transition to agrarian capitalism in the context of a nonabsolutist state which relied upon the participation of broad sections of the landed classes in the affairs of state. Participation of landed gentlemen in the exercise of political power was increasingly seen as a right which flowed directly from ownership of property. Such "liberties" were considered inherent rights of property. Thus, any attack on the participation of landed gentlemen in affairs of state was seen as an attack on property itself.

The Stuart reaction of 1603–1640 was a response to the dispersion of political power in England and an attempt to reconstruct centralized monarchical power. In part, the English Revolution can be seen as a rebellion by landed gentlemen against this tendency towards absolutism and in defence of rights that had been won during the previous one hundred fifty years. To be sure, significant sections of the landed class perceived rebellion against the Crown to be a greater danger than absolutism, since it might ignite a rebellion of the lower orders against authority and property. But it seems fair to say that, although many opposed the road of revolution, the majority of landed gentlemen were markedly hostile to absolutism. Thus this "bourgeois revolution" was a revolution against centralized state power. This characteristic of the English Revolution is perfectly explicable if we see it as an attempt by agrarian capitalist landowners to preserve and protect their property rights, their newfound forms of surplus extraction (and these very surpluses themselves), and their right to participate in the "committee of landlords" ruling England at the local level and increasingly shaping events at the national level (and which they perceived as vital to protect their property and their rents).[21]

The "revolution from below" unleashed by the English Civil War did indeed pose a threat to the traditional privileges of men of property. The popular mobilizations in London and other cities, the formation of Parliament's New Model Army, the abolition of monarchy and the House of Lords, and the execution of the king all contributed to an often-millenarian sense that the old order was finished and that it would be replaced by a democratic and highly egalitarian form of society.[22] Faced with such an upsurge of popular radicalism and an army drawn from the lower orders which opposed a return of the traditional social order, the bulk of the propertied class chose to support a restoration of monarchy and the House of Lords. Even then, however, when Charles II, who took the throne in 1660, attempted to pursue an absolutist policy, he incited the great wave of Whig agitation of 1679–1681 against the court, which culminated in 1688 in the overthrow of his successor, James II.[23]

The drive against the independent powers of the monarchy became even more powerful following the Glorious Revolution of 1688. Despite the fact that 1688 was an event carefully orchestrated to avoid renewed rebellion from below, and despite the fact that the Bill of Rights of 1689 did not go nearly as far as the Whig radicals desired, the bill reinforced the trends towards limiting the powers of the Crown by making extraparliamentary taxation illegal; by ensuring that there should be no standing army without parliamentary approval; and by abolishing the Crown's suspending and dispensing powers.[24] The Triennial Act of 1694 guaranteed regular parliaments and abolished the royal prerogative of summoning and dissolving Parliament. Finally, the Act of Settlement of 1701, subtitled "an act for the further limitation of the Crown and the better preserving the liberties of the subjects," provided that the tenure of judges would be permanent, subject only to good behaviour, and not dependent upon the Crown.

Having achieved a state responsive to their interests, after 1688 the large landowners moved with a passion to enclose and concentrate holdings. Between 1690 and 1750 there was a major shift of property away from the peasantry and lesser gentry and towards the large landowners. The century after 1690 experienced a dramatic decline in the percentage of land held in farms of less than one hundred acres and a sharp rise in the share held by farms of one hundred acres or more. This shift in land ownership involved a doubling of rents, in part a result of the increased productivity of the land brought about by enclosure and improvement.[25] For financial considerations such as these, landlords turned to enclosure on a vast scale. Having taken the reins of government into their hands, they used acts of Parliament to legalize expropriation that has been accurately described as a "massive violence exercised by the upper classes against the lower."[26] In 1710 the first private enclosure act was presented to Parliament. Between 1720 and 1750, 100 such acts were passed. Some 139 acts followed in the subsequent decade. Another 900 acts were passed between 1760 and 1779. The movement reached its peak between 1793 and 1815, when 2,000 acts of enclosure were approved by Parliament. As a result, over the eighteenth and nineteenth centuries more than 6.5 million acres of common fields and commons were enclosed by acts of Parliament—an area equal to nearly 20 percent of the total land of England. In some areas, the amount of land enclosed went as high as 50 percent of the total. The change was thus massive—and, for the small tenant, catastrophic.[27]

Modern historical research has demonstrated the shortcomings of the view that enclosure directly provided the labour force for urban industrialization. In reality, the majority of those who suffered at the hands of enclosure appear to have stayed on the land. This fact has led some writers to claim that the dislocation caused by enclosure has been exaggerated; they have asserted that enclosure and innovation provided work for those members of rural society who no longer held sufficient land or access to land (for example, commons) to support themselves. In this interpretation, enclosure was a largely technical process which benefited most members of the village community through higher levels of output and new prospects for employment.[28] Such an approach so minimizes the social consequences of enclosure as to distort the whole process. Whatever the shortcomings of some Marxist interpretations of the relationship between enclosure and industrialization, the great strength of the Marxist approach has been to see in enclosure a crucial element in a process of social transformation in which the fabric of traditional rural society was rent asunder and a new social structure, based on a propertyless proletariat, created. Enclosure was, after all, as W. G. Hoskins described its effects on the Leicestershire village of Wigston, "the destruction of an entire society with its own economy and traditions, its own way of living and its own culture."[29]

What took place in England during the sixteenth, seventeenth, and eighteenth centuries is what Marx described as the "primitive accumulation of capital." In a nutshell, primitive accumulation refers to those historical processes by which direct producers were separated from the land and transformed into "free" wage labourers.

The freedom of wage labour was for Marx a two-sided phenomenon: on the one hand these workers were "freed" from the land—they neither owned nor controlled means of production adequate to their own subsistence; on the other hand, they were juridically "free" individuals able to enter voluntarily into an agreement to work for an employer. At the heart of primitive accumulation, therefore, is "the historical process of divorcing the producers from the means of production." The separation of labourers from means of production is the crucial historical process which makes capitalist accumulation and production possible. Primitive accumulation creates the unique commodity, labour power that is bought and sold on the market, which distinguishes capitalism from all other modes of production. The creation of a propertyless class of wage labourers establishes the social relationship within which capitalist exploitation and accumulation can develop. The great strength of Marx's analysis was to recognize the critical importance of this social relationship and to grasp the historical fact that "the expropriation of the agricultural producer, of the peasant, from the soil is the basis of the whole process."[30]

However, those most directly affected by enclosure did not, as many early Marxists believed, move in large numbers to urban centers to labour in the workshops of the industrial revolution. Their rural existence was nonetheless radically altered; they became the *rural proletariat* of the farms and village industries. What many Marxists have failed fully to appreciate is that agrarian capitalism formed the connecting link between primitive accumulation and industrial capitalism. By *agrarian capitalism* we refer to that situation in which large farms (usually of two hundred acres or more) were leased out to prosperous tenant farmers who hired wage labourers and produced an agricultural product for sale on a market. The surplus above costs of production (including wages) was then divided between the farmer and the landowner in the forms of profit and capitalist ground rent (as Marx called it). Primitive accumulation thus contributed directly to the creation of a rural proletariat and a system of agrarian capitalism.

Having said this, we must emphasize that the development of agrarian capitalism was neither as direct or unambiguous a process as the economic data alone might suggest. The emergence of agrarian capitalism was constrained by the traditional force of customary rights, to which the small tenant and labourer clung tenaciously. In a very real sense, the full flowering of agrarian capitalism in the eighteenth century represents the victory of property rights over customary rights; but the complete victory of property over custom took place only over centuries in the course of often bitter social conflicts. Agrarian capitalism was anything but a pure social species which leaped fully formed onto the stage of history. On the contrary, it emerged in a hesitant—but nonetheless forcible and sometimes violent—step-by-step process in which it was invariably coloured by the traditional society it was leaving behind.[31]

Proletarianization occurred in a context in which customary rights continued to play an important part in the lives of the direct producers. In the sixteenth and seventeenth centuries in particular, perquisites and customary rights on common lands constituted a significant supplement to the wage. Such rights and perquisites to some extent kept the village labourer from complete subjection to the vagaries of the labour market. For this reason, village labourers objected not so much to their status as wage labourers but rather to those measures which threatened to eliminate such customary rights. This objection is only natural, given that the disappearance of such rights represented their complete proletarianization, the restriction of their sources of livelihood to the price which they could command for their ability to work. It represented, in other words, their total subordination to the rhythms of the capitalist labour market. The parliamentary enclosure in the eighteenth century, therefore, centred as it was on common lands, truly completed the process of proletarianization. For this reason we can echo E. P. Thompson's statement that in the eighteenth century "agrarian capitalism came fully into its inheritance." For it was then that the conflict between property rights and customary rights was resolved decisively in favour of the former.[32]

The growth of large farms and the displacement of small tenants also expanded the home market. The decline of self-sufficient family farming and the growth of specialization forced capitalist farmers, labourers, and landowners to turn to the market to meet their needs for producer and consumer goods. In large measure, the rural proletariat (including semiproletarianized cottagers and the like) provided the labour force for those industries which grew up in response to the demands of England's growing domestic market. In active farming areas, local industries grew up which were devoted primarily to the production of farm and domestic products. Lace-making, straw-plaiting, nailing, needle-production, paper-making, and framework-knitting were the most common industries in such areas. The most significant economic growth took place in less arable areas, such as the Midlands. Here tanners, leatherworkers, fullers, weavers, shearers, clothworkers, and ironmongers dominated the industrial scene.[33] During the sixteenth century, increasing numbers of yeomen and small farmers were drawn into industries such as these. And in the seventeenth and eighteenth centuries, displaced peasants often found employment in these trades as agricultural specialization increased demand for these industrial products. The decline of rural self-sufficiency thus increased the industrial market. In this way, the growth of agrarian capitalism accelerated the growth of an industrial market.

The growth of agricultural productivity, especially during the eighteenth century, played a decisive role in expanding the home market and more than doubling corn exports in the first sixty years of the century. Unprocessed agricultural products as a share of English manufactured exports rose from 4.6 percent in 1700 to 11.8 percent in 1725 and to 22.2 percent by 1750. During this same period, there was no significant increase in industrial exports. As output grew, corn prices fell. In fact, by the 1730s and 1740s, prices were 25 to 33 percent lower than the average for the 1660s. Lower prices for corn contributed to a rise in the real wage and thus brought about an increase in the demand by labourers for domestic manufactures. The terms of trade also moved in favour of manufacturers and gave a boost to the industrial sector, in relatively lower costs of production. By the 1750s, there was a permanent flow of population from the countryside to urban centres like London, Birmingham, Sheffield, and Manchester. Agricultural improvement was thus contributing to the growth of an urban proletariat.[34]

At a certain point—recent research has suggested the 1760s—the expansion of markets and high labour costs induced manufacturers to introduce labour-saving machinery of production.[35] And, once introduced, machinery became central to the process of accumulation. Technological innovation designed to reduce costs became an integral part of capitalist competition. Industrial capitalism—what Marx called "the specifically capitalist mode of production," in which the machinery of production is continually revolutionized in an effort to raise productivity[36]—thus became the order of the day. England had crossed the frontier into the age of modern capitalism. Agrarian capitalism had, however, been the vessel of its crossing.

FRANCE: THE RISE OF ABSOLUTISM

The French nobility was confronted with the problem of declining rents from the middle of the thirteenth century onwards. Peasants enjoyed significant success in struggles over the distribution of output and over access to common woods, pastures, and fisheries; the result was shrinking seigneurial incomes. During the fourteenth and fifteenth centuries, village communities won a corporative status that enabled them to defend their rights. Under conditions of expanding agricultural markets, improved prices for farm products, and a relaxation in the burden of the *taille*, a stratum of middling peasants emerged who reaped the benefits of prosperity.[37]

In order to counteract these trends, during the second half of the fifteenth century the French nobility launched a localized offensive which picked up steam throughout the sixteenth century. In many parts of France, customary grazing rights came under attack. In response to this offensive and to the growth of rural poverty, peasants erupted episodically during the 1540s into resistance they directed especially against various forms of royal taxation. The drift towards anarchy throughout the course of the religious wars was punctuated by major peasant risings between 1578 and 1580. In the midst of widespread famine and economic crisis during the 1590s, massive peasant rebellions shook the social structure of sixteenth-century France. The scale of these uprisings forced the landed ruling class to put its internal differences behind it and to unite against the threat from below. The result was a decisive shift in the direction of monarchical absolutism.[38] Absolutism thus represented, as Perry Anderson has written, "a redeployed and recharged apparatus of feudal domination, designed to clamp the peasant masses back into their traditional social position."[39] Unable to break peasant resistance and to raise levies at the local level, the lords turned to the concentrated power of the centralized state.

Once the absolutist state was set on a secure footing following the civil wars and peasant revolts of the sixteenth century, the political and military weight of a centralized administrative machine was capable of ensuring a substantially increased level of peasant exploitation. Between 1610 and 1644, for example, state exactions from the *taille* rose from 17 million to 44 million livres. Total taxation quadrupled in the decade after 1630. These increases represented a rise in the *real* level of exactions as grain prices stagnated during this period. By 1628, in fact, Normandy alone was providing Louis XIII with revenues equal to all those raised by Charles I in England. By the time of Louis XIV's first war (1667–1668), the French Crown was raising 60 million livres in revenue; no other European power, except Holland, could count on an income a quarter of that amount.[40] However, though absolutism preserved the social relations of feudal exploitation, it did so in a fashion which created new social conflicts and constructed major obstacles to economic development.

The most obvious conflict engendered by absolutism was that between the surplus-extractive demands of the local lords and those of the state. Inherent in the distribution of the surplus product was a conflict between rent and taxes, the latter a "centralized feudal rent" drawn from the seigneurie of the whole realm. Especially in bad years, state exactions could entirely eliminate seigneurial rents. As a result, lords often encouraged peasant resistance directed against tax collectors or their agents.[41]

In order to avoid a full-scale confrontation between the aristocracy and the absolutist state, the Crown strove to integrate sections of the ruling class into the machinery of taxation. The most effective means of doing so was through the sale of offices, which would give their owners a share of the centralized feudal rent exacted by the state. These *officiers* of the state would thus come to identify with the tax system as an important source of their personal wealth. Through the sale of offices the absolutist state provided itself with a measure of stability, since "it could absorb into state office many of those very same lords who were the casualties of the erosion of the seigneurial system."[42] The sale of offices also had another significant effect for the Crown: it provided the state with a source of wealth separate from the surplus product of the peasantry and thus—at least in principle—lessened the direct conflict between rent collection and taxation. Moreover, to the extent to which bourgeois wealth was drawn into the purchase of offices, the Crown was able to tap a financial source largely independent of feudal exploitation.

The sale of offices served as a short-term solution to the basic structural problem of French absolutism. The absolutist state was plagued throughout its history by a chronic inability to raise revenues sufficient to pay its basic costs—especially the costs of war. War forced the state to resort to even more extraordinary measures in an effort to meet its expenses; it relied increasingly on loans. In receiving loans from financiers and wealthy nobles, the Crown agreed in turn to alienate specific revenues from the tax system. While the system of loans enabled the monarchy to meet pressing expenses, its longer term effect undermined the financial strength of the state. The result was that absolutism experienced a sharp conflict between the Crown and those officeholders who claimed a share of royal revenues. So desperate became the situation of the Crown that it often sold fraudulent rights or imaginary supplements to the salaries of *officiers*. And so intense did the conflict between *officiers* and the Crown become that it at times erupted into open insurrection.[43]

A basic contradiction thus ran through the structure of French absolutism: the conflict between Crown and *officiers*. It was a conflict which could not be resolved. On the one hand, the monarchy needed a stratum of nobles and bourgeois whose private wealth it could tap. On the other hand, however serious their grievances, the *officiers* could not fundamentally challenge the absolutist régime; to do so would have deprived them of access to the potential fortunes to be made through participation in the fiscal apparatus of the state. On its own, perhaps, this basic contradiction could have been tolerated. In the long run, however, the extraordinary financial machine of French absolutism siphoned enormous amounts of wealth out of productive activity and into the purely speculative area of state investments. In so doing, the fiscal machine erected an insurmountable obstacle to revitalization of the French economy.

The main focus of bourgeois investment in the eighteenth century was what George Taylor has called "court capitalism," which term refers to "the exploitation by individuals and syndicates of government farms, state loans, and joint-stock flotations and speculations."[44] "Court capitalism" revolved around the speculative activities of financiers, those who were private agents in the collection of state revenues as farmers general, treasurers, and receivers general of finance in the provinces and those who advanced loans to the Crown in exchange for office and *rentes*. In reality, the term is a misnomer. Porshnev's notion of a "feudalization" of the French bourgeoisie is more accurate. In one form or another, through loans either to nobles or to the state, enormous amounts of bourgeois wealth were advanced to the traditional ruling class in exchange for a share of feudal dues from either the local or central level. These feudal dues became a form of interest payment on capital advanced as credit. In this way, bourgeois incomes became dependent upon the system of feudal surplus extraction. Without doubt, the greatest fortunes were to be made through investments in the fiscal machine. In addition, the purchase of venal office could provide noble status while further investments could acquire fiscal exemption and seigneurial rights. The speculative fortunes to be made from lending to the Crown or participating in joint-stock enterprises were immense and stimulated an intricate network of intrigue and influence peddling; state-related investments thus dominated bourgeois pursuit of wealth and status. Consequently, commercial wealth did not flow into productive investments in agriculture and industry, since "the most spectacular operations of old regime capitalism were made possible by royal finance and political manipulation rather than industrial or maritime enterprise."[45]

But perhaps the major obstacle to economic development posed by absolutism had to do with its effects upon the peasantry and the system of agriculture. As in England, significant social differentiation did occur in the ranks of the peasantry during the fifteenth and sixteenth centuries. Unlike England, however, this differentiation did not in France proceed to the point at which a yeoman stratum emerged from the ranks of the peasantry and undertook a form of petty commodity production. The reason for this seems clear: the consolidation of absolutism enabled the state to significantly increase the level of exploitation of the peasants. By raising the level of exploitation, the royal power prevented peasants with larger holdings from amassing surpluses sufficient to improve the productivity of the land, to expand their holdings, and to set in motion the bare beginnings of a genuine agricultural revolution.

Just as absolutism tended to block the emergence of a commodity-producing stratum of rich peasants, so it tended to close off the possibility of lords enclosing land and moving in the direction of agrarian capitalism. Absolutism heightened peasant exploitation; at the same time it also buttressed peasants' rights to property and defended the peasantry against excessive exaction by local lords. The Crown saw clearly that marked rises in rents would prevent full payment of taxes. Furthermore, since the nobility was exempt from taxation, the Crown had a direct interest in the preservation of the peasantry—its primary tax base. As a result, peasants generally received support from the monarchy and especially from its local representatives, the intendants, in their campaigns against enclosures by landlords. For this reason, according to Bloch, "the victory of the absolute monarchy kept the 'feudal reaction' within bounds."[46] Absolutism thus defended the property rights of the peasantry while it heightened exploitation of peasants; and while it blocked the emergence of a prosperous stratum from the ranks of the peasantry, it put major obstacles in the way of agricultural improvement and enclosures by landlords.

Nobles did attempt to enclose, consolidate, and undermine the traditional rights of the peasantry. And in some cases they did demonstrate an orientation to commercial farming.[47] But none of these movements succeeded in transforming France's rural social structure—nor could they have, given the nature of feudal absolutism. Unable to change the social relations of agricultural production, through primitive accumulation, and thereby to boost surplus product with innovations designed to maximize output, the French nobility were left with no real option but to squeeze a greater surplus from essentially unchanged levels of peasant output.

Thus, while absolutism preserved the power of the nobility—in a dramatically altered form—it also undermined the long-term strength of the economy upon which that power rested. The result was that peasants failed to meet the requirements of simple reproduction, to replace the seed, tools, livestock, and labour necessary to sustain a standard level of productivity; and the vitality of the economy was sapped. Consequently, the productivity of the land declined. At the same time, rural poverty blocked the development of a growing home market for domestic manufactures. The maintenance of a mass of small peasant holdings thus guaranteed that absolutist France would not make a breakthrough to self-sustaining economic growth. The sapping of economic vitality also undermined the power of the absolutist state. An impoverished peasantry could not endlessly provide the revenues necessary for a massive, centralized state. Periodic crises, which became endemic by the 1690s, forced the monarchy to tax noble wealth. Yet in so doing the Crown threatened its own often tenuous base of support in the ruling class. The economic and fiscal structure of absolutism thus generated a series of economic and political contradictions, all of which conspired to prevent a capitalist transformation of the agrarian sector and thereby to block a breakthrough to self-sustaining economic growth. In this way, economic crisis sowed the seeds of political crisis.

In 1758—when the physiocratic school first rose to prominence—France was facing a threefold crisis. Her armies were reeling under a series of defeats that were to result in the loss of the Seven Years' War. Foreign trade was ruined and the financial crisis reached alarming heights. Payment of *inscriptions* was suspended, salaries were stopped, and people were urged to bring in their gold and silver ornaments for minting. By this point, absolutism had run its course. The economy was impoverished, the state effectively bankrupt. Theorists like the Physiocrats saw one way and one way alone out of the crisis: an English-style capitalist transformation of the agricultural sector. The physiocratic revolution was not to be, however. The result was that the monarchy stumbled from one crisis to another. By 1789, the annual deficit equaled one-fifth of the state budget while interest payments on the national debt rose to more than half of annual government expenditures.[48] Inability to solve these economic dilemmas of absolutism sealed the fate of the régime, contributing powerfully to the revolutionary crisis of 1789. However, the failure of agrarian revolution continued to haunt the French economy long after absolutism had been laid to rest.

CONCLUSION

Classical political economy, as we noted at the outset of this chapter, originated in England and France in the second half of the seventeenth century. It was during this period that the course of social and economic development for the subsequent century was largely determined. And it was the prospects and problems posed by these patterns of development that occupied the attention of the classical political economists.

In the case of England, the seventeenth century was the century of revolution and of the rise of agrarian capitalism. Transformation of the agrarian social structure was a central feature of this period; the Revolution served ultimately to accelerate this process by fashioning a state which increasingly served the interests of capitalist landowners. Within the structure of agrarian capitalism, rent was the dominant economic surplus and its utilization the key to economic development. It should come as no surprise (to anticipate the next chapter) that the central concern of British political economists of the seventeenth century was understanding those processes which created and increased the rents accruing to the owners of the land.

In France, as we have indicated, consolidation of monarchical absolutism, while preserving noble power, erected major obstacles to economic development. By raising peasant exploitation, absolutism impoverished the rural economy. By defending the rights of peasant ownership, it blocked seigneurial attempts to enclose and consolidate farms and to organize agricultural production on a new basis. Finally, in "feudalizing" the bourgeoisie by integrating it into the apparatus of state credit and finance, it directed non-noble wealth into unproductive channels. The overall result was that a sustained recovery was not triggered and that, every time the lords or the state increased exactions, economic catastrophe loomed.

These economic contradictions of absolutism fundamentally destabilized the monarchy. The financial well-being of the state depended ultimately on the health of the economy. As absolutism undermined the latter, it signed its own death warrant. The most dramatic feature of the crisis of absolutism was its fiscal aspect—the crisis of state revenues. For this reason, the problem of taxation was the central concern of French political economists during this period. The more perceptive theorists recognized, however, that the system of taxation could be reformed in any lasting way only if the economic system—and its agrarian sector, in particular—were radically transformed. The problems of taxation and economic development were intimately connected.

Rent and taxes were thus the major economic categories which dominated the writings of the pioneers of classical political economy. How these categories were constructed, and their place in a general model of economic relations, is the topic of the next chapter.

CHAPTER TWO

Rent and Taxes:
The Origins of Classical Political Economy

Classical political economy developed in societies whose economies were overwhelmingly agricultural. Any theoretical effort designed to grasp the nature of economic development in such societies had almost by necessity to focus attention upon the agricultural surplus product. The utilization of this surplus, which primarily took the form of rent accruing to owners of land, determined the basic economic pattern of these early modern societies. Indeed, an agrarian model of economic reproduction was advanced even in much of the preclassical economic literature of the sixteenth and early seventeenth centuries. This "mercantilist" literature focused upon enrichment of the state as the central objective of political economy, not a surprising objective, given the fusion between state and economy which characterized the societies of early modern Europe. The state was the primary economic agent in regulating wages, curbing imports, encouraging industries, financing commercial and colonial ventures, controlling the mint, and so on. The notion of the economy as something existing independently of the state would have been contrary to experience. Mercantilist economics was thus characterized by what Perry Anderson has called an "indistinction of economy and polity," which reflected the fundamental unity of these two spheres "in the transitional epoch which produced mercantilist theories."[1] However, as England's development departed from the European norm with the rise of agrarian capitalism, English mercantilists came increasingly to view the economy as a mechanism with its own internal laws of development with which the state should not interfere.

Given the different trends in English and French mercantilism, due caution must be exercised in making statements about the general features of mercantilist thought. As a category which embraces the economic thought of several nations during an epoch of social transformation, *mercantilism* is a term which threatens to lose all specificity in its drive for comprehensiveness.[2] Nevertheless, as a number of commentators have argued, the term may serve as "a convenient shorthand." Barry Supple has argued, for example, that it is legitimate to utilize the concept of mercantilism to describe a body of literature which for historical reasons exhibited a preoccupation with questions of a mercantile nature and "displayed a sufficiently common ground of anxieties and modes of discussion."

If we accept that the "common ground of anxieties" refers to the crucial preoccupation of mercantilist theorists with enrichment of the state and that the common "modes of discussion" refer to the tendency to see the expansion of national wealth as depending upon gains made through foreign trade, then the concept of mercantilism may indeed serve as a useful shorthand. To be illuminating, however, the distinctive features of mercantilist doctrine in different nations and at different times must be grasped; and such distinctions must inform our use of the concept. As Supple has shown for the English case, the unity of mercantilist doctrine owed more to "the nature of the economic environment within which men thought out their actions" than it did to a continuity of philosophical or ideological assumptions.[3] We should thus expect that different economic environments would produce different forms of mercantilist thought. And this is precisely what did happen in seventeenth-century England and France, as the central social and economic problems confronted by administrators, reformers, men of affairs, and social theorists in the two countries produced quite different traditions of mercantilist thought.

The scope of the differences in "economic environment" was reflected in England's willingness to depart from the traditional policy of provision—according to which goods essential to domestic consumption were retained and their export prohibited—in favour of a high price for and free export of grain. As early as 1394 all export prohibitions were repealed; the preamble to an act of 1437 asserted for "perhaps the first time in modern history," according to Heckscher, that a low price for corn is injurious to society. The result was that

the country with the most rapidly growing capital, and therefore the one that might be interpreted to encourage imports of food-stuffs, was more interested than any other country in the encouragement of agriculture by the maintenance of high prices and the facilitation of exports.[4]

This is not to suggest that after this period the state abandoned its regulation of food prices and exports. On the contrary, the economic and social problems of the sixteenth century—enclosure, conversion of arable land to pasturage, inflation, and dearth—gave new impetus to the notion that the state was duty bound to intervene to preserve the foundations of a "moral economy" based upon "just prices." Indeed, this notion played an important role in the perspective of the Commonwealth reformers whose contributions to sixteenth-century economic thought will be discussed below.[5] As early as the fifteenth century, however, economic thought increasingly emphasized the benefits of agricultural exports and high prices for foodstuffs, reflecting the changes that would take England down the road to agrarian capitalism. Consequently, mercantilist economic doctrine took on a markedly different shape in the works of English, as opposed to continental, writers. Indeed, English mercantilism displayed an agrarian emphasis unknown to French mercantilism. Furthermore—and another expression of the fundamental differences between the nations—although English mercantilism originated in the writings of statesmen and political reformers during the 1540s, in its classic phase during the 1620s it was the creature of merchants; in France it was largely the concern of royal officials. These differences were significant for the evolution of economic thought.

English Mercantilism: Trade in an Agricultural Commonwealth

English mercantilism emerged from a body of analysis devoted to the crisis of the mid-Tudor economy and society. Towards the end of the 1540s in particular, an identifiable body of political-economic thought had developed which laid the basis for most economic analysis of the subsequent century. In fact, for nearly a century after the writing of

A Discourse of the Commonweal of This Realm of England in 1549, a favourable balance of trade was seen as the main avenue to national wealth and power. The *Discourse* was first published in 1581. It is believed to have been written by Sir Thomas Smith in 1549. Smith had been vice-chancellor of Cambridge University before embarking on an active political career in which he was principal secretary to Edward VI and Elizabeth; a member of Parliament under Edward, Mary, and Elizabeth; privy councillor; and ambassador to France several times.[6] Smith's famous treatise was written while he was a member of the Commonwealth party which rose to prominence under the protectorate of Somerset during the early years of the reign of Edward VI. The Commonwealth party consisted of a group of social reformers who came together during the crisis years of the mid-Tudor period. Their concept of the commonwealth was developed as part of a theoretical response to the manifold social and economic changes brought by emergent agrarian capitalism.

The changes were indeed dramatic. Henry VIII's dissolution of the monasteries had brought about a massive redistribution of land. Between 1536 and 1547, the Crown received about one and one-half million pounds through the sale of land. "This gigantic transfer of land," according to one commentator, "has no parallel in English history, at least since the redistribution which followed the Norman Conquest."[7] More than any other group, it was the gentry which prospered as a result of this redistribution. Whole strata of new gentry were created, while sections of the old gentry significantly expanded their power and influence. This new fluidity of property (the basis also of political power) exerted severe pressure on the social structure. The pressure was exacerbated by the instability brought about by rampant inflation. Leading the inflationary spiral, wool prices doubled in the century after 1450 and provided a powerful incentive to enclosure for pasturage. But the inflationary tide was general. One index of prices for foodstuffs shows a rise from 106 for the decade 1501–1510 to 217 for the decade 1541–1550.[8] The social dislocation created by price inflation, land sales, and enclosure was profound. Poverty and vagabondage increased sharply. Peasant revolts flared nearly every year between 1536 and 1549, culminating in the latter year in the Western Rebellion centred in Cornwall and Devon and in the Norfolk Rebellion led by Robert Ket.

The years 1548 and 1549 formed the peak of a decade of profound crisis. They were also the years in which the Commonwealth party made its greatest political mark and in which several of its leading spokesmen made major contributions to economic analysis. These social reformers used the expression "Commonweal" or "commonwealth" to denote both the body politic and the general good. Their notion of the commonwealth embodied the idea of a just social order whose preservation was the responsibility of the king and his advisors. The commonwealthmen held that it was the role of the Crown to ensure that justice (especially in the treatment of the poor) was preserved amidst the sweeping tides of economic change. The focus of their writings was economic; they addressed problems of enclosure, taxation, inflation, and unemployment. And their fundamental proposition was, as Clement Armstrong put it, that "The holl welth of the body of the realme risith out of the labours and workes of the common people."[9] Accordingly, the main political reform with which the commonwealthmen associated themselves was the enclosure commission of 1548, which sought to protect tenants' rights and restore justice to those harmed by illegal enclosure. In fact, this commission, under the direction of the noted Commonwealth reformer John Hales, actually authorized the destruction of many enclosures.

In the view of the commonwealthmen, the protection of civic virtue—the key to maintaining a just social order—depended upon ensuring that the agricultural basis of the nation was not undermined and that the power of the king was expressed through Parliament. In their political theory they were antiabsolutist; they insisted upon the classical notion of a mixed constitution in which elements of monarchy, aristocracy, and democracy combined in a balanced unity. In their economic theory, they exhibited a definite agrarian bias; while trade and industry were to be encouraged, their ultimate purpose was to stimulate agricultural production to overcome poverty and unemployment. Rooted as it was in the political and economic theorizing which emerged during this decade of social crisis, early English mercantilism was constructed within a generally antiabsolutist and agrarian worldview.

The greatest literary achievement of the Commonwealth party was the *Discourse* of Sir Thomas Smith. Smith has been described as "the most significant thinker among those who wrote on the application of Commonwealth ideals to the economic and social problems of mid-Tudor England." His *Discourse* has been hailed as "the beginning of British political economy." [10] Certainly it is not overstatement to say that no other piece of English economic writing prior to Mun exhibited such analytic sophistication. The central problem posed by the *Discourse* was to explain price inflation amidst plenty, not scarcity, of goods. Rejecting traditional arguments which attributed inflation (or "dearth") to conspiracies of self-interested parties—for example, merchants who greedily increased prices or landlords who raised rents through enclosure—Smith argued that the whole nation, with the possible exception of merchants, suffered from inflation and that its "efficient cause" was debasement of English money. [11] The evidence of debasement was plentiful. Successive manipulations of the English coinage had occurred in 1526, 1542–1544, 1546, and 1549. Between 1542 and 1547 English silver worth about £400,000 was reminted into coins worth £526,000. But Smith's argument transcended empirical observation by positing a systematic interrelationship between the supply of money and the movement of commodity prices. In this respect, the *Discourse* was an analytic achievement of some importance.

In addition to advancing a theoretical treatment of monetary phenomena, Smith also developed a central theme of English mercantilism; he elaborated the view that the wealth of the nation would decline unless imports and exports were kept in balance. Smith did not employ the expression "balance of trade." However, the *concept* of the balance of trade appeared clearly in the *Discourse:* "For we must always take heed that we buy no more of strangers than we do sell them; for so we should impoverish ourselves and enrich them." [12] Smith's treatment of the balance of trade was not particularly novel. Two other economic writers of the period went beyond Smith's notion of the need for a balance of trade (an *equality* of imports and exports) to suggest that national wealth could be increased by a favourable balance of trade (a *surplus* of exports over imports). [13] What distinguished Smith's tract, however, was his unparalleled treatment of the interdependence of economic phenomena. In passages anticipating Thomas Mun's writing of the 1620s, Smith argued that English prices must be internationally competitive if England was to maintain the balance of trade. England could not arbitrarily revalue her coin, Smith asserted, since prices are determined not by the state but by "the universal market of the world":

And I grant, if men might live within themselves altogether without borrowing of any other thing outward, we might devise what coin we would; but since we must have need of other and they of us, we must frame our things not after our own fantasies but to follow the *common market of the world*, and we may not set the price of things at our own pleasure but follow the price of the *universal market of the world*.[14]

Although Smith and the other economic writers of the 1540s can hardly be said to have constructed a general model of economic interdependence, they did develop rudimentary notions about the "circular flow" of economic life. In so doing, they broke from traditional conceptions which saw the flow of money to certain economic agents—for example, merchants or the state—as inevitably involving a loss to others. In demonstrating that the king also suffered as a result of debasement, Smith claimed, for example, that the same money flows from the subjects to the Crown and back again just as water runs from springs to the ocean and back.[15]

Clement Armstrong, in *A Treatise Concerninge the Staple and the Commodities of this Realme*, written between 1519 and 1535, advanced a similar argument to show that government encouragement to manufacturing would enrich, not undermine, agriculture and the state. True to the priority accorded by Commonwealth thinkers to agriculture, Armstrong posited a concept of the circular flow in which agriculture formed the basis of economic life by generating income flows to landlords and the king:

It shall be the gret welth of the kyng and all his lords to sett as moche peple as can be to artificialite, for as moch as they labour and werke all for money, that ther money may alwey ronne owt of ther hands in to the hands of such as occupieth housbandry for ther mete and drynk, which money shuld so ronne owt of the housbonds hands into the hands of the kyng and of his lords of the erth.[16]

Implicit in this argument is the assumption that husbandry produces economic surpluses in the form of rent and taxes which flow into the hands of landlords and the king. On the basis of such assumptions, the essential framework of English mercantilism had been constructed by the end of the 1540s. While sixteenth-century

English mercantilism cannot be said to have constituted a sophisticated body of economic analysis, it had developed some fundamental conceptions that would guide the analysis of economic life over the course of the following century. Two such conceptions stand out most clearly: first, the circular flow of economic life, a flow which originated in agricultural production (husbandry) and whose maintenance was essential to the preservation of a stable commonwealth; second, the balance of trade, especially the notion that a favourable balance of trade was the key to increased national wealth.

After the active period of the 1540s, English mercantilist thought underwent little development until the great economic debates of the 1620s. A severe depression swept the English economy in the early 1620s. Crisis and unemployment gripped the textile industry; exports slumped dramatically; outflows of bullion created a shortage of money. In the spring of 1622, James I ordered a select group to report on the European currency exchange market and its alleged "abuse" to England's disadvantage. This group included Gerrard Malynes, who had been a member of the commission appointed in 1600 by Queen Elizabeth to investigate monetary problems. Malynes developed his basic view of the nature of England's difficulties in a tract written at that time (1601) entitled *A treatise of the Canker of England's Commonweal.*[17] His essential position remained unchanged for the rest of his life. According to Malynes, the outflow of English bullion was the product of a conspiracy by foreign financiers to undervalue English currency. The result of this undervaluation was, Malynes claimed, that high prices for imported goods pushed up the total bill for imports while low export prices brought in an insufficient income on export trade. On the assumption that demand was inelastic and would not rise in response to lower prices—an unvarying assumption in Malynes's argument—the inevitable result of undervaluation would be an unfavourable balance of trade and an outflow of bullion to cover foreign debts. Malynes's solution was for the government to exercise some form of exchange control that would bring about an upward revaluation of English currency. Precisely this was the recommendation of the select group of 1622. Furthermore, Malynes favoured prohibiting the export of bullion, a position James I implemented with the bullion ordinance of 1622.

The report of the select group was referred to a rival committee of merchants. Their report—inspired by the committee's most prominent member, Thomas Mun—rejected the view that the currency exchange market was an independent determinant of prices and specie flows. According to Mun, the rate of exchange was a price and, like all prices, was determined by supply and demand. The supply of and demand for currencies, by contrast, was determined by the balance of trade. In Mun's words, "the over or under ballance of our trade doth effectually cause the plenty or scarcity of mony."[18] Whereas Malynes believed that economic phenomena were the direct result of conscious decisions and could, therefore, be determined by government policies, Mun claimed that there was a natural mechanism at work in international trade which operated independently of the conscious decisions of economic agents:

Let Princes oppress, Lawyers extort, Usurers bite, Prodigals wast, and lastly let Merchants carry out what mony they shall have occassion to use in traffique. Yet all these actions can work no other effects in the course of trade than is declared in this discourse. For so much Treasure only will be brought in or carried out of a Commonwealth, as the Forraign Trade doth over or under ballance in value. And this must come to pass by a Necessity beyond all resistance.[19]

Mun stood out as the most clear-sighted theorist of the 1620s; it was he who truly dealt the deathblow to the perspective formulated by Malynes. Whereas Malynes clung to a static and inelastic conception of international trade in which lower export prices would only aggravate the monetary crisis, Mun recognized that a newly competitive market required lower costs of production for exports at competitive prices. But Mun was more than an insightful merchant who grasped the true character of the new economic environment in which England had to live. He was also an economic analyst of considerable originality. Mun understood clearly that it is commodities, not money, which form the basis of real wealth. Where there are goods, he insisted, there will be money. Consequently, just as it would be absurd to prohibit the export of commodities, so would it be absurd to prohibit the means of circulating them. To keep money in the kingdom would be to raise domestic prices and hurt the export trade.[20]

Although Mun advanced a clear distinction between wealth and money, he persisted in the classical mercantilist position that domestic trade is sterile—since "profit upon alienation" merely involves profit to one individual and loss to another but no net gain to the nation—and that profit to the national economy could come only through a favourable balance of trade.[21] His follower, Misselden, went somewhat further and argued that the balance of trade is the centre of the circle of commerce: "All the rivers of Trade spring out of this source, and empt themselves againe into this *Ocean*. All the waight of Trade falle's to this *Center*, & comes within the circuit of this *Circle*."[22] Thus, in the mercantilist schema of Mun and Misselden, foreign trade was elevated to a causally independent role in economic life; it became the sole determinant of prosperity or poverty.

Though Mun's theory did not break out of the mercantilist mold, which accords priority to exchange within the circular flow of economic phenomena, he nonetheless considerably advanced economic analysis. By focusing on the necessary laws which governed the interaction of prices, the balance of trade, and specie flows, Mun treated economic phenomena as susceptible of analysis which was both scientific and objective, that is, as comprehensible without reference to the "subjective" decisions of individual economic agents. His theory was indeed "the most influential economic doctrine before Adam Smith" precisely because "there had been nothing in English to rival his singleness of purpose, logical analysis, and accomplished manipulation of the economic variables."[23]

Most historians of economic thought accord similar recognition to Mun. His major work, *England's Treasure by Forraign Trade*, is considered to be an almost paradigmatic expression of English mercantilism.[24] What is universally ignored in discussion of Mun's thought, however, is the extent to which economic examples derived from agriculture and discussion of agricultural improvement informed his general theoretical analysis. One commentator has pointed out that "from Mun's *Discourse of Trade* in 1621 onward, seventeenth-century writers discussed the fundamental importance of agricultural improvements."[25] But rarely has it been recognized that agricultural production often served as the basic model which provided explanatory principles for the examination of trade.

There is ample evidence of Mun's awareness of the economic significance of agricultural improvement in *England's Treasure*. In the opening pages of the tract, Mun strongly advocates the development of waste lands as a means of supplying England with various forms of raw produce that would otherwise have to be imported. Furthermore, for both economic and political reasons, Mun believed that the best solution to the unemployment problem was not to expand the cloth industry but rather to encourage "tillage and fishing."[26] In other words, it was to agriculture and primary industries generally—and not to manufacture—that the nation should look for solving unemployment and boosting national output. As suggestive as these passages are, of more significance is the evidence of Mun's conception of the centrality of rent in the national income and his reliance on agriculture to provide general examples of economic phenomena.

With respect to rent and the landed interest, Mun argued that an influx of specie resulting from a favourable balance of trade would boost demand for agricultural goods, raise agricultural prices, and increase rents.[27] As a result of this mechanism, Mun asserted, the interests of the landlords were entirely consistent with those of the merchants. Without a favourable balance of trade, prices of agricultural goods would decline, and land values and rents would fall. On the basis of this analysis, Mun claimed that the merchant's private interest served the public good and that the merchant should therefore be called "*The Steward of the Kingdoms Stock.*"[28] Just as estate stewards were responsible to landlords for the direction and superintendence of landed production in such a way as to render a profit, so it was the job of the merchant to be the steward of the nation's money stock and to increase that stock through foreign trade.

Perhaps the most interesting of Mun's analogies of trade with agricultural production occurs in his defence of the export of gold and silver. Mun continually argued that it was as ridiculous to prohibit the export of gold and silver as it was to prohibit the export of goods in general. The purpose of exporting gold and silver, he claimed, was to sell commodities which would reap a profit. Successful foreign trade required that money be taken out of England in order to allow the buying and selling of goods to take place. But, he argued, the whole point of the operation was to return home with more in gold and silver than was taken out originally. Therefore, to examine only the carrying out of specie by merchants without taking into consideration the import of greater amounts of specie after the completion of a cycle of trade was to ignore the essential motive of foreign trade and specie export—to make a profit which would return to the nation in the form of gold and silver. Condemnation of merchants for carrying gold and silver out of the realm was as absurd as condemning husbandmen for casting away seed. In both cases, the harvests of the original labours are ignored. It is with merchants as it is with husbandmen:

> For if we only behold the actions of the husbandman in the seed-time when he casteth away much good corn into the ground, we will rather accompt him a mad man than a husbandman: but when we consider his labours in the harvest which is the end of his endeavours, we find the worth and plentiful encrease of his actions.[29]

Using this analogy with husbandry, Mun developed a primitive concept of investment. The export of gold and silver for foreign trade was seen as a kind of "advance," like the planting of seed, which would yield a profitable "harvest" in time. This concept of investment, which was merely implicit in Mun's work, was to inform political economy for a century and a half. Although it would be untrue to suggest that Mun's economic writings constituted the starting point for a tradition of economic analysis which would posit the centrality of agricultural production in the circular flow of economic life, his work did demonstrate the influence of agricultural production on the most sophisticated of mercantilist theorists. Mercantilist though he was in his insistence that an increase in national wealth could come only through profit on foreign trade, Mun continually resorted to agricultural analogies in order to explain economic phenomena in general.

One further economic tract of the 1620s is worthy of mention. This is Sir Thomas Culpepper's *Tract Against Usurie* written in 1621 and republished by Sir Josiah Child in his *Brief Observations Concerning Trade and Interest of Money* (1668). Culpepper, like Malynes, Misselden, and Mun, was disturbed by the depression of the early 1620s. In Culpepper's view, however, the collapse of England's trade was a product of an excessively high rate of interest which had pushed up the costs of English goods and lowered land values (and had thereby discouraged agricultural investment). Culpepper's pamphlet did not display the kind of systematic analysis pioneered by Mun. It did, however, utilize a rudimentary concept of capital, and it stressed the significance of landed investment and agricultural improvement for the economy as a whole.

A high rate of interest raises the price of English goods, Culpepper contended, since it increases the cost of money necessary to capital expenditures. The Dutch are able to undersell the English because the cost of "stock" is lower as a result of their lower rate of interest. Furthermore, a high rate of interest discourages borrowing to buy or improve land and therefore causes land prices to sag. Low land prices, in turn, further discourage agricultural improvement. A low rate of interest, however, would encourage investment in land and agricultural improvement on such a scale that "the Riches and Commodities of this Land will near be doubled." With a reduction in the interest rate,

> then would all the wet Lands in this Kingdom soon be drained, the barren Lands mended by Marle, Sleech, Lime, Chalk, Seasand, and other means, which for their profit, mens industry would find out.

Such a boom in investment on the land would benefit "the poor Labourers of the Land" as much as it would benefit "the Landed men." [30]

Culpepper's treatise is by no means as significant as Mun's major work. It is, however, a graphic demonstration of the extent to which the level of rents and the state of agricultural production were considered to be at the heart of the wealth of the nation. Furthermore, its central emphasis on agricultural investment and improvement demonstrates that the agrarian sector was seen as a dynamic part of the economy whose stimulation could enormously contribute to solving the problem of unemployment. Finally, its republication by Child during the economic debates of the 1660s does much to indicate that most economic writers of the seventeenth century gave crucial importance to capital investment on the land.

In the writings of the 1620s, especially those of Mun, English mercantilism received its classical formulation. Between 1549 and 1622, in fact, all the basic elements of English mercantilism were constructed: first, a rudimentary concept of the circular flow, which enabled writers to posit interdependence between a variety of economic phenomena such as price levels, the quantity of money, and specie flows; second, the view that domestic trade was neutral in that one Englishman's loss was another's gain, with no resulting gain to the nation as a whole; and, third, the notion that an increase in the wealth of the nation could be achieved only through a favourable balance of trade. Equally important, however, was the extent to which mercantilist theoretical analysis of economic phenomena relied upon analogies derived from agricultural production and, in some cases, implied a central role for agriculture in the production of national wealth. The Commonwealth writers of the 1540s tended to emphasize the economic and political centrality of agriculture more so than did the writers of the 1620s because their general focus was on the preservation of social harmony in a society suffering the strains of emergent agrarian capitalism. Focusing on problems of a trade depression, the classical mercantilists of the 1620s accorded priority to foreign trade within "the circle of commerce." Nevertheless, agricultural improvement loomed large in their prescriptions for resolving a variety of economic problems. Furthermore, their explication of certain economic processes, such as Mun's defence of the inflow and outflow of gold and silver, often relied upon analogy with production in that sector—agriculture—which still governed the lives of most English people. In the second half of the seventeenth century these agricultural analogies were to be transformed into elements of a much more rigorously theoretical model of the essential relations of economic life.

WILLIAM PETTY AND CLASSICAL ENGLISH POLITICAL ECONOMY

The key figure in the development of an agrarian model in English political economy is William Petty. Petty is widely acknowledged to be a founder of classical political economy. Marx dubbed him "the father of English political economy" and praised his "audacious genius." Max Beer described Petty as "the pioneer of the English economics of production" and claimed that "he must be regarded as the initiator of classical English economics: he laid the foundations on which his successors—Smith and Ricardo—could erect their structures." In the view of Eric Roll, Petty is "the most important, as well as the earliest, English economist who prepared the way for the classical system," while writers such as Schumpeter, Spiegel, and Meek have praised him as the originator of the concept of economic interdependence through the division of labour and of modern income analysis.[31] In *The Origins of Scientific Economics*, William Letwin has written of Petty's major economic work, *A Treatise of Taxes and Contributions*, that "its basic structure must stand as a work of surpassing originality. The quality of its analysis makes it an unmistakable masterpiece of early economic science."[32]

Yet for all the acclaim awarded Petty's economic writings, the literature has made little effort to understand the specific analytical problems which inspired him to initiate a fundamental reorientation in political economy. It has paid insufficient attention to the fact that Petty's major analytic innovation came in a digression in the *Treatise* as he attempted to explain the nature of rent. Furthermore, it has rarely connected Petty's experience as surveyor general in Ireland and as a major landholder to his abiding interest in rent and the value of land and to his novel contributions to classical economics. Finally, it has paid little attention to the fact that a preoccupation with agrarian problems was common to virtually all the seventeenth-century radical Baconian social thinkers amongst whom Petty was a central figure.

The revolutionary period of 1640 to 1660 ushered in tremendous changes in England's social, economic, political, and intellectual life. It was during these two decades that a decisive shift took place in economic literature, a shift which marked the emergence of a scientific economics. This new scientific economics originated as a product of the revolutionary philosophy of the period—social Baconianism. Bacon's philosophy was not new; what was new was its soaring influence in intellectual circles. "Whereas before 1640 Bacon's had been a voice crying in the wilderness," writes one historian, "by 1660 his was the dominant intellectual influence."[33] The turning point came in 1640, the year of the outbreak of the English Civil War, as is evidenced by the fact that more of Bacon's works were published in this year than in the previous fourteen years which had followed his death in 1626.[34] One historian of the scientific movement of this period writes accurately that

Bacon became the most important philosophical and scientific authority of the Puritan Revolution. It is therefore only a slight exaggeration to regard Baconianism as *the official philosophy of the Revolution.*[35]

During the latter part of the sixteenth century and the opening quarter of the seventeenth, Bacon formulated his program for a great intellectual revolution—the reconstruction of science on radically new foundations. More acutely than most of his contemporaries, Bacon recognized that he was living in a period when profound changes were taking place in human affairs. The discovery of the New World; the agricultural revolution; the advance of invention, trade, and industry all heralded the dawn of a new age of improvement. The possibilities of this new age were often interpreted in millenarian terms, as the twin forces of religious reformation and political revolution made their impact on men's minds. Bacon feared, however, that a dogmatic adherence to ancient philosophical systems might prevent fulfillment of the possibilities created by this period of change. The "opening up of the sciences" was the task. It required a new philosophy, a new scientific method. All of Bacon's major works, especially *The Advancement of Learning*, advanced a program to remove all fetters upon the blossoming of knowledge. A thoroughgoing educational reform was to be the precondition for spreading an empirical, experimental, and rational approach to the natural world. Bacon's method did not consist of a crude empiricism. He mistrusted the immediate impressions of the senses. Instead, he recommended a practical, experimental method in which knowledge of nature would be acquired in acting upon it. It is by acting on nature (through "works") that we acquire genuine knowledge of things: "The secrets of nature reveal themselves more readily under the vexations of art than when they go their own way."[36] There is an important element of truth to the claim that "Bacon's scientific method is the trial and error of the craftsman raised to a principle."[37] Bacon wanted, however, to elevate the method of the craftsman (and the practical, improving farmer) to a conscious and systematic philosophy. On the basis of experiment he wished to formulate general propositions. Furthermore, he wanted to collect histories of various trades so that a universal perspective on practical interaction with nature could be constructed. The history of arts, he asserted, reveals the truth about objects because it studies them as "things in motion." In so doing, "it takes off the mask and veil from natural objects, which are commonly concealed and obscured under the variety of shapes and external appearances."[38]

This is not the method of a simple empiricism. Bacon was not suggesting that passive perception of objects constitutes adequate experience for knowledge of things. Rather, he insisted that a conscious, experimental, and practical orientation to things with the intent to transform them according to various human purposes was the only foundation upon which to build knowledge. Further, he maintained that general axioms should be constructed on the basis of such experimental practice. Bacon believed that in the course of studying the effects of practical action upon natural objects—and before proceeding to the elaboration of axioms—there must be a determined effort to measure and to quantify. Things, he argued, must be "numbered, weighed, measured and defined."[39] Such an approach does indeed open the door to a pure inductive empiricism. But in Bacon's case—and that of most of his seventeenth-century followers—such quantification was to preface the formulation of general axioms of knowledge. The overall context for quantification was that of scientific attempts to transform the world. Bacon's philosophy, then, was activist and optimistic in character. It promised a new age of knowledge, improvement, and prosperity if only men would break with the habits of the past and undertake to dominate nature according to human ends.

Bacon's scientific program became the rallying point for Puritan intellectuals after 1640. Baconian science was essentially antiauthoritarian in character. It sided with individual experience against the authority of the written word. It elevated the practical experience of the craftsman, the husbandman, and the improving gentleman above the pseudoknowledge of the priest or the university teacher. During the years 1646 and 1647, the famous Invisible College whose "midwife and nurse," in the words of Robert Boyle, was Samuel Hartlib, consciously set out to advance the Baconian project. Later, during the early 1650s, the Oxford Experimental Philosophy Club— once again inspired by Hartlib—became the focus for Baconian intellectuals. The Oxford Club often met at the lodgings of William Petty and, like the Invisible College, was preoccupied with husbandry, natural philosophy, and mathematics.

Many leading members of the Oxford Club maintained a passionate interest in agricultural problems. Wilkins, Hartlib, and Wren were all enthusiastic advocates of a new design for beehives. Wilkins designed an improved plough which one of Hartlib's followers pursued vigorously. Petty invented a mechanical device for the planting of corn. Several members maintained an abiding interest in the culture of fruit trees. It is no overstatement to say that a scientific approach to agriculture became a major concern of the social Baconians.

The leading figure in the scientific study of agriculture, as in the entire radical Baconian project, was Samuel Hartlib. The son of a Polish or Lithuanian merchant and an English woman, Hartlib made his home in England in 1628. He established an academy at Chichester in 1630 "for the education of the Gentrie of this Nation." Later he became associated with Emmanual College, Cambridge, and was eventually granted an annual pension by Cromwell. Hartlib's project for an Office of Address which would act as a centre for universal education inspired both the Invisible College and the Oxford Club. As the years went by, however, "Hartlib's primary energies were increasingly devoted to the accumulation of materials relating to husbandry."[40] In fact, G. E. Fussell chose in his study of English agricultural tracts to call the period 1641–1660 "The Age of Hartlib."[41] The characterization is appropriate. Hartlib published Richard Weston's *Discourse of Husbandrie used in Brabant and Flanders* in 1651. In that same year he published two works of his own: *Essay on the Advancement of Husbandry* and *The Reformed Husbandman*. The next year he issued his *Design for Plenty*, followed by *Discovery for Division or Setting out of Waste Land* in 1653. In 1659 *The Complete Husbandman* appeared. Most of these works were collections of writings by others. Nonetheless, it was Hartlib who brought them together and popularized them.

Equally important was Hartlib's encouragement of Gabriel Plattes, the leading inventor in the Hartlib circle and the foremost exponent of scientific agriculture, who published tracts on husbandry in 1639, 1640, and 1644 (a posthumous work on agriculture appeared in 1653). Plattes claimed that inefficient agricultural methods had depleted England's soil and impoverished her people. While he supported enclosure as a means of obtaining a greater yield per acre, he opposed its use for pasturage. He believed in protecting tenant rights and in devising plans for the employment of the poor. For Plattes, as for all the Baconian reformers, agriculture was the foundation of the commonwealth. Because declining conditions of husbandry signified economic malaise and political instability, maintenance and improvement of the agrarian sector of the economy were essential to social and economic progress.

In their efforts to stimulate the scientific pursuit of agriculture, several Baconian publicists advocated the creation of a college of husbandry. Although such programs failed to bear fruit, the greatest single contribution of the social Baconians occurred in the study of agriculture. This field attracted more sustained study than any other scientific endeavor during the English Revolution. In fact, the rate of output of works on agriculture doubled between 1600 and 1660. Only mathematics matched this rate of growth in publication.[42]

The purpose of such intense study of husbandry was not merely the pursuit of knowledge as an end in itself. The experimental philosophers believed that reform of husbandry was the key to the reform of the commonwealth. In particular, they saw agricultural improvement as the primary solution to the problem of poverty and unemployment. Consequently, their analyses of agriculture often stressed the economic side of problems of agricultural production. Issues like the costs of production, rent, yields, wages, and employment figured prominently in their writings. As a result, the social Baconians increasingly embarked on theoretical work of an economic nature. In this area of work, as in all others, they sought to apply a strictly scientific method to the phenomena under scrutiny. Baconian philosophy, therefore, constituted the theoretical foundation of the embryonic scientific economics of this period. As we shall see, nowhere is this more clear than in the case of William Petty.

Associated with Baconian social philosophy was a current of political thought which we have come to call *classical republicanism*. This political tradition enjoyed a resurgence in England during the Reformation, especially among Puritan intellectuals. Basing their writings on Aristotle, Polybius, Cicero, and Machiavelli, the classical republicans stressed the virtues of a "mixed constitution" which embodied elements of monarchy, aristocracy, and democracy. Each form of government was held to degenerate inevitably if constituted on its own. Pure monarchy degenerated by nature into tyranny, aristocracy into oligarchy, democracy into anarchy. The task of the political philosopher and legislator was to devise a balance or mixture of the three political forms which would draw upon their strengths and offset their shortcomings. This involved devising a mixed republic or "commonwealth" whose leaders would adhere to the virtues of civic humanism by subordinating private interest to the common good.[43]

Members of the English Commonwealth party of the sixteenth century, and Sir Thomas Smith in particular, were central figures in the English recovery and adaptation of classical republicanism. Often taking their inspiration from contemporary Venice, they developed an *aristocratic republicanism* which emphasized the need for a virtuous aristocracy to prevent the concentration of excessive powers in the hands of either the monarch or the people. They viewed civic-minded gentlemen as guardians of liberty against both tyranny and mob rule. An important development of this classical republican outlook occurred in the course of the English Revolution. Initially provoked into action by the absolutist tendencies of James I and Charles I, the first two Stuart monarchs, the traditional landed ruling class was soon confronted with the spectre of democracy as the revolt against the king triggered an upsurge of popular radicalism. This revolution from below became especially pronounced as parliamentary forces formed the New Model Army in the course of their military struggle with the Crown. Both within and outside the army this protest crystallized in the movement known as the Levellers, which advanced a radical program of social and political demands that called for the abolition of monarchy and aristocracy, emphasized the ultimate sovereignty of the people (as opposed to the divine right of kings), and called for diminishing—and in extreme cases for abolishing—economic inequality between rich and poor.[44]

By 1649, the Leveller movement had been largely defeated by Oliver Cromwell and the generals in the army. With the monarchy and the House of Lords also abolished in that year, a millenarian sense flourished that the political world could be remade to the measure of men. In this context, classical republicanism revived as a significant group of radical gentry, intellectuals, and reformers attempted to chart a political course for England, one which would forestall a revival of absolutism while guarding against the democratic and "levelling" tendencies of the popular radicals. This group, often described by contemporaries as commonwealthmen, believed that it was vital to draw up a constitutional structure appropriate to the English republic. The most significant of the Commonwealth theorists was James Harrington.

Harrington came from a respected landed family. His active career as a political figure and writer was relatively short; during the period from 1656 to 1660 he published a series of works designed to restore parliamentary rule (as an alternative to direct rule by Cromwell and the army) and at the same time avoid the restoration of monarchy. Harrington held it to be a law of politics that the form of government (or political "superstructure") must be in balance with the social distribution of landed property. Ownership of land, he argued, is the basis for control of arms; and the distribution of land and arms expresses the real distribution of political power. Since the time of Henry VII, Harrington maintained, there had been a decisive shift of property from the Crown and the nobility to the people. For this reason, political stability was possible in England only under the form of a "popular government," a commonwealth. Any attempt to reintroduce the "Gothick balance" of the feudal period (based upon a monarchy ruling through bishops and nobles, with a subordinate House of Commons) was doomed to failure. The task was thus to construct a commonwealth—without hereditary monarchy or nobility—in which the balance of power would be in the hands of the people, as was the balance of property.

In the context of the 1650s this was, to be sure, a radical program. At the same time, Harrington's was neither a Leveller program nor an argument for a pure democratic republic. Though rejecting hereditary aristocracy, Harrington believed in the absolute necessity of a "natural aristocracy" of wisdom and virtue which would hold the power of debating and proposing policy to the people. The people would, in turn, hold the sole power of deciding policy, although under no circumstances were they to engage in debate. Harrington claimed that a genuine natural aristocracy was "the deepest root of a democracy that hath been planted"; that without such an aristocracy any republic was doomed—Athens, for example, having collapsed "through the want of a good aristocracy"; that without such an aristocracy of wise and virtuous landed gentlemen England would be left with a commonwealth which would be "altogether mechanic"; and that landed gentlemen who had the leisure to study politics would inevitably constitute a true natural aristocracy.[45] Thus, although Harrington's views on the electoral franchise were close to those of the moderate Levellers (he supported the vote for all but servants), his position as a whole was decidedly more aristocratic, favouring an elected senate composed of natural aristocrats; they, by virtue of their wisdom and public spirit, would have a monopoly of political debate. The people as a whole he considered incapable of meaningful debate, although they were to be trusted to know their common (hence, the public) interest when presented with reasoned proposals from their natural leaders. As he put it in *Oceana*, "As the wisdom of the people is in the aristocracy, so the interest of the commonwealth is in the whole body of the people."[46]

The task confronting England in the crucial period from 1656 to 1660, as it tottered between the false alternatives of military rule and monarchical restoration, was to devise a popular constitution which would be consistent with the existing balance of property (favouring the people, not the Crown or the traditional nobility). Harrington thus set out to explain the true "political anatomy" of England—a term which returns with Petty—and the superstructure of laws which would correspond to it.[47]

It is important to stress, especially because of its significance for Adam Smith and Scottish social thought, that Harrington did not ground his republicanism in the search for those material and moral conditions conducive to civic virtue among citizens. Unlike Machiavelli and earlier classical republicans, Harrington did not hold that public-spirited commitment to the common good instead of to private interest was the sole means of preventing the degeneration or "corruption" of a commonwealth. In place of the problem of civic virtue, Harrington focused on the problem of law. He saw the task of the political legislator not as leading a people down the road to virtue but rather as designing an "empire of laws" in which the actions of citizens would invariably further the public interest even where private interest might dictate the contrary. In other words, even supposing all men evil, an equal commonwealth in which the constitution corresponded to the balance of property would make it impossible for individuals to undermine the public interest. Corruption would thus indicate a defect not in the people but in their constitution.[48]

For Harrington, England was to be an agricultural commonwealth, "a commonwealth of husbandmen," in which excessive accumulation of land was to be limited by an "agrarian law." The purpose of such a law was to preserve the existing ("popular") balance of property and thus avoid further revolutions in government, since a "popular government" of the kind which now suited England was the one based upon public rather than private interests. At the same time—and this, too, is significant for the history of political economy—an agricultural commonwealth was not to eschew trade and commerce. On the contrary; Harrington believed that urban markets stimulate agricultural production and improvement as trade and manufacture absorb the surplus population which cannot subsist on the land.[49] Industry and trade thus have their place in a commonwealth of husbandmen, albeit a clearly subordinate one.

This latter point becomes especially clear in Harrington's economic discussions, limited though they are. Harrington states unequivocally that rent is the "revenue" which is crucial to the power of the state. Indeed, he often treats rent as the sole national revenue, a position common to those who saw it as the basis of state revenues. At the same time, Harrington believed that the "industry" of the people produced revenues three to four times greater than the total income from rent, although it should be emphasized here that he included agricultural wages and profits in his discussion of "industry."[50] What is crucial for our discussion is to recognize that the tradition of Commonwealth theorizing associated with Harrington—which directly influenced William Petty—conceived of the economy in explicitly agrarian terms, but did not advance a nostalgic hostility to industry and commerce. On the contrary, Harrington's "commonwealth for increase" encouraged commercial expansion; but such expansion was to occur in the general context of a commonwealth in which wealth, arms, and power derived principally from ownership of land.

It should be clear, then, that radical Baconianism and Commonwealth political thought converged in their major emphasis upon agricultural production as the basis of national wealth and power. Indeed, quite a few of the social Baconians were themselves commonwealthmen, applying their experimental philosophy to the resolution of the practical political problems posed by the English Revolution. This was probably more true of William Petty than of any of his contemporaries.

Petty was born on 26 May 1623 in Romsey, a Hampshire clothing town which, according to his biographer, was "the outstanding stronghold of non-conformity in Hampshire."[51] The son of a poor clothier, at age fifteen or sixteen Petty joined the Navy for three years. During the Civil War he went to Holland to study medicine and specialized in anatomy. In 1650 he was appointed to a position at Oxford University and was made Reader in Music at Gresham College, London. Throughout this period he was an active member of the Hartlib group and of the Oxford Experimental Philosophy Club. Petty left academic life in 1651 to pursue his fortune in newly reconquered Ireland. There he worked first as a physician to the English army and later as surveyor general in drawing up a division of seized Irish lands to be shared between the conquering soldiers and those speculators who had financed the Irish campaign. Petty's spoils from this undertaking were considerable: over 18,000 acres of profitable land and cash resources exceeding 13,000 pounds. This operation made Petty one of the largest landholders in Ireland. For a time he worked as personal secretary to Henry Cromwell; for several years he was a member of Parliament. Furthermore, during the late 1650s, Petty was an active participant in the Rota Club of James Harrington and his followers. One of Harrington's biographers considered Petty to be the outstanding Harringtonian theorist of the Restoration period.[52] Whether or not we accept this judgement, it is clear that Petty was an important commonwealthman whose thought Harrington decisively influenced. In fact, Petty's position on issues such as the franchise appears to have been more radical than that of Harrington: a recently translated document shows Petty advocating the vote for *all* adult males without restriction.[53]

Petty's theoretical achievements were a product of his membership in the Hartlib circle and his Harringtonian associations with the Rota Club. In 1648, shortly after having made Hartlib's acquaintance, the 25-year-old Petty published *Advice of W. P. to Samuel Hartlib*. In this tract Petty outlined Hartlib's project for an Office of Address, a centre for universal knowledge and education. At Oxford Petty emerged as a central figure in the Baconian circle, and his lodgings often served as the meeting place for the Experimental Philosophy Club. The Baconian outlook characterized Petty's entire intellectual life. In his *Erguastula literaria* Petty produced a plan for the reform of education which had a decidedly practical bent consistent with the Baconian spirit. The curriculum he proposed included practical mathematics, watchmaking, ship design, architecture, chemistry, anatomy, art, optics, botany, and music. Following Bacon's own suggestion, Petty drew up a proposal for a "History of Trades" and actually wrote histories of dyeing, clothing, and shipping for the Royal Society.[54] Even in his writings on economic matters Petty was never reluctant to acknowledge his Baconian inspiration. Thus, in the preface to *The Political Anatomy of Ireland*, which appears to have been written in 1671, he wrote that:

Sir Francis Bacon, in his *Advancement of Learning*, hath made a judicious Parallel in many particulars between the Body Natural and the Body Politick, and between the Arts of preserving both in Health and Strength: And it is as reasonable, that as Anatomy is the best foundation of one, so also of the other.[55]

It is worth recalling that the term "political anatomy" appears to be derived directly from Harrington. Petty's efforts in political anatomy, however, involved a more rigorously quantitative approach to social and economic phenomena than that of Harrington. Petty often called this approach "political arithmetic." In fact, in his *Political Arithmetick* Petty sketches out his method in orthodox Baconian terms. Proceeding from sense experience, he argues, analysis should advance by way of expressing phenomena in terms of number, weight, and measure. His aim in the *Political Arithmetick*, he writes, is

to express myself in Terms of *Number, Weight,* or *Measure;* to use only Arguments of Sense, and to consider only such Causes, as have visible Foundations in Nature; leaving those that depend upon the mutable Minds, Opinions, Appetites and Passions of particular Men, to the Consideration of others.[56]

It was his move to Ireland which stimulated Petty to apply this Baconian method to economic phenomena. Value, rent, and land emerged as the central categories of his analysis. That land should be central was hardly surprising. Oliver Cromwell understood clearly that land was the basis of wealth and power in seventeenth-century England. He understood equally clearly that war was as much a financial operation as a military one. For this reason, he chose to utilize the landed wealth that could be expropriated through the conquest of Ireland as the basis for financing his military campaign. In return for loans to finance the war against Charles I, Cromwell pledged a share of the lands to be confiscated. The land grab which took place was massive. Whereas three-fifths of Irish land had been held by Catholics in 1641, by 1665, on completion of the Restoration settlement, Catholics held a mere one-fifth.[57] As a result of the conquest, a new landed ruling class had come into being. This class then set out to exploit their new properties by rendering these estates as profitable as possible. Many of these new landowners—soldiers and adventurers alike—were radicals identified with the New Model Army. They found the scientific movement a useful tool in the management and improvement of their lands. Consequently, Ireland became a centre of experiment and invention. As Webster has noted, "The investigations into chemistry, metallurgy, agriculture and surveying were to a large degree a reflection of the aspirations of a social group whose primary ambition was to re-establish profitable Irish plantations."[58]

Petty's chief innovation came in the field of surveying. Cromwell and his Ironsides had reconquered Ireland by September 1652. The land of Irish Catholic rebels was to be expropriated in order that the thirty-five thousand Commonwealth soldiers and the adventurers whose speculative fortunes had financed the campaign could be paid directly in land. The English Parliament adopted a plan which reserved the expropriated land in ten Irish counties for the claims of the soldiers and adventurers. But before the land could be expropriated and distributed, it had to be surveyed to determine its extent, boundaries, etc. In June 1653 Benjamin Worsley, an associate of Hartlib, was appointed surveyor general for the "grosse survey" which was to undertake a preliminary estimate of the forfeited lands in order that a provisional distribution could take place. An "exact admeasurement" was to take place afterwards. Worsley's survey encountered innumerable logistical and organizational difficulties. In 1655 Petty, by this time a bitter rival of Worsley, proposed a survey of the whole of Ireland, not simply of the expropriated areas. Petty proposed not only to solve the technical problems involved in the land distribution but also to undertake a scientific survey of Ireland's landed wealth on the basis of quantified geographic and economic information.

Petty startled his commissioners by promising to complete the task within one year and, once he received approval, set about training a crew of surveyors. Petty's job was reduced by his commissioners to a survey of twenty-two Irish counties—still a mammoth undertaking. The results were impressive in the extreme. Despite numerous administrative delays beyond his control, Petty completed the Down Survey in thirteen months. So accurate was his survey that it remained unsurpassed for two centuries. In fact, the Down Survey was a brilliant confirmation of the utility of Baconian principles:

In the first place, it had required a shrewd understanding of the techniques of surveying, which were rationalised, streamlined and adapted to the Irish situation without sacrifice of accuracy. Secondly, a form of organisation using the principle of the division of labour made the survey a model demonstration of the potentialities of Baconian collective enterprise.[59]

For the history of economic thought, the theoretical problems posed by Petty's survey are more significant than his organizational and scientific achievement. For Petty undertook not merely to measure the physical extent of land but also to assess its value or degree of profitability. The practical problem which confronted Petty was that of comparing lands of unequal value. During the survey, Petty attempted to employ various yardsticks, like estimating grain crops by counting the number of seeds from each seed planted or the weight per bushel of planted seed. Similarly, he proposed to assess the value of pasture land in terms of the weight of hay produced or by determining the number of domesticated animals supported per acre. He also suggested that rents, sale prices, frequency of purchase, values of landed inheritances, and improvement of estates could serve as further indices of the value of land.[60]

Like many other seventeenth-century writers, Petty was convinced that England and Ireland were not living up to their productive potential. Agricultural improvement, enlightened administration, and scientific policies of taxation could enormously boost the wealth of the nation. Agricultural improvement loomed large in Petty's analysis. He argued, despite the evidence of unemployment and underemployment, that England was underpopulated. In fact, he claimed, if the lands were "improved to the utmost of known Husbandry," they could support a population twice as large.[61] One means of improvement would be the enclosure of common lands, which he estimated as three million acres.[62] But the major means of improvement would be the application of the principles of scientific husbandry.

Like most members of the Hartlib circle, Petty exhibited a knowledge of the basic principles of agricultural improvement. In his *Political Arithmetick* (probably completed in 1676), for example, Petty referred explicitly to Richard Weston's "Judicious Discourse of Husbandry," which had been published by Hartlib, and praised agricultural improvement by claiming that

bad Land may be improved and made good; Bog may by draining be made Meadow; Heath-Land may (as in *Flanders*) be made to bear Flax and Clover grass, so as to advance in value from one to an Hundred.[63]

Furthermore, Petty claimed that such improvements of land were more productive than the building of furniture or houses.[64] For this reason, he believed that the level of agricultural improvement was the best index of the overall health and well-being of the economy. As he wrote in his proposal for an Irish land registry, "Knowing the fertility and Capacity of our Land, Wee can tell whether it hath not produced its utmost through the labours of the people."[65]

The determination of "the fertility and Capacity" of the land was connected to a critical problem Petty encountered during the course of the Down Survey: how to develop an invariable standard which would allow the common measurement of widely divergent types of land. In 1660, when he advocated the establishment of an Irish land registry, Petty identified its first objective as determining "how not only the naturall & intrinsick, but also the casuall and circumstantiall vallues of Lande in Ireland, may bee ascertayned and brought under Rules."[66] The land registry was also to collect data on the size and boundaries of estates and the ownership of land; to make various calculations of land values; to keep an account of titles, improvements, inhabitants, purchases, and sales. But in all Petty's writings of this period, the central recurring problem is the determination of "the naturall and intrinsick" value of land. Indeed, it was this preoccupation which prompted him to undertake one of the most important analytic innovations in the history of economic thought—the elaboration of a labour theory of value.

This theoretical achievement came by way of a digression in Petty's *Treatise of Taxes and Contributions*, first published in 1662. The *Treatise* was occasioned by an immediate and practical problem, the reorganization of the Revenue by the Restoration Parliament. But for Petty taxation, like any aspect of political policy, had to be established on a genuinely scientific basis. Thus, the *Treatise* does more than advocate a specific approach to taxation; it analyses the very basis of producing wealth and the effects of different taxation policies on generating wealth. The *Treatise* begins by asserting that the wealth of a nation is determined not by its territorial extent but by the size of its population. "Fewness of people," Petty claimed, "is real poverty." But the production of wealth requires that the people be productively employed and well governed. Not all employments, however, are productive. A large number of mercantile pursuits are *sterile*, or unproductive, according to Petty. Although a certain number of merchants are necessary to the state, a large number are entirely parasitical; they merely "distribute forth and back the blood and nutritive juyces of the Body Politick, namely the product of Husbandry and Manufacture." Although many commercial functions are unproductive, state expenditure is, at least indirectly, productive. In substantiating this claim, Petty developed a primitive notion of the circular flow of wealth, according to which state expenditure flows into productive hands. The amounts that the state spends on "Entertainments, magnificent shews, triumphal Arches & . . . [will] refund presently to the most useful; namely to Brewers, Bakers, Taylours, Shoemakers, &c."[67]

The focus of the *Treatise*, however, is taxation. Furthermore, since the basis of taxation in early modern England was landed property, Petty turned to examine the "mysterious nature" of rent, the taxable income from landed property. In a remarkable digression from his main discussion, Petty advanced the argument that rent equals the surplus product of the land—a surplus which is the remaining physical output once the costs of production are deducted:

Suppose a man could with his own hands plant a certain scope of Land with Corn, that is, could Digg, or Plough, Harrow, Weed, Reap, Carry home, Thresh, and Winnow so much as the Husbandry of this Land requires; and had withal Seed wherewith to sowe the same. I say, that when this man hath subducted his seed out of the proceed of his Harvest, and also, what himself hath both eaten and given to others in exchange for Clothes, and other Natural necessities; that the remainder of Corn is the natural and the true Rent of the Land for that year.[68]

This argument constituted a daring and original theoretical departure. In attempting to define rent as a real magnitude, Petty inaugurated a line of inquiry based on a labour theory of value which was to figure prominently in the writings of the classical political economists. As William Letwin has assessed Petty's concept of the "natural and true Rent of Land,"

This definition, in short, applies a formidable theoretical invention—the notion of a 'real' economic magnitude—to a measure, rent, that had always been thought of as a money payment; and it comes very close to saying what again was remarkably original, that real rent is a surplus, not merely— as it had always been considered, and long continued to be—a cost of production.[69]

Petty did not leave his analysis at this point, however. Having defined the real magnitude or value of rent (which in turn determined the value of land), he went on to ask what the money value of this "real Rent" might be. This question led him to a general consideration of the money value of commodities. Petty asked, "how much English money this Corn or Rent is worth?" And he answered,

Let another man go travel into a Countrey where is Silver, there Dig it, Refine it, bring it to the same place where the other man planted his Corn; Coyne it, etc, the same person, all the while of his working for Silver, gathering also food for his necessary livelihood, and procuring himself covering &c. I say, the Silver of the one, must be esteemed of equal value with the Corn of the other.[70]

Contrary to common interpretations, this statement does not say that goods produced with the same amount of labour have equal values. After all, Petty has suggested that the individual who labours to produce silver must simultaneously undertake to feed and clothe himself. Petty's claim is that the *surplus* labour time devoted to producing silver, that is, the labour time beyond that necessary for the maintenance of the labourer, will produce a value of silver equal to the surplus product of corn (again, once the value of the labourer's subsistence has been deducted). It is for this reason that Petty later commented that "the neat proceed of the Silver is the price of the whole neat proceed of the Corn."[71] Nonetheless, this passage strongly suggests the possibility that this method of evaluating the money value of rent might be utilized to analyse the value of all commodities. And this is precisely the suggestion Petty made when he characterized his theory as "the foundation of equallizing and ballancing of values." Furthermore, at a later point in the *Treatise* Petty argued explicitly that the values of goods such as corn and silver are determined by the labour time necessary for their production. He wrote, for example, that "if a man can bring to *London* an ounce of Silver out of the Earth in *Peru,* in the same time that he can produce a bushel of Corn, then one is the natural price of the other."[72]

This statement constitutes the fundament of a simple labour theory of value according to which the value of commodities is determined by the labour time necessary for their production. Yet such a theory was not the solution embraced by Petty despite his use of it at various stages of analysis. While Petty's examples generally focus on the value-determining role of human labour, he remained convinced that land was another constituent of the value of commodities. Thus, he wrote in the *Treatise* that "all things ought to be valued by two natural Denominations, which is Land and Labour." And he contended that "we should be glad to finde out a natural Par between Land and Labour, so as we might express the value by either of them alone as well or better than by both."[73]

Petty did not formulate such a par between land and labour in his analysis in the *Treatise*. Yet the search for such a formulation remained a central preoccupation in his writings. We find the problem discussed in his unpublished papers.[74] Furthermore, in *The Political Anatomy of Ireland* Petty returned to the original problem he had posed nine years earlier in the *Treatise*. In attempting to assess Ireland's wealth, Petty confronted the problem of measuring the value of lands of differing profitability—the same problem he had confronted while undertaking the Down Survey. Once again, he suggested that the value of land is a function of the value of the commodities it produces less their costs of production (defined strictly in terms of wages). Having so formulated the concept of value, Petty returned to his central theoretical question:

And this brings me to the most important Consideration in Political Oeconomies, *viz.* how to make a *Par* and *Equation* between Lands and Labour, so as to express the Value of any thing by either alone.[75]

It is not difficult to understand why Petty was not satisfied with a simple labour theory of value and why he felt compelled to include land as a determinant of value. Rent was the central category in his analysis of economic phenomena. This was so because he understood, as did most other seventeenth-century theorists, that land was the primary form of wealth in England and Ireland at the time. Furthermore, Petty conceived of rent as the basic economic surplus which could be taxed to support the Crown.[76] Rent, therefore, was both the principal determinant of the value of land and the basis of the prosperity of the kingdom. It was natural that Petty should feel compelled to analyse this, to him the most central, economic category. However, Petty saw clearly that the products of the land were not simply the result of the activity of labour. After all, different lands would produce different outputs with similar inputs of labour. Such differences—the basis of differential rents—could be accounted for, he believed, only in terms of the productive powers of nature itself. The value of lands of differing profitability—and, indeed, the value of all products of the land, such as corn and silver—could be determined scientifically only if the productive powers of nature and human labour could be equated, or calculated on the basis of a common standard.

Petty's most ingenious attempt to equate the productive powers of land and labour occurred in *The Political Anatomy of Ireland*. Take two acres of enclosed land, he suggested, and put a calf on it to graze. At the end of twelve months the calf will have put on weight equal to fifty days of food. This increment in food value of the calf constitutes the value of the rent of land: "the Interest of the Value of the Calf, is the value of years Rent of the land." Now, if a man labouring on the same land can in an equal amount of time produce sixty or more days' worth of food, then the surplus of days of food above that produced by nature in the case of the calf constitutes his wages. In other words, wages are "the overplus of days food" after deducting the value of nature's contribution (which accrues to the landowner as rent) from the total output. In this way, the shares of land and labour in the total product (received as income in the form of rent and wages) are both expressed in a single unit, "days food." As Petty wrote, in a passage suggestive of a *corn model* of the economy (that is, the economy as a gigantic farm producing one basic subsistence good): "Wherefore the days food of an adult Man, at a Medium, and not the days labour, is the common measure of Value, and seems to be as regular and constant as the value of fine Silver."[77]

Suggestive though this argument may be, it does not constitute a solution to Petty's problem. To begin with, Petty has slipped here from a discussion of the *determination* of value to a consideration of the *measure* of value. Furthermore, his argument has become entirely circular. Whereas in the *Treatise* he had explained rent as the surplus above wages, here he has explained wages as the surplus product above that represented by rent. It is, of course, fair enough to divide the total product into rent and wages (representing the incomes accruing to the only factors of production in Petty's model, land and labour); but this is simply to define distributive shares, not to explain the determination of value. At times, as we have suggested, Petty approached a strict labour theory of value. Indeed, he quickly reverted to such a theory in *The Political Anatomy of Ireland* when he said that one can value "an Irish Cabbin at the number of days food, which the Maker spent in building of it."[78] But in this case he was not dealing with agricultural production and could thus treat labour as the single value-determining element. When he returned to landed production, Petty immediately found himself back in the quandary of trying to provide a single equation which would account for the value-contributing roles of land and labour.

Despite—indeed in some measure because of—these deficiencies, Petty's theoretical economics was of crucial importance to the further development of classical political economy. More consistently and coherently than any other seventeenth-century writer, Petty grappled with the chief theoretical problem which confronted scientific economics during this period: how to construct a model which comprehended the features of the new form of social production (capitalism) which was developing at a time when agriculture composed the most important sphere of capitalist production. The ambiguities of Petty's analysis reflect, then, not so much the shortcomings of his theoretical equipment as the difficulty of analysing the essential features of capitalist production during the transitional period in which land constituted the most important factor of production and rent the most important form of surplus value. In Petty's model, profit on capital had not yet emerged as the central feature of the capitalist economy; it was eclipsed by rent. His model was based, in other words, on phenomena—land and rent—which were peculiarly unsusceptible to a simple labour theory analysis. Recognizing the differential productivity of land in the case of equal inputs of labour, Petty continually moved from a labour theory to a land-labour theory of value. In the end, he failed to construct a consistent and coherent explanation of value. Nevertheless, by defining the nature of the problem and constructing a model designed to solve the problem, Petty cleared the theoretical terrain for those who were to follow.

The model which Petty passed on to his successors can be accurately described only as an agrarian capitalist one. His anatomy of the economy clearly set forth the triadic structure of landlord, tenant farmer, and wage labourer which was to become the foundation of classical English economics.[79] It is true, however, that Petty did not always clearly set out these relationships. In his writings he tended to replace the tenant farmer by a kind of estate manager whose income Petty treated as a wage (and not as profit). This may well have reflected certain realities of capitalist farming in Ireland after the Cromwellian conquest. Be that as it may, Petty's model presupposed that agricultural production was carried on by hired labourers, that agriculture was organized in terms of the production of foodstuffs for the market, that the increase of the surplus product of the land was vital to economic growth, and that the dominant form of surplus product was rent which accrued to the owners of the land. In these respects, he grasped the fundamental features of emerging agrarian capitalism; and his agrarian capitalist model was to inform theoretical economics for the subsequent century.

RENT AND INTEREST: CHILD, LOCKE, BARBON, AND NORTH

Following Petty's innovative work, an agrarian-based model remained the framework for most sophisticated economic analysis throughout the seventeenth century. This is especially clear when we examine the debate on the rate of interest which occurred first in 1668 and again in 1690. What is equally clear when we examine the debate is that the writings of William Petty were instrumental in defining the conceptual terms and establishing the mode of analysis which dominated it. At the turn of the century, the debate produced one of the most significant outbursts of literature in the early history of political economy.

The debate on the rate of interest had its origins in the establishment of a Select Committee on the State of Trade by the House of Commons in 1667. The following year the king responded, creating a new Council of Trade. The House of Lords got into the act in 1669 by launching its own committee. Active in all these committees was Josiah Child, a London merchant who was in 1673 to become the East India Company's largest shareholder and in 1681 its director. In all of these committees—indeed, throughout the course of his public career—Child consistently advocated a legal reduction in the rate of interest as the key to restoring prosperity in England.

Arguments for a reduction in the rate of interest were not new. But those, such as Culpepper, who had advanced such arguments previously were identified generally with the landed interest. Child presented the case in a new form. His was not the perspective of the landed man whose prodigal lifestyle had led him into the clutches of the usurer. Nor did he advance traditional ethical arguments against usury. Instead, he claimed that the prosperity of all classes, usurers excepted, would improve with a decline in the rate of interest.

Child's theoretical explanation of this claim could not be said, contrary to Schumpeter's view, to constitute a contribution to scientific economics.[80] Indeed, Child's *Brief Observations Concerning Trade and Interest of Money* (1668) was built around unwarranted theoretical generalization from the strictly empirical observation that the rate of interest was lower in Holland than in England. From there, Child makes an enormous conceptual leap. Without anything resembling a theoretical argument, he makes the assertion that "the abatement of interest is the cause of the prosperity and riches of any nation."[81] Constructed as it is, the *Brief Observations* is of little theoretical interest. Of some interest from our perspective, however, is its favourable reference to Petty and his *Treatise*. But the influence of Petty is most apparent in Child's *New Discourse of Trade* (written in 1669 and published in 1693). Also devoted to the debate over money and interest, the *New Discourse* is a work of substantially more intellectual import than the *Brief Observations*. Whether Petty's *Treatise* provided the inspiration for the theoretical structure of the *New Discourse* can only be surmised. Like the *Brief Observations*, this tract includes praise of Petty, "the most Ingenious *Author* of that *Treatise of Taxes and Contributions*."[82] Of more significance, however, is this work's treatment of agricultural improvement and its relation to the rate of interest.

The *New Discourse* reveals a sharp awareness of England's agricultural revolution. Child remarks, for example, upon

what great Improvements have been made these last sixty years upon breaking up and enclosing of Wastes, Forests and Parks, and draining of the Fenns, and all those places inhabited and furnished with Husbandry.

Furthermore, he claims that previous reductions in the rate of interest had been due to "the encouragement which that abatement of Interest gave to *Landlords* and *Tenants*, to improve by *Draining, Marling, Limeing*, etc."[83]

Though the theoretical analysis of the *New Discourse* is far from rigorous, it suggests that a decrease in the rate of interest will contribute to alleviating unemployment. Like most seventeenth- and eighteenth-century writers on economic matters, Child was acutely aware of unemployment and the drain it imposed on the English economy. He appears to have believed that a reduction in the rate of interest would encourage agricultural investment and thereby stimulate industry and trade. Although he does not fully elaborate the argument, Child seems to suggest that the encouragement to landed investment brought about by a lower interest rate will stimulate the whole economy. Certainly his belief that agricultural improvement was the key to solving the problem of unemployment put him in impressive company; Hartlib, Plattes, and Petty, among others, had all made the same claim.

The argument that agricultural improvement is crucial to economic prosperity is made much more explicit in Child's *Discourse of the Nature, Use, and Advantages of Trade*, published in 1694. Here Child claims that "the produce of the Land is the principal foundation of Trade."[84] Moreover, he puts forward a concept of the circular flow throughout the economy of wealth produced by husbandry:

And from this Labour of the Husbandman, are derived many of the Improvements of Trade, in the disposal of those Treasures which he hath raised out of the Earth by his Industry and Pains. His Corn gives Trade and Imployment to the Miller, the Baker, the Maulter and the Brewer.[85]

Finally, in a statement in tune with the Country party's ideology of the period, which saw the preservation of civic virtue by independent landed gentry as the key to health and stability in the body politic, Child calls on "the Gentry of *England*" to "reside in those countries where their Estates lye . . . to preserve good Government and good Husbandry among the many inferiour people in their Neighbourhood."[86]

It is, of course, possible that these arguments represented a conscious rhetorical strategy on the part of Child. Recognizing that landed gentlemen made up the overwhelming majority in Parliament, that they viewed merchants as narrowly self-interested and generally conceived the public interest as founded upon the landed interest, Child may well have shaped his argument to the predispositions of his audience. Be that as it may, his theoretical argument advanced a model of England as a commercial-agrarian commonwealth—that is, a nation whose wealth and prosperity was rooted in agriculture and could be extended through commercial expansion. Compatible in principle with an agrarian-based economy, commercial expansion was thus crucial to agricultural production and improvement.

In both the *New Discourse* and *A Discourse*, Child exhibited a definite agrarian bias which appears to have owed its formulation in part to Petty. Believing that production on the land formed the foundation of national wealth, Child conceived of the stimulus to agricultural improvement which would be brought about by an "abatement" of the rate of interest as critical in restoring England to prosperity. Ironically, Child's major opponent in the controversy over the rate of interest, John Locke, fully shared his agrarian bias yet entirely rejected his theoretical analysis and policy conclusions. Locke came from a social and intellectual milieu similar to that of Petty. One grandfather was a tanner, the other a wealthy clothier. His father, a country lawyer, was a Puritan who fought with the Parliamentary Army from 1642 until its victory in 1649. Locke entered Oxford in 1652—the year after Petty left—and quickly became a member of the experimental philosophy club. Strongly influenced by the Baconian movement, Locke soon fell under the spell of Robert Boyle, the leading experimenter among the Oxford empiricists, and began to assist Boyle in his experiments.[87] Like Petty, Locke became a physician and in that capacity he was invited in 1666 to join the household of Anthony Ashley Cooper, later the first earl of Shaftesbury.

The future leader of the Whig opposition to Charles II, Shaftesbury was one of the central political figures of the seventeenth century and one who maintained a keen interest in trade and colonial expansion. But it was land which was the principal source of Shaftesbury's wealth, and it was agriculture and the landed proprietor which constituted the economic and social centre of his vision. As his biographer has put it, "to the end he remained a country landlord." And even in colonial affairs, this bias came through, for example, in his statement on the founding of an English colony in Carolina that "we aim not at the profit of merchants, but the encouragement of landlords." For Shaftesbury, then, "the basis of society should be the landed interest"; but "commerce and investment had a valuable and respectable contribution to make to the general prosperity."[88] He shared Child's view of the commonwealth as founded upon landed interests yet prospering through commercial expansion.

During the late 1660s, when Locke had just come into his service, Shaftesbury functioned as a member of the Privy Council Committee for Trade and the Plantations and as chief member of the Lords Proprietors of Carolina. In 1672 Shaftesbury enjoyed the greatest success of his official career when he became Lord Chancellor. That same year he inspired the creation of the Council of Trade and Plantations of which he became president. Locke's deep interest in economic problems dates from his service with Shaftesbury. By 1668, Locke had become substantially more than a personal physician to

Shaftesbury; he was also effectively his secretary and confidant. As a result, Shaftesbury secured his loyal supporter several advisory positions in matters of trade and finance. In 1668 Locke was appointed secretary to the Lords Proprietors of Carolina, and in 1673 he became secretary of the Council of Trade and Plantations.

Locke's major economic work, *Some Considerations of the Consequences of the Lowering of Interest, and Raising the Value of Money* was first drafted during the parliamentary agitation of 1668 as a memorandum to Shaftesbury; it was inspired by Josiah Child, who favoured reducing the official rate of interest from six to four percent. The evidence suggests that Locke had read Petty's *Treatise* by this time. Indeed, he employs numerous terms and arguments which appear to have been borrowed from Petty. In 1681 and again in 1691, similar bills—each backed by Child—were presented to Parliament. When one bill was reintroduced in November 1691, Locke had been revising his papers on interest for more than a year. He immediately published *Some Considerations* and appears to have presented his argument during the parliamentary debate on the bill. Nevertheless, in January 1692, the House of Commons passed a modified version of this bill to reduce the interest rate to five percent.

Some Considerations enjoys a curious reputation in the history of economic thought. It has been considered both a traditional mercantilist tract and an early exercise in classical economics, a major statement of the labour theory of value and a pioneering formulation of a subjective-utility theory of value based on supply and demand analysis. Indeed, one analyst has argued that the work employed both value theories simultaneously.[89] What has not been in dispute, however, is the position Locke took on the proposal to reduce the rate of interest. Locke unequivocally opposed all such efforts. He claimed that there were natural laws of trade and "laws of value" which could be violated only to the detriment of the nation as a whole. The rate of interest, Locke argued, is a "natural price" determined by the laws of supply and demand. A forcible reduction in the rate of interest would only provoke lenders to export their money capital to countries where the rate of interest was higher. Such an outflow of specie would cause English prices to decline. As a result, the balance of trade would shift against England since (like Malynes, he assumes that demand is inelastic) the aggregate value of English exports would decline. Furthermore, falling prices would cause rents and land values to collapse. Locke, then, like Child, saw the landed and commercial interests as rising or falling together.

The latter aspect of Locke's argument, that falling prices caused by a reduction in the rate of interest would depress land values and rents, is particularly intriguing. No commentator seems to have appreciated that *Some Considerations* is preoccupied with the effects of a reduced interest rate on rents and the well-being of the landed gentry. To be sure, William Letwin has remarked that "the price of land . . . became the chief matter" of *Some Considerations*. But, considering such an interest idiosyncratic to Locke, Letwin fails to pursue the point and to examine the extent to which this "chief matter," the price of land, and the related matter of rent were the categories around which Locke organized his inquiry into money and interest.[90]

That Locke should have exhibited a pronounced agrarian bias need surprise only those who have taken literally the claim that he was a prophet of commercial and industrial capitalism. As we have noted above, Locke's formative influences were quite similar to those of Petty: a Puritan upbringing, exposure to social Baconianism and the Hartlib circle, participation in the Oxford Club, and an abiding interest in economic—and agricultural—improvement.[91] To this list we can add the powerful influence of Shaftesbury, the great Whig lord whose landed investments and agricultural interest decisively shaped Locke's view of society.

The exact nature of Petty's influence on Locke is difficult to gauge. Given that Petty left Oxford before Locke arrived, it is not certain whether the two ever met. What is certain, however, is that Locke was completely familiar with Petty's major economic works, all of which he possessed. Moreover, one often finds Locke repeating theoretical formulations which originated with Petty. As the author of the only major study of Locke's economic writings has put it, "Often what seems new in Locke had already been at least implied by Sir William Petty several decades earlier." Furthermore, as we have noted above, Locke possessed a copy of Petty's 1667 *Treatise* and may well have read it before writing his economic essay in 1668.[92]

Like Petty, Locke exhibited a distinct awareness of agricultural improvement and its economic importance. In the *Second Treatise*, a work in which the terminology of improvement is employed repeatedly, and which was probably drafted during the years 1679–1681 (that is, after 1668 and before 1692), Locke discusses the advantages of enclosure:

the provisions serving to the support of humane life, produced by one acre of inclosed and cultivated land, are (to speak much within compasse) ten times more, than those which are yeilded by an acre of Land, of an equal richnesse, lyeing wast in common.[93]

It is in this same context that Locke develops his alleged labour theory of value. Discussing the role of labour in increasing the necessities of life he attempts, as Petty does, to compare the output of two equal pieces of land, one uncultivated, the other cultivated. Locke makes the calculation by comparing an uncultivated acre of land in America with a cultivated acre of English land. Again employing Petty's terminology, albeit in a slightly different manner, Locke claims that though the intrinsic values of the two acres may be the same, their market values, measured by the price of their produce, are not. The difference is the value added by the labour expended on the improvement of the English land:

An acre of land that bears here Twenty Bushels of Wheat, and another in *America*, which, with the same Husbandry, would do the like, are without doubt, of the same natural, intrinsick value. But yet the Benefit Mankind receives from the one, in a Year, is worth 5 pounds and from the other possibly not worth a Penny, if all the profit an *Indian* received from it were to be valued, and sold here; at least, I may truly say, not 1/1000.[94]

It is difficult to imagine that this passage does not owe something to Petty's analysis in the *Treatise*. The analogies are profound: Locke chooses agricultural production to illustrate the role of labour in adding value to commodities; he employs the concepts of "intrinsic value" and "natural value"; and he estimates the productive powers of labour in terms of the exchange value of the excess or surplus product beyond that which nature itself will produce. What is true of the *Second Treatise* is even more true of *Some Considerations* (both the 1668 and the 1692 versions), where land and rent occupy centre stage in Locke's analysis. While the essay begins with general deliberations upon money, Locke quickly moves to a circular-flow analysis in which agricultural production forms the fundamental basis of the economy. Locke's presentation of the circular flow is no more sophisticated than that to be found in many earlier theorists, but it is characterized by a greater clarity of exposition:

Money in its Circulation during the several Wheels of Trade, whilst it keeps in that Channel (for some will unavoidably be dreined into standing Pools) is all shared between the Landholder, whose Land affords the Materials; the Labourer, who works them; The Broker, (i.e.) Merchant and Shopkeeper, who distributes them to those who want them; And the Consumer, who spends them.[95]

Not all those who figure in the circular flow of national wealth are of equal importance. It is possible, Locke claims, that there may be too many merchants or brokers who hinder trade "by making the Circuit, which the Money goes, larger, and in that Circuit more Stops." An excess of merchants causes too large a share of the national output to fall into mercantile hands, thereby "starving the Labourer, and impoverishing the Landholder, whose Interest is chiefly to be taken care of, it being a settled unmoveable Concernment in the Commonwealth."[96] Like Petty, Locke here refers to merchants as "gamesters." The settled and unmovable character of landed wealth makes it the *political* foundation of the commonwealth. Locke also had a sound *economic* reason for favouring the landed interest: all taxes are in reality laid on land; the royal revenue is merely a share of the aggregate rent of land.[97] For this reason, landholders are the most important members of the state and ought to be treated accordingly:

the Landholder, who is the person, that bearing the greatest part of the burthens of the Kingdom, ought, I think, to have the greatest care taken of him, and enjoy as many Privileges, and as much Wealth, as the favour of the Law can (with regard to the Publick-weal) confer on him.[98]

This is hardly the voice of a laissez-faire economist or a full-fledged political theorist of democracy. Locke returns repeatedly to the argument that landholders deserve special protection and privileges from the state. Furthermore, the state should endeavour to improve the economic position of their class. The raising of rents "would be worth the Nations Care," Locke maintains. And since rents are high when agricultural prices are high, the state must attempt to prevent actions which would lower the price level. Yet that is precisely what would result from a reduction in the rate of interest (since lenders would turn to foreign investment).[99] For this reason, proposals to reduce the rate of interest must be opposed.

Locke's argument is instructive in several respects. First, despite its ostensible concern with analysis of money and interest, *Some Considerations* focuses on rent and land. Locke states explicitly that the landowner is the most important member of the commonwealth and that rents are the basis of royal revenues (and thus the foundation of state power). For these reasons, the state must guarantee that the interests of the landowners are protected and extended, which in the specific case at hand means opposing a legal reduction in the rate of interest. Second, Locke follows Petty in claiming that the value of land "consists in this, That by its constant production of saleable commodities it brings in a certain yearly Income."[100] Moreover, in his *Short Observations on a Printed Paper* published in 1696, Locke further follows Petty in arguing that the value of land is increased by improvement and that such an increase may be measured by the increased product of the land or by the enlarged money rent that the improved land will yield. Third, Locke claims—again echoing Petty—that interest on money is analogous to the rent of land. Indeed, interest is the rent of money. Fourth, contrary to his popular image as a proponent of commercial and industrial capitalism, Locke adheres to a long tradition of agrarian-based social and political theory by arguing that whereas the interests of the landowners are consistent with the public interest, this is not true of merchants who "may get by a trade that makes the kingdom poor."[101] Finally, Locke's economic model is based upon the assumption that the direct agricultural producer is a "day labourer" who receives a wage for a fixed period of work.[102] Thus, Locke's model generalizes the triadic structure—landlord, tenant farmer, wage labourer—more clearly than did that of any of his predecessors. In all these respects, Locke's economics can be seen to constitute a political economy of agrarian capitalism whose central figure was the landlord and whose central category was rent.

After Locke's writings of the 1690s, no major analysis of agrarian capitalism emerged until Richard Cantillon's treatise appeared in French in 1755. The mode of analysis inspired by Petty and Locke did continue to exercise an important influence, especially on two other late seventeenth-century English economic theorists of distinction—Nicholas Barbon and Dudley North. While neither Barbon nor North was a political economist in the meaningful sense of the term, that is, a social theorist who attempted to comprehend economic relations as a decisive aspect of social life, both produced short pamphlets which exhibited first-rate economic analysis. Barbon and North both came from the London merchant community, although they took conflicting positions on the debate over a legal reduction in the rate of interest. Despite their differences over policy, both framed their arguments in terms of a conscious appeal to the landed interest—stressing a commonality of landed and commercial interest (a common rhetorical strategy in the seventeenth century)—and both employed arguments which described commercial relations in terms often derived from agriculture.[103]

Nicholas Barbon was the son of "Praise God Barebones," the famous leather merchant and radical Puritan after whom the "Barebones Parliament" of the Revolution was named. Like Petty and Locke, Barbon was trained in medicine. He went on, however, to become the largest builder in the City of London and a pioneer in the fields of insurance and banking. Barbon's most important economic tract, *A Discourse of Trade*, was published in 1690 as a contribution to the contemporary debate on the rate of interest. While Barbon differed sharply from Locke and favoured measures to bring about a reduction in the rate of interest, he used the same analogy as the latter in comparing rent and interest. "Interest," he wrote, "is the Rent of Stock, and is the same as the Rent of Land." Just as rent is actually a payment for a share of the goods produced by the land, so interest is paid not on money itself but on the goods ("stock") purchased by money.[104] As did Child, Barbon claimed that interest rates in England higher than those in Holland caused a decay of trade and a decline in rents. And like both Child and Locke, Barbon believed that declining rents were a serious danger to the commonwealth.

According to Barbon, all "settled Forms of Government" are "founded upon Property of Land." Furthermore, "the Land is the fund that must support and preserve the Government."[105] Consequently, the state should pursue economic policies that would raise rents. Most valuable in this respect would be a decline in the interest rate. A high interest rate, Barbon asserted, discourages long-term accumulation of goods for export and therefore reduces the aggregate demand for agricultural goods. The end result is a decline in prices, output, and rents. Barbon did not believe, however, in reducing the rate of interest by means of parliamentary decree. Instead, he favoured an expansion of the money supply by a revaluation of the English currency. Assuming the demand for money to be more or less constant, expansion of the money supply automatically brings about a fall in the rate of interest.

The last major figure to contribute to the debate over interest, Dudley North, whose *Discourses Upon Trade* appeared posthumously in 1691, stands in sharp contrast to Petty, Child, Locke, and Barbon. North was a Tory royalist who opposed the revolutionary influences which had shaped Petty and Locke in particular. Moreover, North's method was Cartesian, not Baconian. North came from an established landed family but made his fortune in trade, becoming one of the most substantial members of the Levant Company and its director in 1680. The following year he was made sheriff of London in Charles II's campaign aginst the Whigs. In 1683 he was made a commissioner of the Customs; and in 1685, the year he was elected to Parliament, he became commissioner of the Treasury.

North's *Discourses* displays a logical structure and a mode of analysis unsurpassed at the time. Like Locke, he claimed that there are natural laws of economic phenomena which defy political control. "This ebbing and flowing of Money," he wrote, "supplies and accomodates itself, without any aid of Politicians." Also like Locke, North maintained that "it is not Interest makes Trade, but Trade increasing, the Stock of the Nation makes Interest low." But undoubtedly the most significant similarity with Locke—and with Petty and Barbon—consists in North's comparison of interest with rent. Interest, he asserted, "is only Rent for Stock, as the other is for land."[106] Furthermore, to bolster his argument against reducing the rate of interest, North claimed that a decline in interest "will bring down the Price of Land" since money holders will not issue loans at a reduced rate and indebted gentry will be forced as a consequence to sell their lands to pay off their debts—thus raising the supply of land on the market and bringing down its price. Whether North was sincere in his concern about the price of land and the well-being of the gentry cannot be determined. Whatever the case, what is most significant is that he felt compelled to appeal to the self-interest of the landowner in making his case against a reduction in interest.

By the end of the seventeenth century, then, a common lexicon and mode of analysis of economic phenomena had been established. Those theorists who conceptualized the economy as a whole tended to employ a rudimentary circular-flow analysis in which wealth was generated fundamentally from the production of goods on the land. Furthermore, the production of an agricultural surplus in the form of rent by hired day labourers was seen as the foundation of the power of the state and also of the most important social class, the landowners. Rent tended to be treated, consequently, as the most significant of all economic phenomena. And that category which dominated analysis and debate during the 1660s and the 1690s—interest—was grasped theoretically by means of analogy with rent. At the same time, it must be noted that seventeenth-century economic writers differed over a number of important issues, not the least of which was the issue of rising incomes and consumption levels among the poor. Some, usually merchants like Barbon and North who were not principally concerned about the organization of production and wage levels, saw consumption in positive terms as a stimulus to industry and trade. Landlords, capitalist farmers, and manufacturers, by contrast, tended to see high wages as a disincentive to labour.[107] Nevertheless, what is crucial for our purposes is the emergence of a framework of analysis in which agriculture was seen as the foundation of national wealth; in which agricultural production was presumed to be carried on by day labourers who worked for tenant farmers, who in turn used a share of their surplus to make rent payments to the proprietors of the land; in which rents and land values were seen as crucial to prosperity; and in which economic policies were analysed and advanced in terms of their impact upon the landed interest.

It is no overstatement to say that at the turn of the century an agrarian capitalist model whose central concept was rent dominated theoretical speculation on economic affairs in England. By way of reflection on a different set of economic and political problems, French economic thought was to arrive at a similar point by the beginning of the eighteenth century.

French Mercantilism: Trade, Finance, and Absolute Monarchy

French mercantilist thought was constituted from a tradition of political discourse which differed sharply from the English version. Whereas English mercantilism built initially on a Commonwealth tradition of political thought which conceived of the health and stability of the state as dependent upon economic relations within a civil society dominated by agriculture, French mercantilism grew from an absolutist political theory which posited the state as the only agency capable of unifying the particular wills which make up civil society. In English mercantilism it was the economic relations of civil society which to an important degree guaranteed the stability and prosperity of the state; in French mercantilism it was the state which guaranteed the unity and harmony of civil society. These divergent intellectual orientations reflected the divergent historical paths taken by English and French society out of the crisis of feudalism discussed in the previous chapter. While in England the state had been transformed in significant measure into an institution which represented the self-organization of landed gentlemen, in France the drive towards absolutism created an explosive tension between centrifugal and centripetal interests. In England, the constitutional monarchy represented in a very real sense the self-centralization of the ruling class; in France, centralization proceeded by way of a constant battle by the Crown against the traditionally dominant elements of civil society.

A series of dramatic events over the course of nearly a century pushed a growing number of French social thinkers in the direction of absolutist political theory (and its mercantilist political economy). The civil wars of the second half of the sixteenth century provoked men like Bodin to swing behind an absolutist-mercantilist concept of state and society. Massive peasant rebellions of 1578, 1580, and almost the entire decade of the 1590s forced the ruling class to unite against the threat from below. Furthermore, representatives of the Third Estate often looked to the monarchy to curb the excessive privileges of the nobility. The draining experience of the Thirty Years' War also exposed the military weakness of an internally divided state. Finally, the crisis of the Fronde demonstrated that no section of society outside the court was capable of creating a unified political force. All sections of the ruling class, and those aspiring to enter it, were involved in a battle for a share of the centralized feudal rent appropriated by the state. To many contemporaries only the monarchy appeared to be above the rampant particularity that was corrupting French society; only the monarchy offered a potential embodiment of the general will. For this reason, political thought began to conceive of the state as the active presence which constitutes the unity of civil society. As one scholar has put it,

> The notion that it is a grave disadvantage for government to be subject to the partial wills of those who are governed, that such subjection is not a source of liberty but of chaos and destruction, distinguishes French theory from the beginning of the sixteenth century, and sets it apart from Anglo-Saxon modes of thought.[108]

French mercantilism emerged in the general context of such theory. Economic prosperity was seen as a central precondition of the reconstitution of state power. Moreover, in a society in which the bourgeoisie sought its fortune, as did most of the aristocracy, by acquiring a political office which entitled it to a share of centralized feudal rent, the task of developing industry and commerce appeared to fall to the state itself. Thus, whereas English mercantilist theory (and those policies corresponding to it) was in the seventeenth century produced by merchants, French mercantilism was largely produced by royal officials. As a noted authority on French mercantilism has written:

> many of the French mercantilist enactments seem to have been handed down from above, rather than demanded from below. It might be worthwhile, even, to call the French developments "royal mercantilism" to mark the difference.[109]

This fact makes the interpretation of French mercantilism particularly difficult. For when we are dealing with figures like Richelieu and Colbert, separating theory from policy becomes extraordinarily difficult. These statesmen were anything but theorists. They were first and foremost pragmatic and ambitious political operators. But they were not pragmatists without design. In fact, they worked with a developed body of ideas which had its roots in absolutist thought. Indeed, in a very real sense, French mercantilism was a category of absolutist political theory—and it is this fact which has prevented many scholars from differentiating the two doctrines and has led some to identify French mercantilism purely and simply with state building.[110] In the minds of men like Bodin and Montchrétien, the notions of an indivisible source of political authority and of national economic self-sufficiency were inseparable. A strong state, capable of waging both military and economic warfare, had to be capable of administering the economy as a whole, even intervening directly in the economic activities of individuals; its centralized political authority had to be able to command the economic resources of the kingdom, to sustain itself. The central state, in other words, had to be both economically and politically self-sufficient.

In political theory, absolutism elevated the state above the Christian ethical principles which were presumed to govern social relations among individuals. Confronted by a fragmented body politic composed of conflicting and competing private interests, absolutist theorists tended to borrow from Descartes the atomic or corpuscular theory of matter to construct a theory of state and society. In their view, the state was not bound by the morality governing individuals. The moral purpose of the state was to *impose* order on the atomic particles which make up society. It was for this reason that some absolutist theorists openly defended the political views of Machiavelli (as did Richelieu). The unity of the state and the harmony of society were the highest worldly good. Any actions which preserved or advanced that unity and harmony were morally defensible as "reasons of state." That could—and often did—induce violence against the king's subjects and against other nations, since all means were justified in the pursuit or defence of the power of the state.

Just as the absolute monarch required sovereign power over his subjects, so he required proprietary rights over the wealth of the nation. French mercantilism envisioned the economy as an extension of the royal household. It is for this reason that the term "political economy" was originated by the French, not the English. The term first appeared in the title of a work in Antoyne de Montchrétien's *Traicté de l'oéconomie politique dédié en 1615 au roy et la reyne mère du roy*. The object of Montchrétien's *Traicté* is improved administration of the national economy. State administration of the economy is conceived to involve an extension of the principles appropriate to the financial organization of the royal household.

Montchrétien's *Traicté* inaugurated a tradition of mercantilist economic discourse in France which extended the Greek concept of *oikonomia* (the economic management of the household) to problems of state finance. It needed, therefore, to distinguish between private economy, the management of a household, and public or *political* economy, the administration of the national economy viewed as an appendage of the royal household. French mercantilism identified the state as the central category of economic analysis. Indeed, it fused the concepts of economy and state; the term political economy implied an indissoluble bond between the two and defined "economics" as a political science. Economic issues were viewed from the standpoint of the fiscal problems of the royal household. Furthermore, the economy was conceived of as constituted in patriarchal terms. The king was seen as the benevolent master who directed and regulated economic activity in the general interests of the political family. It was in Montchretien's *Traicté*, the major text of French mercantilist political economy, that this outlook received its classic formulation.

The starting point of Montchrétien's tract is the statement that the people of France "live in a noble misery." The kingdom is in desperate need of a moral and political renewal; but such a renewal requires economic reform since "the art of politics depends ultimately on the economy." The principles of economic reform are elementary: to apply the rules of domestic economy ("le bon gouvernement domestic") to public or political economy. It is not the extent of its territory or the number of its inhabitants which determines the wealth of the nation. Rather, the wealth of a state is a function of wise administration; and wise administration consists in organizing the economy in such a way that no land is left uncultivated and all individuals are put to work in a manner consistent with their interests and proclivities. Though his mercantilism involved an absolutist conception of the role of the monarch in administering the economy, Montchrétien's was not a despotic absolutism. He held that wise administration should adhere to "natural" rather than arbitrary principles and should be based on a clear recognition of the basic springs of human action—utility and pleasure.[111] People should be encouraged to pursue their self-interest in a general context of economic administration which ensures that they also simultaneously contribute to the good of the state. Montchrétien also claimed that the Third Estate (the political nation beneath the nobility of the cloth and that of the sword) was the foundation of the kingdom and should be protected and preserved. His absolutism thus reflected the views of a member of the Third Estate who looked to the Crown to advance the position of his order in the face of noble opposition.

The basic principle of Montchrétien's doctrine was the need for

France to establish economic self-sufficiency. Like most traditional French mercantilists, Montchrétien held that France was uniquely capable of providing for all her economic needs, whereas other nations were dependent upon France's agricultural exports. As a result, the reduction of imports through the development of domestic industry could in no way diminish French exports. Furthermore, since profit could be made only through foreign trade (since domestic trade was unprofitable to the nation as a whole), a reduction in imports would—assuming inelastic demand for French exports—automatically enrich the nation. In traditional bullionist terms, Montchrétien tended, with rare exceptions, to identify wealth with gold and money. The focus of the *Traicté*, consequently, is on the encouragement of industry and commerce. Not that Montchrétien belittled the importance of agriculture. On the contrary, he claimed that agriculture is the most necessary and fundamental sphere of the economy. But industry is the dynamic sector which alone can contribute to the expansion of national wealth by replacing imports and bringing about a favourable balance of trade—a concept which is implicit in Montchrétien's entire argument.[112]

The central idea underlying the *Traicté* is that of economic self-sufficiency. Moral renewal and economic reform could restore France to full power. Montchrétien advanced, therefore, a system of interrelated ideas: economic self-sufficiency, protection, national development, a favourable balance of trade, tax reform, and encouragement to industry, commerce, navigation, and colonialism were to fit together as aspects of a coordinated program of economic reform. Furthermore, the monarch, employing the basic principles of domestic economy writ large, was to be the agent of this transformation. Despite its proposal to eliminate noble exemption from the main body of taxes, this was hardly a "purely bourgeois" plan, as A. D. Lublinskaya has suggested.[113] Instead, it was a plan for an enlightened and rationalized absolutism which would dismantle certain structures of noble privilege and provide economic incentives to trade and industry. That it failed does indeed say something about the inner contradictions of French absolutism: the restoration of lasting economic prosperity was virtually impossible with a state that consistently expanded royal revenues through increasing exactions from the poorest sections of the population. Nonetheless, Montchrétien's *Traicté de l'oéconomie politique* laid down the basic principles of French mercantilism with a clarity and a systematic exposition that were not to be surpassed.

Cardinal Richelieu was the first major French statesman to espouse economic principles strikingly similar to those of Montchrétien. One author studying Richelieu's economic policies has said of his relation to Montchrétien's *Traicté* that "Richelieu, whether he read it or not, followed its precepts with astonishing accuracy," a view echoed by C. W. Cole.[114] Richelieu's mercantilist notions were rooted in absolutist political philosophy. He conceived of his primary mission as unifying and centralizing the power of the Crown. As he wrote in his *Testament politique*, he had inherited a fragmented kingdom which had sunk in the esteem of other nations; he had set out to rectify this.

I promised Your Majesty to employ all my industry and all the authority which it should please you to give to me to ruin the Huguenot party, to abase the pride of the nobles, to bring all your subjects back to their duty, and to restore your reputation among foreign nations to the station it ought to occupy.[115]

Restoring France's reputation among foreign nations meant building up the kingdom's military power. And for Richelieu, military power was a function of financial strength. War, he argued, consists "less in arms than in the expenditures by which arms are rendered effective."[116] For this reason, the Cardinal undertook to build up French economic strength. The policies he favoured could have been taken directly from Montchrétien: employment of the able-bodied poor in manufacturing; legislation against consumption of imported luxury goods; use of privileges and favours to encourage industry; construction of a colonial empire. Nevertheless, Richelieu did not pursue his economic program with the same fervour he devoted to his political, military, and diplomatic exploits. The attempt to institutionalize mercantilist principles in a systematic fashion awaited the ministry of Jean-Baptiste Colbert.

French mercantilism has been so closely identified with the ministry of Controller General Colbert that it has often been taken to be synonymous with the term "Colbertism." A merchant by early training, Colbert was born in Reims in 1619 and was sent to Paris as a youth. There he quickly established a place for himself in financial and political affairs. Upon the death of Mazarin, in whose employ he had worked, Colbert ascended to the position of controller general, a post he held until his death in 1683. Like Richelieu, Colbert was no economic theorist. He was an intensely practical man of affairs. Nonetheless, Colbert expressed certain mercantilist notions with an unparalleled clarity. Foremost in this respect was his view that international trade was a form of war. "Commerce," he wrote, "is a perpetual and peaceable war of wit and energy among all nations."[117] This outlook was based on an essentially static concept of the European economy. According to Colbert, vital economic resources, from ships to gold, existed in fixed quantities. Consequently, an increase in the wealth of one nation could result only from the loss of another. A nation could build up its wealth and power, therefore, only on the basis of an influx of money from other nations. Everyone accepts the principle, Colbert claimed, "that only an abundance of money in a state may increase its grandeur and power." Thus, the object of French economic policy must be to limit imports in an effort to maintain a favourable balance of trade.

Colbert set about with remarkable persistence to implement policies based on this principle. He imposed tariffs on imported manufactures; he encouraged hothouse industry with huge financial incentives; he organized overseas trading companies; he built up the navy. In all these areas, the controller general encountered opposition. The experience of opposition to his policies drove Colbert to an extreme absolutism. He lashed out at all forms of localism, ancient rights, and feudal privileges, which impeded his ability to organize and administer the national economy. Increasingly he relied upon the *intendants*, the royal officials Richelieu created to represent the Crown in the provinces. Colbert passionately disliked all those particular interests which prevented him from furthering the state interest as he perceived it. For this reason, contrary to those interpretations which see the controller general as a representative of the bourgeoisie, he had a sharp antipathy towards merchants. Merchants, he wrote, "always consult only their individual interests without examining what would be for the public good and the advantages of commerce in general."[118] In this respect, his mercantilism differed sharply from that of Montchrètien, who believed that bourgeois pursuit of self-interest would advance the public good. Despite this difference, Colbert attempted to implement the mercantilist policies developed by

Montchrétien with a determination never again matched in French history. In so doing, he was not carrying out the historic mission of the French bourgeoisie. Rather, he was attempting to advance the interests of the absolute monarchy against private interests within French society. Indeed this battle was as important to him as his battle against rival states. He was a proponent of national—or at least, of *state*—objectives. As C. W. Cole has put it, Colbert was not a representative of the bourgeoisie but rather "a representative of that age-old class, the courtier"; he was, however, a modern representative, one who responded to the new economic, military, and political problems of state building.[119]

But much as Colbert worked with the general interest of society in mind, his policies met with a growing wave of opposition. Aristocrats, merchants, the poor, all came to identify the controller general as the cause of their specific grievances—collapse of trade, famine, or intolerably heavy tax assessments. The depth of this opposition was exemplified in the wave of joy that swept the streets of Paris at the news of Colbert's death in 1683. But opposition to Colbert's policies and their legacy consisted of more than popular hatred of the controller general; by the 1690s "a comprehensive, wholly secular and systematic philosophy of opposition" was in process of construction.[120] Opposition to mercantilism fostered the birth of classical French political economy.

ANTIMERCANTILISM: PIERRE DE BOISGUILBERT
AND CLASSICAL POLITICAL ECONOMY

As influential as mercantilist ideology became during the seventeenth century, it never went unchallenged. Alongside mercantilism grew up competing worldviews which, by the end of the century, gave birth to classical political economy in France. Antimercantilist thought developed out of two distinct—but often related—discourses which opposed the principles of absolute monarchy: constitutionalism and Christian humanism. Constitutionalism had its roots in Christian ethics; its theorists maintained that the state should be constructed on the foundation of a universal system of natural law which would establish the constitutional framework for the relations between the king and his subjects. The morality binding on all parties would be codified in a system of law, derived from principles of natural law.[121] Christian humanism shared the same point of departure in traditional moral discourse; but its emphasis was universalist. Its theorists conceived of world trade as part of a divine plan designed to unite humanity. Providence had determined that no people could be economically self-sufficient. Like individuals, all nations stood in need of relations with others. And contrary to the mercantilist outlook which placed foreign trade beyond moral precepts, the humanists considered that Christian ethics should govern international trade. Just as reciprocal bonds of obligation held together individuals in a single state, so such bonds of reciprocity constituted the basis of international relations. Hugo Grotius, one of the leading theorists in the natural law tradition, clearly expressed this perspective:

> God did not bestow all products upon all parts of the earth, but distributed His gifts over different regions, to the end that men might cultivate a social relationship because one would need the help of another. And so He called commerce into being, that all might have common enjoyment of the fruits of the earth. . . . If you destroy commerce, you sunder the alliance binding together the human race.[122]

Such views were endorsed also by Henri VI's great minister, Sully. Later admired by the Physiocrats for his emphasis on agriculture, Sully preached a universalist ethics. He opposed wars of territorial expansion and developed a plan for universal peace. Like Grotius, he considered commerce a means of establishing harmony among the world's peoples. But influential as a minister like Sully may have been, opposition to mercantilism remained largely the preserve of philosophers and theologians until the crisis of Colbert's ministry brought on by the Dutch war of 1672–1679.

The financial needs of the Dutch war derailed all of Colbert's plans for economic reform. Taxation and more taxation became the order of the day. With almost clocklike precision, excessive taxation triggered a cycle of agricultural crises by preventing simple reproduction of the peasant economy. Economic failure would drive cultivators from the land. Reduced outputs, in turn, would drive up grain prices. Peasant prosperity temporarily restored, prices and incomes would plummet and, as tax assessments hit declining incomes, bankruptcies would usher in a new famine. By the end of the 1670s, France was caught in the grip of an oscillating cycle of poor harvests followed by low prices, which established the conditions for further crop failures. Such a cycle made rural poverty virtually a permanent condition at a time when taxes weighed even more heavily on an impoverished peasantry.

The dominant intellectual response to this crisis has been described accurately as "Christian agrarianism." First enunciated by Claude Fleury during the 1670s, Christian agrarianism became the ideology of a group of reformers within the court grouped around Archbishop Fénelon. Fénelon opposed excessive aggrandisement of the state. Rampant and unjustified taxation, he argued, was bleeding the people dry; the solution was to reduce taxes, so as to let nature and industry support the people and the Crown. Fénelon fell from favour towards the end of the 1690s. But his basic message continued to find an increasingly sophisticated echo. Foremost in this respect was Charles Paul Hurault de l'Hôpital, known as the seigneur of Belesbat, who drafted six memoirs to Louis XIV in September 1692. Belesbat claimed that the withdrawal of the state from economic affairs and the restoration thereby of liberty of commerce would revitalize the French economy. Prosperity restored, the people would then be able to pay rents and taxes. If the king would abide by natural law, he argued, all would be well. The notion that there were natural laws of trade which, if left unimpeded, would automatically establish harmony and prosperity, became a central tenet of antimercantilism. So long as such arguments remained confined to discussion of commerce, they could not construct a coherent and systematic alternative to mercantilism. Such an alternative theory presupposed an analysis of the very basis of wealth creation—an integrated theory of production and exchange. Only when antimercantilist doctrine was taken up in the debate over taxation which emerged in 1695 would a consistently antimercantilist political economy be developed.

Paradoxically, one of the major figures to initiate this debate was himself essentially a mercantilist and a loyal supporter of Louis XIV. Sébastien Le Prestre, seigneur de Vauban, was France's greatest military leader during the reign of Louis XIV. Vauban had provided France with an unsurpassed system of military fortifications, harbours, and canals. He was the leading military engineer of the period and was, in fact, something of a pioneer in geographic surveys and economic statistics. According to his own account, he was shocked by the poverty he found throughout France. During the 1690s, a series of events provoked Vauban to make his concerns public. Following military defeat in 1692, France experienced famine in 1693 and 1694. In order to guarantee the state an adequate income, Louis XIV was forced to adopt the extraordinary measure of taxing the nobility with the *capitation* of 1695. The crisis of the 1690s stimulated an outpouring of literature devoted to reform of the tax system. One of the most important pieces of this literature was Vauban's *Dîme royale*. Vauban first drafted his tract in 1698 merely for circulation within the court. Indeed, he read his manuscript aloud to Louis XIV. But when France's crisis intensified, and as private lobbying at court proved ineffective, he took the step of openly publishing his views. In early 1707, *La Dîme royale* came off the press. It was proscribed immediately and its author exiled from the court, only to die a month later.

The *Dîme* was an impassioned work. Its author spoke out boldly against the impoverished state of the peasantry. Nearly ten percent of the people, he claimed, are reduced to begging; half are incapable of paying any taxes since they can barely sustain themselves; thirty percent are indebted; only the top ten percent are comfortable. His objective, Vauban announced, was to examine "les causes de la misère des peuples" and to propose a remedy. And he had no doubt as to the cause of the poverty of the people—the grinding weight of royal taxation. The king had shown too little regard for the conditions of the poorest sections of the population, "la partie base du peuple," which "by its industry and trade, and by what it pays to the king, enriches him and all his kingdom."[123] Prosperity could be restored and royal revenues, which are nothing other than "une rente foncière," maintained only with the implementation of *la dixième*, a tithe paid by all subjects—nobles, officials, and commoners alike.

Although the publication of Vauban's views—especially his biting description of the poverty of the peasants—was scandalous on its own, perhaps his greatest indiscretion in the eyes of the court was his endorsement of the views of one of the most outspoken and radical reformers of the period. For, in the preface to *La Dîme royale*, Vauban attacked the impoverished state of the French people which had prompted him to search for its cause. And that cause, he claimed, corresponded "perfectly" to that identified by the author of *Le Détail de la France*.[124]

The author of *Le Détail de la France* (1695) was none other than

Pierre Le Pesant de Boisguilbert, son of an ennobled Norman secretary to the king. Boisguilbert's family had a long tradition of royal service. Born in 1646, Boisguilbert was disinherited by his father yet managed to amass a small fortune as a young man and purchase a number of offices including the Presidial Seat of Rouen. Appalled by the deteriorating economic condition of France, Boisguilbert undertook to enlighten royal officials as to the causes of France's crisis. He corresponded with three different controllers general and with Vauban among others. His basic message is captured in one of his letters to Controller General Chamillart in which he states that "the manner in which France is governed will cause her to perish if it is not stopped."[125] But Boisguilbert did not confine himself to denunciations of the inequality of the tax system and appeals to natural law, although both figured centrally in his writings. Instead, he constructed the most sophisticated and systematic political economy of the time, one which was not to be surpassed until the flowering of the classical system at the hands of Smith and Ricardo.[126]

The starting point for Boisguilbert's doctrine was a full-scale assault on the mercantilist concept of wealth. Repeatedly he argued that the decline of the French economy had started in 1660, the beginning of Colbert's ministry. The crucial error of Colbertism was the identification of wealth with money—an error which had brought ruin to the kingdom. Mistakenly, wealth had been equated with gold and silver. "We have made," he wrote in his *Dissertation de la nature des richesses, de l'argent, et des tributs,* . . . (1704), "an idol of these metals."[127] Gold and money have value only, he asserted, through their capacity to provide goods for consumption. Wealth consists in consumption, in the enjoyment of the products of agriculture and industry.

Money should be nothing more than the slave of consumption; its function is to assist in the circulation of goods. Money follows the circulation of goods; it is acquired only via a prior sale. Goods should not follow the movement of money. When the latter inversion occurs, money becomes a false god—indeed, one more tyrannical than those of antiquity: "This devouring god, like a burning fire, never attaches itself to anything, except to devour it."[128] When money becomes a false god and an end in itself, the tyrant rather than the slave of commerce, its supply transgresses its natural boundaries and disrupts the harmony of the state. The natural proportions which establish prices are dislodged. Moreover, hoarding occurs, prices plummet, producers are driven into bankruptcy, and trade collapses.

In Boisguilbert's view, economic recovery presupposed overturning the fetish of money and reconstructing the economy on the basis of a clear understanding of the true nature of wealth. And he left no doubt that, in the case of France at least, the basis of wealth was agriculture; "the principle of all the wealth of France being the cultivation of land," as he put it in his *Traité de la nature, culture, commerce, et intérêt des grains* (1704).[129] People of all other occupations—from lawyers to artisans—subsist on the produce of the land. It is the circular flow of the products of the land that sustains all such social groups. In fact, the reproduction of all social classes presupposes a dual movement of the products of the land and of money which culminates in a return flow of revenue to landowners and agricultural producers, to sustain another cycle of agricultural production. As Boisguilbert wrote in *Le Détail de la France,* all nonagricultural groups derive their subsistence from a "natural circulation" which begins with production on the land, the goods of which "pass through an infinite number of hands" until the "circuit" is complete.[130] Furthermore, the circulation of rent is a central feature of this whole process, since most of those who subsist in nonagricultural occupations live off the rent of land—at least indirectly, via the consumption expenditure of the landowners.[131]

So long as this circular flow maintains "a continual movement," the economy will not suffer. France is ailing, however, because its tax policies have upset this natural movement. Excessive taxation upon agricultural producers has wiped out the small savings which make possible the purchase of animals, the use of fertilizer therefrom, and agricultural improvements.[132] Furthermore, economic pressures on the direct producers are compounded by prohibition of the export of grain. Such prohibitions limit the effective demand for grain and as a consequence depress prices. Low prices cause a contraction of output as those cultivators who fail to meet their costs of production abandon the land. Falling output in turn boosts prices, leading to an inflationary boom which is followed inevitably by rising output and declining prices. Furthermore, agricultural depression becomes generalized throughout the economy. A proprietor who is discouraged from producing will have to curtail his spending. The result will be an extension of the crisis to industrial production.[133]

This cycle—or what Boisguilbert calls "the war" between those forces which cause famine and those which cause high prices—must be broken. The key is to establish free export of grain. A free market in grain will bring about a high yet balanced price which will provide a regular surplus to the producer, a surplus which will guarantee rents, taxes, and agricultural investment. The benefits of a high but balanced grain price will rebound to all members of society: "It is solely the price of grains, although this truth has been little known here, which determines abundance and the wealth of the kingdom." [134]

In order to revitalize agricultural production and thereby guarantee a stable and secure income to the state, Boisguilbert proposed a series of reforms: abolition of tariffs, duties, and sales taxes; establishment of free trade (including export) in grain; replacement of all existing taxes by a single income tax on everyone. Vested interests would, however, attempt to block such reforms, he asserted. In fact, Boisguilbert had had direct experience with such resistance to reform. In 1705 he had convinced Chamillart and de Bouville, intendant for Orléans, to allow him to experiment with his proposals in the *élection* of Chartres. But a torrent of opposition, especially from the president of the Court of Aides in Paris, prevented the experiment from taking place. This experience among others convinced Boisguilbert that reform would have to come from above, from the highest representatives of the state. Yet such reforms need not involve complicated schemas. It was only necessary, he argued, that "one let nature do its work." [135] Nature itself would restore order and harmony to society if only political authorities would disregard the pressures of special interests and let things take their course. Indeed, anticipating Smith's doctrine of the invisible hand, Boisguilbert claimed that if restrictions were removed to the pursuit of individual self-interest, the public good would automatically be furthered. [136]

The natural order established by the free workings of commerce would distribute justice to all through the mechanism of proportional prices. Drawing on the Aristotelian notion of distributive justice, Boisguilbert claimed that the unfettered market mechanism would bring about an equality of purchase and sale. As a result of mutual need everyone would have an equal interest in buying and selling. Consequently, the market would establish an equilibrium ("un équilibre") through which revenue would be distributed proportionally to the value of goods. Such a distribution would maintain just proportions unless an unfair tax system were to distribute the burden of taxes disproportionately. Thus, the main function of the state was to establish and preserve a framework in which natural law and distributive justice could be realized via the self-equilibrating mechanism of the market. The state was not, as the crude absolutists would have it, above "laws of the strictest justice"; like every subject, the state must respect "the laws of nature, of equity and of reason."[137]

Boisguilbert's debt to the Christian agrarian tradition is conspicuous. Yet Boisguilbert far transcended traditional agrarianism by developing a remarkably sophisticated analysis of economic phenomena (and of the market mechanism, money, and depression, in particular). In fact, Boisguilbert formulated an alternative vision of the economic cosmos in which the wealth generated by agricultural production created a surplus above costs of production; and this surplus—primarily taking the form of rent—directly supported rural labourers and, indirectly, all nonagricultural occupations and the Crown. Beyond any doubt, this was a startling anticipation of the physiocratic conception of the circular flow of economic life. It is perhaps for this reason that the Physiocrats consistently acknowledged Boisguilbert as their one true precursor. Reviled during his lifetime as an eccentric and a crackpot, Boisguilbert nevertheless established the foundations of much that was to enter into the construction of the great system of classical political economy of François Quesnay and his disciples.[138]

PETTY, BOISGUILBERT, AND CLASSICAL POLITICAL ECONOMY

By the beginning of the eighteenth century the writings of Petty and Boisguilbert—the "fathers" of English and French political economy, respectively—had established the basic framework of classical economics. For both theorists, the problem of taxation had been their starting point. Petty's *Treatise of Taxes and Contributions* was written as a contribution to the Restoration discussion of English tax policy. Boisguilbert's *Détail de la France* was a direct intervention in the debate over taxation which erupted during the French crisis of the 1690s. Both theorists undertook to address the problem of taxation in terms of a general theory of wealth or value. As a result—and it is this which constitutes their break with mercantilism and truly

makes them classical political economists—they directed their analytic attention not primarily to phenomena related to the circulation
of goods (trade and exchange) but to the fundamental process of
wealth production. No longer was an increase in national wealth considered to be possible only through foreign trade. Instead, Petty and
Boisguilbert each advanced conceptions of wealth as created by human labour applied to nature; and for both theorists, agriculture was
the basis of such wealth. Moreover, only surplus production from
the land was viewed as making nonagricultural occupations (including those involved in the state) possible. The major form taken by
the agricultural surplus was identified by both writers as *rent*. As a
result, the processes by which economic society reproduces itself and
grows were considered to be dependent upon a continuous renewal
of the factors of agricultural production. Thus, it was agriculture
which constituted the foundation of the wealth of nations.

   Writing in Restoration England, Petty, unlike Boisguilbert, was
not bothered by fear of economic collapse. His preoccupation derived from the central concern of social Baconianism: the elaboration
of means whereby state planning could advance the wealth, prosperity, and power of England. Identifying land as the source of
wealth and rent as the decisive phenomenon in determining the
value of land, in supporting the economy as a whole, and in providing revenue to the state, Petty devoted himself to the development of
a general theory of value which could account for the value of both
land and commodities. Boisguilbert, by contrast, was obsessed with
the problem of economic reproduction. The French economy had
been contracting, he believed, since 1660. It was necessary to overthrow the fetish of money which had originated, he believed, with
Colbert and to grasp the true principles of wealth if the road to prosperity were to be found. This required constructing a model of economic interdependence, which would establish the natural relationships between commodities, money, prices, and growth. Concerned
with such problems of economic interdependence, Boisguilbert developed a view of the circular flow of wealth which far surpassed that
of Petty or Locke, just as Petty's theory of value posed problems ignored by that of Boisguilbert.

   But the most important difference between the systems of Petty
and Boisguilbert concerns the social relations of production which
characterized their respective economic models. Petty took for

granted a *capitalist* structure of agricultural production in which the
direct producers were wage labourers—"day labourers," as Petty
called them—who, owning no means of production themselves,
were compelled to sell their labour power to a tenant farmer or landlord and produce a surplus product. It is true, as Marx pointed out
long ago, that Petty equated surplus value with rent and failed to develop a clear concept of profit (in large part because he treated the
income of the tenant farmer as a wage).[139] But in making the wage
labourer, not the peasant proprietor, the direct agricultural producer
at the center of his analytic model, and by making analysis of the
production of surplus value (rent) his central concern, Petty laid the
foundations for a full-fledged theory of agrarian capitalism. Although
neither Petty nor Locke elaborated a complete theoretical model of
agrarian capitalism (in part because they wrote treatises on specific
economic problems such as taxation and interest rather than principles of political economy), both employed modes of analysis which
operated in terms of agrarian capitalist relations of production.

In this respect, Boisguilbert's model differed fundamentally from
that of Petty or Locke. The English writers simply generalized from
the historical process of primitive accumulation which had created—
in fact only in parts of Great Britain at the time they wrote—capital
farms employing a rural proletariat. Their theories of production and
growth were based upon the triadic social relationship of landlord–
tenant farmer–wage labourer which was coming to characterize British farming. But in France these social relationships could not be
taken for granted. For Boisguilbert, the direct agricultural producer
was the small peasant proprietor. The problem of economic reproduction and renewal thus came down to easing the burden of taxation which undermined the vitality of peasant farming. Thus, even
though Boisguilbert tackled the problem of reproduction (the circular flow) with more rigour than any of his predecessors or contemporaries and saw the decisive importance of a growing agricultural
surplus to the regeneration of French economic life, his model was
not a capitalist one. For this reason, appeals to the crown to reform
the policies and structures of French absolutism were crucial to
Boisguilbert's economic program. Whereas Petty and Locke accepted the basic social structure of Great Britain, and the policies
which corresponded to it, and merely advised the state with respect
to specific economic issues of the day, Boisguilbert called upon the

monarchy to implement policies which challenged the basic interests of the French ruling class. The focus of French political economy had to rest upon reasoned appeals to the Crown as the unifying agency in society to carry through sweeping social and economic changes. As the evidence of England's economic superiority mounted during the eighteenth century, the leading French economic theorists of the day, the Physiocrats, thus increasingly called upon the state to sponsor a wide-ranging program of social transformation which would replicate the results of English enclosure and primitive accumulation. The radical innovation of the Physiocrats was to construct a developed economic theory of agrarian capitalism as the basis of French renewal. In so doing they wrote a decisive chapter in the political economy of agrarian capitalism.

CHAPTER THREE

The Paradox of the Physiocrats: State Building and Agrarian Capitalism in Eighteenth-Century France

The science of political economy took a significant step forward during the third quarter of the eighteenth century. The impetus this time came not from England but from France, in the form of the theoretical system known as Physiocracy, in which economic thought received its first genuinely systematic formulation. François Quesnay and his school set out to establish political economy as a science of society. To this undertaking they brought both a well-defined philosophy of economic life and a scientific method to address, for the first time, problems of economic life within the general framework of a theoretical science.

In an important respect, the major theoretical achievement of the Physiocrats was their conception of the economy as a *whole*—as an organic totality in which production, exchange, expenditure, and consumption were inextricably connected. They constructed, as a result, a general model of economic interdependence organized around the circular flow (or "reproduction") of economic life. It is their rigorous and sophisticated concept of the circular flow which establishes the claim of Physiocracy as the first genuine science of economics. As Schumpeter argued, the Physiocrats

made the great breach, through which lay all further progress in the field of analysis, by the discovery and intellectual formulation of the circular flow of economic life. . . . As long as economic periods were viewed merely as a technical phenomenon, and the fact of the economic cycle through which they move had not been recognized, the connecting link of economic causality and insight into the inner necessities and the general character of economics was missing. . . . Before the Physiocrats appeared on the scene only local symptoms on the economic body, as it were, had been perceived, while they enabled us to conceive this body physiologically and anatomically as an organism with a uniform life-process and uniform conditions of life, and it was they who presented to us the first analysis of this life-process.[1]

Such statements would suggest that the interpretation of Physiocracy is a relatively simple matter; that the Physiocrats are essentially to be credited with contributing the concept of general interdependence to the great synthesis of economic thought produced by Adam Smith in 1776. In fact, nothing could be further from the truth. As Norman J. Ware wrote in 1931, "There is perhaps no body of economic theory more misunderstood than that of the Physiocrats." Eight years later, Max Beer claimed that "Physiocracy forms a problem in the history of economics, on the merits and implications of which the most divergent opinions have been current." Thomas Neill, writing a decade after Beer, went so far as to contend that the theories of Quesnay and his followers "have been as grievously misinterpreted as the thought of any group in history." Nor is this problem of interpretation one which was confined to historians and economists writing during the first half of this century. In 1968 Bert Hoselitz, a noted development economist, virtually restating Ware, wrote that "probably no group of economists has been the subject of more varied evaluation than the Physiocrats."[2]

The problem of interpretation posed by the Physiocrats revolves around their unique combination of a theoretical model of capitalist production with a political doctrine which they described as "legal despotism." On the one hand, the Physiocrats conceptualized economic life on strictly capitalist lines (at least within the productive sector of the economy); on the other hand, they were outspoken advocates of a more powerful monarchical absolutism. Furthermore, while extolling the virtues of capital investment and accumulation, they granted social and political priority to landed wealth and denigrated commercial and industrial wealth. The Physiocrats appear to most commentators, therefore, to have constructed a hybrid; a theoretical model of a capitalist economy ruled by a political variant of the feudal state. As a result, most analysts have accorded priority to one or the other side of their thought. But, as Elizabeth Fox-Genovese writes, "none of the many commentators on physiocratic thought has satisfactorily considered legal despotism, the primacy of agriculture, capitalist production and free trade in grain as parts of a coherent whole."[3]

All interpreters have had to wrestle with this central "paradox" of the Physiocrats. Some commentators have chosen to emphasize the capitalist character of the physiocratic model of the economy and their advocacy of private property and laissez-faire. Georges Weulerrse claimed, for example, that in their abstract doctrine Quesnay and his followers expressed "the scientific principles of capitalism, pure and simple, of complete capitalism."[4] Further emphasizing their focus on the importance of capital investment, agricultural entrepreneurs, large farms, technical innovation, and output-maximizing, cost-minimizing production, Weulerrse characterized the physiocratic system as representing "the triumph of the spirit of capitalism."[5] This line of interpretation has been extended by Hoselitz, who attributed to the *économistes* "the development of a full-fledged theoretical system of capitalism." Indeed, Hoselitz argued that the writings of the Physiocrats "constitute the fundament of individualistic capitalism" and that their underlying ideology is "virtually identical with the world-view of the popularizers of utilitarian radicalism and Manchester liberalism in Britain two generations later." Consistent with this view, Guy Routh has asserted that the physiocratic ideal would have constituted "a sort of Chamber of Commerce golden age."[6]

Counterposed to this interpretation are those which emphasize the feudal character of physiocratic doctrine. Dwelling on their advocacy of a strong, centralized monarchy that could direct social and economic development, Warren J. Samuels, in two articles written in the early 1960s, presented a persuasive case for the view that the Physiocrats did not defend absolute individual rights to private property but that, instead, they conceived of rights to property as ultimately subordinate to the social interest. Indeed, Samuels detected "vestiges of a feudal conception of property" in the works of the Physiocrats.[7] This aspect of physiocratic thought has not gone unnoticed by others. Eric Roll remarked in *A History of Economic Thought* upon the "almost feudal air about the physiocratic attitude to land," while Schumpeter claimed that "Quesnay's theories of state and society were nothing but reformulations of scholastic doctrine."[8] Undoubtedly the most extreme argument for the feudal character of the physiocratic system is that developed by Max Beer. According to

Beer, the Physiocrats advocated "a return to the preindustrial era." Furthermore, he asserted that they were proponents of a "rationalized medieval society" characterized by an absence of technological innovation and economic development.[9]

These conflicting interpretations of Physiocracy—based upon different elements of the worldview of Quesnay and his followers— have played havoc with virtually every attempt to analyse the physiocratic system as a whole. To some commentators, however, Marx's perspective on Quesnay and his adherents has appeared to provide a more promising approach. For Marx, the contradiction between the economic theory of capitalism and the political theory of absolutism was resolved into an expression of the contradictory movement of the historical process. The contradictions in physiocratic theory, he argued, "are contradictions of capitalist production as it works its way out of feudal society, and interprets feudal society itself only in a bourgeois way, but has not yet discovered its own peculiar form." Physiocracy represents, therefore, "a bourgeois reproduction of the feudal system."[10]

Marx's notion that the Physiocrats exhibited a kind of "split consciousness," from attempting to analyse a society in transition from one mode of production to another, has informed the studies of Physiocracy undertaken by two modern Marxist writers, Ronald Meek and Elizabeth Fox-Genovese. According to Meek, the "great paradox of Physiocracy" is a result of "certain ideological considerations (in Marx's sense) which prevented the Physiocrats from seeing the capitalist economy of the future otherwise than through feudal spectacles."[11] Elizabeth Fox-Genovese has elaborated upon this line of argument in claiming that Physiocracy represents "a transition from the organic medieval view to the modern economic view" which "attempts to fuse features of both."[12]

Although these interpretations inspired by Marx exhibit a greater sensitivity to the complexity of themes to be found in the writings of the Physiocrats, they do little to resolve the fundamental problem. For, if the Physiocrats were indeed the "first systematic spokesmen of capital," it is difficult to see why they should not have abandoned their allegiance to the monarchy if such a political allegiance violated their economic objectives. The assumption of Meek and Fox-Genovese is that there is a contradiction between the economic and political doctrines of the Physiocrats and that the kind of capitalist economic development favoured by the Physiocrats required the revolutionary overthrow of the monarchy by the industrial and commercial bourgeoisie. Thus, Fox-Genovese claims of Physiocracy that "the ideology in the economic analysis and that implicit in the political economy do not mesh." And she charges Quesnay and his school with "doctrinaire utopianism" for their failure to elaborate a bourgeois revolutionary political program.[13]

But if these eighteenth-century social theorists failed to develop such a program, it may well have been because there was no social basis for such a perspective. No modern commentators have shown that the Physiocrats failed to notice historical possibilities which were recognized by other theorists of the time. Utilizing the classic liberal-capitalist outlook which assumes that capitalism must emerge with the rise of a liberal, urban bourgeoisie, Meek and Fox-Genovese have implied that the Physiocrats failed to construct a consistently liberal-capitalist doctrine. They have treated the physiocratic theory of the state as a kind of historical residue of feudalism, which was destined to disappear with the advancing tides of history. They have failed, however, to put aside the liberal-capitalist historical schema and to confront the possibility that the physiocratic combination of an economic theory of capitalism and a political theory of absolutism was connected quite clearly with some of the most important realities of eighteenth-century French society.

In our view, it is the arbitrary imposition of the liberal-capitalist perspective which has given a paradoxical appearance to Physiocracy. Freed from such a mechanistic schema and inserted in its genuine historical context, Physiocracy emerges as a remarkably consistent doctrine. In the absence of a class (such as England's agrarian capitalists) which undertook a decisive transformation of economy and polity, and troubled by the fragmentation of authority and the plethora of particular interests within civil society, the Physiocrats had little option but to look to the state to undertake a revolution from above which would wipe away feudal rights and privileges, unify and centralize political power, and establish the social and political framework for an English-style transformation of agrarian economy. We shall argue, therefore, that the economic and political theories of the Physiocrats do indeed form a coherent whole; that underlying all aspects of their doctrine was the goal of reconstructing the French state on the basis of agrarian capitalism. Before analysing the history and the doctrine of the movement, however, it will be useful to sketch the social, historical, and intellectual context in which Physiocracy was born.

AGROMANIA AND ANGLOMANIA: THE DISCOVERY OF ENGLISH AGRONOMY AND POLITICAL ECONOMY

Throughout the eighteenth century the central contradiction of French absolutism remained unresolved: on the one hand, economic prosperity presupposed an agricultural revival which could break the recurrent cycle of inflation and depression; on the other hand, to meet the increasing costs of royal administration the state incessantly ground the agricultural producers beneath a growing burden of taxation. Consequently, the immediate fiscal policies of the state eroded the possibility of any lasting prosperity. Following the collapse of Law's system in 1720, the state debt had increased once again. The introduction of the *cinquantième* in 1725, a second *dixième* in 1733, and a *vingtième* in both 1749 and 1756 all failed to tap nobles' income to a degree adequate to overcome the long-term crisis of the absolutist state. The tax burden continued to fall on the rural producers. After a brief respite around midcentury, France found itself back in the midst of severe difficulties by the late 1750s. The French military suffered a humiliating defeat in the Seven Years' War. Under the impact of war, foreign trade slumped dramatically—from 25 percent of gross physical product in the years 1751–1755 to a mere 12 percent in 1758.[14] That same year, the payment of inscriptions was halted, and people were called on to bring in their silver and gold for minting.

It was in these circumstances that the intellectual movement known as the French Enlightenment reached its apex. The Enlightenment represented a movement by French intellectuals (from the clergy, the aristocracy, and the bourgeoisie), originating in the first quarter of the century, to elaborate economic and political solutions to the crisis of French society and the state. In formulating such theoretical solutions, they took their main inspiration from England. England, after all, appeared to offer a sharp contrast to the illness afflicting France. Yet however much England's political arrangements may have fascinated theorists like Voltaire and Montesquieu, it was her economic prosperity that French thinkers most envied. In their minds, there was little doubt as to the basis of that prosperity: it was, they believed, the superiority of English agriculture which underpinned her wealth and power. Thus, in his influential *Lettres d'un Français sur les Anglais*, the abbé Le Blanc told his readers eager for a knowledge of England that

> Whoever has eyes, must be struck with the beauties of the country, the care taken to improve lands, the richness of the pastures, the numerous flocks that cover them, and the air of plenty and cleanliness which reigns in the smallest villages.

The reason England enjoys such comfort and wealth, he claimed, has to do with the attitude towards agriculture of her ruling class:

> What makes the English love planting more than we do, is that those who by birth or riches, are of the greatest distinction in the State, live in the country more than those of the same rank in France. . . . As the nobility sets the fashion to their inferiors, so the farmer plants in imitation of his landlord.[15]

It was through agricultural improvement that the English nobility had elevated their country, Le Blanc wrote; the French would do well to emulate them.

The year after the publication of Le Blanc's *Lettres* Montesquieu's *Esprit des lois* appeared. Public interest in problems of political economy is often said to date from the publication of this work. The year 1748 also saw the appearance of Dupin's *Mémoires des blés*. In 1750 Duhamel du Monceau popularized the methods and techniques of England's agricultural revolution with his *Traité de la culture des terres, suivant des principes de M. Tull, Anglais*. The following year the first volume of the *Encyclopédie* rolled off the press. The first economic article, written by Diderot himself, was entitled "Agriculture" and reflected an awareness of the growing discussion of the new husbandry. But it was Duhamel above all who stimulated discussion of problems of rural economy. For this reason, he has generally been considered to be the father of French agronomy.

Duhamel's treatise advanced a program for a complete reform of traditional husbandry: careful tillage and cultivation; saving of seed; maximization of output; scientific crop rotation and abandonment of the fallow system; use of artificial fodder; improvement of implements, harvesting, and storage.[16] His crusade struck a responsive chord. Five volumes of his work were published between 1751 and 1756, containing reports of practical results sent by Duhamel's correspondents and the author's comments upon them. The efforts of Duhamel and his enthusiasts inspired a growing agronomical movement. In 1757 the first agricultural society was founded in Rennes. During the next decade such societies were formed in every region of France. They published pamphlets, held contests, and experimented with new seeds, livestocks, implements, and techniques.

The French *agronomes* drew their exemplary models from England. Occasionally exiled British writers—particularly Jacobites from Scotland—contributed to the theoretical discussion of French agriculture. Such was the case with the English-born author Henry Patullo, whose *Essai sur l'amélioration des terres* was published in 1765. Patullo was linked closely with the Physiocrats and dedicated his work to Madame de Pompadour, patroness of the group. While focusing on the theory of rotative culture, Patullo also raised the central question of enclosure of land as integral to a program of agricultural improvement: "The practice of enclosing lands began long ago in England and is now nearly widespread there. It was felt that this advantage in itself would not fail to double the value of property."[17]

Beginning about 1760 and lasting some seventeen years, a definite movement developed towards clearing of lands, partitioning of commons, and enclosure. In 1761 a royal edict granted privileges to those who undertook to break up and reclaim land. Companies of capitalists formed by contract with the government to initiate such *défrichements*. In Lorraine, the chancellor, La Galaizière, grouped the tenures on his estates and partitioned the common lands on the *seigneuries*—allegedly with the consent of the inhabitants. These operations were registered by council in 1771. Indeed, Marc Bloch suggested that this registration resembled an English bill of enclosure.[18] The trend towards suspension of common rights and in the direction of enclosure picked up steam around the middle of the 1760s. In 1766 the Estates of Languedoc obtained a judgement from the Parlement of Toulouse against compulsory collective grazing through large parts of the province. Similar acts were passed by the Parlements of Rouen and Paris and the Council of Rousillon. During 1766 and 1767, a series of edicts granted freedom of enclosure in Lorraine, the Three Bishoprics, the Barrois, Hainault, Flanders, the Boulonnais, Champagne, Burgundy, Franche-Comté, Rousillon, Béarn, Bigorre, and Corsica.[19]

As significant as these developments were, moves towards enclosure remained confined to a minuscule percentage of estates. A full-scale agricultural revolution is more than a technical reorganization of farming (as we have noted in chapter 2); it involves a transformation of the social relations of agricultural production. The sophisticated scientific arguments of the *agronomes* ran headfirst into the real-life constraints that the social structure of eighteenth-century France imposed upon such transformation. In a very real sense, the *agronomes* had formulated a program for "primitive accumulation" of capital without taking into account the specific sociohistorical processes such a program presupposed. As André Bourde has noted, enclosure, consolidation of holdings, and extension of farms all implied "the conversion of the peasant proprietor into a paid agricultural labourer."[20]

An agrarian revolution of this character—a revolution not only of technique but, more important, of social relations of production—required more than enlightened propaganda. It would have required a transformation of the relation between the absolutist state and society. For, as we have demonstrated in chapter 2, the absolutist state safeguarded the social position of the peasantry. As a result, "customary rules were too well established and the perpetual character of the tenures presented too many obstacles, for the movement towards integration of plots to result in enclosure on a vast scale."[21] For this reason, those writers concerned with agricultural improvement were forced to confront the problem of the state and its relationship to social classes and the economy as a whole. Increasingly the recognition dawned that France's ailment was as much political as economic; that the structure of state and economy required radical reform if France were to follow the English road to wealth and power. For this reason, many of the *agronomes* were impelled from consideration of problems of rural economy to deliberation upon problems of *political* economy. Thus, with the discovery of English agronomy came the simultaneous discovery of English political economy.

The shift towards political economy was impelled also by the related debate over the grain trade. Throughout the eighteenth century, France maintained the traditional policy of provision, according to which government had the right—indeed, the duty—to direct, regulate, and control the production, transportation, marketing, price, and export of grain in order to avoid dearth and the inevitable social unrest which accompanied it. Under the terms of regulated trade, all dealers in grain had to register with the government; particular groups were prohibited from dealing in grain; and all grain purchases and sales had to be certified by the government. Yet regulation of the grain trade did not eliminate the recurring problem of poor harvests and rising prices, which were followed invariably by rising yields, falling prices, and economic crises for many producers.

Subsistence crises occurred in the Paris region in 1709, 1725–1726, 1738–1742, and 1765–1775.[22] Responding to the failure of regulation of the grain trade, a growing body of writing favoured a policy of economic liberalization—abolition of state regulation to allow free commerce in grain to increase prices and output to equilibrium levels which would ensure abundance of supply and reasonably high and stable prices for the agricultural producers. Central to these arguments was an approach to the grain trade which treated it like any other productive activity by focusing not principally upon the immediate interests of the consumers but rather upon the economic needs of the producers.

One of the most important liberal tracts on the grain trade was Claude-Jacques Herbert's *Essai sur la police générale des grains* (1753). The essay went through six editions in the four years after its publication and popularized many of the economic arguments for liberalization which came to the fore in the 1760s and 1770s. Central to Herbert's position was the view that human beings were motivated fundamentally by "personal interest" and that, if only grain were treated as an "object of commerce" like any other, its supply and its price would readily adjust themselves to the market—thereby stimulating production and eliminating the problem of scarcity. The price of bread would settle ultimately at a reasonable level, but not one so low as to discourage industry on the part of the poor. Herbert's views were echoed in part by Forbonnais, whose *Eléments du commerce* (1754) denounced regulation of the grain trade as "against the order of nature" and advocated a "just equilibrium" of the interests of the consumer and the producer rather than oppression of the latter to serve the former.[23]

The most difficult question for those advocating liberalization of the grain trade was the freedom to export grain. It followed logically that such freedom should be granted if the object was to expand the market for grain to maximize demand and, thereby, the incentive to produce. This, as we have seen, was Boisguilbert's position. But an unqualified right to export grain required accepting the view that even in cases of dearth or famine (which most economic liberalizers discounted as a serious possibility under conditions of free trade) the state would not intervene to assert the priority of subsistence over liberty of commerce—a position which required aggressively asserting the absolute freedom of markets regardless of the conditions of the poor. Yet this was precisely the position taken by the growing "liberty lobby" of the 1750s and 1760s, as well as that taken by the Physiocrats. Moreover, the government itself adopted this position for a time in the 1760s and again in the 1770s—before an aggressive campaign on behalf of traditional policy forced the government to retreat.[24]

Clearly, any attempt to move in the direction of a complete liberalization of the grain trade—and the radical break with traditional policy such a move implied—required the backing of a rigorous and persuasive argument designed to demonstrate the economic, social, and political superiority of markets over regulation. Any such argument had to be constructed, not at the level of special pleading, but in terms of a comprehensive analysis of the general or natural laws of economic life. Thus, as did the debate over enclosure and agricultural improvement, the debate over the grain trade moved in the direction of systematic discussion of political economy. Here again, French writers drew initially upon English economic thought.

The French encounter with English political economy dates also from about 1750. As we have noted above, interest in English political thought grew after the appearance of Montesquieu's *Esprit des lois*. In fact, as early as 1746 Dupré had introduced Locke's economic ideas in the *Essay on Money*. Vincent Gournay, who became *intendant de commerce* in 1751 and who decisively influenced Turgot (among other leading intellectuals), translated essays by Child and Gee, *Interest of Money* and *Causes of the Decline of Commerce* respectively. Throughout the early 1750s the economic writings of Locke, Petty, Child, Davenant, Tucker, and Hume became increasingly well known. Yet, as Weulerrse has argued, "more profound and more remarkable has been the influence of Cantillon."[25] The latter's *Essai sur la nature du commerce en général* appeared in 1755 (although it had been written perhaps twenty-five years earlier). Cantillon is the great link between seventeenth-century English political economy and the system of the Physiocrats. It is no overstatement to say that he constituted the direct connection between the writings of Petty and Quesnay. As Schumpeter wrote, "Few sequences in the history of economic analysis are so important for us to see, to understand, and to fix in our minds as is the sequence: Petty-Cantillon-Quesnay."[26]

Richard Cantillon (1697–1734) went to Paris in 1716 and traded there in wine, silk, and copper. He made his fortune, however, in banking, particularly during the period 1716–1720 when he is reported to have profited enormously through Law's system. By age twenty, Cantillon was a financial success. He returned to London in 1720 and lived there for six years, although he continued to travel widely. He was often in Paris between 1729 and 1733, during which period he appears to have written the *Essai*.[27]

Cantillon brought to political economy a unique combination of practical business experience, broad acquaintance with the literature of political economy (the *Essai* refers to Petty, Davenant, Locke, and Vauban, among others), and a consciously scientific approach to economic analysis (as Higgs pointed out, Cantillon sought to discern the "natural" or "inevitable sequence of effect upon cause" in economic phenomena). Numerous commentators have pointed out that Petty was the major theoretical influence upon Cantillon—upon his general concepts, conceptual framework, and mode of analysis. But although Petty's analysis may have constituted the starting point for many of Cantillon's reflections on economic problems, the *Essai* represented an important advance upon all previous works in political economy.[28]

The *Essai* opens with a modified statement of Petty's assertion that land is the mother of wealth and labour its father. "The Land," Cantillon writes, "is the Source or Matter from whence all Wealth is produced. The Labour of man is the Form which produced it." It is upon the surplus—or, as Cantillon calls it, the "overplus"—produced on the land that all nonagricultural professions subsist. Thus, "all the classes and inhabitants of a State live at the expense of the Proprietors of the Land." For this reason, only the landed proprietors can be said to be truly independent members of society; all others are dependent upon the surplus product of the proprietors' land and upon the latter's expenditure of the revenue they receive from ownership of land.[29]

The wealth of society is thus a function of the productivity of agricultural labour. The example of England has shown that agricultural prosperity requires well-to-do husbandmen who can organize and finance production on large farms. Cantillon's model assumes a pattern of capitalist farming in which the farmer is an "entrepreneur." In fact, he constructs his model upon the assumption that English-style capitalist farming is most advantageous:

> when a Farmer has some capital to carry on the management of his Farm the Proprietor who lets him the Farm for a Third of the Produce will be sure of payment and will be better off by such a bargain than if he let his Land at a higher rate to a beggarly Farmer at the risk of losing all his Rent. The larger the Farm the better off the Farmer will be. This is seen in England where Farmers are generally more prosperous than in other countries where the farms are small.[30]

It is on the basis of such a model of large-scale capitalist farming that Cantillon elaborates a notion of the circular flow, which anticipates the main features of Quesnay's *Tableau économique*. The farmer, he states, produce "three Rents": one goes to the proprietor as payment for the use of land; one covers the costs of agricultural production (including the farmer's subsistence); and one constitutes the profit of the farmer. These three rents are "the mainspring of the circulation of the state." Landlords reside in the towns and spend all their income there; farmers spend one-quarter of their two rents (or one-sixth of the total agricultural output) on urban manufactures. As a result of these expenditures, one-half of the population is able to live in the cities subsisting on the half of the agricultural product (one-third plus one-sixth) spent there. The specific character of the "dependent" professions which subsist upon the expenditure of the agricultural output is determined in large measure by the "Fancy, Methods, and Fashions of life of the Proprietors of the Land in especial."[31] As we shall see below, the basic elements of Quesnay's *Tableau* are here sketched by Cantillon.

Within the general context of this vision of an agrarian-based circular flow of wealth, Cantillon takes up the problem of value. Here the influence of Petty is most apparent. Following Petty, Cantillon distinguishes between the "market price" of a good (which is determined by the interplay of supply and demand) and its "intrinsic value." On the assumption that "in well-ordered societies the market prices of produce and commodities whose consumption is fairly constant and uniform do not deviate much from the intrinsic value," Cantillon proceeds to investigate intrinsic value.[32] Again, he poses the problem precisely as it had been posed by Petty: "the Price or *intrinsic value* of a thing is the measure of the quantity of Land and

Labour entering into its production, having regard to the fertility or produce of the Land and to the quality of the Labour."[33] Cantillon, like Petty, recognizes that such a dualistic theory of value is theoretically unsatisfactory. He undertakes, therefore, the search for a "par or relation between the value of land and the value of labour." Here he acknowledges Petty's priority in the formulation of this problem but he rejects the latter's "solution":

> Sir Wm. Petty, in a little manuscript of the year 1685 [the *Political Anatomy of Ireland*, published in 1691], considers this Par, or Equation between Land and Labour, as the most important consideration in Political Arithmetic, but the research which he has made into it in passing is fanciful and remote from natural laws, because he has attached himself not to causes and principles, but only to effects, as Mr. Locke, Mr. Davenant and all the other English authors who have written on this subject have done after him.[34]

Cantillon attempts to solve this equation between land and labour by expressing labour in terms of land. The value of labour, he claims, is equal to the amount of land necessary for the subsistence of the labourer and two children (assuming that one of the children will die, the usual rate of child mortality, and that the wife manages just to reproduce the value of her own costs of subsistence). What this requires, therefore, is that "the Labour of a free Labourer . . . correspond in value to double the produce of Land needed for his maintenance."[35] Thus, since the value of labour is determined by the amount of land necessary to its reproduction, the amount of land and labour entering into the production of a good can be measured by one member of this value-determining pair—land:

> The intrinsic value of any thing may be measured by the quantity of Land used in its production and the quantity of Labour which enters into it, in other words by the quantity of Land of which the produce is allotted to those who have worked upon it.[36]

This analysis comes close to a "corn-model" solution, by defining the value of labour in terms of a single subsistence unit of landed production. Whether this resolution of Petty's problem represents a significant advance upon its originator's efforts is open to question. Certainly in *The Political Anatomy of Ireland*, the very work Cantillon referred to, Petty comes remarkably close to this solution. Whatever the final judgement of this matter, there can be little doubt that with the appearance of Cantillon's *Essai* in 1755 many of the essential elements of the physiocratic system were ready, awaiting merely the grand architectural efforts of François Quesnay. It may be an exaggeration to say, as did Higgs, that "Cantillon is certainly the Father of Physiocracy";[37] it is nonetheless the case that advocacy of capitalist farming along English lines, definition of the agricultural surplus as the basis of circulation of the aggregate social product, and a *tableau économique* which defines the circular flow of wealth between the different economic classes in society are all to be found in his *Essai*. François Quesnay had only to add the ingredient of his own distinctive genius to produce the theoretical system of Physiocracy.

FRANÇOIS QUESNAY AND PHYSIOCRACY

Born in 1694 to a Norman family, Quesnay studied medicine, became a surgeon, and later a *docteur en médecine*. In 1749 he went to Versailles as physician to the marquise de Pompadour and was promoted rapidly to the position of medical consultant to the king. In 1755 he became *le premier médecin ordinaire* to the king. Quesnay frequented the philosophical discussions at Madame de Pompadour's which included d'Alembert, Buffon, Diderot, Duclos, Helvétius, and Condillac. Indeed, Quesnay agreed to write numerous articles for the *Encyclopédie*, the great undertaking of Enlightenment thinkers. The philosophical article "Evidence" was published in volume 6 in 1756, as was the first of his essays in political economy, "Fermiers." The following year he published "Grains" in volume 7. One other philosophical essay and three economic essays were written but not published at this time because of the suppression of the *Encyclopédie*.

About the same time that the *Encyclopédie* was suppressed, Quesnay appears to have decided to gather around himself a group of disciples of his economic views. In the middle of 1757, he recruited the marquis de Mirabeau, author of the celebrated *Ami des hommes* which had originated as a lengthy commentary on Cantillon's *Essai*.[38] Encouraged by the recruitment of so eminent a first apostle, Quesnay set out to advance his doctrine. His theories soon struck a responsive chord with prominent thinkers and men of affairs like Diderot, Gournay, Turgot, and Mercier de la Rivière. Over the course of 1758–1759 Quesnay constructed three versions of his *Tableau économique*. In 1760 Mirabeau's *Théorie de l'impôt* earned its author a term in prison and a short-lived exile, as a result of its attack on the farmers general. Nevertheless, Mirabeau's pen remained active. In 1763 he published *Philosophie rurale,* the text of which had been carefully scrutinized by Quesnay. The work was of special significance; it represented the generalization of Quesnay's economic theories into a total theory of society. After the publication of *Philosophie rurale,* the reputation of the new school of *économistes* grew by leaps and bounds. During the years 1764–1766 Quesnay and Mirabeau attracted a number of important adherents. Among the new disciples were Dupont de Nemours, who became the school's best-known young spokesman, Guillaume-François Le Trosne, son of a councillor to the king from Orléans, Mercier de la Rivière who had been both a councillor to the first chamber of inquests of the Parlement of Paris and intendant in Martinique, and the abbé Nicolas Baudeau who brought to the school his journal *Ephémérides du citoyen.*

In addition to direct converts, the physiocratic movement began also to exercise a growing intellectual influence. Among the *encyclopédistes,* Diderot, d'Alembert, Duclos, and Helvétius often attended Mirabeau's weekly dinners. Two agricultural societies—one in Orléans, the other in Limoges—openly embraced physiocratic doctrine. Three well-known intendants became strongly identified with the school: le chevalier Méliand in Soissons, Fontette in Caen, and Turgot in Limousin. Courtesy of Baudeau, the movement also had its own journal, the *Ephémérides,* whose subtitle was changed in 1767 from "Chronique de l'esprit national" to "Bibliothèque raisonnée des sciences morales et politiques." In the pages of this journal, Quesnay and his disciples began to sketch out the full social and political implications of their worldview. This process was furthered also by the publication in July 1767 of Mercier's *Ordre naturel et essentiel des sociétés politiques,* which developed the notion of "legal despotism." This work was widely acclaimed—by Diderot among others—and earned its author an invitation from Catherine of Russia to visit her country and help in the framing of a new code of laws. Also in 1767, Dupont brought out a collection of Quesnay's writings under the title *Physiocratie.* Only now did the school become known by this term, coined by Quesnay, which means, roughly, 'rule of nature.'

The new school was, at this time, at the peak of its popularity and success. Indeed, Mirabeau wrote to Rousseau in the middle of 1767 that political economy had become the "new worldly bible" and Quesnay "the venerable Confucius of Europe."[39] Other disciples compared Quesnay to Newton and Leibniz. The popularity and growing influence of Physiocracy was, however, short-lived. By 1769 the climate of opinion began to shift against the group. That year, the abbé Terray, a strong opponent of the school, became controller general and began to undermine physiocratic influence on economic policy (which had, during the late 1760s, grown to sizable proportions). Around the same time, a series of bad harvests stimulated opposition to physiocratic proposals such as free export of and high prices for grain. Finally, the growing dogmatism of the school—increasingly denounced as "une secte"—drove theorists like Voltaire, Mably, Linguet, and Galiani to issue devastating critiques of Quesnay and his followers. After 1770, the fortunes of the school rapidly declined.

The great period of Physiocracy—the period of its genesis, development, and important influence—spanned a mere decade from 1760 to 1770. Nevertheless, the tremendous intellectual energies that it generated produced a body of economic, and to a lesser extent political, theory which decisively influenced the theoretical structure of classical political economy. If it is true that "in many respects Quesnaysian economics *is* classical economics," then a close examination of physiocratic doctrine may provide important insights into the entire theoretical legacy of classical political economy.[40]

Quesnay's *Encyclopédie* Articles

Quesnay's political economy did not burst upon educated French society with any great flash. In fact, Quesnay's first economic article, "Fermiers," published in January 1756 in the *Encyclopédie*, was ignored largely both by his own disciples and by later commentators. Dupont, for example, did not include this article in *Physiocratie*, his collection of Quesnay's economic writings. Modern commentators have generally downplayed the significance of all of Quesnay's *Encyclopédie* articles and have focused attention upon the *Tableau économique*. Without a doubt, "Fermiers" has suffered the greatest neglect.[41] There are many reasons for this. Unquestionably the most important is that later in life Quesnay felt some embarrassment about an article which failed to advance the doctrine of the exclusive productivity of agriculture and which failed to advocate that cornerstone of the physiocratic program, the single tax on land rent. Thus, it was Quesnay himself who chose to deemphasize the importance of his earliest exercise in political economy. Continued neglect, however, has not aided later interpretations of Physiocracy. For, precisely because Quesnay had not yet constructed an integrated system of theoretical concepts, in which all policy recommendations appear to flow logically from a disinterested scientific inquiry, his social and political concerns were stated there more explicitly than in most of his subsequent writings. Yet it is the social and political character of Physiocracy which has been the greatest source of confusion to most interpreters. For this reason, our study of Physiocracy will begin with an examination of "Fermiers" and Quesnay's other *Encyclopédie* articles.

"Fermiers" begins with the statement that farmers are especially important for the support of the state and that the government should pay close attention to the conditions of this class of people. The first paragraph states, for example:

> Farmers, (pol. econ.) are those who strengthen and give value to the goods of the country, and who bring forth the wealth and the resources which are most essential to the support of the state; thus the employment of the *farmer* is a very important object of the kingdom and deserves serious attention on the part of the government.[42]

The article starts, therefore, by stating clearly that Quesnay is adopting the standpoint of the state in analysing economic phenomena. The special significance of farmers derives from their unique ability to provide wealth which is essential to the state. Although the character of this unique importance is not specified at this point, towards the end of the article Quesnay makes it clear that the special importance of the farmer is a function of the fact that agricultural wealth sustains the state. Because it is fixed and visible in character, the physical produce of the land cannot escape taxation as can commercial wealth. Agricultural production alone provides a firm and reliable source of revenue to the state:

> Agriculture is the inheritance of the sovereign: all its products are visible; one can properly subject them to taxation; financial wealth can evade its share of subsidies; the government can take them only through means which are onerous to the state.[43]

In explicitly adopting the standpoint of the state and in making the problem of taxation and royal finances his central concern, Quesnay demonstrates that his is an exercise in political economy in the traditional sense. His starting point is indeed the economy of the royal household; the central problem of royal finances is taxation. Curiously, the full significance of the fact that this preoccupation with taxation and royal revenues constitutes the point of departure of Physiocracy has eluded most writers. Quesnay's adoption of the traditional vantage point of political economy has gone unnoticed in part because he departs radically from the mercantilist conceptions of economic life which infused the preclassical discourse of French political economy. Quesnay rejects the Colbertist concentration on commerce and industry and asserts that it is agriculture which is the source of wealth. It is agriculture, he maintains, which satisfies human needs, increases population, and raises the revenues of proprietors and the state. Commercial or mercantile wealth is fluid and unstable; the wealth employed in agriculture makes up a fixed and stable asset which is a permanent contribution to the nation as a whole.[44] The priority of agriculture, to repeat, is thus for Quesnay not yet a strictly economic fact (as it would become in his subsequent writings); rather, in his eyes agriculture has a *political* priority: agricultural wealth, unlike commercial wealth, remains within the kingdom and its concrete, tangible character guarantees that it is readily accessible to taxation by the state.

Having asserted the priority of agriculture, Quesnay departs further from mercantilist orthodoxy by arguing that it is not poverty but wealth which induces men to work. Poverty, he says, produces poverty; wealth creates wealth. Only rich farmers are capable of purchasing the horses, ploughs, flocks, and implements which make possible the production of a sizable agricultural surplus. Indeed, large farms adequately fuelled by "advances" of capital are capable of doubling the output of the land—as is demonstrated by examining English agriculture.[45] On the basis of this analysis, Quesnay argues that the state should fundamentally reorient its economic policy. The practice of encouraging commerce and luxury contributes to decadence and economic decline. Even though a shift to large-scale capitalist farming on the English model will disrupt traditional social relations, it is preferable to have peasants become wage labourers for rich farmers than to have them work a small plot of land alone. The state should undertake, therefore, to encourage the development of

agriculture—the concentration of ownership and capital investment
on the land—by directing commercial wealth into agriculture:

The government, which gives motion to the springs of society, which ar-
ranges the general order, may find proper and worthwhile expedients for
making them [commercial fortunes] return to agriculture where they will be
more profitable to private individuals and much more advantageous to the
state.[46]

As intriguing as such pleas for state-directed investment in agriculture may be, Meek is undoubtedly correct in claiming that "Fermiers" contains "very little that can properly be called an anticipation of basic Physiocratic theory."[47] The fact that the article does not
proclaim the exclusive productivity of agriculture, advance the concept of the "net product," or advocate the single tax on rent has
served further to discourage scholarly interest in it. Yet, as we have
suggested above, it is precisely its "prephysiocratic" character which
sheds light on the immediate issues which provoked Quesnay to take
up theoretical problems in political economy. The preoccupation of
"Fermiers" with analysing agriculture from the standpoint of the
pressing problems of royal finances indicates that it was the deep-
rooted crisis of state revenues which served as Quesnay's point of departure in political economy.

Nearly two years transpired before Quesnay's next economic writing appeared. Once again, the article had a title, "Grains," which
indicated Quesnay's agrarian concerns. Once again, the article was
published in the *Encyclopédie*, this time in volume 7, which appeared
in November 1757. In "Grains" Quesnay worked, however, with a
more sophisticated conceptual system. Indeed, this article may truly
be called Quesnay's first "physiocratic" essay. There can also be little
doubt that the main theoretical influence on Quesnay during the period between the publication of "Fermiers" and the appearance of
"Grains" was Richard Cantillon. Cantillon's *Essai* appeared in the
middle of 1755, by which time Quesnay had probably completed the
writing of "Fermiers." Quesnay's explicit reference to Cantillon in
"Grains" demonstrates that he was familiar with the latter's work.
Furthermore, as we shall illustrate below, the imprint of Cantillon's
views on the theoretical structure of "Grains" seems overwhelming.

The article commences with a criticism of the manner in which
manufacture of luxuries has "seduced" the French nation and reas-

serts the special significance of agriculture. Excessive expenditure on luxuries, Quesnay argues, lowers demand for agricultural goods (and, therefore, their prices), impoverishes agricultural producers, and creates an exodus of people from the countryside to the towns. From the opening paragraph, then, it is patterns of consumption which are made determinant of general patterns of economic life. It is the division of expenditure between agricultural and industrial goods which determines the social division of the population. Thus, if agriculture is the basis of national wealth, it is the level of consumption of agricultural goods which determines the degree of national prosperity. This is not the case with trading nations which, lacking the climate, land, and resources to produce a sizable agrarian suplus, can grow rich only through saving and economizing. But it is the case with agricultural nations, such as France, which "increase their revenue by means of their consumption."[48]

Increased consumption of agricultural goods provides the high prices that make capitalist agriculture possible. High and stable prices ensure that farmers will recoup investments devoted to increasing agricultural productivity. Not all agricultural producers, however, are in a position to take advantage of high prices. The poor peasant who lives on the margin of subsistence and "who buys nothing and sells nothing, works only for himself: he lives in wretchedness, and he and the land he tills bring nothing to the state."[49] Only rich farmers are capable of taking advantage of high prices to produce a growing surplus product. Quesnay makes it clear that he has in mind just such farmers: capitalists, not simple labourers. Indeed, after quoting Cantillon on the priority of agriculture and the strategic function of landowners, Quesnay paraphrases Cantillon's definition of the capitalist farmer: "We do not here envisage the rich farmer as a labourer who himself works the land; he is an entrepreneur who controls and who makes his enterprise profitable through his intelligence and his wealth."[50] Also indicative of Cantillon's influence on this article is that Quesnay here suggests that the farmer shares in the social surplus. Entrepreneurial profit to the farmer ("des profits aux cultivateurs") is treated as forming, like rent, a part of the net product. Such a conceptualization bears a close resemblance to Cantillon's doctrine of the "three rents," two of which—farmers' profit and proprietors' rents—constitute the surplus.[51]

Utilizing this conceptual framework, Quesnay can not yet ascribe exclusive productivity to the land in the production of new wealth. Treating money still as a form of wealth, he argues that "incomes are the product of land and men," a position he later rejected.[52] "Grains" reflects the still-developing character of Quesnay's economic views, as he gropes for an antimercantilist conception of value and draws inspiration from Cantillon's *Essai*. Before long he will reject Cantillon's view and develop a distinct value theory of his own. Yet "Grains" does advance two notions which were to become central elements of the physiocratic schema: the idea that commerce and manufacturing are sterile, that they produce no surplus beyond their costs of production; and the view that the farmer should be exempted from taxation, that taxes should be imposed exclusively upon that portion of the surplus product appropriated by the proprietor of the land—rent.

Quesnay argues in "Grains" for the first time that agriculture is superior to industry not for political reasons (its accessibility to the tax collector) but because agriculture alone creates a net product, a surplus above costs of production. Industry is not productive in this sense.[53] It follows logically that only the productive sector of the economy—that sector which produces a net surplus product—can provide revenues to the state. Only agriculture, therefore, should be taxed. But taxation of the cultivator would discourage agricultural production and reduce the national wealth. It is the surplus which accrues to the proprietor of the land—rent—which should be taxed by the state. To tax the farmer is to invite disaster:

If the sovereign imposes taxes on the cultivator himself, if they swallow up his profit, there is a decline in cultivation and a diminution in the proprietors' revenue, whence follows an inevitable retrenchment which affects hired people, merchants, workers, and servants. The general system of expenditure, work, gain and consumption is thrown out of gear; the state grows weaker; and the tax comes to have a more and more destructive effect. Thus a kingdom can be prosperous and powerful only through the medium of products which are continually renewing themselves or being generated from the wealth of a numerous and energetic people, whose industry is supported and stimulated by the government.

This passage expresses some of the most important elements of the physiocratic system. And the following passage calls upon the state to direct economic affairs into their proper channels: "The wealth of a state does not maintain itself on its own, but is maintained and increased only in so far as it is made to renew itself by *planning* its employment intelligently."[54]

In the article "Hommes," which was written in 1757 but did not appear at that time since the *Encyclopédie* was suppressed, Quesnay develops several of these themes at greater length and illuminates the character of the state which he believes should direct economic life. The article claims that the level of population is a function of social wealth and that the population of France has fallen by one-third (from twenty-four to sixteen million) over the previous century. But the wealth that sustains population should not be identified with money, which "plays only an ideal role in trade." Genuine prosperity consists not in the quantity of money a state possesses "but in the abundance and the proper price of its exchangeable wealth." Furthermore, the wealth of a state (which determines its military strength) depends upon the surplus beyond their own consumption produced by those engaged in productive labour. "The more wealth men produce over and above their consumption, the more profitable they are to the state," he writes. Contrary to the popular view that the employment of more men on the land increases national wealth, Quesnay maintains that the use of fewer men and more animals increases the productivity of agricultural labour and creates a larger social surplus product. As a result, he advocates the English-style relation between capitalist landlord and tenant, in which the proprietor of the land makes substantial investments in his farm and chooses a prosperous tenant farmer. Furthermore, he advocates the use of "all machines which can contribute to reduce the cost of men's labour."[55]

In "Hommes" Quesnay again asserts the importance of free trade in establishing high prices for primary products. He also clearly states that he considers mining and fishing to be productive industries, that is, industries which produce a net product. In addition, he argues once more that it is the expenditure of the social surplus by the landowning class which drives the entire economy.[56] "Hommes" is most significant, however, for the insights it affords into Quesnay's analysis of French political life. In this article he states more succinctly than ever before his view that the interests of merchants are in opposition to the general interest of society. Merchants grow rich, he maintains, by artificially increasing the prices of goods—something contrary to the general interest. Their interest, therefore, "makes them completely forgetful of the nation's interests."[57] Moreover, by amassing fortunes, merchants obstruct the natural flow of money which makes possible a steady flow of productive wealth.

While he attacks the commercial interest, Quesnay makes it clear that he does not favour the retention (or restoration) of feudal rights and privileges. He denounces "feudal tyranny" and suggests instead that personal liberty and pursuit of self-interest should constitute the basis of the state. He does not, however, argue for a liberal, night-watchman state which merely defends the nation and protects rights to property and personal security. Quesnay is not prepared to sur-render the maintenance of the social order to the free interplay of private interests. Private interests, he argues, "do not lend them-selves to an insight into general welfare. Such advantages can be ex-pected only as a result of the wisdom of the government."[58] But what sort of government should be endowed with the power to direct par-ticular interests in a manner which will further the general welfare? Quesnay makes it clear that classic feudalism is as much character-ized by a tyranny of certain private interests as would be a state based upon the interests of the commercial bourgeoisie. He argues for a monarchical form of government, not an arbitrary monarchy but one which protects and preserves the rule of law and which, in so doing, reconciles particular interests to the general will:

Sovereign monarchical power can subsist only through the authority of the laws and through the balance of the bodies of the state, each restrained in turn by the other; and by the laws which concern them and which limit and guarantee their rights.[59]

In "Hommes," then, we have the fullest view the *Encyclopédie* ar-ticles present of Quesnay's perspective on the relation between state and economy. Although he does not explicitly say so, Quesnay would seem to imply that the state is to undertake the reorganization of the economy along the lines of agrarian capitalism. Clearly, he does not envisage the commercial bourgeoisie undertaking a change which would advance the public interest. Nor does he expect such com-mendable action from the traditional nobility. The monarch, it would appear, must harmonize civil society and direct economic life from above.

The last of Quesnay's articles written for the *Encyclopédie* (but, like "Hommes," never published there) was entitled "Impôts." In many respects, this article does little more than elaborate certain themes found in "Grains." Yet it remains an important piece because it illustrates vividly once again that the point of departure of Quesnay's political economy is his concern with taxation and royal revenues. The article thus begins by denigrating monetary fortunes since they "destroy the stock of productive wealth and evade taxation."[60] Quesnay also dismisses industry and commerce from his analysis of wealth and taxes, since they are *sterile;* that is, they produce no real surplus. Consequently, he states more decisively in this article than in any other of the writings he prepared for the *Encyclopédie* that rent is the basis of national wealth:

> The profits or the revenues which the proprietors draw from their property wealth are thus the true riches of the nation, the riches of the sovereign, the riches of the subject, the riches which pay the taxes imposed for the necessary expenses of government and the defence of the state.[61]

On the basis of this view he reiterates his support for large-scale farming directed by "riches cultivateurs" and calls once again for exemption of all farmers from taxation and placement of all taxes on the rent of land.

I have suggested above that careful analysis of the *Encyclopédie* articles demonstrates that Quesnay's initial undertakings in the field of political economy were stimulated by a preoccupation with the crisis of state revenues in France. This should come as no surprise, given that the Crown had been forced throughout the eighteenth century to adopt extraordinary tax measures to pay its bills and that the financial crisis of the state had been dramatically expressed in France's military misfortunes. Nevertheless, the political objectives which underpinned the physiocratic system have eluded most commentators. This is in part because, as the physiocratic school developed, Quesnay and his disciples chose to present their views as formulations of universal truths. Thus, the connection of physiocratic doctrine to concrete social and historical problems appeared increasingly remote. Furthermore, the level of abstraction employed in the construction of the centrepiece of Physiocracy, the *Tableau économique*, contributed to the view that the Physiocrats were little more than speculative philosophers engaged in purely theoretical work. Illuminated by our reading of Quesnay's early writings, however, the *Tableau économique* appears in an entirely different light.

THE CENTREPIECE: THE *TABLEAU ÉCONOMIQUE*

The most celebrated achievement of the Physiocrats is the *Tableau économique*, the first edition of which Quesnay produced in December 1758. Two more editions appeared the following year. During the 1760s it was republished—and revised—in numerous physiocratic essays and books.[62] To the Physiocrats themselves, the *Tableau* had a near-mystical importance. Mirabeau, for example, claimed that along with writing and money, the *Tableau* represented one of the three great human inventions. Although subsequent commentators were not quite so exuberant in their praise, it has been widely hailed as a brilliant innovation in theoretical economics. Marx, for example, described its conceptual structure as "incontestably the most brilliant for which political economy had up to then been responsible." Schumpeter characterized the notion of economic interdependence which the *Tableau* encapsulated as "a bold abstraction and an innovation which was methodologically most important." These views have been echoed by historians of economic thought for many years.[63]

The *Tableau* was indeed a "bold abstraction." Quesnay made it clear in fact that his diagrammatic representation of the annual interchange of commodities and money between the main economic classes (the "zigzag") involved disregarding secondary details to focus attention on essential economic interrelations. Thus, as he wrote to Mirabeau:

The zigzag, if properly understood, cuts out a whole number of details, and brings before your eyes certain closely interwoven ideas which the intellect alone would have a great deal of difficulty in grasping, unravelling and reconciling by the method of discourse.[64]

In this respect, the *Tableau* represented a new level of abstraction in physiocratic analysis; with it, Quesnay embarked upon the task of model-building. Rather than making social and political policy the centre of analysis, he presented a model of the economy as a self-reproducing system, as an organic totality which creates and recreates itself. The economic mechanism appears, therefore, to be independent of human action; it seems to adhere to natural laws and to follow a causation of its own. Quesnay and his followers were inclined to represent the *Tableau* as a theoretical discovery of natural laws. Indeed, Quesnay claimed that the main interrelations depicted in the zigzag were "faithfully copied from nature." Mirabeau extended and elaborated this theoretical orientation by arguing that the task of political economy was to anatomize the regular movements of "la machine économique."[65]

In depicting the economy as a self-regulating mechanism, Quesnay deemphasized the social and political assumptions of his model. The *Tableau* does rest upon such assumptions. However, they are *implicit* presuppositions of the analytic model constructed in the zigzag diagram (although they are explicitly stated in the text of the *Tableau*) and have escaped the attention of all but the most penetrating commentators. Below we will attempt to reveal these presuppositions of the *Tableau économique*. But first we must examine in some detail the technical features of this "bold abstraction" which so captured the attention of later commentators.

The *Tableau économique* depicts the process of annual economic reproduction as a unity of production and circulation. The cycle begins with the agricultural harvest. The dynamic element of agricultural output is the surplus which cultivators hand over as money rent to the land's proprietors. From that point on, the *Tableau* describes the exchanges of money and commodities between the *productive* (agricultural) class, the landed proprietors, and the *sterile* (manufacturing) class. The best known of the early versions of the *Tableau* (the third edition) represents the process of annual reproduction (illustrated in figure 1, p. 112).

According to this model, the agricultural surplus (the net product) is equal to the working capital (advances) used in agricultural production. These advances produce a surplus at the annual rate of 100 percent. Thus an advance of 600 (million livres) produces 600 (million livres) of rent. Abstracting from taxes on the net revenue and assuming that the proprietors do not save out of their revenue, the *Tableau* depicts first the expenditure of the rent between the productive and the sterile classes. In this version (as in most) the landlords divide their spending evenly between agricultural and industrial goods. Following the expenditure of the aggregate revenue, the productive and the sterile classes enter into a mutual exchange, in which they continually spend one-half of their receipts upon the products of the other class. The diagram also expresses the notion of the exclusive productivity of the land (that is, its unique ability to produce a surplus above costs of production) by depicting the receipts of the

Productive Expenditure	Expenditure of the Revenue	Sterile Expenditure
Annual advances required to produce a revenue of 600 are 600	Annual revenue	Annual advances for the works of sterile expenditure are

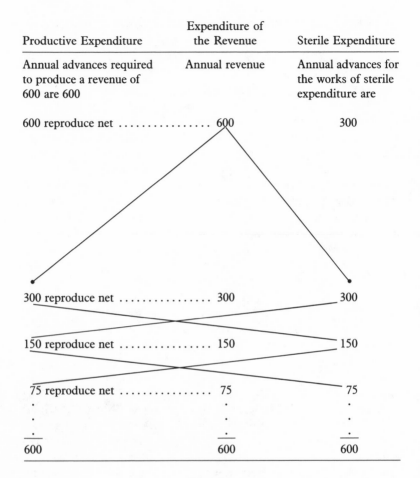

Figure 1.

productive class as generating a new output which accumulates in the centre column and indicates that the productive class will be able to begin the next cycle of economic reproduction with the payment of rent. Within the course of one annual production period, then, the cultivators produce commodities to a value of 1200 (million livres). Of these, 300 are purchased by the proprietors of the land and 300 by the sterile class (the sum of these purchases equals the value of the surplus product). Of the remaining 600 in commodities from the land (equal to the annual advances), 300 are consumed by the agricultural class (farmers and labourers), and the remaining 300 are used to feed and maintain livestock. The sterile class, meanwhile, receives 300 from the proprietors and 300 from the productive class. Of these 600 (million livres) in receipts, 300 are retained for annual advances in the next production period while the other 300 are used for wages. Thus, abstracting from any interest on fixed capital, the annual reproduction is 1200 (million livres). Of this amount, one-half is consumed directly within the productive class (the advances); the other half (the revenue) is spent equally between the productive and sterile classes, which then enter into a period of mutual exchange. At the end of the period of reproduction, then, the productive class has produced another 1200 (million livres), of which one-half is retained as productive advances while the other half goes to pay the rent.

Let us examine the assumptions of the *Tableau* more closely. It represents an ideal model. Quesnay did not believe that the eighteenth-century French economy was reproducing itself year after year in a balanced fashion. The *Tableau* was designed to demonstrate the economic interrelationships that must be maintained to ensure stability and prosperity. In presupposing the essential conditions of prosperity, for example, the model assumes large-scale capitalist farming: "The land employed in the cultivation of corn is brought together, as far as possible, into large farms worked by rich husbandmen."[66] Furthermore, the model assumes that this type of farming produces a surplus equal to the annual advances; the zigzag is designed to show how these essential relations can be preserved year after year. Thus, the *Tableau* sketches out the prerequisites of a simple reproduction and not of growth (expanded reproduction); it depicts a situation of zero net investment.

Next, the model employed in the *Tableau* presupposes complete freedom of trade and export. The *Tableau* also operates with the assumption of equilibrium prices and, therefore, eliminates the possibility that market disequilibria can disrupt the price structure. The capital of the rich farmers (the agricultural advances) determines all of the fundamental economic relations—the size of the revenue, the amount of money necessary for annual reproduction, the level of consumption within the productive class, and the aggregate sterile output. Once we introduce the assumptions that the costs of the industrial sector are half labour costs and half raw materials costs, and further that each class spends half its income on agricultural goods and half on manufactured goods, then the zigzag diagram follows automatically. In this respect, then, the *Tableau* "proves" nothing; it merely illustrates diagrammatically the constraints of Quesnay's model of simple reproduction.

Nevertheless, there are some technical difficulties with the zigzag diagram as it appears. Perhaps the most important of these problems is that the diagram neglects fixed capital. No production process can be carried on with working capital (annual advances) exclusively; the Physiocrats were quite aware of that fact. Indeed, Quesnay claimed that there were three types of advances necessary to agricultural production: *avances foncières*, expenditures on removing stones, weeds, tree roots, and on irrigation, drainage, hedges, and fertilizer; *avances primitives*, fixed capital expenditures on fences, buildings, and farm machinery, and on maintenance or depreciation; and *avances annuelles*, yearly expenditures on raw materials and wages. At no point do the *avances foncières* figure in the text accompanying the *Tableau*. Such is not the case with the *avances primitives;* in the earliest editions, Quesnay discusses the need to replenish these productive elements over time. Nevertheless, the most common versions of the zigzag show no income flow or interest to replace fixed capital. As a result, popular versions of the physiocratic system have represented economic production as strictly annual, all factors of production being replenished each year. This annual reproduction model (with no role for fixed capital) was to create theoretical havoc for classical political economy for years to come.

Quesnay does, however, solve this problem by incorporating fixed capital (*avances primitives*) into his model. Early versions of the *Tableau* mention the need for a fund to maintain and replace the elements of fixed capital. It is only in the *Analyse*, an elaboration of the *Tableau* published in 1766, however, that Quesnay finally introduces interest on fixed capital into the zigzag itself. Working with a base of annual advances (A) of 2000 (as in the version of the tableau he first used in *Philosophie rurale*), Quesnay assumes that the *avances primitives* are five times the value of the *avances annuelles* (5A = 10,000). Furthermore, he assumes that the elements of the *avances primitives* must be entirely reproduced every ten years; one-tenth of the value of fixed capital must be reproduced (via interest) annually. As a result, the *avances primitives* turned over annually constitute a value equal to one-half the value of the *avances annuelles* (5A/10 = 1/2A = 1000). From what source will the productive class obtain the money to pay the interest on fixed capital? In answering this question, Quesnay clears up the confusion surrounding the missing purchase the sterile class makes from the productive class. He states specifically that the sterile class uses its advances of 1000 to buy raw materials from the productive class (the 1000 it receives from the proprietors it uses to buy food from the productive class, as depicted in the zigzag). By accounting for this missing purchase and by introducing the 1000 in interest on fixed capital explicitly into the diagram, Quesnay increases the total reproduction (as always excluding the sterile sector) from 4000 to 5000. In the meantime he has—again in the interest of consistency—ignored the consumption of agricultural produce by livestock since this is an intrasectoral process. Thus, the revised *Tableau* presented in the *Analyse* appears in Figure 2 (p. 116).

As important as is the refinement of the *Tableau*, the technical difficulties of Quesnay's model have tended to obscure its fundamental social and political features.[67] Analysis of the technical operations of the *Tableau* does not, after all, elucidate the purpose of Quesnay's model. Surprisingly, no serious study has probed the problem which Quesnay attempted to illuminate by constructing the *Tableau* or examined the political presuppositions of the economic model it encapsulated. Without a study of this problem, the interpretation of Physiocracy remains grossly one-sided.

The clue to Quesnay's motivation in constructing the *Tableau* may be found in his famous letter to Mirabeau, in which he explains the principles of the zigzag. In passing, Quesnay refers to the *Tableau* as "this Little Book of Household Accounts."[68] With this expression, Quesnay indicates that, for all his analytic innovations, his enterprise

	Productive class Annual advances	Proprietors Revenue	Sterile class Annual advances
	2000	*2000*	*1000*
Sums which are used to pay the revenue and the interest on the original advances	1000		1000
	1000		
	1000		1000
		Total 2000	
Expenditure of annual advances	2000		Of which one-half is held back by this class for the ad-
Total	5000		vances of the fol- lowing year

Figure 2.

remains curiously within the traditional discourse of political economy which conceptualized the economy from the standpoint of—
and as an extension of—the royal household. Quesnay's genius consisted in recognizing that the problem of royal finances could not be
addressed adequately outside a comprehensive analysis of the fundamental interrelations of economic life. Consequently, his "Little
Book of Household Accounts" had to include a treatment of the annual flow of commodities and money between the basic sectors of the
economy. Within the text of the *Tableau* which accompanies the
zigzag diagram, Quesnay states that his objective is to establish a
scientific analysis of the economy as a solid foundation for royal
finances. Indeed, he calls his theory "the science of economic administration in a kingdom," and he writes that "it is in a knowledge
of the true sources of wealth, and of the means of increasing and per-
petuating them, that the science of the economic administration of
a kingdom consists."[69]

   Taking the problem of the economic administration of the kingdom as his point of departure in fashioning the *Tableau*, Quesnay

naturally sets the issue of taxation in the centre of his sights. As in the article "Impôts," he assesses forms of wealth in terms of their contribution to state revenues. Once again he suggests that mercantile trade is not a component of the national wealth since it makes "no contribution to taxes." Commercial wealth, he argues, is not a fixed national asset; it can flee the boundaries of the nation—and the clutches of the tax collector. Monetary fortunes, he writes, "*are a clandestine form of wealth which knows neither king nor country.*" As a result, merchants are "foreigners" to their nation.[70]

Quesnay's denunciation of mercantile activity does not translate itself into praise for other social classes. Quesnay is equally critical of wealthy financiers who adopt the path of "court capitalism" by attempting to "share in the favours of the Court." Likewise, he attacks the "ignorant greed" of the landed proprietors who refuse to understand the economic benefits of exclusive taxation of the net product of the land.[71] These criticisms of the main privileged classes in eighteenth-century France reveal that Quesnay is not looking to any single social class to transform society in the general interest. Quesnay believes that there is no class whose particular interest is identical with the social interest. Indeed, he argues that "the natural order has been turned upside down by individual interests, which always hide under the cloak of the general welfare and make their requests in its name."[72] The only solution to the conflict of competing partial interests within civil society is to construct the state as an autonomous and universal power in society, free from the influence of particular wills, able to impose order and harmony upon society from above. Any conception of the state and the social order as in some sense constituted by the free interaction of individual interests would doom society to faction and conflict. It is necessary, therefore, in Quesnay's view

that there should be a single sovereign authority, standing above all the individuals in society and all the unjust undertakings of private interests. . . . The division of society into different orders of citizens some of whom exercise authority over the others destroys the general interest of the nation and ushers in the conflict of private interests between the different classes of citizens. Such a division would play havoc with the order of government in an agricultural kingdom, which ought to reconcile all interests for one main purpose—that of securing the prosperity of agriculture which is the source of all the wealth of the state and that of all its citizens.[73]

Quesnay's economic theory reveals itself to be *political economy* in the fullest sense of the term. Both analysis of the economic anatomy of society and theory of the state, Physiocracy sought to be "the general science of government."[74] Quesnay's innovation is a radically new conceptualization of the maxim that economic prosperity determines state power; the precondition of a unified state capable of resisting internal and external threats is the continuous production of wealth within civil society. For this reason, Quesnay argues that "the political administration of agriculture and of trade in its produce" is the very foundation "of the department of finance, and of all other branches of administration in an agricultural nation."[75] It is this insight which provides the theoretical point of departure of the *Tableau économique*. In it Quesnay erects an abstract model of the economy which examines these processes from the standpoint of the state. The vantage point of the *Tableau*—indeed, its terminology and conceptual structure—reflects the position of the Crown in relation to the fundamental processes of economic life.

Quesnay profoundly understands that the state can subsist in a lasting and stable way only upon the net product, the surplus of society. It is for this reason that the *Tableau* shows the circulation of the surplus product which derives strictly from agriculture. Although it is not true, as Fox-Genovese asserts, that the *Tableau* exclusively incorporates that movement of the total annual surplus, it remains the case that—both conceptually *and* visually (in the zig-zag)—the circulation of the annual surplus is at the centre of most of the significant economic transactions.[76] The *Tableau* includes those transactions which replace factors of production responsible for a continued surplus within the primary (productive) sector. And it is primarily the circulation of the surplus product by the landed proprietors that replenishes those factors. Furthermore, the pattern of the expenditure of the revenue determines whether the economy will experience simple reproduction, expansion, or contraction. For these reasons, Quesnay places the landed proprietors and their revenue in the centre of the zigzag. Without the landlords and the circulation of the revenue, the economic system would collapse (a view which Quesnay shares with Cantillon).

Those transactions excluded from the *Tableau*—such as intrasectoral exchanges—have no economic significance from a viewpoint concerned with the surplus-producing sector of the economy. Furthermore, in naming the two classes productive and sterile, Quesnay chooses terms that reflect his preoccupation with taxation and royal revenues. The industrial class is sterile not in the sense that its labour fails to create use-values of social importance but rather because it is incapable of producing the "wealth of primary necessity in a state" which contributes to the expenses of government. The *Tableau* thus expresses Quesnay's view that the sovereign is a "coproprietor" of the land and its net product.[77] In fact, the wealth which figures *centrally* in the *Tableau* is that wealth in which the Crown claims a share and which supports it.'

It follows from this argument that "the wealth which gives birth to wealth ought not to be burdened with taxes."[78] Quesnay's *Tableau* returns, therefore, to the position advanced in "Grains" that the cultivator should be exempt from taxes and all levies placed on rent. But Quesnay's prescriptions for state policy transcend those devoted to taxation. The *Tableau* consistently advances the concept of an interventionist state which shapes policies and directs events to encourage agricultural production. In particular, the state must discourage excessive consumption by the proprietors of manufactured goods. Any disruption in the balance of proprietorial expenditure which shifts consumption away from agricultural goods will prevent reproduction of agricultural advances and lead to a decline in the net product and the revenues of the state. Since landed proprietors must be discouraged from excessive consumption of manufactured goods, all of Quesnay's writings exhibit a marked bias against luxury consumption.[79] In fact, Quesnay advocates an active policy by the state to encourage consumption of agricultural goods. He argues, for instance, "that the government's economic policy should be concerned only with encouraging productive expenditure and trade in raw produce, and that it should refrain from interfering with sterile expenditure."[80]

Quesnay's writings are often notoriously vague about the specific measures he would advocate to implement general policies. Nowhere is this more clear than in the case of concentration of landed holdings in the hands of rich farmers. As early as "Fermiers" Quesnay argues clearly that it is preferable for a poor peasant to become a wage labourer than to work the land on his own. In the *Tableau* he continually sings the praises of rich farmers. Indeed, he writes that "more than anything else the kingdom ought to be well furnished with wealthy cultivators." He also claims that "the land employed in the cultivation of corn" should be "brought together, as far as possible, into large farms worked by rich husbandmen." Furthermore, he suggests to the proprietors of the land that they should not entrust the cultivation of their land to poor peasants. Rather, he argues that "it is wealthy men whom you should put in charge of the enterprises of agricultural and rural trade, in order to enrich yourselves, to enrich the state, and to enable inexhaustible wealth to be generated."[81]

Nonetheless, Quesnay does not indicate how the shift to large-scale farming with rich cultivators is to take place. How, for example, are customary rights and practices to be eliminated? Given the contemporary agitation in favour of enclosure, one might expect to find Quesnay openly adopting a similar stance. References to the enclosure controversy, however, are rare in the entire corpus of physiocratic literature. This may well be, as Weulerrse suggested, because the Physiocrats concentrated their energies upon the campaign for free trade in grain.[82] Nonetheless, Dupont did reprint articles favouring enclosure in his journal. Furthermore, we find in Mirabeau's manuscripts a passage explicitly condemning all laws against enclosure:

It is to my sense a barbarous law to impede the proprietor from enclosing his field, his pasture land, his woods. It is to violate the laws of property, basis of the laws: and this prohibition, under whatever pretext it may introduce itself, is unworthy of any legitimate Government and, for all the more reason, of a Government founded on equity and liberty.[83]

The establishment of a just set of laws is for the Physiocrats the most important obligation of the state. The elimination of laws which prohibit enclosure should go hand in hand with general protection of property rights. Quesnay writes, in fact, that "security of ownership is the essential foundation of the economic order of society."[84] And security of ownership means for Quesnay that land is free from the customary claims of tenants. We shall explore the physiocratic conception of law and the state in more detail. For our present purposes it suffices to record the fact that the fundamental precondition of stable economic reproduction in the *Tableau économique* is that the state establish social arrangements which specifically favour a capitalist organization of agriculture at the expense of customary rights. Furthermore, there can be no doubt as to the ultimate objective of the economic analysis in the *Tableau:* its central purpose is to restore the military power of the French Crown.

"It has not been sufficiently recognized," Quesnay writes in the *Analyse,* "that the true foundation of the military strength of a kingdom is the nation's prosperity itself." It is not men but wealth which wins wars, he argues. The military prowess of a nation is, therefore, a function of its prosperity; its degree of prosperity is determined by the size of its surplus product. And from the proposition that military power is a function of wealth it follows inexorably that "it is in the permanent well-being of the taxpaying section of a nation, and in the patriotic virtues, that the permanent power of a state consists."[85]

Thus, however much the "bold abstraction" of Quesnay's *Tableau* may interest us as analytic economics, any interpretation which loses sight of its explicitly political objectives is an impoverished one. At every step in the theoretical argument, Quesnay returns to his preoccupation with political reforms; he advocates overhaul of the system of taxation, abolition of all restrictions on the sale and export of grain, preservation of individual rights to property, concentration of land holdings in the hands of rich farmers, government support to agriculture, and discouragement of luxury consumption. Quesnay understands, however, that all of these reforms depend upon reshaping the French monarchy and its relation to the contending classes in French society. Physiocracy represents, in other words, a theory of the state as much as a theory of the economy. It is to an examination of that theory of the state that we now turn.

"GUARD DOGS OF THE MONARCH": LEGAL DESPOTISM AND THE NATURAL ORDER

Physiocracy originated as a doctrine of *economic* reform intended to overhaul the tax system. As it developed, however, the political dimension of physiocratic theory came increasingly to the fore. The increasing *politicization* of Quesnay's economics is evident even in the theoretical trajectory of the *Encyclopédie* articles. The more Quesnay addressed problems of economic and fiscal reform, the more he was compelled to confront the fundamental problem of the relation between state and society. Furthermore, the more he refined his economic model, the more he tended to present it as a theoretical encapsulation of the principles of the natural order. The same processes occurred with respect to the political doctrine. Increasingly, Quesnay argued that his theory of state and society rested upon universal principles of natural law. Consequently, hand in hand with the politicization of Physiocracy went its *generalization;* from its beginnings as an argument for economic reform it moved towards a general theory of society. In the process, Physiocracy became increasingly abstract, speculative, and philosophical in character.

The generalization of Physiocracy into an all-embracing social theory occurred in 1763 when Mirabeau published his *Philosophie rurale,* a work which was actually a collaborative effort with Quesnay. *Philosophie rurale* symbolized a new phase of physiocratic theorizing which has been interpreted as a *depoliticization* of the doctrine.[86] What this work signified, however, was not the theory's depoliticization but its *dehistoricization;* as it became universal in character, physiocratic thought became increasingly detached from immediate social and political issues. The larger question of the nature and character of political power emerged from the background to become the central issue of physiocratic investigation and reflection. Indeed, Mercier's *Ordre naturel et essentiel des sociétés politiques* (1767)— the work which first systematically advanced the theory of legal despotism—presented the economic order as a product of the political order. Quesnay's growing preoccupation with government and political authority was reflected in his two important essays, published in the same year Mercier's treatise appeared, "Analyse du gouvernement des Incas du Pérou" and "Despotisme de la Chine." In these articles, Quesnay probed the relationship between government and the natural order.

The concept of the natural order was the foundation of Quesnay's theory of state and society. His philosophical inspiration appears to have been Cartesianism.[87] Quesnay frequently described the universe as a gigantic machine which operated according to natural laws of divine origin. The various subsystems of this machine—for example, the economy, the social order, and the state—would operate properly only if they adhered to the laws of the natural order. Similarly, Mirabeau wrote in the *Philosophie rurale* that

> The perpetual movement of this great machine [nature], animated and directed by its own springs, their action well secured and independent, has no need of outside direction. The physical and moral constitution of this system

adheres to a natural and general order, the course of which is regulated by supreme laws.[88]

The principles of the social order are logically deduced from the laws of the natural order. Moreover, these social laws are primarily economic in character. A stable and harmonious society rests upon the continual self-reproduction of wealth: "The natural laws of the social order are themselves the physical laws of perpetual reproduction of those goods necessary to the subsistence, the conservation, and the convenience of men."[89] The social order need only provide the legal and institutional framework which allows the economic machine to reproduce itself. This self-regulating economic mechanism will provide wealth to the citizens and stability to the Crown. The most important economic objective of state policy should be to allow the unhindered operation of the natural laws of the economy. For this reason, the state should abolish all restrictive, prohibitive, and monopolistic trade practices. In the words of Le Trosne, agriculture, industry, commerce, transport, prices, property, and so on "must not be objects of administration and should be left to the free interaction of particular interests."[90]

This emphasis on unrestricted, self-seeking economic activity has led many commentators to see the Physiocrats as prophets of laissez-faire and economic individualism. No doubt laissez-faire and economic individualism do have their place in the physiocratic conception of society. But it is important to recognize that Quesnay and his school do not view the social order itself as constituted by the economic activity of individuals within civil society. Rather, it is only within a preexistent social order that economic individualism can contribute positively to society as a whole. Within an appropriate legal and institutional arrangement, self-interested economic activity can indeed further the general welfare. In this respect, the Physiocrats anticipate Adam Smith's doctrine of the "invisible hand." Unlike Smith, however, they specify the social context which is an indispensable precondition to the operation of the invisible hand. Thus, when Mirabeau writes that "the whole magic of well-ordered society is that each man works for others, while believing that he is working for himself,"[91] his statement presupposes the functioning of "a well-ordered society." In an ill-ordered society, self-interested economic activity could rupture the social fabric. For this reason, the fundamental principles of well-ordered society become a central concern of physiocratic theorists.

It is worth recalling here Quesnay's statement in "Hommes," quoted above, that "private interests do not lend themselves to an insight into general welfare. Such advantages can be expected only as a result of the wisdom of the government." This is one critical reason that Quesnay rejects feudalism's system of provincial estates and French absolutism's "privatization" of state functions; they are not rational forms of political organization. Unlike many British political economists, the Physiocrats cannot take for granted a "well-ordered" civil society in which the state abstains from interference in the private realm. On the contrary, the state has to counter the fragmentation of polity *and* society. In the physiocratic scheme only a unified government is capable of conceiving of society as a whole and of comprehending its general interest. The feudal state cannot properly direct society since, in the words of Le Trosne, it represents "a nation composed of an infinity of particular societies and subdivided to infinity."[92]

The state must stand above the sphere of particular interests if it is to constitute a truly universal power in society. The infiltration of private interests into the state will upset the delicate balance of the social order. As Mirabeau argued,

> The government which wants to secure its authority . . . should anticipate the dangers of anarchical authority which is urged upon it by individual interests; I say anarchical, because authority which disrupts the ties binding society together destroys power, and the annihilation of power destroys authority. . . . Introduce one wrong note into the harmony of society, and the whole political mechanism feels the effect and falls apart, and concord is then as difficult to re-establish as it would be for the world to take shape as a result of the accidental concourse of atoms of Epicurus.[93]

It is for this reason that Quesnay argues for the indivisibility of political authority. The unity and stability of the social order presuppose a centralized political authority which can establish the framework in which private interests unintentionally further the general welfare. Fragmentation of authority results inevitably in the disintegration of social life. As Quesnay writes, "Authority divided between the different orders of the state will become an abusive and discordant authority, which will have neither leader nor meeting point for settling differences and harnessing the interaction of particular interests to the general welfare."[94]

Authority must therefore be singular and indivisible. Yet it is not clear what precise form authority should take. That the Physiocrats supported a monarchical state is indisputable. But what institutional form was the Physiocrats' monarchy to assume? It is evident that they opposed the traditional feudal constitution with its fragmentation of authority. It is equally evident that they derived their notion of unitary, centralized monarchical power in large measure from the experience of French absolutism. Numerous favourable remarks upon absolute monarchy are to be found throughout physiocratic literature. Le Trosne argued, for example, that the absolute monarchy had tamed the nobility and presented royal justice to the people as "a guaranteed refuge and a shelter, which is always open, against violence and oppression." Moreover, achieving autonomy from the nobility, the absolute monarchy established "the most solid constitution, the one most appropriate to administering the laws of the [natural] order."[95] It is no accident, therefore, that their contemporaries often saw the Physiocrats as supporters of the absolute monarchy in its eighteenth-century French form. Their use of the term "legal despotism" to describe their political stance conjured up images of an arbitrary and unbridled absolute power. In important respects, the Physiocrats were supporters of the absolute monarch, as illustrated in Dupont's comment that the *économistes* were like the best "guard dogs" of the royalty.[96] Nonetheless, the concept of legal despotism was substantially more sophisticated than these polemical formulations suggest. It was to provide the basis for a unitary and centralized monarchy which would not exercise arbitrary power or fall prey to seductive private interests.

In advocating a "despotism" the Physiocrats were not proposing an unrestricted monarchical power. On the contrary, the powers of the monarch were to be strictly defined and delimited. Laws were to rule society; the monarch was merely their guardian. The arbitrary rule of a single individual was entirely foreign to the physiocratic outlook. It was their insistence that a powerful, centralized monarchy was essential to the operation of the natural laws of society which made up the physiocratic twist to natural law theory. As early as "Hommes" Quesnay wrote:

Monarchical despotism is a fantasy; it has never existed; and its existence is impossible. A single man could not arbitrarily govern millions of men; sovereign monarchical power can subsist only through the authority of the laws and through the balance of the bodies of the state, each restrained in turn by the other.[97]

In several subsequent articles, Quesnay spelled out the task of the sovereign, to translate the general principles of the natural order into positive laws. There are three fundamental principles of the social order: the right to property; liberty of work, trade, export, and expenditure; and security of person and property.[98] So long as the sovereign preserves these rights and applies a scientific tax policy, the natural order will be preserved. But what guarantees that the sovereign will follow such a path? What is to prevent a singular and indivisible authority from acting arbitrarily? What safeguards prevent the sovereign from violating individual rights and the principles of the natural order? Contemporaries of the Physiocrats posed these questions many times. To this day, there is little agreement among commentators as to the physiocratic solution to the limits upon monarchical power.

The doctrine of legal despotism was to establish the basis for a centralized political authority which would follow the principles of the natural order. As we have argued above, the Physiocrats conceived of the monarch as little more than an instrument of the natural order. Strictly speaking, it was the system of laws, not the monarch, which was to rule. But such a position begged the question of despotic authority. In response to criticism on this point, the Physiocrats were forced to produce a more elaborate response to the problem of arbitrary authority. The most comprehensive answer was advanced in Mercier's *Ordre naturel et essentiel des sociétés politiques*—a work which was written under Quesnay's direction.

In the *Ordre naturel* Mercier developed the notion of judicial control over royal legislation. He argued that throughout history judges had been the mediators between government and the governed; they were "les dépositaires et gardiens des lois." To ensure that a monarchical government truly rules according to natural laws, judges must have power to veto unjust laws. Indeed, it is the moral and political duty of judges not to enforce unjust laws. No magistrate, Mercier wrote, "could undertake to judge according to laws evidently unjust; he would then cease to be a minister of justice and become a minister of iniquity."[99] This judicial power to verify the laws did not imply for Mercier a superiority of judicial over legislative authorities; it merely signified the subordination of both powers to the natural order. Mario Einaudi acknowledges this fact but interprets the physiocratic concept of legal despotism as a doctrine of "judicial control" modeled on the tradition of the Paris *parlement* and analogous to the American doctrine of judicial control.[100]

Einaudi's interpretation of the physiocratic concept of legal despotism is a provocative one. The great merit of his argument is to counterbalance those interpretations which attribute to Quesnay and his followers a doctrine of arbitrary monarchical absolutism. For Einaudi, the concept of legal despotism emphasizes the rule of law over all temporal powers. He sheds light, therefore, upon the strictly defined framework within which the Physiocrats believed the sovereign should operate. In tilting the scales towards a more balanced interpretation of the physiocratic theory of the state, however, Einaudi clearly overstates his case. To suggest that the physiocratic concept of a judicial check on monarchical power constituted an appeal to the tradition of France's *parlements* is simply untenable. As we have pointed out above, Quesnay's writings are full of disparaging remarks about the feudal order with its fragmentation of authority. In "Hommes" he attacks "this feudal tyranny," while in "Despotisme de la Chine" he describes the feudal constitution as "a violent constitution, contrary to nature" and argues that "authority shared between different orders of the state will become an abusive and discordant authority."[101] Such statements do not mesh with Einaudi's view that the Physiocrats were attempting to construct a system analogous to the system of checks and balances in which "magistrates were supreme and the prince had to bow before them."[102]

And it is not only Quesnay who does not fit his argument. Le Trosne, for example, relied upon a council of advisors to the Crown, not upon the judiciary, to ensure that the sovereign adhered to the principles of the natural order—and in this he was following Quesnay.[103] Likewise, Dupont and Turgot were severely critical of the constitution of the United States and the principle of American federalism. Turgot, for example, cautioned his American friends against federalism and the system of checks and balances, arguing that these institutional forms would make of America "a replica of our Europe, a mass of divided powers, disputing territories or profits of trade with themselves, and continually cementing the slavery of peoples with their own blood."[104] It can scarcely be maintained, then, that the notion of an independent judiciary with a right of veto over royal legislation was an integral part of the physiocratic theory of the state.

Despite its shortcomings, Einaudi's interpretation raises a central problem in the physiocratic theory of the state which most commentators have neglected: where in the physiocratic schema are we to locate a check against monarchical despotism? To answer this question we must take seriously the physiocratic claims about their science of government expressed in the political economy of the *Tableau économique*. Physiocracy was, for all its distinctiveness, an intellectual movement within the mainstream of the French Enlightenment. The *économistes*, like the *philosophes* generally, believed that reason should guide the ship of state. Quesnay and his followers firmly believed that their science disclosed universal principles of the natural order. Their task, therefore, was literally one of enlightenment—of educating the public generally and the court specifically as to the true principles of economic and political administration.

"If the torch of reason illuminates the government, all positive laws harmful to society and to the sovereign will disappear," wrote Quesnay in *Le Droit naturel*. For this reason, in the "general maxims" accompanying later editions of the *Tableau*, he argued that statesmen "should be obliged to make a study of the natural order"; and this required that they be guided by "the general science of government" embodied in the physiocratic system. To this end, Quesnay suggested that provincial estates should function as organs of public research and education; they should carefully investigate the economic conditions in their area and propagate the science of economic administration.[105] In the final analysis, public knowledge of the principles of natural law, according to Quesnay, "is the sole safeguard of subjects against monarchical oppression."[106] In addition to public education—stressed by Mirabeau and Le Trosne in particular—it was the king's council of advisors which was to provide a moral and intellectual check to monarchical despotism. Quesnay writes of the reign of Louis XIV that the king was ill advised by Louvois and Colbert and that, as a result, he did not understand "the difference between a great despot and a great King."[107] It is the role of the council of advisors to direct the sovereign to rule as a king, protecting the laws of the natural order, rather than as a despot. In this argument, Quesnay stood squarely in a long tradition of French absolutist thought—a tradition which emphasized the role of councils and estates as guides to the Crown.

Institutionally, then, the Physiocrats envisioned an absolutist state. There were to be no intermediary powers between the Crown and the people. Political authority was to be centralized, not fragmented. Private interests were to be banished from the sphere of state power. Yet this absolutism was to be tempered by "the spirit of the laws"— the universal laws of natural order which apply equally to the Incas of Peru, the emperor of China, and the king of France. This "tempered" absolutism was expressed in the concept of legal despotism. It was enlightened advisors—not provincial *parlements* or independent judges—who were to guarantee the adherence of the sovereign to the natural order. The Physiocrats had no doubt that a sovereign guided by "the torch of reason" would act according to these universal principles. And "the science of economic administration" was the flame which would light the burning torch of reason. In the final analysis, then, the physiocratic theory of legal despotism was a variant of the notion of "enlightened despotism." The absolute monarchy would know no institutional limit to its power; its practice, however, would be limited by knowledge of the laws of nature.

PHYSIOCRACY AND THE DEBATE ON THE GRAIN TRADE

As we have noted in passing, one policy issue stood out above all others in the corpus of physiocratic writing: more than enclosure, or the single tax on rent, it was deregulation of the grain trade which dominated the Physiocrats' discussions of concrete issues of economic policy. It is thus no overstatement when one commentator remarks of the Physiocrats that "virtually all of the major threads of their thinking converged on the question of the grain trade."[108] Central to the physiocratic argument was the view that restrictions on the grain trade (including the right of export) constricted the market, depressed prices, lowered incomes, and undermined investment and productivity on the land. Free trade in grain, therefore, was the key to emancipating those market forces which, by establishing high prices for grain, would raise incomes, investment, and productivity. Enclosure, consolidation of farms, and proletarianization of the direct producers were expected to follow naturally in the wake of deregulation of trade.[109]

By the early 1760s, arguments for liberalization had made a huge impact in intellectual and court circles. Two laws enacted in 1762 and 1764 abolished virtually all restrictions on trade in grain, although freedom of export was still subject to qualification. From the start, the Physiocrats were closely identified with this experiment in liberalization; indeed, Turgot and Dupont contributed to drafting the liberal law of July 1764.[110] During this same period, Le Trosne published "La Liberté du commerce des grains, toujours utile et jamais nuisible" (1765), one of the clearest statements of the physiocratic position on the question. Precisely because of their close association with liberalization of the grain trade, however, the Physiocrats were subjected to growing criticism and abuse when poor harvests and rising prices sparked an agitation in favour of regulated prices and supply.

The years 1769 and 1770 saw a severe subsistence crisis. Supplies contracted, prices rose, and grain and bread riots swept large parts of the country.[111] As early as November 1768, the Assembly of General Police, whose principal responsibility had been regulating the grain trade, adopted a sharply antiliberal and antiphysiocratic tone and came out in favour of a return to the traditional policy. Responding for the Physiocrats, Robaud issued his "Représentations aux magistrats," which asserted that property right "is identical to the right to exist" (and that government regulation of the grain trade violated the right to property), that the subsistence needs of the people "were not rights," that government owed the people nothing but "good laws," and that its regulation was bleeding the countryside of grain on behalf of the "eternally sterile" but "forever devouring" cities.[112]

Despite the theoretical coherence of physiocratic argument, its proponents were by now fighting a losing battle. Reality did not appear to conform to theory; dearth had appeared in the midst of liberalization. The Physiocrats might retort, as they did, that liberalization had been halfhearted and inadequate; but the immediate problem for the rural and urban poor was bread. To those plagued by hunger, the policy of regulated price and supply seemed to provide the clearest solution. It was in this context that the abbé Galiani launched his "bomb" against liberalism and Physiocracy.

Galiani's *Dialogues sur le commerce des blés* was the era's most celebrated assault on the Physiocrats. It simultaneously attacked the intellectual pretension of the Physiocrats, their disregard for the poor, their contempt for tradition, and the ultimately subversive implications of their economic liberalism. Unsystematic and largely negative effort that it was, the *Dialogues* brought together such a range of objections to liberalization of the grain trade, and did so with such wit and sarcasm, that it became the rallying point for antiliberalism and "antiphysiocracy." The crucial theme of Galiani's *Dialogues* was that grain should be treated as "an object of administration" rather than "an object of commerce." Poking fun at the physiocratic concept of long-run economic laws, Galiani pointed out that people starve in the short run, and that precisely this fact necessitated the policy of regulation. He denounced the "fanaticism" and "spirit of enthusiasm" which pervaded physiocratic theory and claimed that economic liberalization would eventually result in the overthrow of the monarchy since the peasants accept the inequality of ranks upon which monarchy is based largely because it in turn guarantees food at moderate prices.[113]

The Physiocrats replied sharply to Galiani, especially through Mercier de la Rivière's *Intérêt général de l'Etat; ou, la liberté du commerce des blés;* but the dearth and social unrest of 1769–1770 had split Enlightenment theorists into two distinct camps on the question of the grain trade. Were liberal thinkers dedicated first to the individual's rights to property or to the people's rights to comfort and happiness? The Physiocrats argued that the two were inseparable; that the people, in their clamour for a return to regulation, were moved by sentiment and misunderstood their own interests. But this response too provoked debate. "Isn't the sentiment of humanity more sacred than the right of property?" asked Diderot.[114] For the first time the *philosophes* had to confront the possibility that the rights of the people and the rights of property were not necessarily compatible; that philosophic individualism might be an inadequate response to the problem of subsistence; that freedom of economic action might run counter to the interests of the majority. The result was that "the crisis of liberalization" became "a crisis of the Enlightenment as well."[115] This same crisis was to reemerge in the mid-1770s during Turgot's tenure as controller general.

TURGOT AND "NEOPHYSIOCRACY"

All the features of physiocratic doctrine we have described—and especially the elaboration of an agrarian capitalist economic model within the political framework of absolute monarchy—received their most sophisticated formulation at the hands of Anne Robert Jacques Turgot. Turgot was one of the intellectual giants of his period and without doubt the most important political economist after Quesnay and before Smith. In his writings we encounter a theory of capital formation which, while constructed on physiocratic terrain, clearly rivals Adam Smith at his best.[116] A careful examination of Turgot's thought thus shows us the physiocratic theory of agrarian capitalism in its most coherent form and the rich theoretical heritage Smith took over from his French contemporaries.

Anne Robert Jacques Turgot was born in 1727 into an old noble Norman family. For generations, "the sons of the family had usually found a career in the royal bureaucracy."[117] Turgot's grandfather had been an *intendant;* his father had held the highest administrative post in Paris, that of *prévôt des marchands*. Like many of his ancestors, Turgot for a time held a post as a master of requests to the Crown. From 1761 until his appointment as *contrôleur général* in 1774, he served as *intendant* in the *généralité* of Limoges. During his period as a master of requests Turgot lived in Paris. There he moved in circles frequented by the *encyclopédistes*, the Physiocrats, and British intellectuals like David Hume and Adam Smith. In addition, Turgot was profoundly affected by Vincent Gournay, who had become *intendant du commerce* in 1748. From 1753 to 1756 Turgot toured France with Gournay, investigating the conditions of industry and trade. Gournay was the first French translator of English economists like Child and Gee; Gournay's strongly laissez-faire ideas made a profound impact upon his young assistant. Turgot participated in the activities of the Society of Agriculture; as *contrôleur général* during the ministry of Bertin (a follower of Quesnay), Turgot introduced a series of physiocratic reforms in Limoges. When Bertin's successor, d'Ivau, was replaced by the conservative abbé Terray in 1769, Turgot threw himself headfirst into the debate over free trade in grain, producing seven *Lettres sur le commerce des grains* in 1770; four letters have survived. When Louis XVI took the throne in 1774, Turgot finally got the chance to try his hand at managing the royal finances.

Turgot was to have but twenty months in the office the king had bestowed upon him. In that time he nevertheless undertook a sweeping program of reform. His first move was to weaken the powers of the farmers general, a move which prompted the financiers to slow down payments to the Treasury in an attempt to thwart reform. When he introduced his famous six edicts in 1776—edicts which, among other things, suppressed the guilds, the corvées, and all duties on grains and cereals in Paris—a combination of reactionary forces in the church and the Parlement of Paris, along with popular forces which asserted the priority of subsistence over principles of political economy, declared war on this minister of reform. Despite the fact that Turgot had radically improved the royal finances, the king caved in and removed his *contrôleur général*. Once again, economic reform had collided with the political constitution of the realm.

As significant as was Turgot's political career, it is primarily as an economic theorist that he is remembered. There can be little doubt that Turgot was a Physiocrat in matters of political economy, albeit with his own distinctive twist (Schumpeter notwithstanding).[118] Turgot's writings are lavishly sprinkled with favourable references to Quesnay and his disciples. In fact, in his 1763 *Mémoires concernant les impositions*, Turgot signalled his acceptance of Quesnay's concept of the net product. "M. Quesnay," he wrote, "was the first to establish the correct notion of the revenue, when he learnt to distinguish the *gross product* from the *net product.*" Furthermore, Turgot strongly hinted that Quesnay's concept of advances underpinned his own theory of capital; he wrote that "M. Quesnay has developed the mechanism of agriculture which is based entirely on very large original advances and requires in addition annual advances which are equally necessary."[119] These passages are more than token gestures towards a respected thinker. The basic tenets of Physiocracy make up the core of Turgot's economics. "The only true wealth is the product of the soil," he wrote in a paper of 1767.[120] Time and time again he asserted that the state could subsist only upon the net product of the land. "The state has not, and cannot have, any strength except for the *net product*," he stated in another paper of the same year. Elsewhere he argued that this net product equaled "the disposable portion of the crop, that gratuitous portion which the soil yields over and above the costs of working it." Again consistent with classic Physiocracy, he claimed that taxes should be assessed exclusively upon the net product of the soil.[121]

Turgot added an uncompromising laissez-faire perspective to these orthodox physiocratic views. Like most of Quesnay's followers, Turgot emphasized that the pursuit of self-interest in the economic sphere furthered the general welfare. This did not mean, however, that the foundation of the state consisted only of self-seeking individual action. On the contrary, for Turgot, as for all the Physiocrats, the monarchy was needed to harmonize particular interests. Yet Turgot's laissez-faire position was more radical and unqualified than that in the writings of any other Physiocrat except possibly Le Trosne. Thus, in his eulogy for Vincent Gournay, Turgot wrote that

in all respects in which commerce may interest the State, unrestrained individual interest will always produce the public welfare more surely than the operations of the government, which are always faulty and of necessity directed by a hazy and dubious theory.[122]

Turgot's real theoretical innovations came, however, in his treatment of "the profit of the entrepreneur farmer" as a regular form of income and in his analysis of saving and capital formation. The traditional physiocratic position was that land rent was the only income which represented the agricultural surplus product. Agricultural entrepreneurs—capitalist farmers—were not depicted as regularly deriving a profit from their investments. Quesnay appears to have felt that the existence of a farmers' profit would have jeopardized the doctrine of a single tax on rent. Quesnay's fear that taxation of farmers would reduce agricultural output may well have prevented him from conceding that cultivators did indeed earn a profit on their capital. Certainly Quesnay realized that under certain circumstances, farmers might earn a profit. For example, those with larger than average farms or those who managed to cut their costs of production would enjoy a profit. Farmers would likewise derive a profit if the price for their product rose during the course of their leases. Quesnay held that none of these, however, were regular conditions of economic life. They represented market irregularities which could not be generalized in the construction of an economic model. For this reason, Quesnay appears to have believed it legitimate to abstract from profit on farmers' capital in the *Tableau économique* and elsewhere.

Later Physiocrats appear not to have shared Quesnay's reservations about treating farmers' profit as a regular phenomenon. The abbé Baudeau, for example, argued that without a regular return on their investment, entrepreneurs would not enter into agricultural production:

we cannot expect that a class which is numerous, wealthy, and well-informed will advance large capitals, give itself continuously a great deal of trouble, expose itself to great risks, without drawing just compensation.[123]

Furthermore, Baudeau generalized capitalist relations to include the industrial sector. He stressed that the sterile class, like the productive class, was divided into those who "guide and direct the work" and those who "do it under their orders."

Like Baudeau, Turgot treated "the profit of the entrepreneur farmer" as a regular form of income.[124] A related innovation came in his analysis of saving and capital formation, where he overthrew the physiocratic bias against saving. According to Quesnay, saving resulted in a reduction in consumer demand which, in turn, reduced the scale of economic reproduction. In the traditional physiocratic schema, it was consumption which determined the level of production. "La consommation est la mesure de la reproduction," wrote Mercier.[125] Saving was conceived of as a diversion of income from consumption and thus as a drain on the production of wealth. In their analysis of advances in agricultural production the Physiocrats did, of course, develop a rudimentary concept of investment. They tended, however, to subsume both the advances of the agricultural entrepreneur and the consumption of the landlords under the general concept of "expenditure." Dupont, for example, argued in a letter to Turgot that "the formation of capitals arises much less from saving out of the expenditure of revenues than from the wise employment of the expenditures."[126]

Turgot broke with the theoretical view which failed to comprehend the investment of savings as a "wise employment of the expenditures" and with the physiocratic bias against saving. In a critique of a physiocratic paper on taxation by Saint-Peravy, he directly challenged Quesnay's view on saving:

The author, and the majority of economic writers [i.e., of the Physiocrats], seem to assume that the whole of the revenue must necessarily be returned directly to the circulation, without any part of it being set aside for the formation of a monetary capital, and that, if it were otherwise, the reproduction would suffer by it. This assumption is far from true: it is sufficient, in order to see its falsity, to reflect on the importance of capitals in all the

profitable enterprises of agriculture, of industry and of trade, and on the
utter necessity of advances for all these enterprisees.

What are the advances, and where lies their origin, if not in the savings
from the revenue?[127]

Turgot makes three essential points in this important passage. First,
he treats advances of capital as necessary to all forms of economic
activity—agriculture, industry, and commerce alike. Second, he
contends that saving is an indispensable part of capital formation.
Third, in what appears slightly paradoxical, he suggests that *all* advances originate in savings from the revenue, the net product of the
land. All of these points are presented with a higher degree of theoretical rigour in the most important of Turgot's writings, his *Réflexions sur la formation et la distribution des richesses*, which was written
in 1766 and published in 1769 in the *Ephémérides* of Dupont.

In the *Réflexions*, Turgot restates his view that "every kind of
work, whether in cultivation, in industry, or in commerce, requires
advances." Such advances originate in savings of values and "these
accumulated values are what is called *a capital*."[128] Turgot proceeds
to argue that such saving of values—the accumulation of capital—
far from being a drain on production and circulation of wealth is,
rather, the precondition of investment and economic growth. Discussing the case of the industrial capitalist, he maintains that

As fast as this capital is returned to him through the sale of the products, he
employs it in making new purchases in order to supply and maintain his
Factory by means of this continual circulation: he lives on his profits, and he
puts into reserve what he is able to save, in order to increase his capital and
invest it in his enterprise, adding to the amount of his advances so as to add
still further to his profits.

Here we encounter an extraordinarily clear and concise formulation of the relationship between profit, saving, capital formation, and
investment—a formulation which rivals the best work of the English
classical school. Turgot goes on then to differentiate the sterile class—
or, as he calls it, the "industrial stipendiary class"—into "capitalist
Entrepreneurs and ordinary workmen." Having thus made capital
accumulation the decisive process within all sectors of the economy,
he asserts that saving is the mainspring of economic prosperity:
"The spirit of economy in a nation continually tends to increase the
sum of its capitals."[129] Here Turgot is on the threshold of developing
an entirely new economics, one which sees saving and investment

out of profit in all sectors of the economy, not just agriculture, as the central feature of economic life. Yet precisely at the point where such a "paradigm shift" might occur, Turgot pulls up short and reinserts his analysis into the physiocratic framework. He writes that all profits are actually "only a part of the product of the land." He insists that, since the surplus product of the land makes industry possible, industrial profit is nothing more than a share of landed revenue. In fact, he argues that all capitals come from the land:

But although capitals are formed in part by means of savings from the profits of the industrious classes, yet, as these profits always come from the land— since all are paid either out of the revenue or out of the expenditure which serves to produce the revenue—it is obvious that capitals come from the land just as the revenue does.[130]

At this point, Turgot's analysis of profit, saving, and capital formation seems to collide with his physiocratic framework. He is caught in the bind of treating profit on capital—be it agriculture, industry, or commerce—as a necessary and regular form of income within the general context of a theory which claims that the only real economic surplus is the net product of the land. As a result, he is forced to reduce industrial profit to a share of the landed revenue which accrues, through the market, to the industrial capitalist. Indeed, a careful reading of Turgot's discussion of industrial profit suggests that he treated it as a result of imperfect competition in the manufacturing sector. He writes,

Although the profits of industry, unlike the revenues of the land, are not a gift of nature, and although the man engaged in industry gets from his labour only the price which is given to him for it by the one who pays his wages; although the latter economises as much as possible in paying these wages, and although competition forces the man engaged in industry to content himself with a lower price than he would like—it is nevertheless certain that this competition was never so extensive or so keen in all the different branches of labour as at any time to prevent a man who was more skilful, more energetic, and above all more economical than others in his personal consumption, from being able to earn a little more than was required for the subsistence of himself and his family, and from putting this *surplus* into reserve in order to build up a little stock of money.[131]

This explanation of profit conflicts, however, with Turgot's professed view that profit must accrue to all capitals to prevent their moving to other spheres. Indeed, Turgot suggests elsewhere in the

Réflexions that the rate of profit is equalized throughout the whole economy precisely because of capital's mobility:

As soon as the profits resulting from one employment of money, whatever it may be, increase or diminish, capitals either turn in its direction and are withdrawn from other employments, or are withdrawn from it and turn in the direction of the other employments.[132]

Logically, then, there would seem to be only one possible explanation for industrial profit as a consistent phenomenon in Turgot's model—that there is a regular, unequal exchange between industry and agriculture which results in a net transfer of a share of landed revenue from the proprietors (and from the cultivators?) to the industrial capitalists. Through the price mechanism of the market, in other words, the economics of imperfect competition would overprice manufactured goods relative to agricultural goods. Turgot does not advance such an argument in the *Réflexions*. However, the Physiocrat with whom he was most clearly associated, Dupont, did develop precisely such an explanation of industrial profit.[133] It is conjectural to suggest that this was also Turgot's view; yet it is at least plausible that he did accept Dupont's argument. Certainly such a position would have rendered his explanation more consistent. In any case, Turgot's continued adherence to Physiocracy was not motivated exclusively by its explanation of economic relations. Turgot's major preoccupation, like Quesnay's, was to regenerate the French economy as the indispensable basis to reconstruct the state. Like all the physiocratic theorists, Turgot supported a state-fostered agrarian capitalism. Indeed, Turgot developed the theoretical principles of agrarian capitalism more rigorously than any of Quesnay's other followers. In particular, his writings stress the crucial significance of the wage labour–capital relation on the land.

In all his writings Turgot emphasized the importance of the distinction between "the agricultural entrepreneur and the rural day labourer," both of whom he considered essential to a productive agriculture. In addition, he made it clear that the rural labourers in his model were to be a classical agricultural proletariat. They were to be free wage labourers, free in the double sense emphasized in Marx's theory of the proletariat: free to dispose of their labour as they chose and free from ownership of any means of production which could enable them to choose other than to work for a wage. He wrote,

"Wage labourers must be *completely free* to work for whom they desire, in order that the employers by contending for them when they need them, may place a just price on their labour."[134] Elsewhere, he made it clear that these wage labourers would have to work for a subsistence wage, since they would have no other means of maintaining themselves: "Wage-earning people, in good and bad years alike, have no other means to live than by working; they will, therefore, offer their labour, and competition will force them to settle for the wage necessary for their subsistence."[135] Moreover, Turgot indicated that he envisioned an economy dominated by an agrarian capitalist sector when he argued that agricultural wage labourers "make up the greatest part of the population."[136]

Turgot's writings project with great clarity the vision of an agrarian capitalist economy. At the same time, Turgot left little doubt that he envisioned this economic system being protected by a highly centralized absolute monarchy. For all his laissez-faire ideas in the economic sphere, Turgot was not content to leave the constitution of the political order to the free interaction of self-seeking individuals. In fact, laissez-faire would be beneficial only under socioeconomic conditions established by the state. As for Quesnay, so for Turgot, self-interested economic activity would further the general welfare only in a political framework where a powerful and unified state ruled according to the principles of the natural order. Self-interested economic activity was acceptable precisely because private interests were to be excluded from influence upon political authority. The "liberty of the king's subjects," he argued, should not be sacrificed "to the exactions and caprices of private interests." Only a political authority standing above the sphere of private interests could safeguard the rights of individuals and the powers of the state. There should be, he maintained, "a paternal government, based on a national constitution whereby the monarchy is raised above all in order to assure the welfare of all."[137]

Turgot's political views were, therefore, in fundamental accord with those of Quesnay and his followers. Born into a family with a long tradition of political service to the Crown, he was naturally alarmed by the crisis of the eighteenth-century French state. Turgot's political economy took as its starting point the central dilemma of France: how to reform the political order in such a way as to break the predominance of peasant farming and the ostensible immunity of noble wealth (or at least of land rents) from taxation. Any prospect of economic revitalization and transformation into agrarian capitalism required that the state carry through a radical shift in the social relations of economic life. Adopting Quesnay's view that only the state had a clear interest in an agrarian capitalist transformation of the French economy, Turgot adhered to an essentially physiocratic program of reform. The physiocratic analysis of state and society, which hinged upon state taxation of a growing agrarian surplus to ensure prosperity and stability, thus provided the theoretical and practical foundation of his political economy. For this reason, a fundamental break from Physiocracy was out of the question for Turgot, although elements of his economic analysis pressed towards such a break. Ultimately, the elements of analysis were subordinate to the theoretical whole which inspired their construction. And that theoretical whole derived from the basic features of eighteenth-century French society and the program for its reform which Quesnay and his school had integrated into their theory of state, economy, and society.

Turgot's attempt to incorporate his theory of profit, saving, and capital into a physiocratic framework illustrates this subordination of his analysis to the general theory developed by Quesnay. Abstractly, it might seem a simple matter for Turgot to have moved towards the view that profit is a category of income which accrues to an owner of capital in return for the new value that productive use of this capital allows. That, however, would have constituted a move towards the notion that any capital, regardless of its sphere of investment, could produce a regular surplus above costs of production—a profoundly antiphysiocratic idea (since it denies the exclusive productivity of agriculture) and one which Turgot ultimately rejected. In the final analysis, Turgot's analytical economics were part of his political economy; and that political economy was physiocratic or, to be precise, neophysiocratic.

To neglect the physiocratic character of Turgot's concept of capital, as Schumpeter proposes, is thus to distort irreparably the character of his doctrine. We encounter in Turgot's finest piece of economic writing, the *Réflexions*, the elaboration of all the elements which entered into the modern concept of capital. Yet these elements could not be so assembled while they remained part of a physiocratic whole. Their reassembly required the existence of a postphysiocratic paradigm of economic life. Turgot did not undertake this job of theoretical reconstruction precisely because he accepted the physiocratic program of reform and the theoretical paradigm of Quesnay and his school. He stretched that paradigm to extremes in an effort to incorporate into it his views on profit, saving, and capital. Yet, in the final analysis, he adapted his conceptual structure to Physiocracy, not vice versa. It is for this reason that we can echo Ronald Meek's statement,

With Turgot, Physiocracy begins to burst its seams: the framework of concepts elaborated by Quesnay can no longer accommodate the basic phenomena of capitalist society. Turgot, however, went much further in preparing the way for Adam Smith than any of his predecessors or contemporaries: with him the 'necessary price' came to include, as it was to do with Smith, a 'normal' return on capital, part of which was available for accumulation. It remained only to remove the Physiocratic integument, and the way was clear for the emergence of the *Wealth of Nations*.[138]

The removal of "the Physiocratic integument" presupposed a markedly different conception of the relationship of the state to civil society. Basing himself on the historical experience of Great Britain and the theoretical legacy of the Commonwealth view of the state, Smith was well situated to produce a new synthesis in classical political economy. Yet Physiocracy and its agrarian-capitalist model of the economy were, as we shall see, a much more significant element of that synthesis than has generally been recognized.

CONCLUSION

The Physiocrats gave political economy its first genuine model of the economy as a self-regulating totality embracing production, circulation, and distribution. And that model was an agrarian capitalist one. Quesnay and his followers constructed their model in conscious imitation of the triadic social organization of English agriculture, in which the relations between landlord, capitalist tenant, and wage labourer formed a commodity-producing agriculture sustained by capital investments on the land. Marx grasped these features of the physiocratic model when he wrote that for Quesnay,

Agriculture is pursued on a capitalist footing, i.e. as the large-scale undertaking of the capitalist farmer; the immediate tillers of the soil are wage-labourers. Production does not just produce articles of use, but their value as well; its driving motive is to obtain surplus value, and the birthplace of surplus value is the sphere of production, not that of circulation.[139]

Nowhere are these capitalist presuppositions of the physiocratic model so explicitly set out as in Turgot's *Réflexions*. There Turgot makes it quite clear that the physiocratic idea of a prosperous, surplus-producing agriculture presupposes "primitive accumulation," the separation of the direct producers from the land and their transformation into wage labourers: "Thus ownership of land had to be separated from the labour of cultivation and soon it was. . . . The landowners began to shift the labour of cultivating the soil on to the wage-labourers." [140]

The Physiocrats thus broke radically from most previous exercises in French political economy, such as grain laws, regulation of food supply in the towns, and guild organization of urban labour. Quesnay and his school treated both food and labour as commodities subject to the self-regulation of the capitalist market. As Turgot's controversial edicts demonstrated, land, labour, and the subsistence of the labouring classes were all to be regulated not by government but by markets. Traditional rights to land and subsistence were to be abolished; capitalist property and the capitalist market were to be the order of the day.

In emphasizing the capitalist character of the physiocratic conception of the economy we must not fall into the trap, as does Bert Hoselitz, of suggesting that the Physiocrats were classical liberals whose worldview was "virtually identical with that of 'utilitarian radicalism and Manchester liberalism.'" As we have demonstrated, the Physiocrats' theory of the state was incontestably absolutist in nature. They did not subscribe to anything resembling a liberal-democratic theory of the state. In fact, in debates with their contemporaries, opponents as often objected to the Physiocrats' view of government and political authority as to their economic principles. Thus, Voltaire in his *Homme aux quarante écus* attacked Mercier's work advancing the concept of legal despotism. "I have read a great part of *L'Ordre naturel*," Voltaire wrote, "and it has put me in a bad humour. It is certain that land pays everything, who is not convinced of this truth? But that a single man should be proprietor of all the land is a monstrous idea." [141] Despite such criticism, the Physiocrats held firm to their theory of the state. It was not some expendable, decorative element—a part of their "sham feudal pretences" as Marx put it. [142] Rather, the doctrine of legal despotism was as much the core of Physiocracy as was the concept of the exclusive productivity of agricultural production. For this reason, any effort at understanding the physiocratic system must treat the economic principles and the political outlook as parts of an integrated whole.

If Physiocracy cannot be reduced to one of its constitutive elements—"bourgeois" economic doctrine or "feudal" political theory—how are we to understand the specific unity of these two features? Several writers, often influenced by a Marxist approach, have opted for an interpretation in which the Physiocrats are seen to represent an identifiable class interest. According to this view, the physiocratic combination of capitalist and absolutist principles must reflect the interests of a specific social class under the conditions of eighteenth-century France. In an influential article published in 1931, for example, Norman Ware argued that Physiocracy "arose out of the special needs of a new landowning class under a bankrupt monarchy and a fiscal system inherited from the past."[143] Ware maintains that a new class of commoner landowners which emerged from the royal bureaucracy wanted to eliminate the many taxes which weighed heavily upon them and to replace them with a single tax on all landowners. Yet even Ronald Meek, who finds Ware's interpretation "very plausible," has pointed out that those who would have gained most from the physiocratic program were not commoner landowners but capitalist tenant farmers—the agricultural entrepreneurs whose capital and profits would be completely exempt from taxation. Ware, however, seems to blur the distinction between landlord and capitalist farmer when he writes of the "cost of production" of the landowner, as if the landowner were also the entrepreneur who organized and directed the production process.[144]

Once we correctly distinguish between landowners and capitalist farmers, then Ware's argument breaks down. If we want to maintain an interpretation which roots Physiocracy in the interests of a social class, we are left with an argument similar to that of I. I. Rubin, according to which the Physiocrats were "defenders of the rural bourgeoisie." Rubin was forced to qualify this argument, however, with the admission that the rural bourgeoisie barely existed in eighteenth-century France. "The Physiocrats did not so much try to rely upon an already existing rural bourgeoisie, which in any case was numerically insignificant and without influence, as to create conditions that would favour this class's economic development."[145] This is a provocative argument which contains an important element of truth. It is developed in a theoretical framework, however, which creates more problems than it resolves. Why, after all, should the Physiocrats have advanced the interests of a virtually nonexistent class? To suggest that their outlook flowed from their "social and class position" as Rubin does, is entirely untenable.[146] It amounts to arguing that the social and class position of the Physiocrats drove them to articulate the interests of a social class which did not exist in any historically meaningful sense. Granting that Quesnay, Mirabeau, Le Trosne, Mercier, Baudeau, Dupont, Turgot, etc., were not themselves rural bourgeois, Rubin can give us no persuasive reason why they should have operated as ideological representatives of such a class—especially when that class was more an ideal than a reality.

All these interpretations of Physiocracy are plagued by a crude form of economic reductionism according to which a major current in social and political thought must by definition be reduced to an ideological expression corresponding to the economic interests of a unique social class. Indeed, it is for failing to elaborate the political program of the bourgeoisie that Fox-Genovese indicts Quesnay and his followers on a charge of "doctrinaire utopianism." Their crime consisted in the fact that they "made no intentional contribution to the development either of the subjective consciousness or the objective interests of the bourgeoisie as it existed under the *ancien régime*."[147] This criticism is based upon uncritical adherence to the liberal-capitalist model—in this case in a Marxist guise—according to which capitalism can be described only in terms of the coming to power of a liberal-democratic bourgeoisie with an individualistic social theory. Indeed, Fox-Genovese condemns the Physiocrats for failing to develop a rigorous and consistent "bourgeois paradigm" or "individualistic paradigm," as if these must automatically flow from any capitalist conception of the economy. Moreover, she uses C. B. Macpherson's interpretation of Locke as a "possessive individualist" to illustrate the theoretical perspective that Quesnay and his followers ought to have adopted.[148]

At no time, however, does Fox-Genovese demonstrate the historical validity of this view. She advances the unexamined postulate that capitalism requires a bourgeois revolution inspired by a liberal-individualist ideology. The Physiocrats are then summarily denounced for failing to develop such an outlook. Yet, as we have shown in chapter 1, in mid-eighteenth-century France there was no revolutionary bourgeoisie driving to transform society in its own image. The bourgeoisie of absolutist France was not a class intent upon transformation of the social order; it sought integration into the structure of power and privilege within the *ancien régime*—not its forcible overthrow. It sought to become part of the privileged stratum which profited from state rents. Ultimately, a major aspiration of the upper bourgeoisie was ennoblement. For these reasons, the bourgeoisie demonstrated no significant desire for sweeping reform—let alone revolution. In fact, France's "bourgeois revolution" later in the century occurred partly as a defensive attempt to preserve upward mobility and access to state rents against a growing aristocratic reaction.[149]

In these circumstances, it was only natural for Quesnay to reject the bourgeoisie—as he had rejected the nobility—as a force for social reform. Furthermore, in a civil society rent by the destabilizing competition of noble and bourgeois interests for political power and influence, prospects for a program of reform to direct self-interested economic activity into socially constructive channels seemed to rest with the state itself. Physiocratic reforms, as Turgot knew, would inevitably encounter the opposition of the dominant classes. Such reforms could be imposed upon society only from above, by a state power capable of commanding the obedience of its citizens and not reliant upon loans and favours for its existence. As Schumpeter wrote, in a particularly insightful passage:

> In the actual situation of eighteenth-century France, the reforms advocated by the physiocrats could have been carried (without revolution) only by the strong hand of a despotic monarch. The hostility of the physiocrats against 'privilege' of any kind was therefore not, as one might think, in contradiction of their allegiance to the monarchy but on the contrary the very reason for it.[150]

Such a position was not unique to the Physiocrats. Because of the array of privileges and acquired rights, all forces within civil society seemed incapable of initiating the changes which were necessary to establish a powerful and unified state. For this reason, political reformers looked to the state power, as embodied in the absolute monarch, to initiate a revolution from above. As Herbert Luthy has written,

In the middle of the eighteenth century, all "progressive" tendencies, beyond their doctrinal quarrels, placed their hopes in an "enlightened despotism"—the only revolutionary force which they could perceive on the horizon—to make a clean sweep of special privileges.[151]

This was certainly the case with the Physiocrats, who desired the elimination of all feudal rights and privileges and the taxation of all landed revenues. But the Physiocrats also knew that a change in the tax system was not enough; the entire system of agricultural production needed to be transformed. As a result, they turned their attention to systematic economic analysis.

From the start, the overriding objective of the Physiocrats was state building. They sought to transform France into a rationalized, modern nation, economically self-sufficient and militarily powerful. This objective was not the product of intellectual speculation; it represented a necessity imposed by the dynamics of state competition in early modern Europe. As Theda Skocpol has put it, "Recurrent warfare within the system of states prompted European monarchs and statesmen to centralize, regiment, and technologically upgrade armies and fiscal administrations."[152] Under the impact of France's losses in the Seven Years' War, the Physiocrats recognized that France's fortunes depended upon emulating the English. England's military prowess, Quesnay argued, derived from her economic wealth. The productivity of English agriculture—which provided a 100 percent return on advances—made possible the wealth to maintain armed forces. Restoring French military power required, therefore, transforming the social and economic structure along English lines. England was the model for the *Tableau économique;* there Quesnay wrote of England:

This nation, inexhaustible by reason of its ever-renascent wealth, maintains military forces on land and sea and sustains severe wars by means of assured revenues which are continually renewed without any decline and which restore its strength.[153]

The physiocratic program of social, economic, and political transformation flowed, then, from their objective of establishing a powerful state. Furthermore, the Physiocrats recognized that no social class had the interest or capacity to initiate a social transformation on the English model. The state, they believed, did have such an interest. Indeed, they believed that the long-term survival of the French monarchy pivoted on such a transformation.

That the interests of the state could serve as the social basis of a theory—especially for those closely tied to the state bureaucracy—has not been fully recognized. Too many commentators—Marxist and non-Marxist alike—have viewed the state as a merely passive or reactive agency which reflects either the interests of the dominant class or the balance of interests within society. Especially in social crisis and change, the state may play a much more active and independent role in social and political life. Indeed, Quesnay's program consisted precisely in developing a genuinely independent state, free from the caprice of private interests. It is fair to say, therefore, that Quesnay's program was constructed upon an analysis of the interests of the state—not as a body within civil society but standing over it—to preserve and improve the lives of its citizens and the position of the nation as a whole. There is an important sense in which such a position was "utopian"; French absolutism was, after all, the locus of particularism. The state exploited private interests in order to finance itself; in so doing, it grounded itself in the private interests of civil society. Still, it did not identify itself with the private interests of any one group or class. And this latter fact was the basis of the physiocratic program.

Depicting the Physiocrats as representatives of a class interest has prevented commentators from accurately perceiving them as spokesmen of the state interest. After capitalism had taken root in England, states in economic, political, and military competition with England recognized their own need to develop the economic strength that underwrote English agricultural productivity, industrial capacity, commercial dynamism, and military prowess. If they were to survive and progress it was essential to imitate at least some aspects of England's social transformation. As one historian of industrialization has put it, "In all industrialization occurring after the British, an element of conscious emulation was present. Nowhere else did it take place as an autonomous and organic process in which even the participants did not know what lay ahead."[154]

The physiocratic system was developed before the onset of Britain's industrial revolution. As a result, Quesnay and his adherents looked upon the critical process which preceded industrialization—

"primitive accumulation," the agrarian revolution in its fullest social sense—as the key to economic and military power. And for that reason, they elaborated a program of agrarian capitalism designed to strengthen the state. Capitalism was not a theoretical ideal of which Quesnay approved; he did not think in terms of the abstract principles of a socioeconomic system. His speculation was motivated by the practical requirements of restoring the power of the French Crown, finding the best means of assuring a large and regular surplus product accessible to royal taxation. It was for this reason that capitalist agriculture became the foundation of his theoretical model of the economy. And it was for this reason, as Rubin perceived but could not explain, that Quesnay advanced a program designed for a social class which barely existed—the "rural bourgeoisie" or, better, agrarian capitalists (and their necessary complement, an agrarian proletariat). Quesnay did not think in terms of capitalism; he tried to have France duplicate the rural transformation which ushered in capitalist development in England. His was a program of "primitive accumulation," designed to create the social conditions necessary for capitalist reproduction and accumulation.

In the conditions of eighteenth-century France, agrarian capitalism represented an ideal. For this reason, the Physiocrats have been accused of being speculative philosophers, who diverted concern over the financial crisis of the monarchy into the realm of theoretical economics, "where practical questions of financial administration seldom entered in."[155] Such a criticism entirely misses the mark. The Physiocrats had an acute understanding of the fact that the French monarchy was confronted not by a short-term fiscal crisis, the result of an immediate problem of maladministration, but rather by a long-term structural crisis of the economy. As a result, they directed their analysis to the most fundamental features of the economic process, and their relation to taxes and royal revenues. Furthermore, they grasped the profound truth that rents and taxes derived from the same social surplus product. Restoration of royal finances presupposed, therefore, the production of ever-larger agricultural surpluses (and those surpluses, in turn, made possible larger advances which could provide growing surpluses).

Large landed revenues alone were not enough. The Physiocrats also sought to ensure the Crown ready access to a share of the annual rents. For this reason, their political theory was built around the idea that the absolute monarch was a coproprietor of the land and of the product it yielded. It is because of this view that Samuels detected "vestiges of a feudal conception of property" in the physiocratic worldview. Individuals do not in the physiocratic schema have an absolute right to private property. Quesnay argued in fact that there were three proprietors of the land—the state, the landowner, and the church. Sovereigns, Quesnay wrote, "are everywhere co-proprietors of the net product of the territory of the nation which they govern." Mirabeau put the point more directly when he asserted in *Philosophie rurale* that the sovereign is the "propriétaire universel du territoire."[156] Quesnay insisted upon this point and in a markedly illiberal argument maintained that taxes are not paid out of the income of the proprietor but rather represent a separate income which accrues to the state as coproprietor of the land:

The possessor of the property should not regard ordinary taxes as a charge laid on his portion, for it is not he who pays this revenue; it is the portion of the property which he has not acquired and which does not belong to him which pays it to those to whom it is due.[157]

This argument forms an indispensable part of the physiocratic outlook. It would be of little value from Quesnay's perspective to increase the productivity of the land if this were not significantly to benefit the state. Yet only a political order which established the Crown's claim to coproprietorship of the land would guarantee that landed improvements worked to the profit of the Crown. The whole history of early modern France is dominated by conflict over the political constitution of the realm. And at the root of these constitutional disputes is the issue of the distribution of the revenue between rent and taxes. To function as a powerful, modern state the Crown needed a steady share of the revenue produced by the surplus labour of the agrarian masses. But the conflicting claims to this surplus continually locked the nobility and the monarch in conflict.

Quesnay's theory started from a realistic understanding of this situation. He hoped, however, that sweeping agricultural improvement could so boost the net product of the land to satisfy the needs of both the landed aristocracy and the Crown. His hope was suspect from the start. But the theoretical analysis which underpinned Quesnay's program of reform was based upon a profoundly realistic appraisal of the social and economic structure of eighteenth-century

France. Herbert Luthy is one commentator who has clearly grasped this crucial fact.

The fact remained no less that the royal resources, essentially, were based on the same agricultural "fixed property" which simultaneously also served as a foundation for ground rent, quit rent, the *dîme*, and taxes. All the constituent parts of the *ancien régime* were co-proprietors, as it were, of the realm. All shared a revenue which was of the same nature and drawn from the same source as that of the King, if not directly deducted from his own. And he apparently could not increase his share without infringing on theirs, that is, by acts of "despotism" which would violate the "fundamental laws of the realm." The long quarrel over finances, which was to be a bitter one from 1765 on and which was really a constitutional quarrel, in effect was fought out entirely within this society of co-proprietors of the "agricultural kingdom"—nobility, clergy, magistry—on the backs of the "husbandmen" in whom nothing hinted at a coming revolt. The struggle remained outside the other classes, which Quesnay called "sterile" and which in fact were so with respect to the tax because the royal fiscal apparatus (not to be the last in this case) was in no way equipped to impose or even detect personal or "monetary" fortunes not manifested in landed property.[158]

The physiocratic schema incorporated all of these fundamental facts of the age in a theoretical model. For this reason, the Physiocrats can truly be said to have penetrated to the underlying structures of their society. Quesnay's *Tableau économique* was not simply an abstract model constructed through idle speculation; "bold abstraction" that it was, it accurately reflected the social structure of the period. And the program which followed from it offered the only reasonable prospect for constructing a solid state power—eliminating feudal privileges and taxing the growing agricultural surplus which a full-scale agrarian revolution would create. That the French monarchy was unable to carry through such a program speaks to the persistence of conflict between the nobility and the Crown—a conflict rooted in the struggle between rent and taxes. The Physiocrats believed that reason could show a better way in the best interests of all. But in their most realistic moments, they recognized that they were up against considerable odds. Turgot, for example, in addressing the need for a single tax on rent wrote: "I confess that this seems completely impossible to me: under this system, the king or the government stands against all."[159]

Yet despite the odds against their project the Physiocrats developed a program of reform which had a solid basis in reality. Since neither nobility nor bourgeoisie gave any indication of initiating or supporting a transformation of the social order which would overturn the relations of agricultural production, stimulate economic development, rationalize the fiscal and administrative structure of the state, centralize political power, and restore military might, the Physiocrats had little option but to look to a state-directed social transformation towards agrarian capitalism. Agrarian capitalism was the key to state building; the state was the key to agrarian capitalism: this historical reality accounts for the Physiocrats' apparently paradoxical combination of capitalist economic principles with a political theory of absolutism. Placed in its historical context, the political economy of the Physiocrats appears as a profoundly realistic analysis of eighteenth-century economy and society—one which historians, economists, and political scientists have ignored to the detriment of their own studies. Moreover, reinserted in their historical context, the Physiocrats appear as the first great theorists of those "revolutions from above" which over the subsequent century reshaped the face of Europe.

CHAPTER FOUR

Commerce, Corruption, and Civil Society: The Social and Philosophical Foundations of *The Wealth of Nations*

To claim that Adam Smith's *Wealth of Nations* advanced a theoretical model of an agrarian-based economy and that it exhibited a marked bias against merchants and manufacturers and in favour of farmers and country gentlemen is to fly in the face of conventional academic wisdom. Smith has traditionally been depicted as "the prophet of the commercial society of modern capitalism."[1] In this view, as Joseph Cropsey has put it, Smith "has earned the right to be known as an architect of our present system of society."[2] Central to this conventional view is the notion that Smith contributed to economics "a theoretical formulation of the phenomena of rising industrial capitalism."[3] Indeed, it often paints Smith as an ideologist in the service of the industrial bourgeoisie. Thus, Eric Roll writes in *A History of Economic Thought* that Smith spoke with "the voice of the industrialists" and that he "gave theoretical expression to the essential interests of the business class."[4] Consistent with this view, Max Lerner claimed in the preface to the Cannan edition of *The Wealth of Nations* that Adam Smith was "an unconscious mercenary in the service of a rising capitalist class in Europe."[5] This perspective takes Smith to be a theorist who provided an intellectual justification for the profit-seeking activities of capitalist entrepreneurs. In fact, it often sees him as a central figure in the "bourgeois individualist tradition" in political thought, a figure whose work represents a "crucial turning point" in the attempt to justify the emerging capitalist society.[6]

The central achievement of this theoretical justification is generally taken to be an individualist social theory which is simultaneously liberal and bourgeois. The liberal-individualist element of Smith's political economy is taken to be that free interaction of self-interested individuals in economic markets produces a stable and self-regulating civil society in which the state does not intervene in the affairs of its citizens. It is taken to be bourgeois insofar as it corresponds to the historical interests of commercial and industrial capitalists in their struggles against feudal privilege and mercantilist restriction. Consequently, Smithian economics appears in this view as a bourgeois doctrine which expressed the interests of merchants and manufacturers in opposition to those of landowners.

Any serious reading of *The Wealth of Nations* should indicate the severe problems which accompany such an interpretation. Smith's famous treatise on political economy contains, as one commentator has put it, "a virtual torrent of abuse" against merchants and manufacturers and a definite bias in favour of agriculture and the lifestyles of farmers and the landed gentry.[7] According to Smith, the interests of landowners and of wage labourers are "strictly and inseparably connected with the general interest of the society." The case is different with merchants and manufacturers. They have "an interest to deceive and even oppress the public." It is only "the clamour and sophistry of merchants and manufacturers" which persuade the public that the particular interests of these groups are equivalent to the general interest of society when, in fact, their interests are "directly opposite to that of the great body of the people."[8]

Smith also argues that rural dwellers "are really superior to those of the town"; that land "constitutes the greatest, the most important, and the most durable part of the wealth of every extensive country"; that England, like France, is primarily an agricultural rather than a trading country; and that "the labour of farmers and country labourers is certainly more productive than that of merchants, artificers and manufacturers."[9] A passage from his *Lectures on Jurisprudence* of 1763 and 1764 seems to express Smith's general view that "agriculture is of all other arts the most beneficent to society, and whatever tends to retard its improvement is extremely prejudicial to the public interest."[10]

These statements are not simply the anomalies of a transitional system of thought which has not entirely freed itself from a traditional discourse. As we shall see below, they form parts of a consistent and integrated theoretical argument in which agriculture is the central and leading sector of economic life. Furthermore, at the same time as he extolled the virtues of agriculture, Smith harshly criticized the "commercial spirit" in modern society. Numerous passages in *The Wealth of Nations* contain one or more elements which the following passage from the *Lectures* summarizes:

These are the disadvantages of commercial spirit. The minds of men are contracted and rendered incapable of elevation, education is despised or at least neglected, and heroic spirit is almost utterly extinguished.[11]

As we shall see, Smith's moral philosophy takes as one of its central problems the corrupting influence of commercial activity upon the moral fabric of society.

In this chapter and the next, we shall attempt to show that Smith's stinging attack on merchants and manufacturers and his glowing comments on agrarian classes are pivotal features of his social theory and are crucial to an adequate understanding of his celebrated treatise on political economy. By situating Smith in his social and historical context, by viewing him in relation to the central intellectual issues of the Scottish Enlightenment, and by taking his writings on rhetoric, morality, the state, and political economy as an essentially unified whole, I shall attempt to demonstrate that Smith was a theorist who fundamentally mistrusted merchants and manufacturers and who presented the case for an agrarian capitalist economy, whose operation would be overseen by a state based upon progressive country gentlemen. While commerce could improve society by raising living standards for the poor and by creating bonds of reciprocal need and sympathy between individuals, such benefits required that the political sphere be constituted on the basis of principles radically different from those which characterize commercial relationships.

SCOTLAND IN THE AGE OF IMPROVEMENT

The Union of the English and Scottish parliaments in 1707 ushered in a new period in the social and economic life of the junior partner to the agreement. Eighteenth-century Scotland was swept by a spirit of improvement which fostered a transformation in the life of her inhabitants. The overall effect of the Union was a subject of heated debate for the half century immediately after the event. By the 1760s, however, as Scotland experienced an economic "takeoff" which triggered her industrial revolution, it was clear that the Scottish economy would not be crushed by the weight of English expansionism. On the contrary, the opening up of the English market provided a substantial stimulus to the Scottish economy. As one economic historian has argued, "in the years after 1707 England was probably the only country with which Scotland had a surplus in her balance of trade." [12] From 1755, when general statistics on Scottish foreign commerce were first kept, until 1771, the official value of imports rose by two and a half times while that of exports (including re-exports) rose three and a half times. If it is true that Scotland's trade was in deficit with all her trading partners save England, then the stimulative effect of the Union seems indisputable. These favourable balance of trade figures seem largely to result from the fact that the Union gave Scotland ready access to Britain's overseas markets. Indeed, between 1755 and 1771, the Scottish share in British foreign trade rose from less than 5 percent to roughly 10 percent of the total. [13]

It was Adam Smith's belief that the greatest single economic benefit of the Union was the increase in long-distance cattle trade with England. Whatever the accuracy of Smith's view, there can be little doubt that changes in the agricultural sector were in the forefront of the transformation of the Scottish economy. Although the Scottish Parliament had passed a series of acts designed to facilitate enclosure long before the Union, the organized movement for agricultural improvement dates from the 1720s. In 1723 the first agricultural society, the Society of Improvers in the Knowledge of Agriculture in Scotland, was founded. Also from this period date some of the most significant efforts at enclosure and experimentation with the new husbandry. [14]

It has been strongly argued that agricultural improvement was not motivated exclusively by economic considerations. Expressing a prevalent view, T. C. Smout has claimed that the motives for improvement "were primarily those of fashion, patriotism and the admiration felt by Scots of all political persuasions for a farming system that made the English so much more affluent than themselves." [15] Motives of pride and emulation did undoubtedly play a role in the projects of Scottish improvers. But emulation required economic improvement "because only efficient estates producing for the market could yield a surplus large enough to support the new standards of luxury consumption." [16] For Scottish landowners, raising the productivity of their estates was especially critical to participation in political life in London. Thus R. H. Campbell maintains that "the demand of an absentee landlord for the fruits of his land may have been the most powerful force making for agrarian change."[17]

Although many failed, the efforts of the earliest improvers bore fruit in the prosperous second half of the century as small and middling landowning gentry followed the example of the handful of aristocratic improvers, carrying through enclosures and estate improvements which resulted in a steady rise in rents, especially after 1763. Particularly dramatic was the increase in land prices. During the decade of the 1780s, prices for land doubled in Lanarkshire, Renfrewshire, and the Barony of Glasgow.[18] An infusion of mercantile wealth further stimulated agricultural improvement. Land had always been an attractive investment for prosperous merchants. Ownership of a substantial estate was the avenue to full participation in the life of the political elite. Furthermore, land was often seen as a stable asset, free from the vicissitudes of trade. By midcentury, however, land also appears to have become one of the most profitable investment opportunities. Especially in the Glasgow area, prosperous merchants moved into estate management on a large scale.[19] The result was a significant interpenetration of the landed and mercantile elites.

More than any other group, landowners were caught up in the spirit of improvement. Their passion for improvement extended to mining, road making, canal construction, banking, and the wool and linen trades. It is no overstatement to suggest that Scotland's industrial revolution was underpinned by the fixed investments—in agriculture, transportation, and mining in particular—and the provision of loans undertaken by Scottish landowners.[20] Modern historians have come to recognize that these investments undertaken by landlords were of much more significance to Scotland's industrial revolution than the profits made through overseas trade.[21] The leading role of landlords in the movement for social and economic progress extended, as we have suggested, beyond agriculture and into industry and banking. Moreover, by midcentury the landed elite were in the forefront of the campaign for institutional reforms—particularly law reform—which would modernize Scottish political arrangements.[22] Yet, despite the diversification of the landed interest, agricultural improvement remained vital to industrial development. The improved agricultural productivity allowed domestic grain production to displace grain imports. As a result, purchasing power was retained at home, the home market was stimulated, and capital was made available for domestic industry.

Agricultural improvement, the growth of industry and foreign trade, and rising living standards contributed to an optimistic vision of Scotland's future. Inspired by the vision of improvement and prosperity, lawyers, teachers, and ecclesiastics lent their intellectual energies to the cause of progress. Agriculture often preoccupied them; as contemporaries noted, conversation among lawyers dwelled as likely on a new breed of cattle or a new strain of turnips as on new ideas in literature or philosophy. Many judges, most notably Lord Kames and Lord Monboddo—both social theorists—constructed model estates based on the new husbandry. Kames wrote a major improvement treatise in 1776, *The Gentleman Farmer,* which went through six editions by 1815. Similarly, the Gordon's Mill Farming Club, founded in Aberdeen in 1758, numbered in its ranks several professors, including the commonsense philosopher Thomas Reid and Principal Chalmers of King's College, University of Aberdeen.[23]

Yet improvement and economic progress, with their desirable effects, raised important questions about the impact of commercial development and economic and social change on individuals, their culture, and their state. Influenced by the spirit of improvement and concerned to direct it to benefit society, a series of major thinkers reflected upon the interrelated issues of historical change, the impact of commercialization, and the relation of the individual to society. Constructing an intellectual framework which embraced jurisprudence, moral philosophy, and political economy, the leading Scottish intellectuals grappled with the problems of what we would now call the rise of capitalism. In this way the age of improvement sparked that process of social inquiry known as the Scottish Enlightenment.

THE SCOTTISH ENLIGHTENMENT: MORAL PHILOSOPHY AND POLITICAL ECONOMY

The origins of the Scottish Enlightenment lie in the period immediately following the Jacobite rebellion of 1745. The rebellion highlighted the Scottish backwardness which troubled those thinkers who wished to guide Scotland's passage through the age of improvement; it illustrated the parochial opposition of a backward-looking section of the landed classes to the Union and threw into sharp relief the anachronistic class structure which prevailed in the Highlands.

The literati perceived eighteenth-century Scotland as a nation at a crossroads: one path, of social, political, and economic integration into English society, led to an age of progress and prosperity; the other path, of isolation and autarky, offered little but economic and cultural slumber. For this reason, the Scottish social theorists were centrally concerned with the concept of *refinement*. The progress of human society from "rude" to "refined" states figured in the writings of Lord Kames, David Hume, Adam Ferguson, Adam Smith, and John Millar—to name the most important representatives of the Scottish Enlightenment. Yet, for all their concern with overcoming backwardness, the Scottish social philosophers were intensely aware of the dilemma of development. Much as they desired the economic and social development of eighteenth-century Scotland, they were troubled by the potential dangers of commercializing social life— luxury, self-seeking, moral decay, and the decline of political virtue. Thus, as they constructed a political economy of Scottish development, these theorists also addressed the problem of moral behaviour in a society dominated by the "new economics." The preeminent Scottish theorists, David Hume and Adam Smith, attempted to construct all-embracing theories of social life to resolve the tension between the imperatives of economic development and the requisites of social ethics.

Rich Country–Poor Country: The Problem of Economic Development
Scottish concern with economic development predated the Union. During the 1690s, Scotland experienced commercial depression and grain famine. An acute sense prevailed of Scotland's economic backwardness relative to England, Holland, and France. Five years before Union, the failure of the much-publicized Darien scheme (organized by the Company of Scotland to establish a self-sustaining colonial trade) sparked a debate in political economy. The debate centred on whether Scottish development could be achieved through commercial (and political) union with England or, rather, through state-assisted autarky. In the event, the argument for Union prevailed. But not until midcentury did it produce visible benefits. Thus when David Hume published his major economic essays during the late 1750s, the issue of economic integration was still hotly disputed. Furthermore, during the 1750s and 1760s the economic and political nationalism fostered by Andrew Fletcher before the

Union enjoyed a significant revival. Fletcher had maintained that economic union could only harm the weaker partner. Scottish industry and agriculture would be swamped, he had claimed, by the products of the more prosperous English economy. Moreover, Scottish society would be infected by the corruption which plagued England. Fletcher had argued for state-directed clearance of the Highlands and for the use of forced labour in industry (to ensure low wages) to provide economic development without the deleterious effects of moral corruption and economic decay which would accompany the Union and any attempts to compete in world markets. Fletcher did not oppose the expansion of industry and commerce; he proposed, rather, to pursue these within a uniquely Scottish context in which a civic-minded landed aristocracy could counter the corruption which plagued England.[24]

Hume's economic writings constituted the most important contemporary challenge to the brand of Scottish nationalism Fletcher had constructed out of the tradition of civic humanism. Hume attacked the view that Scotland would experience disadvantageous terms of trade with England resulting in an outflow of gold and silver and consequently depressing industry, trade, and agriculture. Hume's most sophisticated response to this view took the form of the automatic specie-flow mechanism, the germ of which he first advanced in his essay *Of Money* and elaborated in another, *Of the Balance of Trade*. According to Hume, a country's obsession with its balance of trade and its absolute level of gold and silver is entirely misguided—as is the fear that a rich nation will drain a poor one of its specie if the two enter into free trade.

In the essay *Of Money*, Hume conceded that a rich nation enjoys certain advantages such as "superior industry and skill" and "greater stocks." "But," he argued, "these advantages are compensated, in some measure, by the low price of labour in every country which has not an extensive commerce, and does not abound in gold and silver." For Hume, this lower price for labour is a result of the lower price level in a poor country, since prices are determined by the quantity of circulating money in relation to the volume of marketed goods. Industry will then move into the poor country in search of lower production costs. Hume extended this argument to international trade in the essay, *Of the Balance of Trade*, where he argued that for a nation to attempt to accumulate gold and silver is foolhardy. There is a natural level of gold and silver in every country—a level which corresponds to the nation's relative degree of industry. That level may rise or fall, but it always settles at its natural level in much the same manner as does the level of water between two bodies of water. Suppose, Hume suggested, that four-fifths of all the money in Great Britain were annihilated in one night. Prices for British goods would fall so dramatically that Britain would soon recover her gold and silver by underselling all her competitors and reaping an enormous surplus in foreign trade. Likewise, were the money supply to be multiplied five times overnight, the opposite effect would obtain— British goods would be relatively overpriced, and gold and silver would leave the country until prices were restored to a level consistent with the degree of industry.[25]

On this analytic argument Hume constructed a compelling case for Scottish economic development through integration into world markets. His argument involved several interrelated propositions. First, he dismissed the view that a poor nation would inevitably suffer in its trade relations with a stronger and more advanced partner. To the contrary, he maintained that a poor nation enjoyed decisive advantages in lower production costs which would eventually lead to a balance of economic power between rich and poor nations. Second, Hume exposed as utterly misguided the traditional economic fixation with the nation's money supply. "The want of money," he wrote, "can never injure any state within itself: For men and commodities are the real strength of any country."[26] Third, he claimed that the flow of specie into a country with advantageous terms of trade has a markedly stimulative effect on the economy: "Labour and industry gain life; the merchant becomes more enterprising, the manufacturers more diligent and skilful, and even the farmer follows his plough with greater alacrity and attention."[27] These stimulative effects would prevail, however, only until the price level rose in proportion to the increase in the money supply. The fourth and last link in the chain of Hume's argument was the contention that these stimulative effects could be extended more or less indefinitely. An incease in the national output or an increase in the *marketed share* of the national output could moderate the rise in the level of domestic prices. This point allowed Hume to argue for a more extensive commercialization of Scottish economic life. For an inflow of specie would not boost prices of Scottish goods dramatically if "the sphere of circulation" were to be extended:

But after money enters into all contracts and sales, and is everywhere the measure of exchange, the same national cash has a much greater task to perform, all commodities are then in the market, the sphere of circulation is enlarged.[28]

This analysis allowed Hume not only to defend the Union as economically beneficial but also to argue for encouraging habits of industry and commerce among the Scottish people. For it is commercial habits which ensure that an increased money supply results not in luxury and prodigality but rather in industry which will moderate the rise in prices. It is, therefore, "a change of customs and manners"—a social and cultural process of "refinement"—which is fundamental to sustained growth. The essence of this refinement is that "more commodities are produced by additional industry, the same commodities come more to market, after men depart from their ancient simplicity of manners."[29] Hume's argument pointed, therefore, to the social and institutional presuppositions of economic development. Without a revolution in manners, habits, and customs, he argued, Scotland could not be certain of a future of prosperity and improvement.

Compelling though Hume's argument was, it was not without analytic defects. It pivoted on the assumption that costs of production would necessarily be lower in a poor country than in a rich one. This assumption was challenged by two important critics, James Oswald and Josiah Tucker. Oswald presented his argument to Hume in a lengthy letter written in October 1749, after he had seen *Of Money* and *Of the Balance of Trade* in manuscript. Oswald argued that production for extensive markets often enabled rich countries to hold down their unit costs of production. Furthermore, he claimed that rich countries were often able to prevent a dramatic rise in their wage costs by attracting new immigrants.[30] Similar objections were expressed (and expanded upon) by Josiah Tucker, first in correspondence with Kames and subsequently in his *Four Tracts on Political and Commercial Subjects*.

Tucker maintained that "the poorer Nation cannot rival the Manufacturers of a richer one at a third Place, or in a foreign Market." Nevertheless, he argued, a poor country could often produce competitively for its own domestic market (and use customs duties to this effect); it might well enjoy advantages in specific commodities. "There are," he wrote, "certain *local* Advantages resulting either from the Climate, the Soil, the Productions, the Situation, or even the national Turn and peculiar Genius of one People preferably to those of another." Both rich and poor countries could profit through their mutual exchange; they could provide markets for each other's goods and set examples of industry that each would strive to emulate. "The respective Industry of Nation and Nation enables them to be so much the better Customers, to improve in a friendly Intercourse, and to be a mutual Benefit to each other." Thus, so long as every nation strives to promote industry and commerce, it is quite possible that "every Nation, poor as well as rich, may improve their Condition if they please."[31]

Tucker's argument strongly affected Hume. It is unclear to what extent he came over to Tucker's position. Tucker himself felt confident that "though I cannot boast that I had the Honour of making the Gentlemen a *declared* Convert, yet I can say, and prove likewise, that in his Publications since our Correspondence, he has wrote, and reasoned, as if he was a Convert."[32] Against Tucker's claim stands the fact that Hume never modified the argument presented in his essays *Of Money* and *Of the Balance of Trade*. In his favour, however, stands the fact that the emphasis of Hume's argument shifted somewhat in the essay *Of the Jealousy of Trade*, written in 1759, the year after the Hume-Tucker correspondence.

In that essay Hume conceded that "the advantage of superior stocks and correspondence is so great, that it is not easily overcome."[33] In a letter to Kames, he announced that he was pleased to see that Tucker prophesied continuing prosperity for England "but," he continued, "I still indulge myself in the hopes that we in Scotland possess also some advantages, which may enable us to share with them in wealth and industry."[34] These advantages he now expressed in terms similar to the doctrine advanced by Tucker. "Nature," he wrote, "by giving a diversity of geniuses, climates, and soils, to different nations, has secured their mutual intercourse and commerce, as long as they all remain industrious and civilized."[35] With this argument, Hume returned to his three central concerns: first, to justify a more extensive commercialization of the Scottish economy; second, to argue that free world trade based on an international division of labour was the most direct route to economic development for a poor country (and that for Scottish commerce this meant integration by specialization into English and world markets); third, to state the case for a transformation of the "customs and manners" of the Scottish people to enable them to follow the promise of the age of improvement.

The result of the Hume-Tucker debate was thus to build a persuasive case for Scottish economic development through integration into the English market. Hume's argument represented the most sophisticated treatment of economic development before *The Wealth of Nations* appeared in 1776. In fact, in *The Wealth of Nations* Smith adapted Hume's view by arguing that, although a poor nation could not rival a rich nation in manufactures, it could compete in agriculture—a point to which we shall return in the next chapter. In many respects, Hume's economic writings dealt with the lesser problem which troubled Scottish intellectuals of his era. For, however much they favoured accelerated economic growth, eighteenth-century Scottish theorists worried equally about the moral implications of commercialization. How was ethical life to be preserved in the age of industry and refinement? In many respects, this was the central issue of debate in the Scottish Enlightenment.

The Moral Problem: Social Attraction in Commercial Society The great problem of moral philosophy in the eighteenth century was that "of reconciling the old ethics with the new economics."[36] This problem revolved around the dilemma of finding a unifying principle of social life in a commercial society characterized by competition and individual pursuit of self-interest. How were the atomic individuals of commercial society held together? What was to prevent a society characterized by economic individualism from flying asunder? How was virtue—a commitment to the priority of the body politic over the interests of the individual—to be maintained in an individualist social order? These were the questions which, in one way or another, preoccupied the social theorists of the Scottish Enlightenment.

This problem emerged most clearly in Bernard Mandeville's *Fable of the Bees*. Subtitled "Private Vices, Public Benefits," *The Fable* argued that corruption, fraud, and deceit were economically beneficial. In *The Fable*, elimination of these three vices leads to a collapse of trade and industry. Just as theft makes work for the locksmith, so luxury and extravagance provide a stimulus to many trades. On the basis of this argument, Mandeville prided himself that he had

demonstrated that, neither the Friendly Qualities and kind Affections that are natural to Man, nor the real Virtues he is capable of acquiring by Reason and Self-Denial, are the Foundation of Society; but that what we call Evil in this World, Moral as well as Natural, is the grand principle that makes us sociable Creatures, the solid Basis, the Life and Support of all Trades and Employments without exception.[37]

Mandeville did not insist that all vices are beneficial to the public or that vice is automatically of public benefit. He argued that it required the "dextrous Management of a skilful Politician" to harness private vices in a fashion which would serve the public interest. Nevertheless, his basic proposition was clear: all public benefits derive from actions which are fundamentally vicious in character.

Mandeville's theory posed an enormous challenge to virtually all systems of moral philosophy. Especially threatened were those philosophies which sought to ground social life in a disposition towards benevolent treatment of others. Mandeville had written against Shaftesbury, for example, that men were not drawn together into society by "natural Affection to their Species or Love of Company" but only as a "Body Politick" under the rule of a government. Starting with a perspective similar to that of Hobbes, Mandeville drew out the conclusion that individuals accept the subordination inherent in civil society (that is, society based on government) only to satisfy their basic material needs. Society and government were, therefore, the outgrowth of selfish passions. It was to defend the principle of the natural sociability of men that Francis Hutcheson, friend of Hume and Kames, teacher of Adam Smith, "the personality most responsible for the new spirit of enlightenment in the Scottish universities," undertook to demolish the edifice of Mandeville's system.[38]

Hutcheson wrote as an avowed disciple of Shaftesbury and opponent of Mandeville. The full title of his first published work, which appeared in 1725, reflects the confrontation between Mandeville's new economics and the old ethics; it reads *An Inquiry into the Original of our Ideas of Beauty and Virtue; in two treatises, in which the principles of the late Earl of Shaftesbury are explained and defended against the Author of the Fable of the Bees; and the Ideas of Moral Good and Evil are established according to the Sentiments of the Ancient Moralists: with an attempt to introduce a Mathematical Calculation in subjects of Morality.*

Hutcheson inherited from the third earl of Shaftesbury the ancient Greek concept of the cosmos as a balanced, ordered, and harmonious system. According to Shaftesbury, the universe is a delicately balanced organism in which a strict "oeconomy" obtains in the inter-relationships between the parts which make up the whole. Just as order obtains in the physical universe, so it does in the moral world of social life. But the order of social life is a potentiality; to make it actual, men—or at least "gentlemen of fashion," for Shaftesbury's theory was thoroughly aristocratic—must understand the principles of social harmony and act according to the dictates of moral law. The understanding of moral duty requires aesthetic contemplation, considered reflection upon the beauty which prevails in nature and society. A mind "experienced in all the degrees and orders of Beauty" strives to "rise" from contemplation of the beauty of particular systems to comprehension of the beauty of the whole. Such a mind can direct the soul to its moral obligations since it "views communitys, friendships, relations, dutys; and considers by what Harmony of particular minds the general harmony is composed." Those "fine gentlemen" who appreciate the harmony of the cosmos also appreciate the need for a "balance of the passions." They seek to moderate selfish affections by public or benevolent sentiments, to make their behaviour aesthetically pleasing to others.[39] Shaftesbury's view was thus rooted in the classical civic tradition which held that commitment to and participation in the body politic was the exclusive duty of independent landed gentlemen freed from the exigencies of labour.

Hutcheson built his moral philosophy directly upon Shaftesbury's critique of Mandeville. He added to it a response to the latter's strictly economic arguments. Not only did Hutcheson condemn the moral implications of Mandeville's theory, he also sought to show that the latter's economic arguments were fallacious. Central to Hutcheson's case was the claim that luxury trades or those trades which profit from crime or suffering are not necessary to economic well-being. Income not spent one way will, he claimed, be spent in another. "There may be an equal consumption of manufactures without these vices and the evils which flow from them," Hutcheson maintained.[40]

Hutcheson felt confident that he had refuted the more blatantly pernicious aspects of Mandeville's system, but the problem of the basic springs of social action remained. Although vicious crime could be shown to be unnecessary to economic well-being, selfish interest might still prompt individuals to come together in society and observe its rules. If so, public good might still be said to be the effect of selfish interest. Hutcheson accepted that every individual had a selfish interest in society. The solitary life would be a life without material comfort; only the cooperative activity of individuals in society makes possible that division of labour which increases the wealth available to all members of society. Hutcheson recognized this fact but harboured serious reservations about the commercialization of economic life. He believed that unbridled commercialism leads inevitably to corruption and decline, as had been the case, he believed, with the Roman republic. For this reason he adhered to the Harringtonian idea of an agrarian law which would place limits upon the accumulation of landed wealth; he looked to a virtuous, industrious, and enlightened gentry to counter the pernicious effects of commerce on the morals of individuals.[41] Nevertheless, he continued to believe that society satisfied basic human needs—social as well as material. All humans have, Hutcheson claimed, "a natural impulse to society with their fellows." The impulse toward society comes from natural sociability. The human being is a social creature who craves compassion and friendship. Hutcheson went so far as to make the assertion—directed especially against Mandeville—that all people have an innate concern for the good of society. This concern flows from a distinctive "moral sense," the capacity for benevolence.

In Hutcheson's theory, people are endowed with both selfish and social passions. The central social passion is the "moral sense," or "benevolence" (although in his later writings Hutcheson added to the moral sense two more, a sense of honour and a public sense). In his *Essay on the Passions*, Hutcheson argued that in their action and reaction upon one another, these passions formed a balanced system. This balance of the passions was maintained by a sort of "Newtonian dynamics." Indeed, Hutcheson explicitly compared self-love to the inertial movement of the atoms of the universe and benevolence to the principle of gravitation which subjects inertial movement to strict order and regularity of operation. While self-love is the principle which moves the atoms of society, benevolence is the principle of the whole which acts to moderate, order, and control the selfish impulses. Self-love is not to be repressed but merely regulated, for social life depends upon the balance of these sets of passions. As Hutcheson wrote in his *Inquiry*, "Self-love is really as necessary to the good of the whole as benevolence; as that attraction which causes the cohesion of the part, is as necessary to the regular state of the whole as gravitation."[42]

The decisive claim for Hutcheson's argument is that a force (benevolence) operates in the social world which orders and regulates human affairs, just as gravity or "attraction" regulates the phenomena of the natural universe. Hutcheson's moral philosophy stands or falls on the claim that "this universal benevolence toward all men we may compare to that principle of gravitation which perhaps extends to all bodies in the universe."[43] Without such a principle of moral "attraction" the elementary parts of society—its atomic individuals—would operate in a world of chaos. No general principle could harmonize the disparate and self-seeking activities of individuals into an ordered social whole. Hutcheson believed that the evidence of human experience demonstrated the empirical reality of the principle of benevolence, just as Newton had deduced the principles of gravitation from the evidence of the regular orbits of the planets. But, ultimately, Hutcheson was forced to evoke a teleology of divine origin to support his claim. When we survey the universe, he suggested, "all the apparent Beauty produced is an evidence of the execution of a Benevolent design."[44]

A quite different response to Mandeville was shaped by David Hume, who rejected Hutcheson's resort to teleological argument. As Hume wrote to Hutcheson in 1739, "I cannot agree to your sense of *'natural.'* 'Tis founded on final causes, which is a consideration that appears to me pretty uncertain and unphilosophical." In this letter, Hume maintained that he sought to understand the mind as "an anatomist," not as a painter. The former examines the mind in an effort "to discover its most secret springs and principles" whereas the latter attempts "to describe the grace and beauty of its actions."[45] Moreover, Hume did not believe that it was necessary to counterpose a moral sense to Mandeville's economics. Instead, he believed that moral behaviour pivoted upon intellectual understanding of the processes of commercialization.

Hume did not share Hutcheson's qualms about commercial society. In fact, he believed that the advance of commerce, rather than contributing to corruption and degeneracy, could pave the way for morality, justice, and good government. Hume held that moral behaviour depended upon rational consideration and that commerce, industry, and refinement stimulated the life of the mind. Thus, in his essay *Of Refinement in the Arts*, he maintains against the civic humanists that "refinement on the pleasures and conveniences of life has no natural tendency to beget venality and corruption." On the contrary, refinement in the mechanical arts produces refinement in the liberal arts. "The same age which produces great philosophers and politicians, renowned generals and poets, usually abounds with skilful weavers and ship-carpenters." An age of improvement in the arts and sciences banishes ignorance and allows individuals to "enjoy the privilege of rational creatures." The result is that they come to see the necessity for private property, law, and government. Thus, ages of improvement and refinement need not be ages of corruption. Indeed, moral and political progress are intimately connected to the development of commercial society.[46]

The intellectual commerce in ideas which develops in an age of industry and improvement produces those advances in philosophy and ethics which provide the social and institutional framework for moral action and good government. Indeed, only the intellectual revolution which accompanies an age of progress supplies a solid footing for government and society. Mandeville may thus be right that society emerges out of selfish need, but the process of "humanization" which is associated with the growth of commercial society establishes a more powerful basis for society—human reason itself. This argument emerges clearly in the third book of Hume's *Treatise of Human Nature*.

In the *Treatise* Hume accepts that self-love is the origin of law and government. Nevertheless, since "the self-love of one person is naturally contrary to that of another," competing and conflicting self-interested passions must "adjust themselves after such a manner as to concur in some system of conduct and behaviour."[47] After individuals discover that unbridled selfishness incapacitates them for society, "they are naturally induc'd to lay themselves under the restraint of such rules, as may render their commerce more safe and commodious." As rules of social regulation are developed, they become customary and are passed on to future generations. Eventually people come to cherish the rules which hold society together. They develop a sense of *sympathy* for those who observe social norms. Moreover, they come to model their behaviour in such a way as to be worthy of the sympathy and approval of others. Through custom and education, then, individuals develop a love of praise and a fear of blame. For Hume, moral principles are not innate or providentially inspired. They are practical rules developed in the course of living in society; morality refers to the norms and conventions which prevail there. These norms and conventions can be said to enter into the commonsense view of the world most individuals acquire. Morality is rooted, in other words, in the shared opinions which constitute the common assumptions, the inherited wisdom of individuals living in society. As Hume puts it in the *Treatise*, "the general opinion of mankind had some authority in all cases; but in this of morals 'tis perfectly infallible."[48]

It is sympathy which constitutes the principle of attraction in society. But for Hume sympathy is not an innate propensity as it is for Hutcheson. Rather, it is a capacity derived from experience and modified as the customary rules of social life change. Sympathy has a rational dimension; it derives from the individual's understanding of the necessity for norms of conduct and behaviour. Thus, although "*self-interest is the original motive to the* establishment of justice," as society develops it becomes the case that "*a* sympathy *with public interest is the source of the* moral approbation, which attends that virtue."[49] In the course of experience, then, individuals come to recognize that rules of justice, especially those which regulate property rights, are useful to the order of society.

Hume believed that the forms of human intercourse which characterize commercial society provide the surest foundation for moral behaviour and justice. It is through the experience of those forms of interaction and communication appropriate to an exchange economy that individuals identify the behaviours which sustain the social bonds upon which they rely. Through the customs which characterize commercial society, then, they come to appreciate the necessity for property, law, and justice. They accept the need for—indeed, they will—those institutional arrangements which preserve the social order. They recognize the *usefulness* of the social conventions and institutions which they have created and approve of that which is useful to society. "Public utility" thus becomes the basis of moral decision. As Hume put it in his *Enquiry Concerning the Principles of Morals*, "every-thing which contributes to the happiness of society recommends itself directly to our approbation and good will."[50]

It is certainly true that Hume's argument is constructed within an "essentially jurisprudential framework."[51] That is to say, Hume's primary concern is to establish the conditions which make *justice*— particularly the legal rules governing ownership and transfer of property—possible in a commercial society. His central preoccupation is not, as it was for the civic humanists, to establish the conditions of public virtue. Yet it is misleading to suggest that Hume's position (or that of Smith, which we shall examine below) substitutes the coordinates of natural jurisprudence for those of civic humanism. After all, we have seen in chapter 2 that James Harrington's version of the humanist perspective shifted from specifying the social circumstances conducive to moral behaviour and civic virtue towards delineating the system of laws which could harness selfish passions to the common good. One distinctive feature of eighteenth-century Scottish social theory was that it continued this Harringtonian emphasis on the priority of law in establishing a healthy and stable commonwealth. With this emphasis, it made perfect sense to consider the classical republic in terms of law and jurisprudence, rather than in terms of the moral conditions of citizenship. Moreover, such an approach involved treating the classical civic tradition and the tradition of natural jurisprudence associated with Grotius, Pufendorf, and Carmichael as components of a common enquiry into the science of government. Indeed, we cannot understand the outlook of an influential Scottish theorist like Francis Hutcheson unless we recognize that Scottish writers addressed social development in terms of both the civic problem of corruption and the jurisprudential concern with the evolution of laws and forms of property.

Hume must be seen as operating within this Scottish context of social and political theorizing. Moreover, both his philosophical scepticism and his Ciceronian emphasis on the virtue of moderation would have led him to eschew a rigid attitude towards the classical debate over commerce, corruption, and citizenship. Proponent of commercialization that he was, Hume was deeply concerned that the increase in wealth brought about by economic development might increase the temptation for those in government to exploit public institutions for private advantage—a concern rooted in the civic tradition and its Commonwealth descendant. He was especially concerned with the growth of the public debt—a central issue taken up by the Country opposition of the eighteenth century. Hume worried that growth of the debt would erode the traditional social structure by elevating above all others the holders of the debt, individuals "who have no connexions with the state, who can enjoy their revenue in any part of the globe in which they chuse to reside." Fixed wealth, under such conditions, would no longer be passed from generation to generation. The result would be an end "to all ideas of nobility, gentry and family" and the erosion of "the middle power between king and people."[52]

It was "the middling rank" upon whom Hume hung his hopes for the preservation and growth of liberty, a category which included the landed gentry. Commercialization did not imply a decline in the importance of the gentry; on the contrary, Hume insisted that there was no inherent conflict between the landed and trading classes and that commercial expansion contributed directly to agricultural improvement.[53] It is perhaps worth reminding ourselves also that Hume's model of a "perfect commonwealth" drew directly on Harringtonian ideas and emphasized the integrity of local communities in which landed gentlemen exercised a significant influence in political affairs.[54] Hume appears also to argue that one of the advantages of commercial progress is that it will allow larger sections of the population to achieve the material and moral prerequisites of citizenship (most important, economic independence). For this reason, John Robertson seems close to the mark when he argues that "the suggestion that commerce has the potential to universalize citizenship was sufficient to enable Hume to realign the civic ideal of political community with the individualism of his jurisprudential theory of government."[55] Hume's resolution of the new economics with the old morality—his unique mix of natural jurisprudence and civic humanism—did not settle the Scottish debate over commerce and virtue. One of the most important challenges to Hume's position was framed by Adam Ferguson, whose *Essay on the History of Civil Society* (1767) Pocock has rightly called "perhaps the most Machiavellian of the Scottish disquisitions" on the problem of virtue and corruption in commercial society.[56]

Ferguson's position was not a wholesaie rejection of commercial society. He had no doubt that social division of labour increased the wealth of a nation. He also accepted that as an individual pursues his own commercial gain "he augments the wealth of his country." Indeed, for this reason he took an essentially laissez-faire position on trade, arguing that "private interest is a better patron of commerce and plenty, than the refinements of state." However economically beneficial it might be, commercial society had adverse social and political effects. Ferguson saw social development as a contradictory process: "Every age hath its consolations, as well as its sufferings." In the case of modern civil society—the commercial society in which exchange turns "the hunter and the warrior into a tradesman and a merchant"—the suffering has to do with the damage done by commerce to the moral fabric which sustains the political order.[57]

The central problem of commercial society is that economic competition and the pursuit of profit become the model for all human intercourse. All social relations tend to be reduced to those which characterize the cash nexus. Individuals become little more than objects in the path of selfish action. Ferguson wrote of commercial society:

It is here indeed, if ever, that man is sometimes found a detached and a solitary being: he has found an object which sets him in competition with his fellow-creatures, and he deals with them as he does with his cattle and his soil, for the sake of the profits they bring.[58]

The great danger associated with commercializing all social relations is that the principles of profit-seeking can come to dominate the political system. It is when individuals approach political affairs with an eye to their private advancement that we are confronted with a full-fledged process of corruption. The decline of civic virtue—a dedication to the interests of society above those of the individual—signals the decay of the moral and political substructure of society. Thus, although commercial society is always fraught with the dangers of corruption,

The case, however, is not desperate, till we have formed our system of politics, as well as manners; till we have sold our freedom for titles, equipage and distinctions; till we see no merit but prosperity and power, no disgrace but poverty and neglect.[59]

According to Ferguson, corruption was not an inevitable consequence of commercial society. It was inevitable only if the ruling class failed to recognize the dangers posed by "the spirit which reigns in a commercial state" and failed to erect safeguards which would prevent this spirit from infiltrating the "system of politics, as well as manners." In a very real sense, the *Essay* was written to counsel the Scottish political elite regarding the commitment to civic virtue which was necessary if the age of commerce and improvement were not to destroy the civic virtues which sustained the political order. Ferguson bemoaned the fact that "in too many nations of Europe, the individual is everything, and the public is nothing." And he reminded his readers that "to the ancient Greek, or the Roman, the individual was nothing and the public everything."[60] He thus appealed to the landed classes to play the role of enlightened and public-spirited gentlemen who would preserve in the political realm the virtues which could counter the corrupting influence of the commercial spirit.

For Ferguson the principles operative in the political sphere can and should counter those which prevail in economic relations. It is the duty of the political actors, virtuous men of affairs, to design and promote political arrangements which offset the corrupting influence of commerce. The statesman, the public-minded leader, ought to strive to construct a framework of laws based not on his particular selfish interests but on his understanding of the general interest of society. These laws must then operate to "weaken the desire of riches, and to preserve in the breast of the citizen, that moderation and equity which ought to regulate his conduct."[61] Ferguson's argument thus presupposes civic activism. The direction of society is not simply the unforeseen outcome of interacting selfish interests operating in a system of exchange relations. The interventions of public-spirited individuals do matter in the overall social scheme. For Ferguson, one of the most important means to maintain political virtue was through military engagement; for this reason, he supported the Scottish campaign for a citizens' militia. The social division of labour is not to be extended to the military sphere; if military activity becomes a specialized professional function, then the citizenry will never know the experience of risking death to preserve the commonwealth—an experience which forces citizens to rise above narrow particularity and to become one with the general will.[62]

Although he does not repudiate commercial society, Ferguson rejects the Humean identification of commerce with the development of social ethics. He sees commercial society as a thoroughly contradictory phenomenon. The benefits of wealth are offset by the damage it does to virtue. Only a conscious use of law and government to prevent the infiltration of the commercial spirit into the moral fabric of society can preserve justice and virtue.

The Scottish Enlightenment produced, therefore, several responses to the problem of reconciling the new economics with the old ethics. In the case of Hutcheson, a superior moral sense was to moderate and direct the selfish passions which are central to a commercial society. For Hume, commercial society was the best framework to elaborate rules of social conduct which would preserve the social and political order. In Ferguson's system, public-minded civic action was to immunize political life against the corrupting influence of the commercial spirit of an exchange economy; the exchange economy was thus a necessary evil—necessary to economic growth but evil when its principles and imperatives came to dominate the body politic. It was in the context of these previous approaches that Adam Smith penned his answer to the question of the relation between economic activity and moral conduct. His answer culminated in his celebrated work, *The Wealth of Nations*. And that work was the end product of an ingenious attempt to resolve the central problem which preoccupied all thinkers in the Scottish Enlightenment.

ADAM SMITH: THE SOCIAL AND INTELLECTUAL HERITAGE

Adam Smith was born into the age of improvement. In fact, the year of his birth, 1723, was also the one in which the first agricultural society was founded; his intellectual development cannot be understood outside the context of the Scottish Enlightenment. Student of Hutcheson, admirer of Kames, friend of Hume, Adam Smith framed the most profound response to the problems which preoccupied the social theorists of eighteenth-century Scotland.

Smith's father, who died a few weeks before his son was born, followed the family tradition of administrative service. He was judge advocate for Scotland and private secretary to the Scottish Minister, the earl of Loudon, before being promoted to comptroller of Customs at Kirkaldy in 1714. The elder Adam Smith and his cousin were both associated with the Customs. And it was to the post of commissioner of Customs that his son, Adam Smith, moved after completing *The Wealth of Nations*. The association of the Smith family with state service has been described as "curious" by one biographer, while another has commented on the appointment of the author of *The Wealth of Nations* to the post of commissioner of Customs that it was "an odd reward for the Apostle of Free Trade."[63] Odd and curious though it may seem, this tradition of involvement in state service related to taxation is of no little significance. Certainly it goes some way towards explaining Smith's lifelong preoccupation with problems of public finance. And as we shall see, it also assists our understanding of his treatise on political economy.

Just as family tradition created an interest in issues of public finance, so it created a concern with problems of agriculture. Smith's mother, Mary Douglas, came from a long line of landowners with medium-size estates. Smith visited his relatives' estates often; it was through them that he acquired his "early interest in agriculture which endured."[64] The significance of this agricultural connection has been noted by W. R. Scott:

The visits which he made with his mother, or later alone to relatives, who were Fifeshire lairds, would familiarize him with agriculture. Indeed, *The Wealth of Nations* contains several little vignettes based on these early impressions which were amplified by later visits.[65]

As we have seen, others shared Smith's interest in agriculture. In 1754 a number of prominent intellectuals and political figures founded a debating club known as the Select Society, which met weekly in Edinburgh. Among its members were Lord Kames, Lord Monboddo, David Hume, Adam Ferguson, and Adam Smith; the majority were wealthy landowners. Smith was closely involved with the project from its inception. In fact, it was he who was entrusted with the duty of explaining the nature of the proposed society at its founding meeting. The Select Society was the most significant centre of intellectual life in mid-eighteenth-century Scotland. It addressed the moral and political issues at the heart of the Scottish Enlightenment, debating "whether a nation may subsist without public spirit"; "whether commercial and military spirit can subsist in the same nation"; and so on.[66] From the start, the society also centred its attention on questions of an economic nature; its overriding concern soon became issues of agrarian economy. According to contemporary records, the group debated the merits of large and small farms, the division of farms into arable and pasturage, the most advantageous length for farm leases, methods of enclosure, land drainage, fertilization of land, ploughing, the most beneficial level of rents, money rents versus rents in kind, and so on. The society launched a special agricultural branch; in 1756 the society voted, with Smith's enthusiastic support, to admit some "practical farmers" into membership in order to improve its discussions.[67] Over the years the society seems to have identified "the problem of introducing a free market in land on the English model" as the central problem of Scottish improvement.[68] Many of the important political and intellectual figures with whom Smith associated were agricultural improvers. This was true of Kames who has been called "the first of the improvers";[69] true also of the geologist James Hutton, one of the executors of Smith's literary estate; of John Sinclair, a lifelong friend and the founder of the Board of Agriculture; and of another longtime friend, John Callender, a practicing advocate in Edinburgh. Smith was acquainted as well with Charles Townshend, a prominent member of one of the great Whig landowning families; in 1763 Smith accepted the post of travelling tutor to Townshend's nephew, the duke of Buccleugh. It is of some interest that the duke chose not to go into politics—as had been expected of him—and instead lived on his Scottish estates and became "a powerful and enlightened promoter of all sound agricultural improvement."[70] Certainly we must recognize these associations as being at least as significant as Smith's connection through the Political Economy Club with leading Glasgow merchants, when we consider that many of these merchants, especially the tobacco lords, were also large landowners.[71] As we shall see in the next chapter, during his stay in France (1764–1766) Smith was further exposed to intense theoretical discussions of agrarian economy, particularly those discussions which took place in physiocratic circles. The evidence for his abiding interest in agricultural improvement is thus substantial. From an early age Smith was also initiated into the theoretical debates at the centre of the Scottish Enlightenment. This exposure began when, as a student at Glasgow, he came under the influence of Francis Hutcheson.

Smith always acknowledged a profound intellectual debt to "the never-to-be-forgotten Hutcheson" as he described his great teacher. "If he was any man's disciple," wrote Rae, "he was Hutcheson's."[72] Smith was particularly inspired by Hutcheson's doctrine of natural liberty—the doctrine that every man has an inalienable right to the disposition of his labour and the fruits of this labour (his property) so long as he does not transgress the principles of justice set out by society.

Added to the early influence of Hutcheson was the later influence of Hume, Smith's dearest friend in Edinburgh. It was to Hume, until his friend died in 1776, that Smith entrusted the execution of his literary estate, as Hume made Smith his literary executor. Hume was more than a friend; he was also a powerful intellectual influence on the younger Smith. In *The Wealth of Nations* Smith described Hume as "by far the most illustrious philosopher and historian of the present age."[73] Hume transmitted to Smith a profound mistrust of teleologically based natural rights arguments. As we have noted above, Hume rejected the naturalistic teleology developed by Hutcheson and ascribed the origin of property, law, and government not to nature but to the evolution of human society. Hume's argument, as we shall see, made a strong impact on Smith. In an important sense, we can say that Smith had two prominent mentors—Francis Hutcheson and David Hume. In fact, Smith's moral and political philosophy developed in the course of an ongoing intellectual exchange with the systems of Hutcheson and Hume.

Interest in problems of taxation, concern with agricultural improvement, preoccupation with the responses Hutcheson and Hume gave to problems of commercialization and the social basis of morality: these ingredients made up the social and intellectual heritage of Adam Smith. To these ingredients he added his unique genius, making a decisively important contribution to the problems posed by the Scottish Enlightenment.

SMITH'S EARLY WRITINGS: TOWARDS A SCIENCE OF SOCIETY

Smith's political economy developed in the context of the central concerns of the Scottish Enlightenment. Like most of his colleagues, Smith was preoccupied with improving the Scottish economy and refining Scottish society. In fact, economic progress and social refinement were inseparable; Smith treated the basic phenomena of economic life—division of labour and economic exchange—as specific aspects of human interaction in general. Economic relations presupposed social interaction; and crucial to all human interaction was the art of communication—the ability to convey ideas and feelings. If we are fully to appreciate Smith's science of economic relations, we must grasp the basic features of his science of society sketched out in his early philosophical writings, which predate *The Moral Sentiments* and *The Wealth of Nations* (some of these writings were published after his death; the majority were burned upon his orders shortly before he died). What remains available to the modern reader, however, is crucial to understanding the whole of Smith's intellectual project.[74] As we review these early writings and the development of his thought in this chapter, it will become clear that Smith turned to the political order to establish the institutional settings which would prevent commercial relations from corrupting social life, and that *The Wealth of Nations* attempted to set out the political framework in which the energies of economic individualism would contribute to the public interest. *The Wealth of Nations* is thus immersed in the discourse of Smith's moral philosophy; indeed, any interpretation must suffer if it neglects the social and moral theory which underpins Smith's political economy.

■ ■ ■

The crucial problem of Smith's theory of society concerns the human capacity for communication. Communication presupposes that we possess images and thoughts which we can express to others. Communication thus raises an epistemological problem: how do we develop images and ideas about the world around us? Smith's response is to advance a *conventionalist* epistemology according to which, though we can never come entirely to know the "things-in-themselves" which make up the extramental world, we can erect a shared symbolic system which forms the intersubjective basis of all experience.[75] Perception itself is impossible without such a symbolic system. Although there may be "no resemblance between visible and tangible objects," Smith writes in the essay *Of the External Senses*, there is "some affinity and correspondence between them." This affinity and correspondence are analogous to the relation between words and objects. Indeed, in analyzing vision Smith refers to "the language which nature addresses to our eyes."[76] Such references are anything but arbitrary. Smith regarded language as the foundation of thought—the structure of our ideas, he wrote, "seems to have arisen more from the nature of language, than from the nature of things"—and as paradigmatic of all intellectual efforts to understand the world around us.[77]

Language develops by way of generalization from particular experiences. It involves the passage from concrete particulars (for example, a river) to abstract universals ("river" as a generic term) and thus requires "more metaphysics than we are apt to be aware of."

But language is more than a metaphysical undertaking; it is also an aesthetic project. Indeed, the rules of grammar are a product of the "love of analogy and similarity of sound."[78] Language emerges by way of a dual process of division and combination. In order to represent the continuous flux of experience to themselves "mankind have learned by degrees to split and divide almost every event into a great number of metaphysical parts, expressed by the different parts of speech, variously combined in the different members of every phrase and sentence." These principles of division and combination are exemplified in the division of words into letters with the creation of an alphabet.[79] The notion of language as requiring division of experience and its recombination into a humanly ordered pattern presents, as we shall see, a close analogy with Smith's concepts of division of labour and economic cooperation in commercial society.

Smith treated language as a prototype of all the imitative arts. All such arts—poetry, drama, painting, etc.—are, as Ralph Lindgren puts it, "efforts to formulate systems of conventional signs."[80] The same applies to science and philosophy. Smith considered these liberal arts also to be systems of signification. Philosophical systems are efforts to overcome our sense of wonder in the face of the phenomena of nature. As with language, the mind divides the continuum of experience into genera and species and then establishes "customary connections" between ideas. The function of philosophy is to construct a "chain of invisible objects" which joins together events in our experience. In this way, philosophy calms the mind by representing the world as regular, orderly, and predictable.[81]

We have noted Smith's view that language is a system based upon division and combination of words. What, however, are the consequences of the fact that systems change over time? In the case of language, Smith believed that language was simplified when various people with different tongues met and strove to communicate with one another. In its basic principles language became more simple, while in its principles of combination it became more complex. This is the case also with machines:

Language becomes more simple in its rudiments and principles, just in proportion as it grows more complex in its composition, and the same thing has happened in it, which commonly happens with regard to mechanical engines.[82]

This simplification of the elements of language and the growing complexity of its composition may serve to render communication easier, but it also renders language "less agreeable to the ear." What is gained in utility is gained at the expense of beauty. The end result of this process is "the prolixness, constraint and monotony of modern language."[83] If, as we have suggested, language was for Smith paradigmatic of all systems of human communication, then these comments upon the decline in the beauty of modern language may have some implications for his views on problems of modern social organization. As we examine Smith's moral, political, and economic theories—in that order, the order in which he dealt with them in his lectures in moral philosophy at Glasgow—we shall see that such is indeed the case and that the conflict between beauty and utility is central to his theory of commercial society.

SMITH'S MORAL PHILOSOPHY

Smith's general social philosophy forms the background to his moral theory. As we have seen, Smith is concerned fundamentally with the problem of communication. In this respect, his project lies within the mainstream of the Scottish Enlightenment. The problem of communication is for Smith one of social harmony. Unless they can communicate their sentiments, thoughts, and experiences to one another, how can independent individuals—especially ones who are self-seeking—cohere to form a unified social whole? This is the central problem of "social Newtonianism": what principle of attraction binds the atoms of human society? Smith states explicitly in *The Theory of the Moral Sentiments* that without a system of justice and a political order, human society "must in a moment crumble into atoms."[84] But before considering justice and politics, Smith needed to establish the philosophical principles of social intercourse which make civil society possible; this is the basic objective of the *Moral Sentiments*. Indeed, it would appear that having grappled with the problem of language, Smith felt compelled to backtrack to establish the social-psychological presuppositions of language and communication. In the sixth of his *Lectures on Rhetoric and Belles Lettres*, Smith hints at the course his argument will take in the *Moral Sentiments*. Speaking of the beauty of language, he states that

Whenever the sentiment of the speaker is expressed in a neat, clear, plain and clever manner, and the passion or affection he is poss(ess)ed of and intends, *by sympathy*, to communicate to his hearer, is plainly and cleverly hit off, then and then only the expression has all the force and beauty that language can give it.[85]

This passage suggests that the ability of a speaker to communicate his sentiments or thoughts depends upon his *sympathy* with his audience. As the basis of all social relations, a mutual bond of sympathy (by which Smith means "fellow-feeling") between an actor and spectator(s) of the action is a prerequisite to the community of sentiments which makes social life possible. Conversation and social convention require that individuals construct a network of common sentiments to share in some measure in the feelings of one another.

Smith believed (with Shaftesbury and Hutcheson) that "conversation and society" provide pleasure to individuals. This pleasure "arises from a certain correspondence of sentiments and opinions, from a certain harmony of minds, which, like so many musical instruments, coincide and keep time with one another."[86] This harmony of minds is based upon a structure of shared moral sentiments and opinions. But what makes shared sentiments and opinions possible? According to Smith, sympathy is the basis of the social bond. But sympathy requires a specific mechanism to produce moral sentiments; this mechanism Smith calls "the impartial spectator."

Smith's moral theory is predicated on the view that it is in the nature of human beings to desire a harmony between their sentiments and those of others. We must emphasize, since Smith is popularly conceived to be the apostle of self-interest as the driving force in human affairs, that sympathy according to Smith "cannot, in any sense, be regarded as a selfish principle."[87] The *Moral Sentiments* is in fact a sustained attack upon the "selfishness school," represented by Hobbes and Mandeville, which reduces social sentiments to selfish interest. Smith concedes that self-love is a major human passion; like Hutcheson, however, he insists that the foundation of social life is the subordination of self-love to sympathy. Thus, the opening sentence of the *Moral Sentiments* clearly states that Smith's objective in the work is to explore our sentiments of fellow-feeling:

How selfish soever man may be supposed, there are evidently some principles in his nature, which interest him in the fortune of others, and render their happiness necessary to him, though he derives nothing from it, except the pleasure of seeing it.[88]

All individuals have, according to Smith, a capacity for sympathy with others. By an act of the imagination we are all inclined to consider how we would feel if we were to have the experience which befalls another. This imaginary transference of ourselves into the position of others (imagining what we would feel were we "in their shoes") allows us to sympathize with the reaction of others to their experience. In our imagination, in other words, we exchange our position with that of another. This ability to exchange experience through an imaginary operation based upon sympathetic identification with others is the fundamental basis of society. The imaginary operation in which one individual attempts to assume the position of another can never give a spectator the total experience of an actor. To receive the sympathy of spectators, actors must strive to moderate their joy or sorrow over what has befallen them, just as spectators must endeavour to heighten their sensitivity to the feelings of the actors. The actors, thus, must try to reduce the intensity of their feeling; they must try to react to their experience as would *impartial spectators* who observe it from a distance.

Social life requires, therefore, that all individuals attempt to transcend their immediate interest to some degree. They must all endeavour to adopt the standpoint of the impartial spectator who, as one commentator has put it, may be said to represent "the average reaction of ordinary observers of human conduct."[89] In order to receive the approval of others (something which every person passionately desires), an individual learns to control selfish desires, to keep them within socially acceptable bounds. Social life requires that all individuals subordinate their passions to the norms of conduct which characterize a given community. As Smith writes,

If he would act so as that the impartial spectator may enter into the principles of his conduct, which is what of all things he has the greatest desire to do, he must upon this, as upon all other occasions, humble the arrogance of his self-love, and bring it down to something which other men can go along with.[90]

In order to maintain that community of sentiments upon which society depends, all individuals must subject their behaviour to the standards of an imagined impartial spectator. This standard may be said to represent the moral code which prevails within a given society. During the course of our daily experience of those actions which elicit approval and those which elicit disapproval we form ideas concerning what behaviour is morally acceptable. The moral code of a society thus consists of general rules derived by induction from the moral judgements which we daily make. When such general rules have been formed and "when they are universally acknowledged and established by the concurring sentiments of mankind, we frequently appeal to them as to the standards of judgement."[91]

Smith's is indeed "a common sense morality."[92] In fact, in his *Lectures on Rhetoric,* Smith argues that all the rules of morality, like those of criticism, "when traced to their foundations, turn out to be some principles of common sense which every one assents to."[93] Such a position is fraught with difficulties. What, after all, are the consequences if society is in a state of corruption? If degeneracy prevails, to what extent can acting according to social norms be said to be truly moral? Such questions were posed to Smith after the appearance of the first edition of *Moral Sentiments.* In later editions he tried to solve the problems raised by such questions by distinguishing between the "impartial spectator" and the "ideal spectator."

Whereas the impartial spectator represents the judgement of the average member of society, the "ideal spectator" represents judgement on a higher moral plane. When individuals govern their behaviour according to the dictates of the ideal spectator, they act not out of desire for praise but out of love for praiseworthiness. They act, in other words, not on the basis of public opinion but on the basis of a truly refined conscience. With this construct, Smith appears to have saved conscience from subservience to public opinion. But his solution is more apparent than real. What, after all, provides the basic moral code adhered to by conscience and the ideal spectator? Clearly, if moral judgements are not implanted in human beings by God or nature—positions which Smith rejects—they must be produced by the human community. Thus, the ideal spectator can simply be said to represent the moral rules of society freed from the partiality which sometimes affects public opinion. Occasionally, the ideal spectator may use the moral sentiments of society to reject the opinion which prevails in the community at a given point in time. But such moral judgements remain based upon the moral standards of the community. As we shall see, Smith's solution to the problem of moral action in a corrupt society is not an entirely convincing one.

It is the tendency of people to identify more with wealth than with virtue which poses the greatest moral threat to society. Infatuation with wealth and indifference to the poor are, according to Smith, "the great and most universal cause of the corruption of our moral sentiments."[94] Since human beings are more inclined to sympathize with pleasure than with pain, most humans feel inclined to pursue riches. Wealth elicits admiration; and for this reason most individuals strive to emulate the rich.

Although reputed to be a proponent of economic individualism and the pursuit of personal wealth, Smith pours scorn on wealth and the wealthy. "Wealth and greatness are mere trinkets of frivolous utility," he writes; and those "in the superior stations of life" pursue that empty vanity, a "gaudy and glittering" life. In the circles of the rich and powerful, "flattery and falsehood too often prevail over merit and abilities."[95] Moreover, those of poor and middling rank who suffer and labour to attain the station of the rich can never achieve the happiness and security they desire. The poor man's son, Smith claims, through his whole life "pursues the idea of a certain and elegant repose which he may never arrive at." His headlong pursuit of wealth wastes his body "with toil and diseases." In "the languour of disease and the weariness of old age," the pleasures of the vain and empty distinctions of greatness disappear. He then sees power and riches in their true light, as "enormous and operose machines" which "threaten every moment to overwhelm the person that dwells in them."[96]

If we consider the satisfaction provided by objects of wealth in an "abstract and philosophical light" it inevitably appears "contemptible and trifling." But this is not the perspective of most individuals, easily seduced by the beauty, elegance, and order of the system which produces wealth—just as they are enamoured of the operation of a complex machine. When people contemplate the satisfaction provided by wealth, "we naturally confound it in our imagination with the order, the regular and harmonious movement of the system, the machine or economy by means of which it is produced."[97] The manner in which the imagination confounds the beauty of the system of wealth production with the satisfaction it provides serves a useful

social function. It is a classic case of an unintended social consequence of a propensity found in most individuals. Indeed, it is in this
context that Smith first uses the phrase "an invisible hand."
Nature deceives human beings by causing us to identify wealth
with happiness. But, Smith writes,

It is well that nature imposes upon us in this manner. It is this deception
which arouses and keeps in continual motion the industry of mankind. It is
this which first prompted them to cultivate the ground, to build houses, to
found cities and commonwealths, and to invent and improve all the sciences
and arts, which ennoble and embellish human life.[98]

Thus, this deception imposed by nature has beneficial consequences.
And these consequences are not restricted to the effects of industry
which produce prosperity, government, art, and science. Another
unintended consequence of the pursuit of personal wealth is that the
rich end up providing the means of subsistence necessary to the
poor, as we can see when we consider the case of a landlord who im-
proves his estate. It is impossible that the landlord should consume
the increased produce which results from his improvements. In fact,
his consumption can only marginally exceed that of "the meanest
peasant." The rest of his produce "he is obliged to distribute among
those who prepare, in the nicest manner, that little which he himself
makes use of." The result is a distribution of the national product
which is markedly beneficial to all members of society:

The produce of the soil maintains at all times nearly that number of inhabitants which it is capable of maintaining. The rich only select from the heap
what is most precious and agreeable. They consume little more than the
poor; and in spite of their natural selfishness and rapacity, . . . they divide
with the poor the produce of all their improvements. They are led by an
invisible hand to make nearly the same distribution of the necessaries of life
which would have been made had the earth been divided into equal portions
among all its inhabitants; and thus, without intending it, without knowing
it, advance the interest of the society.[99]

However much Smith may have been pleased with the social consequences of the pursuit of wealth, his *Theory of the Moral Sentiments*
had still not solved the problem of morality in a corrupt society. Certainly it is clear that Smith had little use for the habits and lifestyle of
the rich; he belittled their vanity and denounced their "natural selfishness and rapacity." Yet it would appear that Smith believed that
"men in the inferior and middling stations of life" learn habits of

economy, industry, frugality, and self-control in the course of their everyday affairs of business—habits which are conducive to moral behaviour.

The wise and firm individuals who are shaped by "the bustle and business of the world" learn the habits of self-command; they learn under all conditions to maintain their composure. Such individuals discover through experience that "real and solid professional abilities, joined to prudent, just, firm and temperate conduct, can very seldom fail to success." Not born into wealth, people of inferior or middling station learn that industry and frugality are applauded by all and they grow to appreciate a life of comfort and security. They disavow faction and intrigue but are ready to defend their country in time of need. The prudent individual learns that "pursuit of the objects of private interest" must be held within socially acceptable bounds, that it "ought to flow rather from a regard to the rules which prescribe such conduct, than from any passion for the objects themselves." These individuals of inferior and middling stations learn as well that their professional success "almost always depends upon the favour and good opinion of their neighbours and equals; and without a tolerable regular conduct, these can very seldom be obtained." Such individuals are generally respectable and law-abiding citizens. Their situation forces them to be so since, unlike the rich and powerful, they "can never be great enough to be above the law, which must generally overawe them into some sort of respect for, at least, the more important rules of justice." Unlike the rich, most individuals of inferior and middling rank learn the virtues of prudence, moderation, industry, frugality, and respect for the law through the experience of commercial life. They learn to govern their behaviour according to the rules of propriety necessary to commerce. This is all to the benefit of society; and, "fortunately for the good morals of society," people of these stations form "by far the greatest part of mankind." [100]

Smith clearly believed that beneficial social effects were produced by the economic activity of lower- and middle-class people (amongst whom he included at least the bulk of the landed gentry) in commercial society. Those of the inferior and middling sort developed the habits of industry and moderation which are vital to social stability. Yet Smith himself would willingly have conceded that such a society would not necessarily be a virtuous one. Industrious members of commercial society need merely observe those rules which are useful to the preservation of the social order; there is nothing in their daily business in the world which teaches them love and benevolence towards others. A commercial society might well adhere to the principle of utility while neglecting the more virtuous principle of benevolence:

Society may subsist among different men, as among different merchants, from a sense of its utility, without any mutual love or affection; and though no man in it should owe any obligation, or be bound in gratitude to any other, it may still be upheld by a mercenary exchange of good offices according to an agreed valuation.[101]

Although commercial life binds people together in a nexus of reciprocal need, this is not sufficient to maintain virtue. Smith did not consider that action on the basis of utility—in this case the usefulness of preserving the social bond—was the essence of virtue. In fact, he dismissed Hume's view that moral behaviour is a product of considerations of social utility. Smith agreed that what is socially useful is indeed pleasing; but the pleasure derived from useful objects and practices does not derive from reflection on their utility. Such a view would, he maintained, degrade our concept of virtue; it would involve judging virtuous action on the same basis as we judge a human contrivance like a chest of drawers.[102] Smith seems, in fact, to have been troubled by the idea that the considerations of utility which dominate the economic life of a commercial society might come also to dominate its political life. In addressing this problem, he clearly indicated the depth of his worries about the general social effects of commerce and the division of labour.

We have seen that people are inclined, according to Smith, to confound the beauty of a system of production with the satisfaction it provides. Our love of the system, order, and beauty of a form of wealth production causes us to attribute its qualities to the products themselves. We confound, in other words, the process with its results, the means with the ends. The same thing happens with respect to political institutions. "The same principle, the same love of system, the same regard to the beauty of order, of art and contrivance, frequently serves to recommend those institutions which tend to promote the public welfare."[103] Forms of government ought to be judged in terms of the extent to which they promote human happiness. Our love of system often causes us to admire "the political machine" as an end in itself. We marvel at "the connections and dependencies of its several parts, their mutual subordination to one another" and confound the order and harmony of its system with the result (human satisfaction) which it is designed to produce.[104]

This "spirit of system" is especially pernicious when it infiltrates the political realm. It produces "the man of system" who attempts to mold and shape social life and political institutions according to the beauty of an imaginary plan. The man of system "is so often enamoured with the supposed beauty of his own ideal plan of government, that he cannot suffer the smallest deviation from any part of it." He disregards the established norms of the community and erects "his own judgment into the supreme standard of right and wrong." He treats the members of society in purely instrumental terms—as parts of a grand scheme who can be manipulated according to plan much like the different pieces on a chessboard. The man of system, Smith writes,

> seems to imagine that he can arrange the different members of a great society with as much ease as the hand arranges the different pieces upon a chessboard; he does not consider that the pieces upon the chess-board have no other principle of motion besides that which the hand impresses upon them; but that, in the great chess-board of human society, every single piece has a principle of motion of its own, altogether different from that which the legislature might choose to impress upon it.

When the principle of motion imposed by the hand of government overrides the principle of motion which adheres to the invisible hand of social interaction, "the game will go on miserably, and society must be at all times in the highest degree of disorder."[105]

There seems little doubt that Smith was concerned that the spirit of system in a commercial society would direct politics. His basic reason was simple: he believed that the division of labour posed quite serious problems to maintaining shared moral sentiments and opinions. In all of his works, Smith held to the view that the habits, feelings, opinions, and beliefs of individuals are intimately connected to their social situation. People are not prisoners of their social situation, but they do react to different situations in ways which are shaped by those situations themselves. Situational reactions become habitual; they are the foundation upon which is erected a superstructure of beliefs and opinions.[106]

By fixing individuals in markedly different situations, the specialization which accompanies division of labour threatens to disrupt the moral fabric of society. If their situations become radically dissimilar, there is the danger that individuals will no longer share a common set of assumptions about moral conduct. This is especially a problem in terms of the class of industrial labourers. In *The Wealth of Nations* Smith argues that the debilitating and stupefying effects of the division of labour reduce the intellectual horizons of urban workers and render them incapable of comprehending their own interests or the general interest of society. This poses a serious problem for a theory which seeks to find a moral basis for government in the shared sentiments and opinions of citizens. This problem is exacerbated by the tendency of specialization to alienate government from society as a whole.

According to Smith, as division of labour becomes more complex, government becomes an increasingly specialized function. This specialization raises severe problems with respect to the moral foundation of government. For what guarantee is there that rulers and ruled will continue to share a common set of moral preferences? The division of labour which accompanies commercial society may well tend to make government less responsive to the moral sentiments of the ruled. Ralph Lindgren is one of the few commentators to have recognized the severity of this problem for Smith:

As political authority becomes institutionalized the activities and responsibilities of sovereign and subject become increasingly diverse . . . each begins to cultivate those habits and perspectives which are peculiarly suited to their separate functions. . . . Each acts from a "particular turn or habit" and that forecloses the very possibility of either being able to morally sympathize with the concrete practical situation of the other.[107]

It would seem that the best that a statesman can do in such a situation is to act on the basis of considerations of utility. In fact, Smith argues early in the *Moral Sentiments* that a moral judgement which refers to objects or actions which do not touch us, which we do not experience as affecting us, can be made only on the basis of utility. Where sympathy does not draw us into a situation, we have no other basis for judgement.[108] Needless to say, such a situation is especially troublesome when it characterizes the relationship between government and the governed. For when political judgements are made not on the basis of values but rather according to the purely aesthetic criterion of utility, then the machinery of government is treated as an end in itself, as an object of beauty, as a complex system approaching perfection, and not as a means to realize shared social goals. Inevitably, then, the spirit of system becomes the foundation of political relations.

Smith did not formulate this dilemma as clearly as we have expressed it. Yet it runs like a recurring theme through the pages of the *Moral Sentiments*. Furthermore, as his attention turned increasingly to problems of political economy, the evidence suggests that Smith grew ever more troubled by this problem. There is in the *Moral Sentiments*, however, the sketch of a solution to this problem of preserving the moral foundations of government in a commercial society. It is a solution which returns us to the notion of the "ideal spectator."

In developing his concepts of conscience and the ideal spectator, Smith sought to elevate virtue above public opinion. Indeed, as D. D. Raphael has shown, in successive editions of the *Moral Sentiments* Smith became more distrustful of the opinions which reigned in commercial society; he relied increasingly upon the imagination to direct the individual towards the correct course of action.[109] Smith believed, however, that only a select few were capable of rising above public opinion, of disregarding approval and praise, and of ordering their lives according to the moral ideals of conscience. Those individuals who accede to the realm of virtue necessarily abandon vanity and the desire to emulate the rich. In so doing, they reject the disposition to admire the rich and powerful, the disposition which constitutes "the great and most universal cause of the corruption of our moral sentiments." Such individuals acquire the respect of mankind "by the study of wisdom and the practice of virtue"; their character consists of "humble modesty and equitable justice." Smith does suggest that those who develop the characteristics of prudence may ascend to the life of virtue. But they can do so only by directing their industry to "greater and nobler purposes than the care of the health, the fortune, the rank, and the reputation of the individual." It is an inferior prudence which is preoccupied with such goals; "superior prudence" is directed to the advancement of the public good.[110] Unlike the rich and powerful, virtuous individuals are largely ignored by most members of society. The "real and steady admirers of wisdom and virtue" are, says Smith, "but a small party."[111] Nonetheless, such individuals, many of whom may be drawn from the ranks of the industrious middle class, can play a decisive role in political affairs.

It would appear that Smith looked to public-spirited action by individuals of virtue to preserve the moral integrity of government. "The man whose public spirit is prompted altogether by humanity and benevolence" will not attempt to impose an ideal system upon society. Instead, "he will accomodate, as well as he can, his public arrangements to the confirmed habits and prejudices of the people." Unlike the man of system who takes his personal views as the standard of right and wrong, the virtuous man respects the sentiments and opinions prevailing within the community; he will attempt to introduce only those reforms which the people can be brought to accept. Thus, "like Solon, when he cannot establish the best system of laws, he will endeavour to establish the best that the people can bear."[112]

With this argument, Smith shifts the whole direction of his discourse. With respect to the problem of corruption and commercial society, his work on moral philosophy now opens onto the vistas of political philosophy. He shows commercial society to be characterized by the absence of virtue. Nevertheless, such a society may preserve itself "as among different merchants, from a sense of its utility, without any mutual love or affection." Benevolence is not a necessary condition of society—admirable though it may be. In fact, Smith states that benevolence "is less essential to the existence of society than justice." Benevolence is, of course, a beautiful virtue; but "it is the ornament which embellishes, not the foundation which supports the building." Justice, however, is not optional; without its maintenance society "must in a moment crumble into atoms." Justice "is the main pillar that upholds the whole edifice" of society.[113]

If the correct rules of justice are to prevail, the legislator must be capable of rising above the considerations of utility which dominate the day-to-day practice of individuals in commercial society. He must reject the identification of wealth with happiness and the tendency to admire the complex and elegant system of the political machine more than the ends it is designed to produce. The statesman must, in other words, rise above the daily practices and sentiments which characterize a commercial society. In this respect, Smith shared aspects of the civic humanist perspective as expressed by Francis Hutcheson and Adam Ferguson—particularly the view that, however beneficial commercial society might be from a purely economic point of view, it is necessary to insulate the political sphere against the spirit of commerce. On this score, then, Smith was decidedly less optimistic than Hume about the link between commerce and civilization. As we shall see in the next chapter, *The Wealth of Nations*, Smith's "very violent attack . . . upon the whole commercial system of Great Britain," as he described his treatise, was precisely an attempt to free British politics—and especially its commercial regulations—from those groups most infected with the defects of the spirit of commerce: merchants and manufacturers. Smith's moral theory thus took him to the threshold of a program of political reform, a program addressed to virtuous individuals of public spirit who might be the vessels of moral and political reform. Before turning to look at the program advanced in *The Wealth of Nations*, we must first examine the general principles of Smith's political philosophy.

"SCIENTIFIC WHIGGISM": SMITH'S POLITICAL PHILOSOPHY

Smith's political philosophy was designed in part to address the tension between commerce and virtue which permeated his moral theory. Smith in fact considered moral philosophy in its classical sense to embrace many of the issues of political philosophy or, as he preferred it, "jurisprudence." Thus, in *The Wealth of Nations* he approvingly describes the object of ancient moral philosophy as the study of "wherein consisted the happiness and perfection of a man, considered not only as an individual, but as the member of a family, of a state, and of the great society of mankind."[114] Consequently, Smith's transfer of the problem of commerce and virtue from a strictly moral problem to a generally political one was not a move from one framework to another but rather a shift within a broad framework of analysis which embraced both moral theory and jurisprudence.

In Smith's view, admiration of wealth has two important effects. First, it inspires people to industry and in so doing increases national wealth and provides employment and income for the poor. Second, it binds individuals together in a nexus of interdependence in which they discover that economic exchange requires the observance of specific norms. The benefits of commerce, however, are not unmixed. The social bond which prevails in a commercial society is one characterized by utility, not benevolence; its members need one another, but they do not necessarily act from considerations of the public interest. While the principle of utility is adequate to the smooth functioning of the economy, it is not adequate to the practice of government. Indeed, considerations of utility distort government when the "system" or "machine" of administration comes to be admired as an end in itself, rather than as a means to the happiness of its citizens. For this reason, government should be based on an entirely different principle from that which dominates commercial relations. That principle is benevolence—the public-spirited concern for the social good.

It is the responsibility of individuals of wisdom and prudence to shed light on the moral and political principles that should guide government. In fact, the only guarantee that commercial relations will not shred the moral fabric of society is the creation of an institutional framework which sets bounds upon their self-interested action. Though the maintenance of society does not require that its members behave benevolently towards one another, it does require justice, "the main pillar that upholds the whole edifice" of society. And justice can be the creation only of those wise and prudent leaders who have risen above concern with public opinion and who, striving to be praiseworthy, elaborate those laws and policies which are "the best that the people can bear."

The constitution and preservation of the moral basis of society is a political task—the construction of the institutional framework that members of commercial society will be forced to acknowledge should they desire, as do all, success and the esteem of their fellows. For these reasons, Smith considered jurisprudence to be the most important aspect of moral philosophy. As he wrote in the *Moral Sentiments,* natural jurisprudence is "of all sciences by far the most important," and he maintained that the principles of this science "ought to run through, and be the foundation of, the laws of all nations." [115] Smith's jurisprudence, like his moral philosophy, took shape through a dialogue with the philosophies of Hutcheson and Hume. The final product was in each case unique. But reflection on its Hutchesonian and Humean ingredients is critical to its full understanding.

Hutcheson was probably the greatest mid-eighteenth-century representative of the radical Whig or Commonwealth tradition in British political thought. The Commonwealth tradition arose during the Tudor period as part of a theoretical response to the manifold social and economic changes that were disrupting the traditional patterns of English life. The notion embodied a just social order whose protection was the responsibility of the king and his advisers. During the middle of the sixteenth century a number of theorists associated with the protectorate of Somerset used the expression "commonweal" or "commonwealth" to denote both the body politic and the general good.[116] These social reformers known as commonwealthmen believed that it was the role of the Crown to preserve justice (especially in the treatment of the poor) in the face of the changes sweeping English life. As we have shown in chapter 2, their writings often focused on economic problems; in particular they addressed the issues of enclosure, inflation, and unemployment.

The Commonwealth reformers believed that economic individualism threatened the social order and that the pursuit of private interest would result in corruption and political decline. Holding that the social order derived from maintaining civic virtues in the body politic, they advanced a program of moral and political reform centred on educating the king and the nobility in the principles of a learned and virtuous life. Their role as philosophers was thus to be advisers to the court who would oversee the moral reform of the aristocracy.[117] The commonwealthmen also advanced a definite set of political views. They held that maintenance of civic virtues required strengthening of the agricultural basis of the kingdom (to offset the growing power and influence of "moneyed interests"), participation of independent landed gentlemen in the affairs of state, and preservation of a political order in which the king ruled through Parliament. Their political theory was distinctly *anti-absolutist;* they rediscovered the classical notion of the mixed constitution in which elements of monarchy, aristocracy, and democracy were combined in a balanced unity.

In the face of the dramatic reshaping of the social and economic order of Tudor England, the Commonwealth perspective could have led to a backward-looking opposition to commercial and industrial development and to a romanticizing of agriculture and the old feudal order. As we have seen in chapter 2, however, this was not the case with the most important of the Commonwealth writings, Sir Thomas Smith's *Discourse of the Commonweal of This Realm of England.* Smith advocated free trade in corn to resolve the economic problems facing peasants and farmers. Moreover, he understood that a stable commonwealth could be maintained only if the statesmen, rather than resisting economic individualism, directed economic self-interest into socially desirable channels. The *Discourse* thereby combined the idea of a just republic with that of a state founded upon the self-interested activity of individuals, in a framework established by wise rulers. From this orientation, the most important writings in the Commonwealth perspective brought together a traditional concept of the just social order with an economic individualist conception of its members.

During the century prior to 1640 important sections of the English gentry and aristocracy came to see the Commonwealth in terms of a civil society in which individuals were free to pursue their economic well-being so long as they adhered to the laws instituted in the public interest by the king in consultation with virtuous landed gentlemen (who were increasingly to be found in the House of Commons). In the course of the Civil War, when these prosperous and improving gentlemen found their acquired rights and privileges challenged by the Crown, this outlook took on a more radical character. The central figure in the radicalization of the Commonwealth doctrine was James Harrington.

Harrington wrote as an English exponent of the classical civic tradition. In his view, a just and stable commonwealth would have to be based on husbandmen ruled over by a landed gentry. The rule of the gentry, however, would be subject to an elaborate scheme of democratic regulation. Harrington believed a commonwealth based on husbandry to be "the least subject to innovation or turbulency" because it would be based on a stable asset, land, as opposed to an unstable one, money. Furthermore, he believed that so long as an agrarian law prevented excessive social differentiation, the nobility and gentry would be "the very life and soul" of a "popular government." The nobility and gentry were not, however, to exercise arbitrary power. Rather, they were to administer the rule of law. It was the "empire" of laws which assured liberty; and the most important laws were those which preserved the property of the individual. Finally, Harrington modeled the revenue of the state on the rent of the landowner—a notion which was to be of great importance to the development of British political economy.[118] In Harrington's hands, then, the Commonwealth tradition became one in which civic virtue would depend upon a "popular" distribution of land, one in which the ideal commonwealth would be based upon the rule of law administered by landed gentlemen, conforming to various popular regulations.

A definite Harringtonian perspective can be detected in many writings of the social Baconians of the seventeenth century. In fact, Harrington had an important influence upon those figures who connect Sir William Petty to Adam Smith. Petty was a friend and associate of Harrington's; he is considered to have maintained the Harringtonian tradition of political argument during the Restoration period.[119] In the writings of John Locke (especially his economic works), and in the speeches and pamphlets of his mentor, the first earl of Shaftesbury, we also find neo-Harringtonian themes concerning the priority of landed wealth and the claim that the general interest of the nation is founded on the self-interest of the landowner.[120]

A Commonwealth perspective derived from Harrington informed the basic political outlook of the Country party and the Real Whig opposition movements of the closing years of the seventeenth century and the bulk of the eighteenth century. The notion of a country opposition to the Crown originated in the 1620s; by the 1640s the House of Commons generally expressed the view that independent gentlemen had a duty to represent the interest of the country against the corrupt clique dominating the court of Charles I.[121] Between 1640 and 1660, the landed class divided over the question of whether the greater threat to the rights and liberties of men of property stemmed from the tyrannizing tendencies of the court or the levelling impulses of the people. After the restoration of monarchy and House of Lords in 1660, however, country attitudes became associated with the Whig agitation of the 1670s and 1680s when Shaftesbury, Algernon Sidney, and others drew on the armoury of classical republicanism to mobilize opposition against a court allegedly intent on introducing popery and slavery by corrupting the House of Commons and invading the rights and liberties of English subjects. Both Shaftesbury and Sidney held to a decidedly less democratic and more aristocratic variant of republicanism than had Harrington. Shaftesbury made the doctrine less radical yet by wedding to the Harringtonian preoccupation with a natural aristocracy of landed gentlemen the notion of an ancient or Gothick constitution which had been sharply criticized by Harrington.[122]

Although the Glorious Revolution of 1688–1689 appeared to vindicate radical Whig principles of popular sovereignty over Tory notions about the divine right of kings, the reality was more complex. Moderate Whigs were anxious to dissociate themselves from any democratic or levelling tendencies; the ascent to the throne of Anne (herself a Stuart) in 1702 created the space for an aggressive Tory revival which attacked all notions of popular sovereignty and condemned Protestant dissent.[123] Fears about corruption, absolutism, and a possible Catholic succession to the throne fueled a resurgence of radical Whiggism, which linked itself explicitly to Harringtonian principles and the Commonwealth tradition of the mid-seventeenth century.

In 1697 Andrew Fletcher's *Discourse on Government* appeared, stating the case for restoring the Gothick balance described in largely Harringtonian terms as a republic of freeholders. That same year two "independent Whigs," John Trenchard and Walter Moyle, issued *An Argument, Shewing, that a Standing Army is inconsistent with a Free Government.* That year also saw the publication of Milton's *Works.* In 1698 both Fletcher and Trenchard brought out further works; the Civil War *Memoirs* of the Republican Edmund Ludlow were published, as were the *Discourses concerning Government* of the Great Whig martyr Algernon Sidney. The following year John Toland brought out the first collected edition of Harrington's political works. Central to this whole body of writing—which constituted a political argument of some force—were the views that English liberty was imperilled, that the constitution remained biased in favour of the Crown and against Parliament, that the increase in the number of "placemen" (those who accepted an office from the Crown) in the House of Commons threatened its independence, and that maintenance of a standing army in peacetime was an instrument for the introduction of absolutism and the destruction of free government.

These "True Whigs" rejected the notion of the absolute right of kings; they believed that the authority of the king was limited by the powers of Parliament; and they held that all subjects possessed inalienable rights—of life, liberty, and property—which were embodied in the tradition of English law. Classical Whigs were neither republicans nor democrats. They believed in a constitutional monarchy just as they opposed any notion of full political rights (in contrast to legal rights) for the propertyless and the poor. They believed that the exercise of political power should rest with those persons of substance who were the natural leaders of the commonwealth.

When moderate Whiggism secured its hold on power with the accession of the Hanoverian prince in 1714, "Court Whigs" increasingly came to emphasize the more conservative, traditional, and

undemocratic elements of Whig ideology. The Court Whigs emphasized fear of the poor (the "mob" or the "rabble") and argued that
only increased powers to the Crown could counter the enemies of the
constitution (all of whom they tended to label "Jacobites"). To this
end they passed the Septennial Act in 1716 to prevent frequent elections from making the House of Commons too receptive to public
opinion. The Court Whigs also favoured curbing the powers of the
Commons as a way of shoring up the stabilizing powers of the Crown.
For this reason they even defended the practice, commonly identified as a form of corruption, of allowing the king to grant a place or a
pension to an individual.

Opponents of the establishment Whiggism of the Court party
turned to the armoury of Commonwealth thought for their ideological weapons in constructing a Country party. The Country party,
which came ultimately to embrace radical Whigs and reconstructed
"Tories" who accepted the principles of the Whig settlement of
1688, attempted to mobilize country gentlemen in a crusade to defend civic virtues and the constitutional order. The Country party
advanced the view that tyranny could be avoided only by excluding
officeholders or "placemen" from the House of Commons, by guar-
anteeing frequent elections to Parliament, and by ensuring that in-
corruptible, independent landed gentlemen were able to exercise
sufficient power to curb the infringements of government upon the
liberties of men of property. Country ideology saw political power as
rooted in landed property and civic virtue as dependent upon possession of sufficient land to render individuals truly independent. The
Country interest advocated cheap and honest government, opposed
the creation of a standing army, and often supported increased property qualifications for members of Parliament as a way of keeping dependent and corruptible elements out of the Commons.[124]

The most eloquent defence of the Country Whig perspective came
from the third earl of Shaftesbury and his Irish disciples.[125] The
members of Shaftesbury's circle, whose central figure was Robert
Molesworth, considered themselves "Old Whigs" and vigorously
advanced an aristocratic Harringtonianism. A definite tension
existed within the body of Old Whig thought. Defence of the principles of an agrarian commonwealth ruled by virtuous landed men
took both conservative and radical forms. Thus, Andrew Fletcher,
who combined traditional humanism and Scottish nationalism with

an acceptance of economic progress, was associated with the Molesworth circle, as was a radical Harringtonian like Walter Moyle, who emphasized equality, democracy, and the need for an agrarian law. In important respects, attitudes towards commerce were central to these differences. All the "High Whigs," as Shaftesbury described his group, distrusted the influence of merchants in political affairs. Many of them, however, believed that the expansion of trade was economically and socially useful. Shaftesbury himself favoured free trade and opposed protectionism.

Such Country ideologists were concerned about the effect of commerce on morality, virtue, and the social order at the same time as they recognized its indispensability to economic prosperity and military power. Their solution was to let commerce expand while leaving political power in the hands of a natural aristocracy of landed gentlemen and using public education to instill civic values in the people.[126] In this way, the Country outlook—or at least its most sophisticated version—accepted the necessity of commercial development while retaining the commonwealth bias in favour of grounding the state in the landed interest. This strain of Old Whiggery, which supported the development of commerce within the framework of a state based on the landed interest, is to be found in the writings of Francis Hutcheson, who, as we have indicated above, was also closely associated with the Shaftesbury circle.

Molesworth was a good friend of Hutcheson's and immersed the latter in the theories of Milton, Harrington, and Locke. Probably the strongest influence on Hutcheson came from the writings of Harrington. Locke, too, figured as a major influence on Hutcheson's thought, although it is important to recognize that the Scottish philosophers interpreted Locke as an advocate of agricultural society on the classical republican model, not as a spokesman for commercial society.[127] Hutcheson strongly endorsed Harrington's view of the relationship between property and government. Moreover, he supported the latter's notion of an agrarian law which would limit excessive accumulation of property by the rich. Hutcheson further endorsed Harrington's positions on a popular assembly and a senate which proposed legislation (that is, a purely consultative body), both based on a system of rotation. He was also one of the strongest eighteenth-century defenders of the right of resistance; he believed that tyranny was largely a result of the fact that men had generally been too tame. Hutcheson held the view that everyone—including the poor, women, and children—had certain natural rights which should not be violated. He similarly supported a high degree of religious freedom.

While holding to these positions, Hutcheson adopted a "progressive" perspective on commerce. He saw the division of labour as an important form of social cooperation; he supported international trade as a means of breaking down national rivalries; he saw plentiful consumption as a stimulant to industry; and he supported the removal of most—but not all—mercantilist restrictions on trade.[128] Yet it must be noted that for Hutcheson, as for most of the Scottish philosophers, commercial progress was rooted in agricultural improvement. In this respect, he reflected the "improving spirit" of the period. For example, he urged the rich to forego wasteful consumption in favour of investment in "clearing forests, draining marshes, maintaining foreign commerce, making harbours, fortifying cities, cultivating manufactures and ingenious arts, and encouraging the artizans [*sic*]."[129]

It is significant that agricultural clearing and improvement figure so prominently on Hutcheson's list. But this is entirely consistent with his vision of a commercialized agricultural society, as with his view that political power should rest not with the few in the high aristocracy, nor with the propertyless poor, but rather with the sober, moderate, and progressive gentry.[130] What Hutcheson transmitted to his students, therefore, was a radical Whig outlook which stressed natural liberty, the right of resistance, the rule of law, the virtues of moral and economic improvement, and the need for a public-spirited gentry to direct the body politic.

In some important respects, Adam Smith's political philosophy may be seen as an elaboration of that of Hutcheson—albeit an elaboration of a highly original character, one which involved significant modification of his predecessor's outlook. There is much truth to Rae's remark about Smith that "if he was any man's disciple, he was Hutcheson's."[131] Particularly in his *Lectures on Jurisprudence*, Smith advanced arguments which were derived largely from the classical Whig tradition. Yet Smith tended to adopt a much more cautious, detached, and at times sceptical attitude to Whig orthodoxy than did Hutcheson. Here the influence of Hume played a decisive role.

In his political writings, Hume inclined to a moderate Whig ap-

proach which rejected the theoretical basis of classical Whig orthodoxy. He rejected the notion of government deriving from an original contract among the people, seeing it instead as a product of
opinion and the habit of obedience; he dismissed as little better than
myth the Whig fetish of the ancient constitution as a bastion of English liberties; he refused to accept that the Stuart kings were no
more than wicked; he mistrusted the use made of the doctrine of
a natural right of resistance; he dismissed the idea that civilized
monarchies like the French were tyrannies; and he defended the
Crown's use of 'corruption' as a necessary to prevent Britain from
becoming a republic.[132] At the same time, his support for a citizen
militia, his diatribe against the deleterious effect of the public debt
on the traditional ruling class, and the landed and republican bias of
his model for a "perfect commonwealth" indicate that his approach
involved an attempt to balance Court Whig with Country principles.

Smith shared many of Hume's criticisms of classical Whiggism; at
the same time he was decidedly less optimistic about the progress of
commercial society than was his friend. Smith's politics represent a
continuation of that project undertaken by the most sophisticated of
the commonwealth theorists: to find a means of preserving a body
politic resting on universal principles of justice within a commercial
society characterized by extensive division of labour and individual
pursuit of economic self-interest.

In explaining the origin of government, Smith followed Hume in
arguing that government was the product not of a contract but of the
emergence of property. Government, he wrote, "arose, not as some
writers imagine from any consent or agreement . . . but from the
natural progress which men make in society."[133] This natural progress represents the transition from rude and barbarous conditions to
those characterized by relations of private property. Property in turn
requires government; the form of government shapes the prevailing
form of property.[134] Government is thus an institution designed primarily to preserve inequality of property and to protect the property
of the rich from the incursions of the poor.[135]

Government is not, however, simply an instrument of oppression.
Because of the admiration which the rich naturally inspire, they
come to acquire authority in society. To them, then, is entrusted the
management of the affairs of state. In fact, in his *Lectures on Jurisprudence* Smith referred his listeners to the *Moral Sentiments* for an

explanation of the psychological principle which induces people to confer authority upon the rich. Elsewhere in the *Lectures*, Smith referred to the inequality of property as a "usefull inequality" since the enjoyment of wealth by the leading members of society would spur the poor to industry, in an effort to emulate them.[136]

The crucial function of government for Smith, as for Hume, is to establish a juridical framework which guarantees liberty of life and property. The great achievement of the English constitution is that it enshrines these rights—an achievement rooted in a unique path of historical development. Following the Union with Scotland, no foreign invasion was to be feared as the "dominions were then surrounded by the sea." As a result, Britain had no need to maintain a standing army; without a standing army the sovereign was obliged to call Parliament to procure revenues. Parliament in turn demanded numerous concessions in return for granting taxes. In this way, liberty of speech and the necessity for parliamentary consent to taxes were established. Parallel with this development was the ascent of the House of Commons above the House of Lords. Thus was established a "system of liberty" rooted in fundamental rights such as habeas corpus and in guarantees of frequent parliaments and an independent judiciary. This unique process of historical development resulted in a "mixed constitution" in which sovereign power was lodged "in the king and Parliament together"; it was "a happy mixture of all the different forms of government properly restrained and a perfect security to liberty and property."[137]

Smith's praise for the liberties provided by the English constitution is entirely in the mainstream of the Whig tradition. We should not be surprised to find, therefore, that he defended the right of resistance to arbitrary authority and treated the Glorious Revolution as a legitimate exercise of that right.[138]

Smith's *Lectures on Jurisprudence* provide some evidence of his influence by the classical Whig perspective. But it is in *The Wealth of Nations* that we find the clearest expression of his absorption of a series of Radical Whig or Country concerns which manifest themselves in a decidedly agricultural bias, hostility to merchants, and defence of the view that government should be based upon a natural aristocracy of landed gentlemen. In *The Wealth of Nations* Smith puts forward the view that merchants and manufacturers are not fit to rule within the body politic. Like the ideologists of the Country interest,

Smith held that a merchant's possession of movable wealth makes him an unreliable citizen:

A merchant, it has been said very properly, is not necessarily the citizen of any particular country. It is in great measure indifferent to him from what place he carries on his trade.

And he argued with respect to the wealth of a merchant that "no part of it can be said to belong to any particular country, til it has been spread as it were over the face of that country, either in buildings, or in the lasting improvement of lands."[139] Smith repeated the point by way of contrast between landed and movable wealth in Book 5 of *The Wealth of Nations:*

The proprietor of land is necessarily a citizen of the particular country in which his estate lies. The proprietor of stock is properly a citizen of the world, and is not necessarily attached to any particular country.[140]

The stability of society resides in the landed interest. Furthermore, only those who live independently on the land—"country gentlemen and farmers"—are free from "the wretched spirit of monopoly."[141] Smith did not, however, favour rule by an hereditary nobility. Rather, in true Commonwealth fashion, he advocated the direction of political affairs by a natural aristocracy of the country, those prosperous, improving country gentlemen who embody the civic habits (and the class interests) necessary to political stability. Indeed, he argued that a standing army was no threat to liberty if it was commanded by "the principal nobility and gentry of the country."[142] Smith further argued:

Upon the power which the greater part of the leading men, the natural aristocracy of every country, have of preserving or defending their respective importance, depends the stability and duration of every system of free government.[143]

Smith was quite willing to accept that men who had made their fortunes in commerce should make up part of the natural aristocracy, although he would appear to have believed that they should move part of their fortunes into landed investment. Smith believed that such individuals in fact made the best landowners. Thus, he favoured the "commercialization" of agriculture and the investment of commercial wealth in land:

When land is in commerce and frequently changes hands it is most likely to be well managed; those who have raised a fortune by trade or otherwise have generally more money besides what they lay out. They are generally also men of scheme and project, so that they for the most part have both the desire and the ability of improving.[144]

Consistent with this view, Smith favoured elimination of primogeniture and all entails upon land and supported long leases which would provide the tenant farmer with the security to undertake the investments crucial to improvement. Smith favoured, in other words, an agrarian capitalist arrangement in which prosperous landowners made the investments necessary to improve the estates which they leased to wealthy farmers; these, in turn, could be expected to make a reasonable profit on their annual investments. This social arrangement has political as well as economic implications since Smith "pinned what hopes he had for the survival of a free society upon the intelligent and commercially-minded gentry."[145] We shall pursue these points at more length in the next chapter. For our present purposes, what most matters is to recognize that while Smith saw certain important advantages to commercial society—particularly its generation of material security and independence for a large section of society (a point to which we shall return)—he did not conclude from this that merchants and manufacturers should take over the reins of political power. On the contrary, he saw landed wealth as the foundation of the public interest and country gentlemen as most suited to participate in political affairs. In this sense—and it is not an insignificant one—he shared many of the concerns of the Country or Real Whigs. Nevertheless, he believed that commerce had played a vital role in fostering social and economic progress in England, among other nations, and that the social relations characteristic of commercial society were a vast improvement on feudalism. Thus in Book 3 of *The Wealth of Nations*, he argued that the expansion of commerce and the attendant growth of manufacture had "gradually introduced order and good government, and with them the liberty and security of individuals" throughout much of Europe. And he credited Hume with being "the only writer" to have taken note of this process.[146]

After the fall of the Roman empire, Smith maintained, anarchy and despotism characterized the basic relations of society. Towns, however, managed—usually by charter from the Crown—to carve out small oases of liberty in the midst of feudal despotism. Over time, "order and good government" came to prevail in the towns even though rural dwellers were constantly "exposed to every sort of violence." [147] Towns were also the centres of commerce and industry. Slowly and imperceptibly, the commercial and industrial wealth which accumulated in the towns came to undermine the feudal relations which prevailed in the countryside. The basic causes of the decline of feudalism were economic. First, the towns encouraged agricultural improvement by providing a market for agricultural goods. Second, some merchants bought land and applied their habits of order and economy to improvement. Third, the penetration of trade and manufacture in the countryside "gradually introduced order and good government." [148]

As significant as these three processes were, the most important effect of commerce was that it undermined the very basis of feudalism, the dependence of peasants upon their lords. Under classical feudalism, claimed Smith, lords could not possibly consume the total surplus product of the land. As a result, they shared their surplus—usually in the form of rent in kind—with their tenants and retainers. However, the expansion of foreign trade changed all this. Suddenly, lords could exchange their surplus product for foreign luxury goods. Driven by vanity, they released their dependents so as to acquire countless precious objects. In so doing, they undermined the economic basis of their authority over others.

This process had an important economic effect as well as an important political one. Economically, the process improved the land by bringing about the dismissal of "the unnecessary part of the tenants" and the consolidation of lands into large farms which came to be worked by "independent" tenant farmers, who hired the number of labourers strictly necessary for production. Politically, the decline in the authority of feudal lords meant that "they became as insignificant as any substantial burgher or tradesman in a city." Consequently, "the great proprietors were no longer capable of interrupting the regular execution of justice," and a "regular government" was introduced in the countryside. [149]

It is important to recognize that in praising the effects of commercial growth upon the feudal order, Smith was not attributing the progress of liberty to the conscious action of men of commerce and industry. On the contrary, Smith's account of the decline of feudalism is a paradigmatic case of his doctrine of the unintended social consequences of individual action. Neither lords nor merchants set out to transform society. Yet this was precisely the net effect of their actions:

A revolution of the greatest importance to the publick happiness, was in this manner brought about by two different orders of people, who had not the least intention to serve the publick. To gratify the most childish vanity was the sole motive of the great proprietors. The merchants and artificers, much less ridiculous, acted merely from a view to their own interest, and in pursuit of their own pedlar principle of turning a penny wherever a penny was to be got. Neither of them had either knowledge or foresight of that great revolution which the folly of the one, and the industry of the other, was gradually bringing about.[150]

Smith's argument has frequently been interpreted as implying that under all conditions the commercial activities of men will ultimately overturn the ill effects of a violent and unnatural political constitution. Certainly there are times when Smith appeared to say precisely this sort of thing.[151] Yet the general thrust of Smith's argument indicates that such "economic determinism" was foreign to him; if anything, Smith would appear to have assigned a determining role to political institutions. Thus, discussing the relative poverty of Spain and Portugal, he wrote that "the civil and ecclesiastical governments of both Spain and Portugal, are such as would alone be sufficient to perpetuate their present state of poverty, even though their regulations of commerce were as wise as the greater part of them are absurd and foolish."[152] Likewise, analysing China's alleged "stationary" state, he maintained that though that nation "had possibly long ago acquired that full complement of riches which is consistent with the nature of its laws and institutions," he suggested that "this complement may be much inferior to what, with other laws and institutions, the nature of its soil, climate, and situation might admit of."[153]

From this perspective it follows that the link between commercial progress and progress of liberty presupposes certain institutional arrangements which are conducive to the protection of the life, liberty, and property of the individual. Without such institutional arrangements "the universal, continual and uninterrupted effort" of human beings to better their condition will be thwarted by conditions of personal insecurity. True, Smith held that people's efforts to better their condition had overcome political obstructions and carried England "towards opulence and improvement," but he also held that this had occurred because their striving had been "protected by law and allowed by liberty to exert itself in the manner that is most advantageous." [154]

In elaborating the nature of the institutional arrangements necessary for political liberty, Smith revealed the degree to which his Whiggism was scientific rather than vulgar. Orthodox Whiggism maintained that Britain was uniquely "free." All other peoples were oppressed, to greater or lesser degrees, by arbitrary authority. Only the peculiar historical evolution of England towards constitutional monarchy had brought liberties to the people of Great Britain. Smith followed Montesquieu and Hume in asserting that an absolute monarchy could also realize the true ends of government, forming "a government of laws, not men." For Montesquieu, Hume, and Smith, "political liberty" could exist in a state which was not "free," in the sense of a government based on participation of the natural aristocracy in the affairs of state and the separation of legislative and executive powers. [155] Critical to Smith's notion of liberty, moreover, was a regime of justice which protected property rights. On this argument, then, for Smith France would have qualified as a state based on liberty. In fact, in Book 5 of *The Wealth of Nations*, Smith asserted that France "is certainly the greatest empire in Europe which, after that of Great Britain, enjoys the mildest and most indulgent government." [156] This is an especially un-Whiggish position; orthodox Whiggism depicted France as an arbitrary and despotic state. By maintaining that France, too, enjoyed a régime of liberty, Smith implied that the progress of commerce could carry that nation to a condition of opulence.

There can be little doubt that Smith's positive, albeit highly qualified, attitude towards commerce had important roots in the tradition of natural jurisprudence, which emphasized the conditions of the regular administration of justice rather than the achievement of civic virtue. Smith was decidedly pessimistic about the capacity for public virtue in commercial society. But he believed that commercial society could be organized in such a way as to bind men together in a system of sympathetic communication in which they would respect the principles of justice. Moreover, commercial society had the important advantage that it provided a decent level of subsistence for "the sober and industrious poor." And for Smith there was much to be said for such a result, since "no society can surely be happy or flourishing, of which the greater part are poor and miserable."[157] Thus, if civic virtue was not possible on any significant scale in commercial society, justice and opulence certainly were (although commercial society by no means guaranteed them).[158] Furthermore, as I have indicated, Smith did believe that a natural aristocracy dedicated to prudence could be developed—particularly from the ranks of the progressive gentry. Indeed, Smith's project in *The Wealth of Nations* must in large measure be seen as scientific counsel addressed to those who would heed the call of wisdom and benevolence.

Smith saw his task as contributing to "the science of the legislator, whose deliberations ought to be governed by general principles which are always the same." Moreover, he defined political economy as "a branch of the science of a statesman or legislator."[159] Thus, *The Wealth of Nations* can best be seen as a piece of scientific counsel addressed to the legislator, the "prudent lawgiver," who attempts, like Solon, to frame the best laws that the people will accept, which in this case means it is addressed to the natural aristocracy who should rightfully possess legislative power. As we shall see in the next chapter, this scientific counsel was constructed as a response to the tension between commerce and virtue—a response which favoured an agrarian capitalist commonwealth based upon the civic activism of a natural aristocracy of country gentlemen.

CHAPTER FIVE

Agrarian Capitalism and *The Wealth of Nations*

All interpretations of Adam Smith's social theory must come to terms with his great classic, *The Wealth of Nations*. Significant as the *Theory of the Moral Sentiments* or the *Lectures on Jurisprudence* may be, Smith's reputation rests upon his treatise on political economy. That work, as we have indicated at the opening of the previous chapter, is generally taken to offer extended praise for the division of labour, commercial expansion, and the accumulation of capital. It is perfectly true that *The Wealth of Nations* does advance such praise. But this praise is linked to a plea for the formulation of policies and the establishment of an institutional framework which will ensure that no one abuse the economic process or distort economic relations so as to profit at the expense of the community. Contrary to the widespread view that *The Wealth of Nations* represented the definitive break of positive from normative economics, of economic science from ethics, we shall demonstrate that *The Wealth of Nations* was constructed on normative foundations, that it offered a sustained critique of those policies which had served the narrow interests of merchants and manufacturers, that it advanced a stirring plea for a new set of policies which would ensure that commercial activity served the general interest, and that it conceived of an agrarian capitalist commonwealth as the social foundation of a modern system of liberty and justice.

In setting out this argument, we shall pursue two main lines of argument. First, we shall demonstrate that *The Wealth of Nations* is steeped in the ethical theory of the *Moral Sentiments* and cannot properly be understood outside that context.[1] In particular, we shall show that Smith's theory of value is constructed on moral foundations; that it is designed to specify those conditions in which all goods exchange at their "natural price" and, therefore, in which distributive justice is preserved (that is, in which no economic agent can distort market processes in a fashion detrimental to society as a whole or any of its members). To this end, Smith denounced the monopolizing tendencies of merchants and manufacturers—tendencies which distort the natural laws of the market—and argued for conditions of "perfect liberty," to ensure that market competition would prevent these capitalist groups from exploiting the economics of imperfect competition to discriminate against labourers, farmers, and landlords.

The second line of argument which we shall pursue in this chapter concerns the agricultural model central to the theoretical structure of *The Wealth of Nations*. We shall show not only that Smith preferred the habits and practices of those social classes associated with agriculture but also that he considered agriculture to be the most productive economic sector, whose development was essential to balanced economic growth. Moreover, a careful analysis of Smith's theory of growth and accumulation demonstrates that he inherited his concepts of capital and growth from the Physiocrats and that his general model of capital accumulation makes sense only on the basis of an agricultural model of the economy. As this last point is especially controversial, we shall develop it at some length in probing the agrarian capitalist basis of Smith's theoretical economics. We shall conclude by discussing the vital role of the state in shaping the agrarian capitalist order of society.

THE SOCIAL PSYCHOLOGY OF COMMERCE

The Wealth of Nations opens with Smith's rapture for the division of labour. Schumpeter wrote that "nobody, either before or after A. Smith, ever thought of putting such a burden upon division of labour. With A. Smith it is practically the only factor in economic progress."[2] That Smith believed the division of labour and its extension were crucial to the increase of national wealth is indisputable. What is generally neglected by commentators, however, is the fact that the division of labour had more than an economic significance for Smith; it had a profound social significance as well. In fact, chap-

ter 2 of Book 1 of *The Wealth of Nations,* entitled "Of the principle
which gives occasion to the Division of Labour," establishes a definite connection between Smith's concept of division of labour and
his theory of language and communication discussed in our previous
chapter.

The division of labour, Smith claims in the opening paragraph of
this chapter, is a consequence of "the propensity to truck, barter,
and exchange one thing for another." This well-known statement
has often been taken as proof that Smith treated market activity as
essential to human relationships (which he unquestionably did).
However, most commentators have ignored the interesting paragraph
which follows this statement. There Smith states that his present
work cannot attempt to determine whether this propensity derives
from human nature "or whether, as seems more probable, it be the
necessary consequence of the faculties of reason and speech." Yet,
Smith cannot resist saying something more on the subject—something which elaborates on the "probable" view that the propensity
for exchange arises from the faculties of reason and speech. This propensity, he writes, "is common to all men, and to be found in no
other race of animals, which seem to know neither this nor any other
species of contracts." To illustrate this point, Smith compares dogs
with human beings:

Nobody ever saw a dog make a fair and deliberate exchange of one bone for
another with another dog. Nobody ever saw one animal by its gestures and
natural cries signify to another, this is mine, that yours; I am willing to give
this for that.[3]

This passage clearly links the propensity to exchange with language
and communication. Smith refers to "gestures" and "cries" which
"signify" the terms of exchange. He thus implies that exchange presupposes the same capacity essential to moral relations—the ability to
change places with another in the imagination. Exchange presupposes
the capacity to imagine how I could benefit from the item which belongs to another, just as another could benefit from that which belongs
to me. It further presupposes the ability to communicate this idea by
gestures and cries. It is thus readily apparent why Smith thinks it
"probable" that the propensity to exchange derives from reason and
speech. Without them the comparison between my situation and that
of another could not be made and communicated.

Exchange is thus by its nature a social process. Division of labour is predicated for Smith not on competition but on cooperation. Division of labour involves an extensive network of cooperative activities. Human beings cannot live in a society characterized by division of labour without the cooperation, however unconscious, of thousands. The human animal is distinguished from other species by this dependence on others and is thus the preeminently social animal. Economic life in commercial society constitutes a vast network of cooperation. Yet it is a network of cooperation based on utility, not love. In the *Moral Sentiments* Smith had written that "society may subsist among different men, as among different merchants, from a sense of utility, without any mutual love or affection." Now, in *The Wealth of Nations*, he claims that in commercial society every individual "lives by exchanging, or becomes in some measure a merchant."[4] It is for this reason that

It is not from the benevolence of the butcher, the brewer, or the baker, that we expect our dinner, but from their regard to their own interest. We address ourselves, not to their humanity but to their self-love.[5]

As we saw in the previous chapter, Smith believed that society could subsist without benevolence but not without justice. The maintenance of justice in commercial society required that justice prevail in the economic relations among its members and that the state takes measures "to prevent the almost entire corruption and degeneracy of the great body of the people."[6] Smith's concern about corruption is based upon his analysis of this problem in the *Moral Sentiments*. As in that work, Smith maintains in *The Wealth of Nations* that wealth confers great authority in commercial society and that the poor naturally aspire to emulate the rich. The rich, however, are driven by "avarice" and "giddy ambition." Those of the inferior and middle ranks cannot conduct themselves in the fashion of the rich. Their situation forces them to obey "the principles of common prudence."[7] Most people desire to better their condition in order to win esteem in the eyes of their fellows. They work and save to increase their wealth and to enjoy the respect that wealth brings:

An augmentation of fortune is the means by which *the greater part of men* propose and wish to better their condition. It is the means the most vulgar and the most obvious; and the most likely way of augmenting their fortune is to save and accumulate some part of what they acquire.[8]

Vulgar though such a desire may be, it has important social effects. Most important is that "the uniform, constant and uninterrupted effort of every man to better his condition" is capable of overcoming enormous obstacles and carrying society to a state of opulence.[9] Nonetheless, Smith is concerned that distortions in the commercial system of Great Britain could undermine prudence and frugality. The prevalence of monopoly—which is based upon "sophistry," "vulgar prejudices," and "giddy ambition"—could thwart the industry and frugality of the vast majority.[10] The high profits which attend monopoly "destroy that parsimony which in other circumstances is natural to the character of the merchant." They render "sober virtue" superfluous and endow the monopolizer with "expensive luxury." This is especially dangerous to the nation, since the example of the great merchants "has a much greater influence upon the manners of the whole industrious part of it than that of any other order of men."[11] True, "the morals of the great body of the people are not *yet* so corrupt" as the morals of those who have clamoured for the institution of oppressive and monopolistic statutes.[12] But Smith is worried, nevertheless, that without corrective measures the moral fabric of society could become irreparably damaged. And, as we shall see in the course of this chapter, *The Wealth of Nations* presents a program of reform designed to avert this possibility.

The Wealth of Nations is thus firmly based upon the psychological and moral principles developed in the *Moral Sentiments*. Smith treats commerce as a distinct mode of communication and argues that individuals seek the respect of their neighbours; the majority are driven by the desire for approval to adopt "the principles of common prudence." Yet, as in the *Moral Sentiments*, Smith raises grave concerns that a commercial society might undermine the moral foundations upon which justice depends. In this respect he is particularly worried about the corrupting example set by the monopolizing tendencies of merchants and manufacturers—and he also sees these tendencies as generating poverty and economic injustice. He sets out consequently to establish the conditions of distributive justice in a market society. This, indeed, is the crucial concern which underpins his theory of value and his argument for perfect competition.

THE THEORY OF VALUE AND DISTRIBUTION

The centrality of the concept of value to Smith's theoretical economics is widely recognized. What is not generally recognized is the ethical dimension of his theory of economic value. Yet, as much as it offers a "scientific" theory of value and price, Smith's analysis provides the basis for making theoretically informed moral judgements about the economic power and practices of social classes. As we shall see, Smith's judgements tend to be markedly critical of the economic practices of merchants and manufacturers.

The starting point for Smith's theory of value is his concept of wealth. He is unequivocal in defining wealth in terms of consumption. "Consumption," he writes, "is the sole end and purpose of production." National wealth is measured by the size of "the stock reserved for immediate consumption."[13] As Samuel Hollander has pointed out, Smith here defines wealth in terms of the quantity of consumer goods.[14] What is most important to Smith, however, is not the aggregate social consumption but rather the level of consumption of the ordinary member of society, of the working poor: the higher the level of consumption of the average member, the greater the wealth of the nation. The vast majority of society are productive labourers, "the sober and industrious poor." National wealth can be approximately measured, therefore, in terms of the standard of living of common labourers. For this reason Smith strongly defends rising real wages as advantageous to society and maintains that promoting "cheapness of commodities" is one of the principal objects of political economy.[15]

It is with these thoughts in mind that Smith opens chapter 5 of Book 1 of *The Wealth of Nations* with his famous statement, "Every man is rich or poor according to the degree in which he can afford the necessaries, conveniences and amusements of human life." Every person derives the greater part of the goods he consumes from others. His consumption thus depends upon the labour of others. By exchanging the product of his own labour, each man acquires a share in the labour of others. In fact, a man's wealth may be measured, Smith asserts, by his command over the labour of others. But does not the value of labour itself change? And if so, how can it provide an invariable measure of value? Smith answers this question by suggesting that there is an invariable unit of disutility which will allow us to measure value.[16] All production involves a constant physical drain on the labourer; this unit of disutility is the only real standard of value:

> The real price of everything, what everything really costs to the man who wants to acquire it, is the toil and trouble of acquiring it. What everything is

really worth to the man who has acquired it, and who wants to dispose of it or exchange it for something else, is the toil and trouble which it can save to himself, and which it can impose upon other people.

Moreover, this disutility of labour is invariable:

Equal quantities of labour, at all times and places, may be said to be of equal value to the labourer. In his ordinary state of health, strength and spirits; in the ordinary degree of his skill and dexterity, he must always lay down the same portion of his ease, his liberty and his happiness.

It follows that

Labour alone, therefore, never varying in its own value, is alone the ultimate and real standard by which the value of all commodities can at all times and places be estimated and compared.[17]

These passages have often been taken to constitute a labour theory of value. Yet such an interpretation is untenable. Nowhere here does Smith say that the value of goods is *determined* by the labour time necessary for their production. In the subsequent chapter he does say that goods exchange on the basis of labour time in the "early and rude" state of society prior to accumulation of capital and private property in land. But all he says in these passages is that labour—or, rather, its disutility—provides an invariable *measure* of value. The question of the determination of value has not yet been raised.

Before proceeding to discuss Smith's theory of value, we must note one other point: while defining the value of a good in terms of the share of social labour it can command in exchange, Smith also introduces the notion that wealth is power. Since wealth equals command over a certain amount of the labour of society, it can be taken as equivalent to a power over others. "Wealth, as Mr. Hobbes says, is power," Smith writes. The possession of wealth confers "a certain command" over the labour of society. In fact, a man's fortune is equal "to the quantity either of other men's labour, or, what is the same thing, of the produce of other men's labour, which it enables him to purchase or command."[18] It follows from this—and it is a point whose full significance will become clearer below—that anything which artificially increases the wealth of certain groups or classes in society at the expense of others can be said to increase artificially (and unjustly) the power of these groups or classes.

Smith turns to the determination of value in chapter 6 of Book 1, "Of the component Parts of the Price of Commodities." The chapter title gives away the essence of Smith's position: value or "natural price" equals the sum of its parts or "components." What, then, are the components of price? Smith's answer is unequivocal: "Wages, profit, and rent, are the three original sources of all revenue as well as of all exchangeable value." These forms of revenue accrue to the three basic classes in society—wage labourers, capitalists, and landlords. Smith's theory of value is in fact also a theory of distribution. The value of every commodity is composed of (some fractional share of) those components which make the national income.[19]

This theory of value—what Sraffa called an "adding-up theory"—is up to this point purely descriptive. If the value of a commodity "resolves itself" into rent, profit, and wages, what determines the value of the factors of production—land, capital, and labour—to which these revenues accrue? It is remarkable how little attention has been directed to this crucial problem in Smith's theory of value. This lack of attention is particularly remarkable given that chapter 7 of Book 1, "Of the natural and market Price of Commodities," opens with a clear statement of Smith's theory of value, or natural price:

There is in every society or neighbourhood an ordinary or average rate both of wages and profit in every different employment of labour and stock. This rate is naturally regulated, as I shall show hereafter, partly by the general circumstances of the society, their riches or poverty, their advancing, stationary, or declining condition; and partly by the particular nature of each employment.

There is likewise in every society or neighbourhood an ordinary or average rate of rent, which is regulated too, as I shall show hereafter, partly by the general circumstances of the society or neighbourhood in which the land is situated, and partly by the natural or improved fertility of the land.

These ordinary or average rates may be called the natural rate of wages, profit, and rent, at the time and place in which they commonly prevail.

When the price of any commodity is neither more nor less than what is sufficient to pay the rent of the land, the wages of the labour, and the profits of the stock employed in raising, preparing and bringing it to market, according to their natural rates, the commodity is then sold for what may be called its natural price.[20]

This "adding up" theory of value is far from consistent. Throughout *The Wealth of Nations* Smith treats wages and profit as factors which determine price; yet he generally treats rent as a factor determined by price. Thus, to use rent as an element in measuring price is an entirely circular undertaking: it is to measure price by price. In strictly logical economic terms, then, Smith's theory of value is inconsistent. There have, however, been various attempts to render Smith's theory of natural price consistent with one or another major view in modern economics. Either one can construct a cost of production theory of value on the assumption that there is a tendency in Smith's model towards an equalization of returns to the factors of production—land, labour, and capital—or one can construct a supply and demand theory of price. Smith seems to want it both ways.[21] However, the imputation to Smith of concerns which dominate modern economics has obscured some central features of his theory of value. Although Smith looks in part to purely economic explanation of the natural rates of wages, profit, and rent, he does not treat these rates as strictly technical-economic data. In fact, Smith constantly emphasizes the social factors which enter into the determination of wages and rent, although he does tend to look exclusively to perfect competition to determine that natural rate of profit—a point to which we shall return below.

The wages of labour, Smith writes, "are every where necessarily regulated by two different circumstances; the demand for labour, and the ordinary or average price of provisions."[22] The wage rate, in other words, revolves around a basic subsistence level yet rises or falls according to the relation between the demand for and the supply of labour. Smith does not treat the subsistence wage as equivalent to what is physically necessary to support the labourer and reproduce a new generation of workers. He argues, on the contrary, that there is a *customary* level of subsistence which prevails in a given society at a given point in time. This customary "basket of wage goods" is not determined for the most part by demand and supply for labour. It is determined in large measure by social conditions— by the tastes, expectations, and moral standards which prevail in society:

By necessaries I understand, not only the commodities which are indispensably necessary for the support of life, but whatever the custom of the country renders it indecent for creditable people, even of the lowest order, to be without. . . . Custom . . . has rendered leather shoes a necessary of life in England. The poorest creditable person of either sex would be ashamed to appear in publick without them. . . . Under necessaries therefore, I comprehend not only those things which nature, but those things which the *established rules of decency* have rendered necessary to the lowest rank of people.[23]

In other words, short-term movements in the real wage rate can be understood in terms of supply and demand. But the level around which the wage rate moves—the "natural rate" towards which it gravitates—defies strictly economic determination. The natural price for labour is determined not by the market but by custom and convention.

The natural rate for rent, too, is determined by largely social factors. J. M. A. Gee has shown that attempts at neoclassical formulations of Smith's doctrine of rent have proved to be inconsistent with his theory. One important reason for this inconsistency is that the neoclassical framework makes institutional assumptions markedly different from those of Smith.[24] Smith makes the natural rate of rents a function of property laws, leases, price movements, and the tastes of the landlords. The degree of monopolization of land, laws of inheritance, and so on, determines the social distribution of land, the activity of the land market, and to some degree the price of land. Leases reflect the social power of landlords and tenants and influence the distribution of the landed produce between wages, profits, and rent. Demand for the various products of the land influences agricultural prices and, thereby, rents—although Smith holds that rent is less affected by changes in demand than are wages and profit. Finally, the tastes of the landlords play an important role in determining the general rate of the economy's growth and, consequently, in determining the level of rents. The greater the share of their revenues which landlords spend on manufactured (luxury) goods, rather than on personal retainers, the higher the rate of growth of industry and commerce. And the higher the rate of industrial and commercial expansion, the higher the demand for agricultural goods to feed urban workers and supply raw materials for industry. In this way, landlords inadvertently affect their own incomes.[25] It is obvious, therefore, that the natural rate of rent is largely determined by custom and convention. No purely economic determination of rent makes sense in the Smithian schema.

Smith's discussion of the natural rate of profit differs in important respects from his discussion of wages and rent. Smith opens chapter 9 of Book 1, "Of the Profits of Stock," not with an explanation of profit and its natural rate but rather with a discussion of the way in which "the increase of stock, which raises wages, tends to lower profit."[26] Much of the chapter is devoted to explaining why rising wages and falling profits are associated with economic progress. Smith does suggest, however, that there is a "lowest ordinary rate of profit" which is determined by the "occasional losses to which every employment of stock is exposed."[27] Smith's focus on "the lowest ordinary rate of profit" may at first seem surprising. It is not so, however, if one recognizes that Smith hoped to see the profit rate fall to its lowest possible rate—the rate which would be just sufficient to maintain economic activity. Smith wished, in other words, to see the average rate of profit fall to its "lowest ordinary rate." In fact, *The Wealth of Nations* may be seen in large measure as a sustained argument to promote policies which would dampen the rate of profit.

Smith's attitude towards profit derives from his general conception of wealth. As we have seen, Smith defines wealth in terms of the level of consumption of the majority of society, the working poor. This level of consumption is a product of the level of wages and the prices of commodities. In Smith's theory of natural price, it follows that, if we take the wage rate as given, the lower the prices of commodities, the higher the real standard of living. Whatever conspires to raise the prices of goods (assuming a fixed wage rate) diminishes the wealth of society. Consequently, any obstruction which keeps the market price of goods above their natural price ought to be removed. As Smith writes in his *Lectures:*

> Whatever police tends to raise the market price above the natural, tends to diminish the public opulence. Dearness and scarceity [*sic*] are in effect the same thing. When commodities are in abundance, they can be sold to the inferiour ranks of the people, who can afford to give less for them, but not if they are scarce. So far therefore as goods are a conveniencey [*sic*] to the society, the society lives less happy when only the few can possess them. Whatever therefore keeps goods above their natural price for a permanencey [*sic*] diminishes [a] nations opulence.[28]

Smith returns to this theme in *The Wealth of Nations* where he argues that monopolies tend to raise the market price of a commodity above its natural price.[29] He grants that exclusive corporations, statutes of apprenticeship, and so on tend to raise the market price for labour above its natural price; he maintains nonetheless that "high profits tend much more to raise the price of work than higher wages." And he denounces the hypocrisy of merchants and manufacturers, who bemoan the effects of high wages:

Our merchants and master-manufacturers complain much of the bad effects of high wages in raising the price, and thereby lessening the sale of their goods both at home and abroad. They say nothing concerning the bad effects of high profits. They are silent with regard to the pernicious effects of their own gains. They complain only of those of other people.[30]

Smith's discussion of value or natural price does not present a flawless analytical model designed to conform to the standards of modern economics. Indeed, as we have suggested, Smith's theory of value is riddled with inconsistencies. Smith was concerned primarily about economic growth and the social distribution of wealth. As we shall see below, Smith did not object in principle to high wages or rents; he believed that both wages and rents would rise with economic progress and that this would be in the best interest of society. He believed also that, under conditions of "perfect liberty," rates of profits would tend to fall with economic growth. However, merchants and manufacturers had conspired to thwart that natural process; in so doing, they oppressed the poor by forcing up the price of goods and by appropriating to themselves an unreasonably large share of the national income.

Smith's theory of natural price was thus at its heart a theory of distribution; it was designed to show that by distorting the laws of value (or natural price), merchants and manufacturers had brought about an unjust distribution of income. Obsessed by these unjust activities of merchants and manufacturers and the unjust effects of their high profits, Smith launched in *The Wealth of Nations* what one commentator has rightly called "a virtual torrent of abuse" against these capitalist groups. It is to that dimension of *The Wealth of Nations* that we must now turn before considering the question of value and natural price.

A DIATRIBE AGAINST MERCHANTS AND MANUFACTURERS

Smith's attack on merchants and manufacturers in *The Wealth of Nations* is so sweeping and so devastating that one is astonished to read statements such as those quoted at the beginning of the previous chapter, that Smith was "the prophet of the commercial society of modern capitalism," that he performed the function of "an unconscious mercenary in the service of the rising capitalist class in Europe," and that he "has earned the right to be known as an architect of our present system of society." The direction of Smith's argument was not lost, however, upon his immediate contemporaries. Hugh Blair of the Church of Scotland, a close friend of Smith's, and from 1762 to 1764 a professor at Edinburgh, wrote in congratulatory terms to the author of *The Wealth of Nations* shortly after the book's appearance. "You have done great service to the World," he wrote, "by overturning all that interested Sophistry of Merchants, with which they had confounded the whole Subject of Commerce." Similarly Adam Ferguson, Smith's friend and an important social theorist in his own right, wrote to Smith after the publication of *The Wealth of Nations* that "you have provoked, it is true, the church, the universities, and the merchants."[31]

Smith bases his attack on merchants and manufacturers on his belief that the interests of these groups run counter to that of the general public. As we have noted above, the natural progress of opulence will lower the rate of profit by increasing competition. Merchants and manufacturers have, therefore, an interest in resisting a process which serves the public interest. By conspiring to maintain high profits, they maintain prices at an artificially high level (and thus diminish the consumption and satisfaction of the majority) and slow down the overall rate of economic growth. As Smith writes towards the end of chapter 9 of Book 1, "Of the Rent of Land":

The interest of the dealers . . . in any particular branch of trade or manufactures, is always in some respect different from, and even opposite to, that of the publick. To widen the market and to narrow the competition, is always the interest of the dealers. To widen the market may frequently be agreeable enough to the interest of the publick; but to narrow the competition must always be against it, and can only serve to enable the dealers, by raising their profits above what they would normally be, to levy, for their own benefit, an absurd tax upon the rest of their fellow-citizens.

Smith goes on from this passage to describe merchants and manufacturers as "an order of men, whose interest is never exactly the same with that of the publick, who have generally an interest to deceive and even to oppress the publick, and who accordingly have, upon many occasions, both deceived and oppressed it."[32]

The interests of this group drive them to attempt to establish monopolies in trade and industry. In a particularly vitriolic passage in Book 4, Smith denounces "the mean rapacity, the monopolizing spirit of merchants and manufacturers," and condemns them for their "impertinent jealousy." More bothersome to Smith than their "monopolizing spirit" is the fact that merchants and manufacturers have connived to deceive the public; they have duped the latter into believing that what serves the interest of these capitalist groups automatically serves the public interest. "The interested sophistry of merchants and manufacturers," Smith writes, "confounded the common sense of mankind."[33] Landlords, farmers, and labourers are the dupes of particular interests dressed up in the guise of the public interest. "The clamour and sophistry of merchants and manufacturers easily persuade them that the private interest of a part, and of a subordinate part of the society, is the general interest of the whole."[34] The result of this clamour and sophistry is the mercantile system—a system entirely prejudicial to society.

The mercantile system is brought about, Smith claims, by deception and intimidation. Merchants and manufacturers exploit the "generosity" of country gentlemen (the largest percentage of the electorate) to persuade them that the interest of the former group, not the latter, is "the interest of the public." While merchants and manufacturers rely upon the good nature of country gentlemen for the advancement of their "vulgar prejudices," where necessary they clamour and cajole in an effort to subordinate the legislature to their private interest. "Like an overgrown standing army," Smith writes of master manufacturers, "they have become formidable to the government, and upon many occasions intimidate the legislature." It is in this way that "the sneaking arts of underling tradesmen" have been "erected into political maxims for the conduct of a great empire" and that Great Britain has become "a nation whose government is influenced by shopkeepers."[35]

The basic principle of the mercantile system is monopoly—the restriction of competition to suppress output and sustain unnaturally high prices and profits. Economic and market restrictions are a violation of the natural liberty of individuals to exercise their labour in the trade which they choose. Under the mercantile system and its plethora of restrictions, "the boasted liberty of the subject" is "plainly sacrificed to the interests of our merchants and manufacturers." Furthermore, the mercantile system inverts the proper relationship between production and consumption. "The sole end and purpose of production" ought to be consumption. "But in the mercantile system, the interest of the consumer is almost constantly sacrificed to that of the producer."[36]

Equally pernicious is the effect of the mercantile system on the rate of economic growth—and, consequently, on the standard of living of landowners and labourers whose incomes naturally rise with the progress of opulence. The monopoly of the colonial trade has drawn towards it a disproportionately large share of the capital of Great Britain. Foreign commerce is, however, the least productive employment of capital. In Book 2 of *The Wealth of Nations* Smith maintains that agriculture is the most productive employment of capital, followed next by manufacture, then by the wholesale trade, and finally by the retail trade. The more distant the retail trade, the less frequent its returns and, according to Smith, the lower its productivity.[37] As a result, by directing capital to its least productive employment, the mercantile system "has in all cases, therefore, turned it, from a direction in which it would have maintained a greater quantity of productive labour, into one, in which it can maintain a much smaller quantity."[38] As a consequence, this system will lower the wages of labour, since the aggregate demand for labour will be lower. Smith pays less attention to this consequence of mercantilism, however, than to its effects on landed revenues. "By raising the rate of mercantile profit," he writes, "the monopoly [of the colonial trade] discourages the improvement of land." This is the inevitable effect of drawing capital away from agriculture and into foreign trade, since rent will naturally rise with agricultural investment and improvement.[39] In fact, to encourage trade and manufacture at the expense of agricultural improvement is the very essence of the mercantile system:

It is the object of that system to enrich a great nation rather by trade and manufacture than by the improvement and cultivation of land, rather by the industry of the towns than by that of the country.[40]

If this is the essence of the mercantile system, Smith's attack must be designed in part to reverse this process—to redirect capital into agriculture even if this will hurt certain sectors of trade and manufacture in the short term. As we shall see below, Smith believed that such a reversal would not require extraeconomic direction but would automatically follow the elimination of the system's restrictive practices.

Smith mistrusts merchants and manufacturers for another reason—one that has nothing to do with the mercantile system but stems rather from the Commonwealth tradition of political thought.

According to Smith, commercial and industrial wealth—unlike agricultural wealth—is mobile and hence, from the standpoint of the nation, unstable. Whereas landowners have a fixed interest in the country in which they reside, mercantile and industrial wealth has no loyalty to any particular nation. It will move according to the vagaries of the profit rate. A stable commonwealth cannot therefore be built upon commercial and industrial capitalists, nor can the state rely upon stock and its profits for revenue:

Land is a subject which cannot be removed; whereas stock easily may. The proprietor of land is necessarily a citizen of the particular country in which his estate lies. The proprietor of stock is properly a citizen of the world, and is not necessarily attached to any particular country.[41]

It follows that a stable and prosperous commonwealth must be based upon the landed interest and should promote (or at least remove disincentives to) those policies which are conducive to agricultural improvement. As for merchants and manufacturers, they "neither are, nor ought to be the rulers of mankind." Indeed, the state should take measures to ensure that their "mean rapacity" is "prevented from disturbing the tranquility of anybody but themselves."[42] It follows from this attack on merchants and manufacturers that barriers should be erected against their influence on the legislature and that commercial policies should be designed which will reduce or eliminate their ability to "oppress the public" through restrictive practices.

Smith's proposal with respect to the influence of merchants and manufacturers upon legislation is straightforward: every legislative proposal from these groups ought to be treated "not only with the most scrupulous, but with the most suspicious attention."[43] With respect to the monopolizing actions of merchants and manufacturers, Smith argues not that the state should attempt to reform their character but rather that it should pursue policies which guarantee that these orders have no access to any situation in which they could oppress the public. It is in the nature of commerce that any "dealer" will attempt to monopolize his trade. Smith makes this point clear when, after condemning the merchants of the East India Company, he states that "it is the system of government, the situation in which they are placed that I mean to censure; not the character of those who have acted in it. They acted as their situation naturally directed."[44]

The obvious conclusion is thus that the state must construct an institutional setting in which merchants and manufacturers are denied access to situations in which they can monopolize their trade. This, in fact, is the whole point of Smith's advocacy of a system of perfect competition, or, as he puts it, "perfect liberty." The economic function of competition is to prevent monopoly and to push profits down to their "lowest ordinary rate"; it will guarantee low prices and make the necessities and conveniences of life available to the vast majority. Competition has more than an economic function, however: it also has a social function. As we shall see in the next section, competition compels merchants and manufacturers to behave according to acceptable standards of propriety.

PERFECT COMPETITION, PROPRIETY, AND NATURAL PRICE

The set of policies which Smith advances as a corrective to monopoly is remarkably simple. It consists in his system of natural liberty. In that system

> Every man, as long as he does not violate the laws of justice, is left perfectly free to pursue his own interest his own way, and to bring both his industry and his capital into competition with those of any other man, or order of men.[45]

The most important consequence of the system of perfect liberty is that prices will fall to their natural level. The natural price is "the price of free competition" and is "the lowest which can be taken, not upon every occasion, indeed, but for any considerable time together."[46] The natural price is thus that price most conducive to the wealth of the nation. Wealth is defined in terms of the real standard of living of the ordinary labourer; and the lowest price consistent with continued production makes the largest range of commodities accessible to the most people in the long run. It is clear, therefore, that Smith's concept of natural price has a moral dimension. The natural price is not a purely economic construct; it has a normative element—it is that price which provides the largest range of satisfactions to the bulk of the population while providing a fair profit to the capitalist. It is here that Smith's concept of natural price finds its point of intersection with the scholastic notion of the just price. This is not to say that *The Wealth of Nations* is constructed upon the same terrain of moral discourse as the economic writings of the scholastics. It is to note, however, that Smith's price theory was designed in part to serve moral ends—to eliminate unjust monopolies and to further the wealth of the common people. Marian Bowley is one of the few authors to have appreciated the connection between Smith's "natural price" and the "just price" of the scholastics. She writes:

Adam Smith's reliance on competition to eliminate the divergences [between market prices and natural prices] was wholly consistent with the acceptance by some of the later Schoolmen of the price ruling in a competitive market as the just price. The requirement of competition by such Schoolmen was of course due, as with Adam Smith, to the need to prevent individuals, or groups, from obtaining and taking advantage of favourable bargaining positions to raise prices.

As Bowley further points out, such a connection between Smith and the scholastic doctrine should not be surprising, given that Hutcheson brought the young Smith into contact with the work of Samuel Pufendorf, who had commented extensively upon scholastic economic thought.[47]

There is a further moral element in Smith's treatment of competition—one which again connects *The Wealth of Nations* with the *Moral Sentiments*. Not only does competition lower prices and profits (and thereby raise national wealth), it also forces merchants and manufacturers to adhere to customary standards of propriety. It would seem that Smith had come to despair of the ability of the moral mechanism of the impartial spectator to moderate the selfish passions of most individuals in commercial society. As we have seen, commercial society was for Smith a social system based not on benevolence but on utility. In commercial society, considerations of utility would force merchants and manufacturers to behave in a frugal and well-mannered fashion if competition tended to reward such qualities. In this way, the necessities of price competition might produce the socially acceptable behaviour produced in a less corrupt society by the mechanism of the impartial spectator. The discipline of the market thus enforces moderate behaviour:

The real and effectual discipline which is exercised over a workman, is not that of his corporation, but that of his customers. It is the fear of losing their employment which restrains his frauds and corrects his negligence.[48]

What connects this discussion even more clearly with the argument of the *Moral Sentiments* is Smith's claim that the low rate of profit produced by free competition forces capitalists to behave like the prudent individual described in the *Moral Sentiments*. High profits, by contrast, destroy parsimony and frugality. Moreover, the corrupting influence of high profits does not affect the moral character of the merchants alone. The poor, as Smith stresses in the *Moral Sentiments*, generally strive to emulate the character and practices of the rich. Since "the owners of the great mercantile capitals are necessarily the leaders of the whole industry of every nation," it follows that

their example has a much greater influence upon the manners of the whole industrious part of it than that of any other order of men. If his employer is attentive and parsimonious, the workman is very likely to be so too; but if the master is dissolute and disorderly, the servant who shapes his work according to the pattern which his master prescribes to him, will shape his life according to the example which he sets him.[49]

Smith's praise for the invisible hand of the market is thus more than admiration of its allocative efficiency. It is not praise for market society or its major representatives—merchants and manufacturers. On the contrary, Smith, as we have demonstrated, is profoundly critical of commercial society and of those who embody commercial habits and values. Smith's praise for the market is praise for a mechanism which he believes can counteract the corrupting influence of commerce on the behaviour of those most closely connected with commercial activity. As Nathan Rosenburg has commented, "So long as profits are difficult to earn, and so long as competitive pressures keep the rate of profit low, the system itself may be relied upon to force the capitalist to display the traditional virtues of his class."[50] In fact, the self-seeking activities of merchants and manufacturers can further the public interest so long as competitive markets constrain their "mean rapacity" and "monopolizing spirit." Yet, although Smith was satisfied with his solution to the problem of the oppressive business practices of merchants and manufacturers, he still considered those social groups based on trade and manufacture inferior to those based on agriculture. Unlike later theorists of perfect competition who looked to the market to channel and control the selfish passions of all members of society, Smith was concerned almost exclusively with the imposition of market discipline upon merchants and manufacturers whose selfish interests—unlike those of landowners and labourers—run directly counter to that of the public.

FARMERS, COUNTRY GENTLEMEN, AND THE PRIORITY OF AGRICULTURE

Smith's claims for the superiority of country life are at times rapturous. In Book 3 of *The Wealth of Nations*, after commenting upon the attractiveness of landed investment because of its security, he adds an aesthetic dimension to his argument for agricultural investment:

The beauty of the country besides, the pleasures of a country life, the tranquillity of mind which it promises, and wherever the injustice of human laws does not disturb it, the independency which it really affords, have charms that more or less attract everybody; and as to cultivate the ground was the original destination of man, so in every stage of his existence he seems to retain a predilection for this primitive employment.[51]

It is not only those who enjoy the independence of country life who are superior to urban dwellers; country labourers are also superior to their urban counterparts. "How much the lower ranks of people in the country are really superior to those of the town, is well known to every man whom either business or curiosity has led to converse much with both," Smith writes.[52]

Smith's argument for the superiority of country labourers appears positively paradoxical if we take him to be the prophet of commerce and industrial specialization. For it is precisely the limited character of the division of labour in agriculture which elevates rural labourers above their urban counterparts. Excepting the liberal arts, Smith claims, "there is perhaps no trade which requires so great a variety of knowledge and experience" as husbandry. Compared to "the mechanick who lives in a town," a "common ploughman" has a comprehensive understanding of nature. "His understanding . . . being accustomed to consider a greater variety of objects, is generally much superior to that of the other, whose whole attention from morning till night is commonly occupied in performing one or two very simple operations."[53] It is worthwhile recalling here that Smith defines philosophy as the science of the connecting principles of nature. He characterizes philosophical inquiry as the search for connections, for invisible chains, which bind phenomena together. An industrial labourer who works exclusively at one or two operations in a vast network of integrated activities fails to grasp the connections which link individual labours into the total process of production. Husbandry, however, requires a range of interconnected skills. Since the division of labour cannot be extended as far in agriculture as in industry, the practitioners of the former tend to have wider intellectual horizons.

Smith returns to the theme of the debilitating effects of the industrial division of labour in Book 5. There he makes it clear that the division of labour tends—unless the state takes countervailing measures—to render industrial workers incapable of judging as to the best interests of society:

> The understandings of the greater part of men are necessarily formed by their ordinary employments. The man whose whole life is spent in performing a few simple operations, of which the effects too are, perhaps, always the same, or very nearly the same, has no occasion to exert his understanding. . . . He naturally loses, therefore, the habit of such exertion, and generally becomes as stupid and ignorant as it is possible for a human creature to become. The torpor of his mind renders him, not only incapable of relishing or bearing a part in any rational conversation, but of conceiving any generous, noble or tender sentiment, and consequently of forming any just judgment concerning many even of the ordinary duties of private life. Of the great and extensive interests of his country, he is altogether incapable of judging.[54]

The knowledge of society available to the industrial worker is inferior to that of a member of a "barbarous" society. "In such societies the varied occupations of every man oblige every man to exert his capacity." In this way, "invention is kept alive" and people's minds do not "fall into that drowsy stupidity, which, in a civilized society, seems to benumb the understanding of almost all the inferior ranks of people." Moreover, everyone in a barbarous society is involved to some degree in political and military affairs. Consequently, "every man too is in some measure a statesman, and can form a tolerable judgment concerning the interest of the society, and the conduct of those who govern it."[55]

The superiority of the inhabitants of the country does not consist simply in an intellectual superiority; it involves as well a moral superiority. The rural labourer is a known member of a tightly knit community. He strives to win the approval of his neighbours and to govern his conduct according to conscience and the moral standards of the community. The labourer who moves to a city soon loses this moral bond; "He is sunk in obscurity and darkness. His conduct is

observed and attended to by nobody, and he is therefore very likely
to neglect it himself, and to abandon himself to every sort of low prof-
ligacy and vice." [56] If country labourers are superior to their urban
counterparts, this is even more true of the rural upper and middle
classes. Country gentlemen and farmers are in nearly every respect
superior to their urban counterparts, merchants and manufacturers.
Country gentlemen and farmers (and here Smith would seem to exclude the traditional, but not the improving, landed aristocracy) are
industrious, generous, and public-minded individuals whose chief
shortcoming is their good nature, which merchants and manufacturers strive to exploit. "Country gentlemen and farmers are, to their
great honour, of all people, the least subject to the wretched spirit of
monopoly." They are characterized by a "generosity which is natural
to their station" and strive to share, rather than to hide, the secrets of
agricultural improvement. [57] It is true that landlords are often lazy
and indolent and thus fail to grasp their own best interest and the
genuine interests of society; but this is true primarily of the large
landowners descended of the nobility, not of the prosperous and improving gentry. In any case, all landlords experience rising incomes
as a result of the increasing opulence of society. They have no interest, therefore, in thwarting the natural progress of the economy. For
this reason, their legislative advice can be trusted: "When the publick deliberates concerning any regulation of commerce or police, the
proprietors of land never can mislead it, with a view to promote the
interest of their own particular order." [58]

These arguments constitute a powerful claim for the superiority of
agrarian social classes. If we take seriously the claim that Smith's political economy was a branch of his moral philosophy and a subsec-
tion of his jurisprudence, it would seem that he is constructing,
among other things, a forceful argument in *The Wealth of Nations* for
resting social and political power upon those classes which are least
corrupted or stupefied by commercial society and industrial specialization. Yet it might still be objected that these are merely romantic and nostalgic yearnings for a simpler life, which do not affect the
theoretical structure of *The Wealth of Nations*. Such an objection cannot be sustained. The entire argument of *The Wealth of Nations*—
and especially of Books 2, 3, and 4—is built upon the notions that
agriculture is the basis of all improvement, that agricultural investment is the most productive employment of capital, and that mer-

cantile policy has dampened down the overall growth rate of the economy by diverting capital from agriculture to commerce.

Smith's claim that the growth of agricultural productivity is fundamental to the growth of industry would appear to be unobjectionable. It is based on the simple proposition that, in the progress of human affairs, subsistence is prior to conveniency and luxury; development of the arts related to the former is a precondition to development of those related to the latter.[59] What is controversial is Smith's claim that agriculture constitutes the most productive field for capital investment. This claim is no mere quirk on Smith's part. It is, as we shall see, central to the policy prescriptions in *The Wealth of Nations*.

Smith's view is based upon the claim that "no equal capital puts into motion a greater quantity of productive labour than that of the farmer. Not only his labouring servants, but his labouring cattle, are productive labourers. In agriculture too nature labours along with man."[60] The superiority of agriculture is manifested in the fact that, unlike industry and trade, it supplies a surplus above wages and profit. This surplus—rent—"may be considered as the produce of those powers of nature, the use of which the landlord lends to the farmer." Rent is a surplus unique to agriculture. Thus, a capital invested in agriculture reproduces the largest total product (and thus the largest surplus product). "Of all the ways in which a capital can be employed, it [agriculture] is by far the most advantageous to the society." Furthermore, the capital invested in land, unlike that invested in stock, constitutes a fixed and permanent asset to the country in which it resides. For all these reasons, "the natural course of things" dictates that capital will flow first into agriculture and only subsequently into manufacture and commerce. This natural order of progress has, however, "in all the modern states of Europe, been, in many respects, entirely inverted."[61] Because agriculture was discouraged during the feudal period, stimulation of progress fell to trade and manufacture, which slowly but inevitably reached the stage where they could react upon the quiet and unchanging world of agriculture. In this way trade and industry inspired agricultural improvement by penetrating the nearly frozen sphere of agriculture.

Beneficial though it may have been to society that expanding commerce and industry should bring general economic improvement, this course of progress, "being contrary to the natural course of things, is necessarily both slow and uncertain." This slower rate of growth is caused, first, by the remnants of feudal property relations that impede agricultural improvement. Second, and more significant, it is caused by the growth of trade and manufacturing classes who use their new social power to bring about the restrictive and monopolizing measures of the mercantile system.

As we have indicated above, Smith believed that the overriding object of the mercantile system was "to enrich a great nation rather by trade and manufacture than by the improvement and cultivation of land." He further maintained that such a system would slow down the progress of opulence by diverting capital from its most productive employment (agriculture) to its least productive employment (the colonial trade) (see this chapter's discussion of merchants and manufacturers). This was one main reason that Smith favoured dismantling the mercantile system. Abolition of mercantile restrictions would induce a flow of wealth into landed investment. "Merchants," after all, "are commonly ambitious of becoming country gentlemen." The flow of mercantile wealth into agriculture would have benefits beyond the increase of capital investment on the land. Agriculture would benefit also from the application of the mercantile habits of "order, oeconomy and attention." Because of these habits, merchants, once they become country gentlemen, "are generally the best of all improvers."[62] The nation derives a further advantage from the flow of commercial wealth into agriculture: for the first time the capital of the merchants forms part of the permanent wealth of the country:

> The capital . . . that is acquired to any country by commerce and manufactures, is all a very precarious and uncertain possession, till some part of it has been secured and realized in the cultivation and improvement of its lands. . . . No part of it can be said to belong to any particular country, till it has been spread as it were over the face of that country, either in buildings, or in the lasting improvements of land.[63]

These passages clearly indicate that Smith's agrarian bias did not consist in a romantic attachment to a noncommercial (or noncapitalist) agriculture. On the contrary, Smith strongly favoured the commercialization/capitalization of agriculture; this was the reason that he praised the improving habits of merchants who purchase land. Moreover, Smith argued that it was the duty of the proprietor of land to undertake those landed investments which are essential to the profitable working of the land. The landlord, Smith argued, should "keep his estate in as good condition as he can, by building and repairing his tenants houses, by making and maintaining the necessary drains and enclosures, and all those other expensive improvements which it properly belongs to the landlord to make and maintain."[64]

The tenant farmers, on the other hand, cultivate the land "with their own stock" and should "lay out part of their capital in the further improvement of the farm." So long as tenant farmers enjoy the security of long leases, they will recover their investment "with a large profit, before the expiration of the lease." The other duty of capitalist farmers is to use their capital to hire labourers. Economic security is essential for the farmers to fulfill both duties. Such security is the secret of Britain's prosperity. Smith argues, for example, that "those laws and customs so favourable to the yeomanry, have perhaps contributed more to the present grandeur of England than all their boasted regulations of commerce taken together."[65] Moreover, Smith makes it clear that he prefers the triadic arrangement, in which the landlord leases out part of his estate to tenant farmers while he personally works the rest, to one in which he personally attempts to oversee the whole estate with the aid of bailiffs. Because the capital of the landlord "is generally greater than that of the tenant" and, as a result, "the landlord can generally afford to try experiments," Smith recommends that the landed proprietor "be encouraged to cultivate a part of his own land." At the same time, Smith is opposed to the idea that landlords should try to farm the whole of their lands, since this requires that they employ "idle and profligate bailiffs" who have no direct interest in agricultural improvement. Instead, he advocates leasing lands to "sober and industrious tenants, who are bound by their own interest to cultivate as well as their capital and their skill will allow them."[66]

Taken as a whole, Smith's model can be seen to be an agrarian capitalist one. He envisages landlords who undertake long-term fixed investments on land, who initiate agricultural experiments while themselves cultivating part of their lands, and who rent a large amount of their lands to prosperous, independent farmers who in turn make further short-term investments and who hire country labourers, all with a view to turning a profit on their capital. This model bears a strong resemblance to that of the Physiocrats, in particular to their analysis of the different kinds of "advances"—the *avances foncières* and *avances primitives* of the landowners and the *avances annuelles* of the farmer—necessary to "la grande culture." Given this resemblance, we shall consider the degree to which Smith's theoretical economics were influenced by the agrarian capitalist model of the economy developed by the Physiocrats.

CAPITAL ACCUMULATION AND THE CIRCULAR FLOW: SMITH'S PHYSIOCRATIC INHERITANCE

There is a distinct similarity between certain arguments produced in *The Wealth of Nations* and elements of the physiocratic system. We have examined above Smith's bias in favour of landlords, farmers, and country gentlemen and have noted his belief that land was the most valuable and enduring form of national wealth. We have also drawn attention to his conviction that agriculture constituted the most productive field for capital investment—a conviction based on the claim that in agriculture nature labours along with man. Further, as we shall see below, Smith's notion that rent is a component of price—a view to which Hume took exception[67]—would also appear to result from his contact with Physiocracy.

These points are generally belittled in the literature on Smith. Most commentators have seen these similarities as of little significance to the general theoretical structure of *The Wealth of Nations*. In fact, it has become almost orthodoxy to maintain that Smith had worked out the basic theoretical structure of *The Wealth of Nations* before his trip to France in the mid-1760s and that the physiocratic influences on his great work were of minimal importance. Schumpeter wrote, for example,

It is not necessary to infer that Smith was under heavy (and largely unacknowledged) obligation to the physiocrats, whom he had met (1764–6) and presumably read before he settled down to work at Kirkcaldy. The Draft discovered by Professor Scott proves that this may go too far: the Draft clearly foreshadows the scheme of the Wealth.[68]

We shall consider the relationship between the "Early Draft" and *The Wealth of Nations* below. For the moment, however, let us continue to consider the treatment of Smith's indebtedness to the Physiocrats in some of the more important secondary literature. It is perhaps Edwin Cannan who inaugurated the modern tradition of downplaying Smith's debt to Quesnay and his followers. In his editor's intro-

duction to *The Wealth of Nations,* Cannan asserted that "the introduction of the theory of stock or capital and unproductive labour in
Book II, the slipping of a theory of distribution into the theory of
prices towards the end of Book I, Chapter 6, and the emphasizing of
the conception of the annual produce" were all inspired by the physiocratic system. Taken together, these elements of physiocratic influence might be considered to constitute an inheritance of considerable
importance for Smith's economics. Not so, according to Cannan. In
fact, it was Cannan's view that these aspects of *The Wealth of Nations*
could be deleted without serious loss to the work as a whole:

> These changes do not make so much real difference to Smith's own work as
> might be supposed; the theory of distribution, though it appears in the title
> of Book I., is no essential part of the work and could easily be excised by
> deleting a few passages in Book I., chapter vi., and a few lines elsewhere; if
> Book II were altogether omitted the other Books could stand perfectly well
> by themselves.[69]

This is a truly remarkable statement; it amounts to claiming not
only that *The Wealth of Nations* could stand perfectly well without
the theory of distribution developed in Book 1 but—more startling—that it could just as well do without the theory of capital, accumulation, and growth presented in Book 2. In recent Smithian
literature, such extravagant claims are rarely made. This tendency
has not, however, led to a greater emphasis on Smith's physiocratic
inheritance. Instead, it has led to statements that go further even
than Cannan's and downplay the physiocratic influence on Smith's
theories of distribution, capital, and growth. Samuel Hollander, for
example, after enumerating those aspects of *The Wealth of Nations*
which Cannan attributed to physiocratic inspiration, writes that
"even Cannan's limited attributions are probably exaggerated."[70]

All these views—that of Schumpeter, that of Cannan, and that of
Hollander—operate upon the assumption that the essential theoretical structure of *The Wealth of Nations* was erected in Smith's *Lectures*
and in the Early Draft and that Smith's contact with the Physiocrats
could therefore have affected only some secondary features of his
text. Physiocratic influence is, in this argument, largely superficial—
not something which affected the theoretical core of *The Wealth of
Nations*. This position does not fare well when subjected to critical
examination. A thorough comparison of Smith's *Lectures* and the
manuscript which has become known, following W. R. Scott, as the

Early Draft with *The Wealth of Nations* demonstrates conclusively that Smith's theory of value underwent a profound change after the *Lectures* and the Early Draft and that only in his treatise on political economy did he develop a model of capital accumulation and growth. As we shall demonstrate below, all the evidence suggests that it was Smith's contact with the Physiocrats which was responsible for these fundamental changes in his theoretical economics. Given that the Physiocrats developed a rigorous model of agrarian capitalism, we should not be surprised to see such a model erected in *The Wealth of Nations*.

The most obvious contrast between the *Lectures* and *The Wealth of Nations* is that the *Lectures* do not deal with the issues which make up Books 2 and 4 of *The Wealth of Nations*. In his *Lectures* of 1762–1763, for example, Smith states that his treatment of opulence will cover the following topics:

1st		The rule of exchange, or what it is which regulates the price of commodities.—
2 Money as		1st The measure by which we compute the value of commodities (as measure of value)
	3dly	The causes of the slow progress of opulence and the causes which retarded it, which are of two sorts: 1st Those which affect the improvement of agriculture 2 Those which affect the improvement of manufactures
4th		Taxes or as no part of pu(b)lick law so much connects with publick opulence has such an influence upon it; as ill revenue contrived laws relating to commerce and taxes have been one great drawback upon opulence.—
5th		The effects of commerce, both good and bad, and the naturall remedies of the latter.[71]

This arrangement of Smith's economic materials in the *Lectures* of 1762–1763 can easily be compared with the general structure of *The Wealth of Nations*. Smith's first and second items, price and money, are treated in Book 1; his third topic, the progress of opulence, constitutes the subject of Book 3, and his fourth and fifth topics—taxation and the laws of commerce on the one hand and the social effects of commerce on the other—form the bulk of Book 5. What is conspicuously absent is any discussion of capital and growth—the subject of Book 2—and any treatment of the doctrines of political economy—the topic of Book 4. Also absent is any section which corresponds to the division of the annual produce into wages, profit, and rent and to the way in which these three figure in the natural price of commodities. These topics are missing also from the *Lectures* of 1763–1764 and from the manuscript known as the Early Draft.

Before comparing these elements added to *The Wealth of Nations* with the conceptual framework of the Physiocrats, let us review the historical record of Smith's contact with and attitude towards Quesnay and his school. Smith arrived in Paris from Toulouse around Christmas of 1765 and spent the better part of 1766 in Paris. The year 1766 was a high point of physiocratic activity. The school had just secured control of the *Journal de l'agriculture, du commerce, et des finances;* Turgot was writing his *Réflexions* and Mercier his *Ordre naturel*. Smith thus encountered Quesnay's circle at the height of its influence and creative energy. He attended its regular meetings in Quesnay's apartment and met regularly with Turgot, for whom he developed a special admiration.[72]

It is hard to imagine that direct contact with so prominent and influential a group of economic theorists should not have had a profound effect on Smith. The evidence suggests that this was indeed the case. We have it on the authority of Dugald Stewart that Smith intended to dedicate *The Wealth of Nations* to Quesnay—until the latter died shortly before its publication.[73] Furthermore, Dupont later described himself and Smith as being in those days "fellow disciples of M. Quesnay." And Smith's biographer, John Rae, felt confident in declaring that his subject was "a very sympathetic associate of this new sect, though not a strict adherent."[74] After he returned to Britain, Smith maintained a connection with Turgot. Although the story usually attributed to Condorcet that the two corresponded has now been discredited, Turgot did send Smith copies of his *Mémoires concernant les impositions,* a work which Smith quoted frequently in *The Wealth of Nations,* as well as a copy of the *procès verbal* of the *lit de justice* concerning his famous six edicts of 1776. Furthermore, Smith had at least two-thirds of Turgot's *Réflexions* as it first appeared in serial form in the *Ephémérides du citoyen* in November and December 1769 and January 1770.[75]

Clearly, Smith's contact with the Physiocrats was extensive and his attitude towards them one of admiration and respect, as confirmed by his comments upon physiocratic doctrine in *The Wealth of Nations*. There, Smith described Physiocracy as a "very ingenious system," which was the product of "the speculations of a few men of great learning and ingenuity in France." He characterized the doctrine of Quesnay and his followers as a "liberal and generous system" and Quesnay himself as "the very ingenious and profound author of this system." Furthermore, though Smith differed with major tenets of Physiocracy, he described the system as "the nearest approximation to the truth that has yet been published upon the subject of political economy," as a system which had been of service to the French nation, and as a doctrine which would be "well worth the consideration of every man who wishes to examine with attention the principles of that very important science" of political economy.[76]

Despite his praise, Smith criticized the Physiocrats for representing artisans, merchants, and manufacturers as unproductive and for attempting to prescribe the course to a healthy state.[77] These criticisms demonstrate that Smith's general vision of economics differed in important respects from that of Quesnay. Yet it is also worthy of note that some younger Physiocrats—and especially a neophysiocrat like Turgot—did modify their master's orthodoxy concerning sterility of the industrial sector (that is, its alleged inability to produce a surplus); they moved towards a laissez-faire position quite similar to that of Smith (see discussion of Turgot and Neophysiocracy in chapter 3). In any case, Smith's discussion of Physiocracy in *The Wealth of Nations* is a decidedly sympathetic treatment of the doctrine of the *économistes*. Certainly his generally favourable discussion of the school suggests that on certain points Smith might have been influenced by, or even adopted, the physiocratic perspective.

Evidence of physiocratic influence on the conceptual structure of *The Wealth of Nations* emerges from the first sentence of that work. Smith introduced his treatise with the statement, "The annual labour of every nation is the fund which originally supplies it with all the necessaries and conveniences of life which it annually consumes." This statement indicates that Smith had adopted the physiocratic concept of the annual reproduction period. Indeed, Smith had so completely absorbed the notion that production and consumption should be treated as an annual circular flow that he did not seem to recognize that he was introducing entirely new concepts into British economics. Before Smith others, like Petty, had tried to assess Britain's national wealth by aggregating the value of its capital stock or its accumulated possessions—land, buildings, houses, mines, etc. Smith shifted from the capital stock framework to an "annual income" framework. This new approach could have come only from contact with the Physiocrats. As Cannan wrote, "Adam Smith adopted Quesnay's 'annual riches' as the subject of his inquiry regarding the wealth of nations without seeing very clearly that he was thereby breaking with the traditional meaning of the phrase."[78]

Equally significant is the fact that right after the introduction to *The Wealth of Nations* Smith put the concept of distribution developed by the Physiocrats into his title for Book 1. That title reads: "Of the Causes of the Improvement in the productive Powers of Labour, and of the Order according to which its Produce is naturally distributed among the different Ranks of the People." Like annual reproduction, this notion of distribution was foreign to British economics prior to Smith. Again, Cannan recognized the significance of this point. "Before Adam Smith," he writes, "English economists did not talk of 'distribution' or of the manner in which wealth or produce is 'distributed'."[79] Cannan also attributes Smith's use of distribution to the influence of Quesnay and his school. It is perhaps worthy of note that the concept appears in the title of Turgot's major economic treatise, *Réflexions sur la formation et la distribution des richesses.*

Smith made one further contribution to British economics which Cannan considered original. This was the explicit use of the triad land, labour, and capital.[80] To be sure, this triad can be found, implicit, in the writings of Petty, Locke and Cantillon. Yet Cannan is correct to claim that this triad did not become an integral part of the explicit conceptual structure of economics until Smith formulated his theory of the component parts of prices. Again, this Smithian contribution to British political economy appears to owe much to physiocratic influence. As we have shown above, this triadic structure moved into the foreground in Turgot's writings, especially in the agrarian capitalist model he developed in the *Réflexions* (discussed in chapter 3).

It seems evident, therefore, that the general theoretical framework Smith used in *The Wealth of Nations* relied upon important elements of the physiocratic perspective. For the first time in the history of British political economy, *The Wealth of Nations* employed the notion of a circular flow of wealth in which national output was annually produced, distributed, and consumed. Furthermore, Smith developed the neophysiocratic insight that national income is divided among landlords, labourers, and capitalists (in the form of rent, wages, and profit) into the central feature of his theory of value and distribution. It seems improbable that these concepts could, as Cannan suggests, be omitted without damage to Smith's theory as a whole. They entered into the ground level of Smith's theoretical framework.

The evidence is also conclusive that Smith's physiocratic inheritance entered into the theory of value developed in *The Wealth of Nations*. In the *Lectures* and the Early Draft, Smith often advanced a pure labour theory of the measure of value of the sort which he rejects in *The Wealth of Nations* as applicable only to a rude state of society. In Smith's early view, wages were the best measure of value; profit and rent were not treated as components of price.[81] It is instructive in this respect that one of the aspects of *The Wealth of Nations* to which Hume took exception was Smith's claim that rent was a component of value. It would appear that Smith was breaking with convention with his tripartite "adding-up" theory of value developed in Book 1. There is also little doubt that it was the theory of distribution which he took over from Quesnay and Turgot and modified to suit his own needs which caused him to revise his theory of value. For, as we have shown above, Smith reasoned that if the value of the annual produce resolves itself into wages, profit, and rent, then this must likewise be true of the value of all—or nearly all—commodities. Incorporation into Smith's value theory of the physiocratic view of reproduction as a unity of production and distribution would on its own be a significant influence on Smith's theoretical economics. This influence becomes even more obvious, however, when we turn to his theory of capital.

Nowhere in any of Smith's writings prior to *The Wealth of Nations* is there anything resembling an extended treatment of capital. Yet Smith's concept of capital has been taken by many modern commentators to be the central organizing concept of the whole work. Ronald Meek, for example, wrote of Smith's achievement in *The Wealth of Nations* that "it was Smith's great emphasis on the economic role of profit on capital and capital accumulation which more than anything else gave unity and strength to the structure of *The Wealth of Nations*."[82] If this is so, then *The Wealth of Nations* must owe much more to physiocratic inspiration than most commentators have been willing to concede. For there can be little doubt that the introduction of capital and its accumulation into the theoretical structure of *The Wealth of Nations* was a result of Smith's contact with Quesnay and his school. We should not be surprised to find, therefore, that Smith's concept of capital is an essentially physiocratic one. In fact, as we shall show, Smith often reverted to a vulgar-physiocrat position in his treatment of capital, a position which treats capital as consisting exclusively of annual advances, a position which was markedly inferior to the theory of capital developed by Quesnay and Turgot.

The most obvious similarity between the Smithian and physiocratic concepts of capital is that Smith follows his French contemporaries in treating capital as an "advance" made by employers to labourers. Thus, in his chapter on wages in Book 1, Smith writes that "in all arts and manufactures the greater part of the workmen stand in need of a master to *advance* them the materials of their work, and their wages and maintenance till it be compleated." [83] But more significant—and here his doctrine involves a regression from Physiocracy—is that, in his famous third chapter of Book 2, "Of the Accumulation of Capital, or of productive and unproductive Labour," Smith tends to treat capital as identical with the *avances annuelles* of the Physiocrats. It is instructive that in the title of this chapter Smith takes the accumulation of capital to be equivalent to the employment of productive labour. The whole chapter is constructed with an annual reproduction model in mind. Thus, without any explanation, Smith ignores the fact (which he acknowledges elsewhere) that a certain share of capital must take the form of fixed investments such as buildings, fences, machines, livestock, and so on. Indeed, he tends also to forget that even "the capital annually employed" must consist of raw materials annually turned over. He writes, for example, that "that part of the annual produce of the land and labour of any country which replaces a capital, never is immediately employed to maintain any but productive hands. It pays the wages of productive labour only." [84] This passage constitutes a classic definition of capital as a wage fund—as a fund of money or consumer goods for maintaining labour during the (annual) production period. It is only with this conception in mind that we can explain Smith's claim that "what is annually saved is as regularly consumed as what is annually spent, and nearly in the same time too; but it is consumed by a different set of people." Saving and investment, in other words, divert a share of the annual produce from landlords and capitalists to "labourers, manufacturers, and artificers." Thus, Smith concludes this passage on saving with the statement that "the consumption is the same, but the consumers are different."[85]

Smith tends to see accumulation exclusively as a process which increases the demand for and the wages of labour. Smith's growth model thus conceives capital as a fund to maintain productive labourers—a fund which is annually reproduced. Accumulation thereby becomes synonymous with production of an ever larger fund of consumer goods. A larger national output seems to require a larger productive workforce. Such a view involves, however, neglecting the role of fixed capital in the accumulation process. As Marian Bowley has written, once Smith had made the assumption that the number of productive labourers would automatically increase in proportion to the increase in the capital annually accumulated,

> It was easy for him to forget that part of the net output of an investment of £x will be due to the use of capital invested in materials, tools, etc., and output will not therefore increase in proportion to the number of productive labourers employed. Indeed it is easy to show the reverse may be the case.[86]

Bowley's claim that Smith's theory of capital accumulation tended to "forget" about "the use of capital invested in materials, tools, etc." constitutes a major challenge to the view of Samuel Hollander, who depicts Smith as an economic theorist who constructed an analytic model appropriate to industrial capitalism. Hollander contends that "Smith's analytic structure was largely designed for factory, rather than domestic, organization."[87] But can we fairly describe someone as a theorist of factory production when his "analytic structure" in certain important respects—especially in the theory of growth—neglects the role of fixed capital investments? Certainly one would expect a theorist of the factory system to accord a central place to fixed investments such as buildings and machinery. Hollander does acknowledge that Smith often treats capital as a fund of subsistence goods for labourers. Moreover, he accepts that Smith's growth model did not incorporate fixed capital and suggests that this failing may have been a result of Smith's lack of adequate "analytic tools." Nevertheless, he rejects the attribution to Smith of a wage fund theory with the claim that "it is, however, very unlikely that this was Smith's position in view of the attention paid to fixed capital and its maintenance."[88] How are we to assess this claim?

There can be little doubt that Smith does pay attention to the role of fixed capital in *The Wealth of Nations*. Chapter 1 of Book 2 is devoted in part to explaining the distinction between fixed and circulating capital. Yet as soon as Smith moves to a dynamic model in discussing accumulation, fixed capital disappears from sight. It is difficult to believe that this "logical error," to use Hollander's term,[89] is a result of Smith's lack of appropriate "analytic tools." After all, as we have shown in chapter 4, Quesnay's *Tableau* (at least in its later versions) incorporated a depreciation fund to replace fixed capital. In developing his value theory, however, Smith explicitly rejects the notion that, in addition to wages, profit, and rent, the value of a commodity ought also to resolve itself into a fourth component or fund to replace fixed capital. In discussing this issue, Smith chooses his example from agriculture—the price of corn, to be precise—but he makes it clear that his argument applies to all goods. After stating that the value of all goods is equal to the wages, profit, and rent paid to marshal the factors of production, he continues:

A fourth part, it may perhaps be thought, is necessary for replacing the stock of the farmer, or for compensating the wear and tear of his labouring cattle, and other instruments of husbandry. But it must be considered that the price of any instrument of husbandry, such as a labouring horse, is itself made up of the three same parts; the rent of land upon which he is reared, the labour of tending and rearing him, and the profits of the farmer who advances both the rent of this land, and the wages of this labour.[90]

It is interesting that Smith draws his example from agriculture. It is also significant that his first example of fixed capital is "labouring cattle" used in farming. Elsewhere in *The Wealth of Nations* Smith describes "labouring cattle" at one point as fixed capital and at another point as productive labour. The first case occurs in chapter 1 of Book 2, where he discusses the distinction between fixed and circulating capital. There, he states that the farmer's "labouring cattle is a fixed capital in the same manner as that of the instruments of husbandry." Yet when he comes to chapter 3 of Book 2 on accumulation, Smith says of the farmer that "not only his labouring servants, but his labouring cattle, are productive labourers."[91] This shift in perspective is instructive because it demonstrates that in his growth model Smith defines capital as a consumption fund for productive labourers. In order to hold consistently to this view he thus redefines as "productive labour" an element he previously described as "fixed capital." How are we to understand Smith's shift when he turns his attention to growth?

The significance of this shift cannot be appreciated unless we recognize the degree to which the question of growth came to dominate Smith's concerns by the time he wrote *The Wealth of Nations*. As we have shown above, so long as all restrictive practices were eliminated, growth had social consequences of which Smith morally approved—the raising of wages and rents, the lowering of profits, and the employment of the industrious poor. The evidence seems compelling that Smith, moral philosopher as well as political economist, felt that the commercialization of economic life was morally justifiable only if it contributed to opulence, that is, to raising the income of the labouring poor. For this reason he was inclined to treat the growth process as a process which automatically raised real wages. But how was such growth in opulence to be measured? After all, for Smith wealth consisted of real consumption, not money incomes. For this reason, he sought an invariable standard of value which would be free from the fluctuations of money prices. In searching for such a standard, Smith came to rely upon a primitive corn model which abstracted from the existence of fixed capital.

The essence of a corn model has been aptly defined by Hollander. He writes that

> The main characteristics of the model are that the only form of capital is circulating or working capital advanced from past produce; that there is only one kind of circulating capital good, namely 'corn'; and that the period of its circulation is the agricultural year. Labour is the sole variable factor, currently producing either corn—in which case it is defined as 'productive'—or luxury services when it is defined as 'unproductive.' This model casts light on the forces determining the growth rate of the economy—where the national dividend is defined in terms of physical product (corn output)—under various conditions of productivity, labour supply, and allocation of employment between the two categories of labour.[92]

Hollander rejects the attribution of such a model to Smith because it presupposes that "Smith's basic concern . . . is with the increasing of material wealth rather than the efficient allocation of scarce resources among alternative ends."[93] According to Hollander's interpretation, Smith is a precursor of general equilibrium theory; his prime concern is with the way in which the price mechanism allocates capital, labour, and materials among scarce and competing ends. A corn model is clearly of little value to such a theoretical undertaking. Hollander concedes, however, that it is a useful abstraction for a theorist concerned primarily with growth. Since I am among those who consider the latter topic central to Smith's political economy, let me briefly consider the evidence of Smith's use of a corn model in *The Wealth of Nations*.

Smith's corn model emerges in Book 1, where he discusses the measure of value. His initial concern is with measuring the real as opposed to the nominal value of commodities. To measure the value of commodities presupposes that we can measure the value of the labour which produces them. Money wages give us, in Smith's view, a merely nominal measure of the value of labour. The real value of labour can be determined only by its real wage, which is best measured by the commodity upon which labourers spend the bulk of their income. That commodity is corn. "Equal quantities of labour," Smith writes, "will at distant times be purchased more nearly with equal quantities of corn, the subsistence of the labourer, than with equal quantities of gold and silver, or perhaps of any other commodity."[94] It is interesting that Smith returns to this question in chapter 11 of Book 1 on rent, when he discusses the problem of measuring real rents. Again, he advances a corn model of the value of labour:

Equal quantities of corn will, in every state of society, in every stage of improvement, more nearly represent, or be equivalent to, equal quantities of labour, than equal quantities of any other part of the rude produce of land. Corn, accordingly, it has already been observed, is, in all the different stages of wealth and improvement, a more accurate measure of value than any other commodity or sett of commodities.

Smith develops this argument further in Book 4, chapter 5, where he discusses the bounty on the export of corn. There he argues that the price of corn regulates the price of all manufactured goods since it regulates the price of labour:

By regulating the money price of labour, it [corn] regulates that of manufacturing art and industry. And by regulating both, it regulates that of the compleat manufacture. The money price of labour, and of every other thing that is the produce either of land or labour, must necessarily either rise or fall in proportion to the money price of corn.[95]

Thus far, Smith's argument is simply that corn can be treated as the single consumption good of workers and that, if labour is considered to be the single determinant of value, the value of goods can be measured by the price of corn necessary to maintain labourers during the time they produce a given good. Such a view certainly creates problems with respect to Smith's "adding-up" theory of value in which capital and land are also constituents of natural price. But when it comes to constructing a growth model, the simplifying assumptions that labour is the single productive factor and that corn is the single consumption good of workers are of substantial service. Nowhere in *The Wealth of Nations* does Smith construct a full-fledged growth model. Nevertheless, chapter 3 of Book 2 does advance a theory of growth which makes sense only upon the assumption of a corn model. This fact has been recognized by several commentators. John Hicks, for example, points out that in the "pure model" of growth developed in Book 2, chapter 3, all capital is circulating capital (that is, there is no fixed capital), and the production period, represented by the agricultural year, begins with an initial capital stock consisting of a certain quantity of corn from the previous year's harvest. If the average wage is given, then the number of labourers is determined by the size of the capital stock, which is nothing more than a wage fund.[96] Once we accept this elementary circular flow model, all inputs and outputs of production are treated as quantities of corn. It thus becomes a simple matter to measure changes in national output. Since fixed capital is ignored, all output in the productive sector—excepting that seed which is needed for the next planting period—is taken to consist of the one commodity consumed by workers. All productive investment thus translates into a greater quantity of wage goods and the employment of more workers (perhaps at higher wages) during the next production period. For Adam Smith, then, as Marx put it, accumulation comes to mean "nothing more than the consumption of the surplus product by productive workers."[97]

Such a view has important implications for Smith's concept of capital. In the Smithian theory of accumulation, capital constitutes a part of the annual produce, since it is transformed—via the wage fund—into productive labour which produces consumer goods. Smith makes no allowance in his growth model for excluding from the annual produce that part of the capital of society to be added to the fixed stock of society. Such a position makes sense only, as Cannan pointed out, if we assume that Smith had adopted the physiocratic concept of annual reproduction in which all capital is treated as a "flow" which is reproduced during the production period. Cannan writes:

> But how can a particular part of the year's produce be the same thing as a particular part of the accumulated stock? The answer is that Adam Smith had evidently imbued himself with the physiocratic idea of 'reproduction.' . . . So, if the whole stock of provisions, materials, and finished work be supposed to be consumed and reproduced, or to be 'turned over' or 'circulated' in a given period, it becomes much the same thing as the part of the produce which during that period replaces the stock; the produce of one period becomes the stock out of which the wants of the next period are supplied.[98]

In truth, as Cannan points out elsewhere, such a view represents a regression with respect to physiocratic theory since it is based on an "imperfect understanding or partial adoption of the physiocrat theory of *avances primitives* (original capital) and *avances annuelles.*"[99] In other words, when he turns to the process of accumulation, Smith adopts a "vulgar-physiocrat" view in which all capital is taken to consist exclusively of annual working capital. Such a view amounts, as we have pointed out, to neglect of the role of fixed capital in accumulation. And, if we accept Hicks's view that Smith intended his chapter on accumulation "to be regarded as the centre-piece of his whole work," then such neglect has important implications for Smith's theory as a whole.

The recognition that Smith adopts a primitive circular flow model allows us to make sense of other aspects of *The Wealth of Nations.* We have seen above that Smith employs the physiocratic notion of "the annual produce of the land and labour" and that he tends, despite the attention he sometimes pays to fixed capital, to treat capital as a wage fund. Furthermore, as Cannan pointed out, Smith consistently describes the rate of profit as a percentage of a sum called "the capital annually employed," thus ignoring the existence of fixed capital stock in determining the rate of profit.[100] Finally, in *The Wealth of Nations* Smith consistently argues that the price of corn is the most accurate measure of value. Thus, it makes a certain analytic sense to conceive of the national economy as a giant corn-producing firm with one input and output of production. Such a conception squares nicely with Smith's neglect of fixed capital in his theory of growth. In fact, in Book 5, Smith discusses taxes on the annual produce of the land and treats seed as the only part of that produce which does not enter into consumption. Once again he ignores the costs of maintaining and replacing the elements of fixed capital: "The whole annual produce of the land of every country, if we except what is reserved for seed, is either annually consumed by the great body of the people, or exchanged for something else that is consumed by them." [101]

It seems clear, therefore, that Smith's theory of accumulation conforms quite closely to the characteristics of a corn model as outlined by Hollander. That model is characterized by one form of capital—circulating capital—reproducing itself during a period of circulation defined by the agricultural year. Obviously such a model is of little use to a theorist of industrial capitalism who is concerned about the allocation of capital, labour, and resources between sectors, as Hollander depicts Smith. Such a model is of value, however, if agriculture is taken to be the fundamental and strategic sector of the economy and if the primary concern of the theorist is with measuring increases in the output of the basic wage good. Moreover, the actual conditions of eighteenth-century Britain were such as to lend plausibility to such a model. As Hla Myint has written,

> In the light of economic conditions existing at that time, there is much to be said for such a method of abstraction. In those days, wage goods in fact consisted of a few primary products which could be lumped together under the head of a single commodity, "corn," and the output of "corn" could then be used as a convenient index of the output of consumers' goods in general. [102]

As we have noted above, Smith's approach to the question of growth is shaped by his concern for the level of real wages—for the standard of living of the "industrious poor." This concern predates *The Wealth of Nations*. Only in that work, however, does he construct a model of growth which defines accumulation in terms of growth of consumption (that is, as expansion of the wage fund) and which in so doing neglects the role of fixed capital in the growth process. In constructing such a model, Smith relies heavily upon the physiocratic concept of reproduction. In fact, by identifying capital with annual working capital (*avances annuelles*), Smith simplifies the physiocratic schema to present the economy as a system which entirely reproduces itself over the course of the agricultural year. This is far from being a pure physiocratic model. It is, however, a model which Smith could not have constructed without adapting certain basic physiocratic concepts. There can be little doubt that Smith's very concept of capital owes much to the Physiocrats. The debt comes out especially clearly when we examine his discussion of the "employments of capital." As we have noted above, in his claim for the superior productivity of agricultural investment Smith ranks the "employments" of capital by the amount of productive labour they set in motion. It has been noted accurately that "the peculiar and new terminology of 'employments of capital'" originated with Turgot's *Réflexions*. Moreover, Smith's four main employments of capital are clearly derived from the five such employments listed by Turgot.[103] Furthermore, as Schumpeter pointed out, Smith's view that saving "immediately" creates a new source of consumption since "what is annually saved is as regularly consumed as what is annually spent" would also seem to be derived from Turgot. Referring to this section of Smith's discussion, Schumpeter questions the originality of Smith's line of thought:

Turgot also says that, at least in the case of entrepreneurs, savings are converted into capital *sur-le-champ* (his italics). But Smith's 'immediately' certainly is the exact translation of *sur-le-champ*. And this is not unimportant; on the contrary, . . . it is an essential feature of both theories and indeed their most serious shortcoming. That such a slip should occur independently in two texts is indeed quite possible; but it is not likely.[104]

The unlikelihood of Smith's having developed this view independently is further confirmed by comparison of Smith's treatment of capital with that of Turgot. Several commentators have demonstrated a quite startling terminological correspondence between the theories of capital developed in *The Wealth of Nations* and the *Réflexions*.[105] Both Smith's theory of capital and his theory of growth, then, owe a profound debt to the Physiocrats. From them he derived a vision of economic dynamics which allowed him to translate his agrarian capitalist outlook into a growth model of the whole economy as a gigantic farm. From them, in other words, he inherited concepts of capital, accumulation, and reproduction which he assembled into a model of agrarian-based growth. And this model was a capitalist one. As we have shown in the previous chapter, the Physiocrats erected their reflections on English economic development into a rigorous analytical model of agrarian capitalism, one they based on replacing small peasant production by wage labour and using the agricultural surplus for capital investments on the land. In taking over and adapting physiocratic concepts, Smith was thus drawing upon a sophisticated agrarian capitalist model—a model which underpinned key elements of his economic analysis of society.

POLITICAL ECONOMY AND THE STATE

Smith has been seen often as a theorist in the tradition of those who construct "a non-political model of society," in which order and harmony are generated out of the free interaction of self-seeking individuals. In this conception, society seems "to sustain its own existence without the aid of an outside political agency." [106] Accordingly, the pursuit of private interest spontaneously creates an ordered pattern of social relationships which require no regulation by the political agency of the state. Society, therefore, is an intricate mechanism whose driving principle is self-interest; the state is a purely protective agency which functions as the defence of last resort for the system of economic individualism.

Our analysis of Smith's writings indicates that there are severe difficulties with such an interpretation. Smith's moral philosophy expresses a consistent concern about the erosion of the social bond in a commercial society. Likewise, his political economy—and his critique of mercantilism in particular—turns upon a vigorous denunciation of self-interested attempts to subvert the natural laws of the free market. In both cases, Smith looks to the state to correct these problems: first, by maintaining the principles of justice ("the pillar which supports the whole edifice" of society), and, second, by establishing and preserving an institutional framework which makes self-interested distortion of market relations virtually impossible.

Smith's worries about the social effects of the pursuit of self-interest surface at many points throughtout *The Wealth of Nations*. Private interests, he believes, constitute a formidable obstacle to political reform and economic progress. Discussing the prospects for establishing freedom of trade in Great Britain, for example, he writes that "to expect, indeed, that the freedom of trade should ever be entirely restored in Great Britain, is as absurd as to expect that an Oceana or Utopia should ever be established in it. Not only the prejudices of the publick, but what is much more unconquerable, the private interests of many individuals, irresistibly oppose it." The only solution to this problem is for the legislature to rise above the sphere of contending private interests and to establish laws and policies which are directed "not by the clamorous importunity of private interests, but by an extensive view of the general good." [107]

The Wealth of Nations thus puts a special emphasis upon the social and political setting in which self-interested economic activity takes place. In fact, if we examine Smith's theory of social determination—of the causes of economic and social progress—it becomes apparent that Smith accords priority not to strictly economic factors but, rather, to the social and institutional framework of society. Smith is often depicted as a theorist for whom private economic activity inevitably overcomes the obstacles to progress created by the ignorance and folly of governments. Indeed, Ronald Meek, among others, has painted Smith as an "economic determinist" for whom developments in the economic sphere set the basic patterns of social development. [108] Yet, throughout *The Wealth of Nations*, Smith continually suggests that economic progress is impossible without political arrangements which guarantee liberty of work and investment, and security of property. Smith does assert that "the natural effort of every man to better his own condition" is capable of "surmounting a hundred impertinent obstructions with which the folly of human laws too often encumbers its operations"; but he makes this process contingent upon a political order which maintains the liberty of the individual. Smith's much misunderstood passage actually makes this condition clear.

The natural effort of every individual to better his own condition, *when suffered to exert itself with freedom and security,* is so powerful a principle, that it is alone, and without any assistance, not only capable of carrying on the society to wealth and prosperity, but of surmounting a hundred impertinent obstructions with which the folly of human laws too often incumbers its operations. [109]

Elsewhere, Smith spells out in more detail those conditions of freedom and security which are prerequisites of economic progress and prosperity:

Commerce and manufactures can seldom flourish long in any state which does not enjoy a regular administration of justice, in which the people do not feel themselves secure in the possession of their property, in which the faith of contracts is not supported by law, and in which the authority of the state is not supposed to be regularly employed in enforcing the payment of debts from all those who are able to pay. [110]

It is, in other words, the system of justice and law which is essential to economic development; Smith states explicitly that England's progress has been supported by her unique political trajectory. "The security which the laws in Great Britain give to every man that he shall enjoy the fruits of his labour, is alone sufficient to make any country flourish." Conversely, as we noted earlier, he attributes the poverty of Spain and Portugal to their "civil and ecclesiastical governments" which would block economic progress regardless of the wisdom or folly of their commercial regulations. It follows, therefore, that the state must undertake to preserve the institutional order necessary to opulence. The science of political economy must consequently do more than analyze the natural laws of the market economy; it must illuminate those government policies which will satisfy the economic objectives of the wise legislator. Smith leaves little doubt as to what those objectives should be. In the introduction to Book 4 he writes that

Political oeconomy, considered as a branch of the science of a statesman or legislator, proposes two distinct objects: first, to provide a plentiful revenue or subsistence for the people, or more properly to enable them to provide such a revenue or subsistence for themselves; and secondly, to supply the state or commonwealth with a revenue sufficient for the publick services. It proposes to enrich both the people and the sovereign.

Elsewhere he writes that "the great object of the political economy of every country, is to encrease the riches and power of that country."[111]

It is pursuit of these social objectives—and not a dogmatic adherence to laissez-faire—which guides all of Smith's policy recommendations in *The Wealth of Nations*. In fact, a careful consideration of these recommendations indicates that he is quite prepared to violate the principles of laissez-faire in order to increase the opulence and security of the nation. In the case of the rate of interest, for example, Smith supports state regulation to prevent the legal rate from rising much above the lowest market rate.[112] Bentham subsequently attacked Smith for violating the principles of laissez-faire in this way. Unlike Smith, at this stage in his thinking Bentham elevated economic individualism above all other social principles. For Smith, however, public objectives can override the liberty of the individual: "But those exertions of the natural liberty of a few individuals, which might endanger the security of the whole society, are, and ought to be, restrained by the laws of all governments."[113]

This principle applies especially in the case of national defence. Smith hails the Act of Navigation, which sought to ensure that all British trade was carried in British ships. He acknowledges that the act was not favourable to the progress of opulence yet defends it on the grounds that defence "is of much more importance than opulence." Similarly, he supports bounties upon the export of British-made sailcloth and gunpowder, since these commodities are essential to national defence.[114]

Smith ascribes three essential functions to the state: maintenance of national defence; preservation of a system of justice; and erection and maintenance of public works and institutions.[115] National defence involves a standing army and those economic measures which protect defence-related industries. The system of justice, as we have shown above, requires an independent judiciary and separate executive and legislative functions of government. With respect to public works and institutions Smith elaborates a program of state activities which makes the state substantially more than a purely protective agency. He assigns to the state the responsibility for running the mint and a national postal service and for creating and maintaining roads, bridges, canals, and harbours; he also assigns it the job of constructing forts in the colonies to protect the colonial trade.[116] With respect to the educational system, however, Smith designates a particularly active role for the state.

The special significance that Smith attaches to education derives from his concern about the debilitating effects of the division of labour. Unlike some forms of society, commercial society is such that "some attention of government is necessary in order to prevent the almost entire corruption and degeneracy of the great body of the people." Despite his dexterity at a particular trade, the industrial labourer will experience a decline in "his intellectual, social and martial virtues"—a decline which is inevitable "unless government takes some pains to prevent it."[117] The specific measure which Smith favours as a corrective is a state-funded system of public education. So strongly does he feel about the necessity for such a system that he believes that the public has a right to "impose upon almost the whole body of the people, the necessity of acquiring those most essential parts of education." The way in which Smith proposes to impose education upon the poor clearly constitutes a case of violating principles of individual liberty in favour of a higher social good:

The publick can impose upon almost the whole body of the people the necessity of acquiring those most essential parts of education, by obliging every man to undergo an examination or probation in them before he can obtain the freedom in any corporation, or be allowed to set up any trade either in a village or town corporate.[118]

What this discussion demonstrates is the degree to which Smith's fundamental moral concerns—in this case, the deleterious effects of the division of labour—take priority over the premises of individual liberty. In cases such as this, it is the role of the state to initiate those programs or implement those policies which will correct the defects of commercial society. Smith's undertaking is thus *political* economy in the fullest sense of that term—advice to legislators on the political policies they ought to follow in the pursuit of national wealth and power—a pursuit whose ultimate purpose is to ensure a decent life for the labouring poor. As we have noted above, Smith defines political economy as in part "the science of the legislator." *The Wealth of Nations* is an exercise in political economy addressed to the wise legislator "whose deliberations ought to be governed by general principles which are always the same." Elsewhere, Smith refers to the "prudent law-giver," a term reminiscent of the *Moral Sentiments;* and he makes it clear that it shall fall to "the wisdom of future statemen and legislators" to determine precisely how to introduce the system of perfect liberty.[119]

Smith leaves little doubt, however, as to what should constitute the most fundamental objective of the legislator and the sovereign:

The principal attention of the sovereign ought to be to encourage, by every means in his power, the attention both of the landlord and of the farmer; by allowing both to pursue their own judgment; by giving to both the most perfect security that they shall enjoy the full recompence of their own industry; and by procuring to both the most extensive market for every part of their produce.[120]

This examination of his discussion of the functions of the state should indicate that Smith's was anything but "a non-political model of society." On the contrary, Smith considered the political order to be the crucial determinant of the economic state of society. Indeed, as we have shown, Smith ascribed a much more active role to the state than is generally recognized. Important as these modifications of the traditional image of Smith may be, however, they should not blind us to the crucial differences between Smith's theory of the state and that of the Physiocrats. Quesnay and his school responded to the fragmentation of the French polity, advocating a major program of social and economic intervention by the state. The state was to be the active agency of social and economic transformation; and this interventionist state was to be a rationalized absolute monarchy constituted above civil society and was to direct selfish action into socially acceptable channels—a monarchy "raised above all in order to assure the welfare of all," as we have quoted Turgot's words. For the Physiocrats, in other words, the state was to shape the overall direction of civil society. For Smith, by contrast, the state was to abstain from intervention in the economic relations of private individuals. The state was to establish an equitable framework for economic activity; it was not to attempt to direct or shape that activity. In this respect, Smith's was a more thoroughly laissez-faire position (recognizing all the qualifications we have introduced on this score) than that of Quesnay.

In an important sense, these different perspectives on the state reflected the different historical trajectories of French and British development. For the Physiocrats, unlike Smith, agrarian capitalism was not a reality to be protected but an ideal to be constructed. In a country suffering from economic stagnation and conflicting struggle among the dominant classes to privatize sections of the state, only the absolute monarchy appeared able to carry out a general reconstruction of the social and economic order. The crucial social and economic changes envisioned by the Physiocrats pivoted upon primitive capitalist accumulation—establishment of individual property in land, dissolution of traditional rights, transformation of the direct agricultural producers into wage labourers separated from the land. Since the political constitution of the kingdom blocked any single social class from initiating such a process, Quesnay and his followers looked to the absolutist state to carry through a capitalist reorganization of the state and agrarian economy. In so doing, they elaborated the theoretical program for an agrarian capitalist revolution from above.

Whereas the conditions of prerevolutionary France forced the Physiocrats to construct a political program for the separation of the direct producers from the land, Adam Smith could take such a process for granted. As Marx wrote, "in Adam Smith's writings this process of separation is assumed to be already completed."[121] Consequently, Smith did not need to invoke the agency of the state to establish the social relations of agrarian capitalism. Given the right institutional arrangements, the self-regulating mechanism of the market would continually reproduce the social division of labour upon which capitalist relations rested. Smith's agrarian capitalist model reflected what he took to be the dominant existing relations of production. For Smith, the commonwealth was a self-regulating organism in which state activities (unquestionably necessary in defence, justice, and public works) were to be regarded with some distrust. For the Physiocrats, the agricultural kingdom could be unified only through the active agency of the state, whose role it was to impose universality upon a civil society ravaged by particular interests; for Smith, the commonwealth could regulate itself, given the correct institutional and policy arrangements, and advance the public interest based on the self-seeking activity of individuals. All that was required—albeit a tall order, in Smith's view—was that the state ensure that it could not be swayed by the self-interested deceit of those whose interests ran counter to those of the public—that is, merchants and manufacturers. Given a state directed by an enlightened natural aristocracy of civic-minded landed gentlemen and correct policies with respect to justice, defence, and public works, the state could abstain from intervention in the economic relations of its citizens and allow the natural laws of the market to regulate the actions of individuals in civil society.

CONCLUSION

It is obvious from the foregoing discussion that the conventional picture of Smith as prophet of and propagandist for industrial capitalism is a gross distortion. If anything, Smith was a critic of industrial and commercial capitalists, but one who hoped to harness the productivity of the capitalist economy to moral ends. Smith hoped that commercial forces could be used to hurry the development of an agrarian-based capitalism guarded by a state run by a natural aristocracy of landed gentlemen. These aspirations were anything but foreign to the Scottish Enlightenment. Scotland's capitalist transformation was tied to agriculture, and Smith, like so many other leading Scottish intellectuals of the time, took a special interest in agricultural innovation and development. And in *The Wealth of Nations* he consistently sings the praises of rural life and argues that agriculture, by virtue of its superior productivity, ought to be the leading economic sector.

Agrarian-based development was contingent for Smith upon dismantling the mercantile system by which merchants and manufacturers had artificially increased prices and profits (thereby diminishing opulence) and diverted capital from its most productive to its least productive employment. The elimination of monopolizing activities by these groups required the establishment of a system of perfect competition; it would drive profits down to their "lowest ordinary level," increase opulence by lowering prices and boosting levels of personal consumption, and impose standards of propriety upon all participants in the market economy. Critical to the balanced development of agrarian capitalism was an institutional framework which would prevent selfish abuse of political and economic processes. It required that the state be based upon the most enlightened section of the landowning class (including those merchants who had bought land), a class whose basic interest was consistent with the public interest in unfettered economic growth. Smith's political economy was designed to develop a program for just such a social arrangement. It was, therefore, anything but an apology for industrial and commercial capitalists. On the contrary, it was a sustained attack on these groups and an argument for agrarian-based capitalist development in a landed commonwealth ruled by prosperous and public-spirited country gentlemen.

Conclusion: Political Economy and Capitalism

The history of landed property, which would demonstrate the gradual transformation of the feudal landlord into the landowner, of the hereditary, semi-
tributary and often unfree tenant for life into the modern farmer, and of the
resident serfs, bondsmen and villeins who belonged to the property into agricultural day-labourers, would indeed be the history of the formation of
modern capital.[1]

So Marx wrote in his famous preparatory notebooks for *Capital*.
What Marx had in mind in this passage is that the genesis of capitalism crucially involved dissolving the bonds between labourers and
the land which had characterized all previous modes of production.
The essential precondition of capitalism—what Marx called "the
primitive accumulation of capital"—is creation of a growing class of
propertyless labourers. And creation of such a class presupposes the
(often forcible) separation of producers from the land: "the expropriation of the agricultural producer, of the peasant, from the soil is
the basis of the whole process."[2] The ultimate result of this historical process of separation is the triadic social order of landowners,
capitalists, and wage labourers, which characterizes agrarian capitalism. In the actual course of events, however, all kinds of in-
termediate social arrangements are possible. In fact, it was quite
common in the seventeenth century for the improving landlord to
function as the principal economic agent organizing capitalist production on the land and for the farmer to appear as a wage labourer
of sorts. The pioneer analysts of the emerging economic system thus
often identified surplus value with ground rent and capitalist profit

258

with wages. Within this developing system of agrarian capitalism they had not yet grasped the essential features of that industrial capitalism which would emerge in the course of time. As Marx wrote,

Petty, Cantillon and all those other writers who stand closer to the feudal period assume that ground-rent is the normal form of surplus value, while profit for them is still lumped indiscriminately with wages or at most appears as a portion of this surplus-value extorted from the landowner by the capitalist. They therefore base themselves on a state of affairs in which, firstly, the agricultural population are still the overwhelming majority of the nation, and, secondly, the landowner still appears as the person who appropriates in the first instance the excess labour of the immediate producers, by way of his monopoly of landed property. Landed property thus still appears as the chief condition of production.[3]

The pioneers of classical political economy thus wrote with an emerging agrarian-based capitalism in mind. Their theoretical preoccupations were shaped by those changes which transformed the nature of agrarian economy rather than by industrial development. They envisioned the economy as a circular flow of wealth animated by the agricultural surplus product; the primary economic agents were farmers, landlords, and country labourers. Merchants and manufacturers, although necessary within a commercial economy, were considered of subsidiary importance; indeed, in some cases these groups were depicted as actually detrimental to economic and social well-being. Even when these groups were seen as fulfilling an economically necessary role, their functions were emphasized as subordinated to the leading economic sector—agriculture.

This theoretical orientation is clear in the earliest period of classical political economy, the late seventeenth century. In the case of William Petty, the pioneer of classical British economics, we have shown that rent was the central concept in his system of economic analysis. Petty was preoccupied with determining the relative value of land and labour inputs in agricultural products and that agrarian income which he considered most significant—rent. As we have demonstrated in chapter 2, Petty's conceptual structure centrally informed the economic writings of Child, Locke, Barbon, and North. A similar approach informs the pioneer of classical French political economy—Pierre de Boisguilbert. Although Boisguilbert's primary concern was the relation between taxes and the generation of wealth, he saw the continuous production of an agricultural surplus as critical to the economic and political health of France; the economic and fiscal policies of the Crown should derive first and foremost from encouraging peasants and landlords to improve agriculture and expand their output. Thus, although Boisguilbert's analytic point of departure differed from Petty's, he too arrived at the view that economic well-being hinged on a growing agrarian surplus.

In the third quarter of the eighteenth century the analyses of Petty and Boisguilbert were integrated into a rigorous and coherent model of economic relations. Building on Richard Cantillon's refinements of Petty and Locke, the physiocratic school developed the first genuine system of theoretical economics. Quesnay and his followers saw themselves as reconstructing at a theoretical level the basic economic practices of English agriculture. They took agriculture to be the only surplus-producing (or "productive") sector and saw rent as the only form of this surplus. Thus, the generation and utilization of rent became the crucial phenomena of the physiocratic model. Moreover, the Physiocrats saw the agrarian economy in clearly capitalist terms. Central to their model was the triadic social structure which had become the distinctive feature of English agriculture, the relationship of landlord, tenant farmer, and wage labourer in agricultural production. They thus constructed their model on large "capital farms" which employed hired wage labour and produced for the market.

The same triadic structure occupies a central place in Adam Smith's vision of the economy. Indeed, it crucially informs his theory of value, in which the value of every good "resolves itself" into rent, wages, and profit; these incomes accrue respectively to landlords, labourers, and capitalists.[4] Moreover, though Smith rejects the physiocratic doctrine of the exclusive productivity of agriculture, he does consider it to be the most productive sector of the economy. This view is fundamental to his critique of mercantilism, which he faults for diverting wealth away from its most productive use (landed investment) into less productive areas. Furthermore, as we have demonstrated in chapter 5, Smith's theory of capital accumulation rests upon an agricultural model of the economy. His growth theory treats the economy like a giant corn-producing enterprise, in which all capital is reproduced during the course of the annual agricultural cycle (and in which there is thus no fixed capital). Though this model does not incorporate all the essential features of industrial capitalism, it points to some central aspects of growth, as defined in terms of a per capita increase in the most important consumer good—corn. Moreover, Smith's analysis of growth in an agricultural economy clearly assumes capitalist production relations; it assumes that all feudal or precapitalist forms of organization have given way to those based on capital and wage labour. It is this assumption, integrated into an economic model, which clearly distinguishes the classical political economists from Petty to Smith as theorists of agrarian *capitalism*.

A capitalist model of economic relations presupposes a labour market; it presupposes that feudal social relations have been severed, communal and customary rights to land in large measure eliminated, and the direct agricultural producer "proletarianized," that is, reduced to the status of a rural day labourer. The rudimentary model of Petty and Locke explicitly incorporates the wage labourer. Unable to take the results of primitive accumulation for granted, the Physiocrats advocated state policies which would create capitalist relations of production on the land. Smith, by contrast, simply accepts without analysis the results of primitive accumulation; and, in chapter 6 of Book 1 of *The Wealth of Nations*, he quickly plunges his readers into a social setting inhabited not principally by independent commodity producers like butchers, brewers, and bakers but rather by three main social classes: landowners, capitalists, and wage labourers.

Some classical political economists thus made explicit reference to those processes of primitive accumulation which are a prerequisite of capitalist development; others simply presupposed this unique result of historical change. But in either case, there can be little doubt that classical political economists prior to Ricardo paid significant attention to those historical processes which constitute the origins of capitalism, an attention they shared with Marx. But the pre-Ricardian classical economists differed sharply from Marx; they saw these historical changes as creating a social relation (wage labour) consistent with the natural order of things and thus as indispensable to economic prosperity and social harmony. These economic theorists thereby naturalized and eternalized historically specific relations of production. The result, as Marx put it, is that for the political economists "there has been history, but there is no longer any."[5] It is this ahistorical and naturalistic treatment of capitalist production relations which gives the work of these theorists its uncritical and apologetic character.

Although they accepted the need for primitive accumulation, however, the political economists had profound reservations about the general effects of commercialized economic relations on social and political life. It is here that their treatments of the state become important—and it is here that our analysis departs again from the traditional interpretation of classical economics. As we have pointed out in the introduction, this interpretation sees classical political economy as a species of economic liberalism. According to this view, the political economists developed a liberal-individualist account of economic relations which buttressed the liberal theory of the state. Indeed, this view generally credits the classical economists with identifying market relations—personified in merchants and capitalist manufacturers—as the vital precondition for liberal political arrangements. In this way, it says, they made commercial and industrial capitalists the agents of liberty.

Our analysis has shown that such a view suffers from grave defects. To be sure, the classical political economists we have studied were, to differing degrees, advocates of laissez-faire insofar as they believed that self-seeking action by independent individuals produced beneficial social effects. Yet they held that this pertained only under very definite conditions. And it was the role of the state to create those conditions—conditions which would ensure that market processes were not distorted to give monopolistic power to any economic agents. Only if the state created institutional arrangements which protected society against attempts to manipulate economic processes for selfish ends would self-seeking activity in economic markets operate for the good of society.

To say that, however, is to recognize that for these economic theorists the state had to be constructed on principles different from— indeed, antagonistic to—those which prevailed in civil society. The early classical political economists did not treat the state as an emanation of civil society, as a special institution rooted in market relations and constructed on principles consistent with those which regulated the economic relations between private individuals. On the contrary, as we have suggested, they believed that the state should function as a bulwark against the intrusion of private economic interests into the political sphere. To this end, they argued that the state should be immunized against the disease of "particularism" and constituted as a general order above the sphere of private interest. In this sense, then, the principles of the political order were the ultimate key to prosperity and harmony. Theirs was thus anything but a nonpolitical theory of society. They assigned to the state the task of creating and maintaining the legal and political framework in which self-seeking economic activity, rather than harming society, would further its general interests.

It followed from this argument that the state should not be based upon those groups which excelled at the enterprise of private economic advancement. Useful though such groups might be in a well-ordered society, they should not be allowed to influence the principles of the political realm. On this point the Physiocrats and Adam Smith were united, however much they differed in their overall conceptions of the state. For the Physiocrats, no group in civil society was to be allowed to exercise influence over state policy. Civil society was characterized by rampant particularism. For this reason, Quesnay and his school argued, the state must exist in the form of an absolute monarchy in which an indivisible political power is constructed over and against civil society. Only such a state can defend the general interest of society against the pleadings of special interests; and only such a state can intervene to eliminate those economic and fiscal practices instituted in order to win the favour of private interests. The absolutist state—a form of enlightened despotism—was for the Physiocrats, then, the essential precondition for reorganizing society from above in such a way that it could move towards agrarian capitalism.

Adam Smith shared the physiocratic opposition to the intrusion of selfish interests into the political sphere. Unlike the Physiocrats, however, Smith held that certain groups in civil society had interests consistent with the general interest. These were the groups connected with agriculture and the dominant agrarian class, the landed gentry, in particular. There were many reasons for Smith's bias in favour of the landed gentry. Two are worthy of emphasis in the present context. First, Smith held that landlords, unlike merchants, have a fixed and permanent interest in their country of residence. They have a permanent interest, therefore, in seeing that society is prosperous and well-governed. Second, Smith held that since rent rises with the general progress of opulence, landlords have no special interest in obstructing the natural course of economic development. The same is not true for merchants and manufacturers. Since economic growth tends to depress the average rate of profit, these groups have an interest in creating monopolistic arrangements which artificially raise their prices, slow down the overall rate of growth, and increase the prices of consumer goods (thereby lowering real living standards).

From this perspective it follows that merchants and manufacturers should be prevented from influencing state policy. Instead, political power should be based upon the landed gentry—or at least its enlightened members who truly perceive the fusion between their interests and that of society. Only a commonwealth rooted in a natural aristocracy of landed gentlemen can create the framework in which self-seeking economic activity furthers the public interest. Thus, however much Smith may have admired the economic effects produced by the activities of merchants and manufacturers in a framework of perfect competition, he considered that economic progress and social stability were possible only if the state were founded upon principles foreign to those which governed the activities of merchants and manufacturers in market society. A state so founded could, moreover, be decidedly more liberal than the state envisioned by the Physiocrats. Unlike his French counterparts, Smith believed that there were groups in civil society whose private interests were consistent with the public interest. If the state were based on these groups, and if these groups were properly enlightened as to the economic and political principles necessary to the well-being of society, then the legal and institutional context could be created for private individuals to simultaneously pursue their economic self-interest and further the public good. The state could, *under these conditions*, play a noninterventionist role in economic life—an option which was not available in the physiocratic schema.

Our analysis makes it clear, therefore, that it is a serious misreading to depict classical political economy before Ricardo as an apologia for industrial capitalism. On the contrary, the classical political economists examined in this study—and especially their most famous representative, Adam Smith—were deeply suspicious of the commercial spirit and its potentially destructive impact upon society and the state. They did, of course, see social benefits if that spirit were to be harnessed for useful ends—benefits such as improved living standards and a strong and stable state. Nevertheless, they were profoundly worried about the dangers posed by the commercialization of social life. To circumvent these dangers, they proposed a structural tension between polity and economy. They proposed to found the state on principles foreign to those which governed economic relations in a market society. In the case of the Physiocrats, this required an *absolute autonomy* of the state from civil society. Smith, by contrast, believed that there was a class in civil society whose mode of life suited it for civic responsibilities—the landed gentry, or at least its most enlightened representatives. For Smith, this agrarian group could provide the required political counterbalance to the growing economic weight of merchants and manufacturers. In fact, it would appear that Smith welcomed the expansion of agrarian capitalism partly as a means of bolstering the wealth and power of the landed ruling class. By counterposing polity and economy in this way, these classical political economists, and Smith in particular, adopted an implicitly critical stance towards developing capitalism. They asserted the priority of values—distributive justice, benevolence, the priority of consumption over production—foreign to the purely economic system of capitalism. In this respect they provided the basis for a moral critique of capitalism. Yet we would not go as far as to say, as does Ralph Lindgren, that we can find in Smith a "concrete and feasible" alternative to the critique of capitalism developed by Marx.[6]

Smith's critique of industrial capitalism was by its nature partial and seriously compromised from the start. Like all the political economists examined in this study, Smith accepted the necessity of the basic social relations of capitalism. His vision of a society based upon natural liberty presupposed those processes of primitive accumulation which had transformed the direct agricultural producer into a wage labourer bereft of land. He did so for purely economic reasons: he believed that capitalist agriculture and industry were the best means of increasing the division of labour and raising aggregate output. Yet, as we have seen, he recoiled from the inevitable consequences of generalizing these relations—intellectual fragmentation, physical stultification, and corruption. His attempt to use state policy—especially in the field of education—to combat these trends amounts to little more than an attempt to resist the symptoms of capitalist development. This ambivalence vitiated Smith's critique of industrial capitalism. To accept the social relations of capitalism offered him little logical choice but to accept the inevitable consequences of capitalist development.

Smith was saved that choice. He lived and wrote in a period of transition, in which the ultimate direction of social and economic development was not yet clear. His ambiguous stance towards capitalism was not a tenable position, however, for social theorists and political economists of the next generation. Political economists like Jeremy Bentham, David Ricardo, and Jean-Baptiste Say recognized the direction of development and allied themselves to it. They shaped political economy into a doctrine of industrial capitalism. They jettisoned its moral and historical dimensions and its agrarian bias.[7] For them, the social relations *and* the direction of capitalist development were justified as natural to all forms of economic life. Classical political economy became through their labours a more rigorous doctrine; but it also became, as it had not previously been, an apologia for industrial capitalism. Once so constructed, it appeared as the goal of Smith and the Physiocrats—although their theoretical tools had been inadequate to the task. And it is that interpretation which has dominated histories of political economy. Seen through the prism of Bentham, Ricardo, and Say—rather than on their own terms— Quesnay, Turgot, and Smith appear as brilliant, although occasionally muddled, prophets of industrial capitalism, prophets whose work was merely systematized at the hands of the next generation of political economists.

Our study has shown that this view seriously distorts the richness of thought to be found in the classical political economists of the seventeenth and eighteenth centuries, and in Quesnay and Smith in particular. In their writings we find an important dimension of historical analysis (a recognition that the preconditions of capitalism must be explained) and the treatment of economic theory as *political* economy in the fullest sense of the term—a body of thought which sees political organization and its legal and institutional arrangements as decisive to the processes of economic life. Furthermore, because their political economy was constituted on the terrain of moral and jurisprudential discourse, we find in their writings themes which anticipate a critique of industrial capitalism. But any critique constructed upon these foundations could only be an inconsistent and ambivalent one. For as theorists of agrarian capitalism, Quesnay and

Smith accepted as necessary and desirable those historical processes of primitive accumulation which transformed the mass of society into a proletariat, created a potential home market, and established certain essential preconditions of industrial capitalism. In the final analysis, their acceptance of the social relations of capitalist production rendered weak and ineffective their moral opposition to certain consequences of that form of social production.

It was the burden of Marx's critique of capitalism to demonstrate that the original alienation of producers from the land and their transformation into wage labourers necessarily produced exploitation and general forms of capitalist alienation—alienation of workers from the products of their labour (which dominate them in the form of capital, an alien wealth and power); from their own labouring activity itself (which is performed under the dictates of capital); and from the materials and instruments of labour (the means of production).[8] For Marx, overcoming alienation and exploitation thus requires overturning the separation of producers from the means of production (including land), which is the essential precondition of capitalism; it requires in other words the expropriation of capital, that alien power produced by workers which dominates their lives in capitalist society: "What is now to be expropriated is not the self-employed worker, but the capitalist who exploits a large number of workers." Such an expropriation "does not re-establish private property, but it does indeed establish individual property on the basis of the achievements of the capitalist era: namely cooperation and the possession in common of the land and the means of production produced by labour itself."[9] Recognizing that capitalism was constituted on the grounds of an historical process of alienation (separation) of producers from the means of production, Marx, unlike Smith, developed a critique which struck at the roots of capitalism in demanding the abolition of alienated wage labour. For this reason, his critique remains to this day the only comprehensive—and thus "concrete and feasible"—critique of capitalism. But that is another story, one far beyond the scope of the present study.

Notes

INTRODUCTION

1 I make no great claim for the originality of this argument. It is essentially derived from Marx's important discussion of the "primitive accumulation of capital." See Karl Marx, *Capital*, vol. 1, trans. Ben Fowkes (Harmondsworth: Penguin, 1976), pt. 8.

2 Harold J. Laski, *The Rise of European Liberalism* (London: Unwin, 1936), 119.

3 Hiroshi Mizuta, "Moral Philosophy and Civil Society," in *Essays on Adam Smith*, ed. Andrew Skinner and Thomas Wilson (Oxford: Oxford University Press, 1975), 115.

4 Eric Roll, *A History of Economic Thought*, 4th ed. (London: Faber and Faber, 1973), 150, 86.

5 Joseph Cropsey, *Polity and Economy: An Interpretation of the Principles of Adam Smith* (The Hague: Nijhoff, 1957), vii.

6 It needs to be emphasized that my argument applies to classical political economy *prior* to Ricardo. In certain respects, Ricardo's work represents a turning-point in the development of economics equally significant to the "neo-classical revolution." Ricardo severs the explicit connection of economic analysis to a broader social philosophy. The considerations on morality, justice, and government which figured centrally in the writings of Smith and Quesnay are entirely foreign to Ricardo's *Principles*. Ricardo jettisons the normative dimension of political economy; we are left to reflect simply upon the laws of economic distribution.

Ricardo's inappropriateness to our thesis stems from other considerations, his hostility to the landlord and his concern that the surplus accruing to the agricultural sector (rent) would inevitably diminish the surplus accruing to the industrial capitalist (entrepreneurial profit). Ricardo still conceives of the economy in agrarian terms. Indeed, as Keith Tribe writes (*Land, Labour, and Economic Discourse* [London: Routledge and Kegan Paul, 1978], 133), "For Ricardo, political econ-

269

omy is the investigation of the system of distribution in an agrarian capitalist economy." But it is Ricardo's contention—and here the break from Smith, Quesnay, Locke, and Petty is decisive—"that the interest of the landlord is always opposed to the interest of every other class in the community" (see David Ricardo, "Essay on Profits," in *The Works and Correspondence of David Ricardo*, ed. Piero Sraffa, vol. 4 [Cambridge: Cambridge University Press, 1962], 21).

CHAPTER I. FROM FEUDALISM TO CAPITALISM:
THE HISTORICAL CONTEXT OF CLASSICAL
POLITICAL ECONOMY

1 Karl Marx, *Grundrisse*, trans. Martin Nicolaus (Harmondsworth: Penguin, 1973), 883.

2 Throughout this work I shall use the modern spelling of Boisguilbert and not the version (Boisguillebert) used by Marx. It should also be noted that Petty, although born in England, spent much of his adult life in Ireland. Even there, however, he was in every sense an Englishman, working for many years on behalf of Cromwell's régime in its conquest and settlement of Irish lands.

3 Michael Postan, *The Medieval Economy and Society* (Harmondsworth: Penguin, 1975) 194. For discussion of the notion of a feudal crisis see Rodney Hilton, "A Crisis of Feudalism," *Past and Present*, 80 (1978): 3. Marc Bloch's view can be found in his *French Rural History*, trans. Janet Sondheimer (Berkeley: University of California Press, 1966). Two other attempts to assess the crisis of feudalism are worthy of note. They are Edouard Perroy, "A l'origine d'une économie contractée: les crises du XIVe siècle," *Annales. Economies, Sociétés, Civilisations* 4 (1949) and Rodney Hilton, "Y eut-il une crise générale de la féodalité?" *Annales. Economies, Sociétés, Civilisations* 6 (1951).

4 Marc Bloch, *Feudal Society*, trans L. A. Manyon (Chicago: University of Chicago Press, 1961), 1: 69–71; Georges Duby, *Rural Economy and Country Life in the Medieval West*, trans. Cynthia Postan (Columbia: University of South Carolina Press, 1968), 71–80.

5 See for example Harry A. Miskimin, *The Economy of Early Renaissance Europe: 1300–1460* (Englewood Cliffs, N.J.: Prentice-Hall, 1969), 25.

6 Duby, 298–300; Guy Bois, *Crise du féodalisme* (Paris: Presses de la Fondation Nationale des Sciences Politiques, 1976), pt. 1.

7 Robert Brenner, "The Agrarian Roots of European Capitalism," *Past and Present* 97 (1982): 29, 34–35; idem, "Agrarian Class Structure and Economic Development in Pre-Industrial Europe," *Past and Present* 70 (1976): 49; Witold Kula, *An Economic Theory of the Feudal System*, trans. Lawrence Garner (London: New Left Books, 1976), 29–39, 102–5; Michael Postan, *Essays on Medieval Agriculture and General*

Problems of the Medieval Economy (Cambridge: Cambridge University Press, 1973), 15; Emmanuel Le Roy Ladurie, *The Peasants of Languedoc*, trans. John Day (Urbana: University of Illinois Press, 1974), 236.

8 Rodney Hilton, *The Decline of Feudalism in Medieval England* (London: Macmillan and Co., 1969), 36; idem, *Bond Men Made Free: Medieval Peasant Movements and the English Rising of 1381* (London: Methuen and Co., 1973), 156–63; Christopher Day, "A Redistribution of Incomes in Fifteenth-Century England?" in *Peasants, Knights, and Heretics*, ed. Rodney Hilton (Cambridge: Cambridge University Press, 1976); Maurice Dobb, *Studies in the Development of Capitalism*, rev. ed. (New York: International Publishers, 1963), 49–52.

9 Hilton, *Decline of Feudalism*, 39, 43.

10 Postan, *The Medieval Economy*, 158.

11 William Lazonick, "Karl Marx and Enclosures in England," *Review of Radical Political Economics* 6 (1974): 20; Eric Kerridge, "The Movement of Rent, 1540–1630," *Economic History Review* 6 (1953): 28–29.

12 William George Hoskins, *The Midland Peasant: The Economic and Social History of a Leicestershire Village* (London: Macmillan and Co., 1957), 141; Rodney Hilton, *The Economic Development of Some Leicestershire Estates in the Fourteenth and Fifteenth Centuries* (Oxford: Oxford University Press, 1947), 105; R. H. Tawney, *The Agrarian Problem in the Sixteenth Century* (1912; reprint, New York: Harper and Row, 1967), 56–57.

13 Mildred Campbell, *The English Yeoman Under Elizabeth and the Early Stuarts* (New Haven: Yale University Press, 1942), 104.

14 Tawney, 152.

15 David Underdown, *Revel, Riot, and Rebellion: Popular Politics and Culture in England, 1603–1660* (Oxford: Oxford University Press, 1985), 26.

16 On this point see Rodney Hilton, *The English Peasantry in the Later Middle Ages* (Oxford: Oxford University Press, 1975), 168.

17 On rising rents see Lawrence Stone, *The Crisis of the Aristocracy, 1558–1641*, abridged ed. (Oxford: Oxford University Press, 1967), 153–59. The estimate on the amount of enclosure to have taken place by 1700 comes from Eric Kerridge, *The Agricultural Revolution* (London: George Allen and Unwin, 1967), 24.

18 For a useful discussion of the economics of the new husbandry see C. Peter Trimmer, "The Turnip, the New Husbandry, and the English Agricultural Revolution," *Quarterly Journal of Economics* 83 (1969): 375–95.

19 These are the dates suggested by F. M. L. Thompson, "The Social Distribution of Landed Property in England since the Sixteenth Century," *Economic History Review*, 2d ser., 19 (1966): 510–11, although Thompson himself remains sceptical about such a redistribution of property. On this point and on the sales of church lands see Gordon E. Mingay, *The Gentry: The Rise and Fall of a Ruling Class* (London: Longman, 1976), chaps. 2 and 3.

20 On these points see Lawrence Stone, *The Causes of the English Revolution, 1529–1642* (London: Routledge and Kegan Paul, 1972), 92; and G. R. Elton, *England Under the Tudors*, 2d ed. (London: Methuen and Co., 1974).

21 The phrase "committee of landlords" was coined by Barrington Moore, Jr., in his *Social Origins of Dictatorship and Democracy* (Boston: Beacon Press, 1966), 19, in reference to the eighteenth century.

22 Among the best accounts of the revolution from below during the 1640s are Brian Manning, *The English People and the English Revolution* (1976; reprint, Harmondsworth: Penguin, 1978) and Christopher Hill, *The World Turned Upside Down* (1972; reprint, Harmondsworth: Penguin, 1975). See also idem, *The Experience of Defeat* (New York: Viking Penguin, 1984) and H. N. Brailsford, *The Levellers and the English Revolution*, ed. Christopher Hill (1961; reprint, London: Spokesman, 1976). For an important study which qualifies the overall picture of popular politics in terms of regionally-based popular cultures see Underdown.

23 On this period see Christopher Hill, *The Century of Revolution, 1603–1714* (1961; reprint, London: Cardinal-Sphere Books, 1974), 174–76 and 202–9; J. R. Jones, *The First Whigs: The Politics of the Exclusion Crisis, 1678–1683* (London: Oxford University Press, 1968); and K. H. D. Haley, *The First Earl of Shaftesbury* (Oxford: Clarendon Press, 1968).

24 Lois G. Schwoerer, "The Bill of Rights: Epitome of the Revolution of 1688–89," in *Three British Revolutions: 1641, 1688, 1776*, ed. J. G. A. Pocock (Princeton: Princeton University Press, 1980), interprets the Bill of Rights as an essentially radical document. For views which emphasize the more moderate and conservative character of the bill see W. A. Speck, *Stability and Strife: England, 1714–1760* (London: Edward Arnold, 1977), 12–15; and Hill, *Century of Revolution*, 237–40.

25 Gordon E. Mingay, "The Size of Farms in the Eighteenth Century," *Economic History Review*, 2d ser., 14 (1961–62): 481; and idem, *English Landed Society in the Eighteenth Century* (London: Routledge and Kegan Paul, 1963), 20. On the overall importance of landed investment at this time see also Barry Holderness, "Capital Formation in Agriculture" and the subsequent "Comment" by F. M. L. Thompson, in *Aspects of Capital Investment in Great Britain, 1750–1850*, ed. J. P. P. Higgins and Sidney Pollard (London: Methuen and Co., 1971) and J. D. Chambers and Gordon E. Mingay, *The Agricultural Revolution, 1750–1850* (London: B. T. Batsford, 1966), 84.

26 Barrington Moore, Jr., 29.

27 Charles Wilson and Geoffrey Parker, eds., *An Introduction to the Sources of European Economic History, 1500–1800*, vol. 1 (London: Methuen and Co., 1977), 121; Lazonick, 26–27.

28 One of the more sophisticated versions of this argument can be found in Chambers and Mingay.

29 Hoskins, 255.

30 Karl Marx, *Capital*, trans. Ben Fowkes (Harmondsworth: Penguin, 1976), 1: 875–76.

31 See, for example, Eric Hobsbawm and George Rudé, *Captain Swing: A Social History of the Great English Agricultural Uprising of 1830* (New York: W. W. Norton, 1975), 32.

32 E. P. Thompson, "The Peculiarities of the English," in *The Poverty of Theory and Other Essays* (London: Merlin Press, 1978), 42; see also 44. On the victory of property rights over customary rights see idem, *Whigs and Hunters: The Origin of the Black Act* (New York: Pantheon, 1975).

33 E. L. Jones, "Agricultural Origins of Industry," *Past and Present* 40 (1968): 58–71; W. H. B. Court, *The Rise of Midland Industries, 1600–1838* (1938; reprint, London: Oxford University Press, 1953), 36–38; and E. L. Jones, editor's introduction to *Agriculture and Economic Growth in England, 1650–1815* (London: Methuen and Co., 1967), 37. See also Joan Thirsk, *Economic Policy and Projects* (Oxford: Oxford University Press, 1978), chap. 5.

34 A. H. John, "Agricultural Productivity and Economic Growth in England, 1700–1760," *Journal of Economic History* 25 (1965): 19–34; and idem, "Aspects of English Economic Growth in the First Half of the Eighteenth Century," *Economica* 28 (1961): 176–90.

35 For a provocative argument about the timing of the industrial takeoff see John, "Aspects of Economic Growth," 189.

36 Marx, "Immediate Results of the Process of Production," *Capital*, 1: 1021, 1024, 1054–55.

37 J. H. M. Salmon, *Society in Crisis: France in the Sixteenth Century* (1975; reprint, London: Methuen and Co., 1979), 30, 40–41; see also Le Roy Ladurie, 94; and Bois, 141–43.

38 Salmon, 291–92. For the overall context of the rise of absolutism see Robin Briggs, *Early Modern France 1560–1715* (Oxford: Oxford University Press, 1977) and Max Beloff, *The Age of Absolutism, 1660–1815* (London: Hutchinson and Co., 1954).

39 Perry Anderson, *Lineages of the Absolutist State* (London: New Left Books, 1974), 18.

40 Pierre Goubert, *Louis XIV and Twenty Million Frenchmen*, trans. Ann Carter (New York: Vintage, 1970), 107. It should be noted that a sizable share of revenues came from the sale of offices. For data on price levels during this period see Wilson and Parker, 178–80.

41 See Boris Porshnev, "The Bourgeoisie and Feudal Absolutism in Seventeenth-Century France," in *France in Crisis, 1620–1675*, ed. and trans. P. J. Coveney (London: Macmillan and Co., 1977), 124, 128–29. On lords encouraging peasant resistance to the Crown see Hubert Methivier, "A Century of Conflict: The Economic and Social Disorder of the 'Grand Siècle,'" in *France in Crisis*, 75.

42 Brenner, "Agrarian Roots of Capitalism," 81.

43 Julian Dent, *Crisis in Finance: Crown, Financiers, and Society in Seven-*

teenth-Century France (Newton Abbot, England: David and Charles, 1973), 39, 43, 51; Goubert, *Louis XIV*, 114–39; Boris Porshnev, "Popular Uprisings in France before the Fronde, 1623–1648," in *France in Crisis*, 164; Roland Mousnier, "The Financial *Officiers* during the Fronde," in *France in Crisis*, 203.

44 George V. Taylor, "Types of Capitalism in Eighteenth-Century France," *English Historical Review* 79 (1964): 479.

45 Ibid., 491; see also Taylor, "The Paris Bourse on the Eve of the Revolution, 1781–1789," *American Historical Review* 67 (1962).

46 Bloch, *French Rural History*, 134.

47 See, for example, ibid., 221–28; and Robert Forster, *The Nobility of Toulouse in the Eighteenth Century: A Social and Economic History* (Baltimore: Johns Hopkins Press, 1960), 77–82.

48 Beloff, 75.

CHAPTER 2. RENT AND TAXES: THE ORIGINS OF CLASSICAL POLITICAL ECONOMY

1 Perry Anderson, *Lineages of the Absolutist State* (London: New Left Books, 1974), 36*n*34.

2 This is precisely the criticism often made of the classic study by Eli Heckscher, *Mercantilism*, trans. Mendel Shapiro, 2d ed., 2 vols. (London: George Allen and Unwin, 1955). For critical perspectives see D. C. Coleman, ed., *Revisions in Mercantilism* (London: Methuen and Co., 1969) and Joseph Schumpeter, *History of Economic Analysis* (New York: Oxford University Press, 1954), 335.

3 Barry Supple, *Commercial Crisis and Change in England* (Cambridge: Cambridge University Press, 1959), 228–29.

4 Heckscher, 2: 144.

5 On the sixteenth-century revival of notions of the regulated economy see Lawrence Stone, "State Control in Sixteenth-Century England," *Economic History Review* 14 (1947): 103–20; and John Walter and Keith Wrightson, "Dearth and the Social Order in Early Modern England," *Past and Present* 71 (1976): 22–42. The persistence of such ideas is analyzed by E. P. Thompson, "The Moral Economy of the English Crowd in the Eighteenth Century," *Past and Present* 50 (1971): 76–136.

6 On Thomas Smith see Mary Dewar's introduction to *A Discourse of the Commonweal of This Realm of England*, by Thomas Smith (Charlottesville: University Press of Virginia, 1969).

7 S. T. Bindhoff, *Tudor England* (Harmondsworth: Penguin, 1950), 114.

8 For a discussion of the causes of this period of inflation see R. B. Outhwaite, *Inflation in Tudor and Early Stuart England* (London: Macmillan and Co., 1969), 10.

9 Clement Armstrong, "Howe to Reforme the Realme in Setting Them to Werke and to store Tillage," in *Tudor Economic Documents*, ed.

R. H. Tawney and Eileen Powers (1924; reprint, New York: Barnes and Noble, 1963) 3: 115. On Armstrong's life and writings see S. T. Bindhoff, "Clement Armstrong and His Treatises of the Commonweal," *Economic History Review* 17 (1944): 64–73.

10 Whitney R. D. Jones, *The Tudor Commonwealth, 1529–1559* (London: Athlone Press, 1970), 37; and Max Beer, *Early British Economics* (1938; reprint, London: Frank Cass and Co., 1967), 86.

11 Thomas Smith, *A Discourse of the Commonweal of This Realm of England*, ed. Mary Dewar (Charlottesville: University Press of Virginia, 1969), 79, 101–2. In a revised edition of the *Discourse*, apparently written in 1581, Smith came (having perhaps been influenced by Bodin) to lay much more emphasis upon the influx into Europe of precious metals from the Americas.

12 Ibid., 63.

13 See Armstrong, "Howe to Reforme the Realme," 129, and the anonymous "Policies to Reduce this Realme of England Unto a Prosperous Wealthe and Estate," in *Tudor Economic Documents*, 3: 318; see also 3: 321.

14 Smith, 86; my emphasis.

15 Ibid., 85.

16 Armstrong, 105.

17 See Gerrard Malynes, "A treatise of the Canker of England's Commonweal," in *Tudor Economic Documents*, 3: 386–404.

18 Thomas Mun, *England's Treasure by Forraign Trade* (1664; reprint, Oxford: Basil Blackwell, 1928), 40.

19 Ibid., 87. A similar conception of the functioning of necessary laws of economic life was elaborated by Mun's disciple Edward Misselden in *The Circle of Commerce* (1623; reprint, Amsterdam: Theatrum Orbis Terrarum, 1969), esp. 112.

20 Mun, 16–17; see also Misselden, 95. Even this level of analysis indicates more sophistication than that attributed to the mercantilists by Adam Smith. This is not to imply, however, that Mun had a theoretically adequate concept of money or of value. On the contrary, the social preconditions for such a theory, rooted in production based upon "abstract human labour" (Marx), did not yet exist.

21 Mun, 52.

22 Misselden, 142.

23 Supple, 213, 216.

24 See for example Eric Roll, *A History of Economic Thought*, 4th ed. (London: Faber and Faber, 1973), 78: "*England's Treasure* is a clear synthesis and development of the most advanced mercantilist theories."

25 Joyce Oldham Appleby, *Economic Thought and Ideology in Seventeenth-Century England* (Princeton: Princeton University Press, 1978), 202n5.

26 Mun, 7, 73.

27 Ibid., 21.

28 Ibid., 1.

29 Ibid., 19.
30 Thomas Culpepper, "A Tract Against Usurie," in *Selected Works of Josiah Child, 1668–1697* (Farnborough Honts, England: Gregg Press, 1968), 1: 27, 28. All of the works reprinted in this selection are paginated independently so that page numbers repeat within a single volume.
31 Karl Marx, *A Contribution to the Critique of Political Economy*, trans. S. W. Ryazanskaya (Moscow: Progress Publishers, 1970), 53*n;* Beer, 167–68; Roll, 99; Schumpeter, 213; Ronald Meek, *Studies in the Labour Theory of Value*, 2d ed. (London: Lawrence and Wishart, 1973), 39; Henry William Spiegel, *The Growth of Economic Thought* (Durham, N.C.: Duke University Press, 1971), 126, 129.
32 William Letwin, *The Origins of Scientific Economics* (London: Methuen and Co., 1963), 146.
33 Christopher Hill, *The Century of Revolution, 1603–1714* (1961; reprint, London: Sphere Books, 1974), 159.
34 Christopher Hill, *The Intellectual Origins of the English Revolution* (1965; reprint, London: Granada Publishing, 1972), 116.
35 Charles Webster, *The Great Instauration: Science, Medicine, and Reform, 1616–1660* (London: Duckworth and Co., 1975), 25; my emphasis.
36 Francis Bacon, *The New Organon*, ed. Fulton H. Anderson (Indianapolis: Bobbs-Merrill Co., 1960), 95. On Bacon's critique of crude empiricism see 67.
37 Hill, *Intellectual Origins*, 110.
38 Bacon, "Preparative Toward Natural and Experimental History," in *New Organon*, 277.
39 Ibid., 279.
40 Webster, 427.
41 George Edwin Fussell, *The Old English Farming Books from Fitzherbert to Tull, 1523–1730* (London: Lockwood and Son, 1947), chap. 4.
42 Webster, 489–90.
43 For a useful introduction to this tradition of political thought and its early modern reception and modification in England see Zera S. Fink, *The Classical Republicans*, 2d ed. (Evanston: Northwestern University Press, 1962), chap. 1.
44 Among the best treatments of this revolution from below during the 1640s are Christopher Hill, *The World Turned Upside Down* (Harmondsworth: Penguin, 1975); Brian Manning, *The English People and the English Revolution* (Harmondsworth: Penguin, 1978); and H. N. Brailsford, *The Levellers and the English Revolution*, ed. Christopher Hill (1961; reprint, London: Spokesman, 1976) (see also note 22 of chapter 1).
45 J. G. A. Pocock, ed., *The Political Works of James Harrington* (Cambridge: Cambridge University Press, 1977), 284, 259, 257. For Harrington's use of the term "natural aristocracy" see 173, 262, 284, 416; for his attacks on "levellers" see 292–93, 429–30, 658.

46 Ibid., 173.

47 Harrington's use of the term "political anatomy" can be found in "The Art of Lawgiving," ed. Pocock, 656.

48 Ibid., 170, 179, 320–21, 401, 415, 658.

49 Ibid., 470.

50 Ibid., 292–94, 304, 429–30.

51 E. Strauss, *Sir William Petty: Portrait of a Genius* (London: Bodley Head, 1954), 18.

52 H. F. Russell Smith, *Harrington and His Oceana* (Cambridge: Cambridge University Press, 1914), 131.

53 Frank Amati and Tony Aspromourgos, "Petty *contra* Hobbes: A Previously Untranslated Manuscript," *Journal of the History of Ideas* 66 (1985): 127–32.

54 *The Petty Papers: Some Unpublished Writings of Sir William Petty,* ed. Marquis of Lansdowne (London: Constable and Co., 1927), doc. 60, 1: 205–7.

55 William Petty, "Political Arithmetick," in *Economic Writings of Sir William Petty,* ed. Charles Henry Hull (1889; reprint, New York: Augustus M. Kelley, 1963), 1: 129.

56 Ibid., 1: 244.

57 Marie O'Brien and Conor Cruise O'Brien, *A Concise History of Ireland,* 2d ed. (London: Thames and Hudson, 1973), 69.

58 Webster, 67.

59 Ibid., 437.

60 See Petty's discussion of his survey in his proposal for an Irish land registry, in *The Petty Papers,* doc. 25, 1: 77–90.

61 Petty, "Observations of England," ibid., doc. 61, 1: 208.

62 Petty, "Inclosing Commons," ibid., doc. 118, 2: 129.

63 Petty, "Political Arithmetick," in *Economic Writings,* 1: 249.

64 Ibid., 1: 249, 269.

65 Petty, "Irish Land Registry," in *Petty Papers,* doc. no. 25, 1: 90.

66 Ibid., doc. no. 25, 1: 77.

67 Petty, "A Treatise of Taxes and Contributions," in *Economic Writings,* 1: 34, 28, 33.

68 Ibid., 1: 43.

69 Letwin, 144.

70 Petty, "Treatise," in *Economic Writings,* 1: 43.

71 Ibid.

72 Ibid., 1: 50; emphasis in original.

73 Ibid., 1: 44–45.

74 Petty, "Of Lands and Hands," in *Petty Papers,* doc. no. 58, 1: 196.

75 Petty, "Political Anatomy of Ireland," in *Economic Writings,* 1: 181.

76 Petty was not, however, an advocate of a single tax on land or land rent. Instead, he favoured taxing consumption as a way of encouraging saving. See "Treatise," 1: 91–94.

77 Ibid., 1: 181.

78 Ibid., 1: 182.

79 Petty did not devote great attention to discussing the phenomenon of wage labour, in large measure because he consistently took it for granted. From time to time he did, however, make explicit his implicit assumption that the direct agricultural producer was a wage labourer; see for example "Treatise," 1: 87.

80 Schumpeter treats Child throughout his *History* as a major theorist of distinction; see especially 242, 290–91, 362–64. However, as Letwin has pointed out (*Origins*, 46n2), Schumpeter mistakenly attributes to Child a pamphlet which expressed relatively sophisticated views. Letwin is correct to claim that "Child never set down any systematic analysis of economic relations" but is clearly in error when he claims that Child had no important influence on the development of economic thought. As I point out in the next chapter, Child's work played a central role in transmitting English political economy to France.

81 Child, "Brief Observations Concerning Trade and Interest of Money," in *Selected Works of Josiah Child*, 1: 10.

82 Child, "A New Discourse of Trade," ibid., 1: 140.

83 Ibid., 1: 181, 19; emphasis in original.

84 Child, "A Discourse of the Nature, Use, and Advantages of Trade," in *Selected Works*, 2: 14. On the unemployment problem in seventeenth-century English economics see N. G. Pauling, "The Employment Problem in Pre-Classical English Economic Thought," *Economic Record*, 27 (1951): 52–65.

85 Child, "A Discourse of the Nature of Trade," in *Selected Works*, 2: 7–8.

86 Ibid., 2: 27.

87 Karen Iversen Vaughn, *John Locke: Economist and Social Scientist* (Chicago: University of Chicago Press, 1980), 14. On Locke's Baconian heritage see Neal Wood, *The Politics of Locke's Philosophy* (Berkeley: University of California Press, 1983), chap. 4.

88 K. H. D. Haley, *The First Earl of Shaftesbury* (Oxford: Clarendon Press, 1968), 705, 251. For discussion of Shaftesbury's landed investments and his interest in agricultural improvement see 210–11, 218–19, 234. From this discussion it should be clear that my interpretation of the social and political thought of Shaftesbury and Locke is quite different from that advanced by Richard Ashcraft (*Revolutionary Politics and Locke's Two Treatises of Government* [Princeton: Princeton University Press, 1986]), whose failure to come to terms with the issue of agrarian capitalism clouds his understanding of the social outlook of the early Whigs. This issue is discussed at more length in my forthcoming article, "Locke, Levellers, and Liberty: Property and Democracy in the Thought of the First Whigs," to be published in *History of Political Thought*.

89 For a treatment of Locke as a scholastic-mercantilist see Beer, 128, 234–35. Vaughn considers Locke the great anticipator of a marginal-type theory of value, whereas Meek (21–23) sees him as a formulator of the labour theory of value who had not entirely shaken off the heri-

tage of mercantilism. Guy Routh, *The Origin of Economic Ideas* (London: Macmillan and Co., 1975), 47–49, maintains that Locke adhered to both a marginalist and a labour theory of value.

90 Letwin, 168.

91 The influence on Locke of the seventeenth-century agricultural revolution and literature of agricultural improvement is examined in Neal Wood, *John Locke and Agrarian Capitalism* (Berkeley: University of California Press, 1984), chap. 2.

92 Vaughn, 17. On Locke's debt to Petty see Wood, *Locke and Agrarian Capitalism*, 34–37, 125n.14.

93 Locke, "The Second Treatise of Government," in *Two Treatises of Government*, by John Locke, rev.edn., ed. Peter Laslett (New York: New American Library, 1965), 336.

94 Ibid., 340. Strictly speaking, this is not a pure labour theory of value, since the value of labour is calculated in terms of the market values of the commodities it produces. On this point see Vaughn, 87.

95 Locke, "Some Considerations of the Consequences of the Lowering of Interest, and Raising the Value of Money," in *Several Papers Relating to Money, Interest, and Trade*, by John Locke (1696; reprint, New York: Augustus M. Kelley, 1968), 30–31.

96 Ibid., 42.

97 Ibid., 88, 90.

98 Ibid., 100.

99 Ibid., 84.

100 Ibid., 44.

101 Locke, "Short Observations on a Printed Paper," in *Several Papers*, 21, 55–56, 87. It should be noted that these echoes of Petty did not necessarily derive directly from the latter's writings since many of these ideas were in the air at the time. Yet the combination of some unique terminology and lines of argument which appear to derive from Petty and the fact that Locke possessed Petty's main works, along with the obvious political and intellectual affinity between the two men, suggests that Petty should be considered a significant source of Locke's economic analysis.

102 For a discussion of Locke's concept of the wage earner see Wood, *Locke and Agrarian Capitalism*, 40–41, 44–45.

103 For a discussion of the increasing tendency in seventeenth-century economic literature to assert the harmony of commercial and landed interests see J. A. W. Gunn, *Politics and the Public Interest in the Seventeenth Century* (London: Routledge and Kegan Paul, 1969), esp. 258–63.

104 Nicholas Barbon, *A Discourse of Trade*, ed. Jacob Hollander (1690; reprint, Baltimore: Johns Hopkins University Press, 1905), 20.

105 Ibid., 27, 42.

106 Dudley North, *Discourses Upon Trade*, ed. Jacob Hollander (1691; reprint, Baltimore: Johns Hopkins Press, 1907), 17.

107 This issue is perceptively discussed by Joyce Oldham Appleby, "Ide-

ology and Theory: The Tension between Political and Economic Liberalism in Seventeenth-Century England," *American Historical Review* 81 (1976): 499–515.

108 Nannerl O. Keohane, *Philosophy and the State in France* (Princeton: Princeton University Press, 1980), 34.

109 Charles Woolsey Cole, *Colbert and a Century of French Mercantilism* (1939; reprint, Hamden, Conn.: Archon Books, 1964), 1: 553–54.

110 Such a conflation characterizes the very valuable study by Lionel Rothkrug, *Opposition to Louis XIV: The Political and Social Origins of the French Enlightenment* (1943; reprint, Princeton: Princeton University Press, 1965). Cole, *French Mercantilism, 1683–1700* (New York: Octagon Books, 1965), 5, employs the same approach.

111 Antoyne de Montchrétien, *Traicté de l'oéconomie politique dédié en 1615 au roy et la reyne mère du roy*, ed. Théodor Funck-Brentano (Paris: Librairie Plon, 1889), 5, 17, 31, 18, 20.

112 Ibid., 23–24, 141–42, 140, 40–41, 45.

113 A. D. Lublinskaya, *French Absolutism: The Crucial Phase, 1620–1629*, trans. Brian Pearce (Cambridge: Cambridge University Press, 1968), 131.

114 Franklin Charles Palm, *The Economic Policies of Richelieu* (1922; reprint, New York: Johnson Reprint Co., 1970), 19. See also Cole, *Colbert*, 1: 146.

115 Henry Bertram Hill, ed. and trans., *The Political Testament of Cardinal Richelieu* (Madison: University of Wisconsin Press, 1961), 11.

116 As quoted by Cole, *Colbert*, 1: 138.

117 As quoted in ibid., 1: 343. See also William F. Church, ed. and trans., "Lettres, instructions, et mémoires de Colbert," in *The Impact of Absolutism in France* (New York: John Wiley and Sons, 1969).

118 As quoted by Cole, *Colbert*, 1: 334. In his *French Mercantilism*, 224n1, Cole had argued, "Mercantilism was in essence bourgeois and that class was the one most benefited by the application of its tenets." By the time of his study on Colbert he seems to have abandoned this view.

119 Ibid., 1: 333.

120 Rothkrug, 364.

121 Keohane, chaps. 1 and 14. There were, of course, different traditions of constitutionalism in early modern France. For the sake of simplicity, I have had to ignore such distinctions. On the various forms of French constitutionalist thought see Quentin Skinner, *The Foundations of Modern Political Thought* (Cambridge: Cambridge University Press, 1978), vol. 2, *The Age of Reformation*, pt. 2.

122 Quoted by Rothkrug, 73–74.

123 Sébastien Le Prestre de Vauban, *La Dîme royale* (Paris: Bibliothèque Nationale, 1872), 11–12, 23.

124 Ibid., 10.

125 Quoted by Hazel Van Dyke Roberts, *Boisguilbert: Economist of the Reign of Louis XIV* (New York: Columbia University Press, 1935), 41.

126 Cole wrote that Boisguilbert "made statements that have the ring of the nineteenth or twentieth century rather than the seventeenth" (*French Mercantilism*, 244). Roberts argues the rather extreme thesis that Boisguilbert's "Dissertation" served as the "prototype" for *The Wealth of Nations* (*Boisguilbert*, chap. 16).

127 Pierre de Boisguilbert, "Dissertation de la nature des richesses, de l'argent et des tributs . . . ," in *Pierre de Boisguilbert ou la naissance de l'économie politique* (Paris: Institut National d'Etudes Démographiques, 1966), 2: 974; my translation.

128 Ibid., 2: 1000; my translation.

129 Boisguilbert, "Traité de la nature, culture, commerce, et intérêt de l'argent" in *Pierre de Boisguilbert ou la naissance de l'économie politique*, 2: 833; my translation. See also "Le Détail de la France," ibid., 2: 588.

130 Boisguilbert, "Le Détail," 2: 584; my translation.

131 Ibid., 2: 619.

132 Ibid., 2: 599, 645.

133 On the agricultural cycle and the nature of depressions see Boisguilbert, "Traité," 2: 847–52.

134 Ibid., 2: 857; my translation.

135 Boisguilbert, "Dissertation," 2: 933; my translation.

136 Ibid., 2: 991.

137 Boisguilbert's letter of July 1704 as quoted by Roberts, 51. On distributive justice see "Le Détail," 2: 648–49; on equilibrium see "Traité," 2: 840, 862, 874; and on proportional prices see ibid., 2: 874, and "Dissertation," 2: 993.

138 See Louis Salleron, "Boisguilbert, précurseur des physiocrates," and Jean Molinier, "L'Analyse globale de Boisguilbert ou l'ébauche du 'Tableau économique,'" in *Pierre de Boisguilbert ou la naissance de l'économie politique*, vol. 1.

139 Karl Marx, *Theories of Surplus Value*, trans. Emile Burns, ed. S. W. Ryazanskaya (Moscow: Progress Publishers, 1963), 1: 356–57. See also Meek, *Studies*, 36, and Isaac Ilyich Rubin, *A History of Economic Thought*, trans. Donald Filtzer (London: Ink Links, 1979), 72.

CHAPTER 3. THE PARADOX OF THE PHYSIOCRATS:
STATE BUILDING AND AGRARIAN CAPITALISM IN
EIGHTEENTH-CENTURY FRANCE

1 Joseph Schumpeter, *Economic Doctrine and Method*, trans. R. Aris (London: George Allen and Unwin, 1954), 43–44. See also Eric Roll, *A History of Economic Thought*, 4th ed. (London: Faber and Faber, 1973), 130; and Michael Bleaney, *Underconsumption Theories: A History and Critical Analysis* (New York: International Publishers, 1976), 84. It is beyond the bounds of this discussion to take up the question as to what constitutes a "scientific" economics. My own approach to this

question begins from Marx's distinction between classical and vulgar political economy. See Karl Marx, *Capital*, trans. Ben Fowkes (Harmondsworth: Penguin, 1976), 1: 174*n*–75*n*.

2 Norman J. Ware, "The Physiocrats: A Study in Economic Rationalization," *American Economic Review* 21 (1931): 607; Max Beer, *An Inquiry into Physiocracy* (1939; reprint, New York: Russell and Russell, 1966), 17; Thomas P. Neill, "Quesnay and Physiocracy," *Journal of the History of Ideas* 9 (1948): 153; Bert F. Hoselitz, "Agrarian Capitalism, the Natural Order of Things: François Quesnay," *Kyklos* 21 (1968): 638.

3 Elizabeth Fox-Genovese, *The Origins of Physiocracy: Economic Revolution and Social Order in Eighteenth-Century France* (Ithaca: Cornell University Press, 1976), 13.

4 Georges Weulerrse, *Le Mouvement physiocratique en France (de 1756 à 1770)* (1910; reprint, Paris: Editions Mouton, 1968), 2: 148; my translation.

5 Ibid., 2: 684–85; my translation. Weulerrse does recognize that there are "feudal vestiges" in the physiocratic system, although he downplays their importance; see 2: 710.

6 Hoselitz, "Agrarian Capitalism," 637, 650, 657; Guy Routh, *The Origin of Economic Ideas* (London: Macmillan and Co., 1975), 79.

7 Warren J. Samuels, "The Physiocratic Theory of Property and the State," *Quarterly Journal of Economics* 75 (1961): 110. See also idem., "The Physiocratic Theory of Economic Policy," *Quarterly Journal of Economics* 76 (1962).

8 Roll, *History of Economic Thought*, 135; Joseph Schumpeter, *History of Economic Analysis* (New York: Oxford University Press, 1954), 228.

9 Beer, *Inquiry*, 13, 169–70.

10 Karl Marx, *Theories of Surplus Value*, trans. Emile Burns, ed. S. W. Ryazanskaya (Moscow: Progress Publishers, 1963), 1: 152.

11 Ronald Meek, "The Case of the French Physiocrats," in *Events, Ideology, and Economic Theory*, ed. Robert V. Eagly (Detroit, Mich.: Wayne State University Press, 1968), 55. The same perspective informs Meek's *The Economics of Physiocracy* (Cambridge, Mass.: Harvard University Press, 1963) (hereafter cited as *EP*).

12 Fox-Genovese, 235.

13 Ibid., 265, 58, 61.

14 Jan Marczewski, "Some Aspects of the Economic Growth of France," *Economic Development and Cultural Change* 9 (1961): 370.

15 Abbé Le Blanc, *Letters on the English and French Nations*, 2 vols. (London, 1747), as quoted by André Bourde, *The Influence of England on the French Agronomes* (Cambridge: Cambridge University Press, 1953), 18–19.

16 See Bourde, chap. 4.

17 Patullo, *Essai*, as quoted in ibid., 83; my translation.

18 Marc Bloch, "La lutte pour l'individualisme agraire dans la France du XVIIIe siècle, 2e partie," *Annales d'histoire économique et sociale* 2 (1930): 536.

19 Marc Bloch, *French Rural History: An Essay on its Basic Characteristics,* trans. Janet Sondheimer (Berkeley: University of California Press, 1966), 221–22.

20 Bourde, 103–4.

21 Bloch, *French Rural History,* 206.

22 Stephen L. Kaplan, *Bread, Politics, and Political Economy in the Reign of Louis XV* (The Hague: Nijhoff, 1976), 1: 86.

23 My discussion of Herbert and Forbonnais relies on ibid., 1: 101–4, 111–12.

24 Ibid., 1: chap. 3.

25 Weulerrse, *Le Mouvement physiocratique,* 1: 34.

26 Schumpeter, *History,* 218.

27 The most reliable biographical information on Cantillon is provided by Joseph Hone, "Richard Cantillon, Economist—Biographical Note," *Economic Journal* 65 (1944). W. Stanley Jevons's article, "Richard Cantillon and the Nationality of Political Economy," was first published in the *Contemporary Review,* January 1881, and is reprinted in Richard Cantillon, *Essai sur la nature du commerce en général (Essay on the Nature of Trade in General),* trans. and ed. Henry Higgs (New York: Augustus M. Kelley, 1964). See also Henry Higgs, "Richard Cantillon," *Economic Journal* 1 (1891); and idem, "Cantillon's Place in Economics," *Quarterly Journal of Economics* 6 (1892).

28 On the influence of Petty on Cantillon see Higgs, "Cantillon's Place," 438; Roll, 124; and Schumpeter, *History,* 217*n*, 218–19. For an assessment of Cantillon's theoretical achievements see Joseph J. Spengler, "Richard Cantillon: First of the Moderns," parts 1, 2, *Journal of Political Economy* 62 (1954).

29 Cantillon, *Essai,* 3, 15, 43.

30 Ibid., 123. Schumpeter, *History,* 222, writes that "Cantillon had a clear conception of the function of the entrepreneur (ch. 13)." Cantillon did not, however, work with a model based upon capitalists and wage labourers; indeed, in the *Essai* he includes labourers and beggars in his category of "entrepreneurs."

31 Cantillon, *Essai,* 123, 47; see also 61–63.

32 Ibid., 31.

33 Ibid., 29; my emphasis.

34 Ibid., 43.

35 Ibid., 35.

36 Ibid., 41.

37 Higgs, "Cantillon's Place," 454. For Cantillon's influence on Physiocracy see Schumpeter, *History,* 242; and Vernon Foley, "An Origin of the *Tableau économique,*" *History of Political Economy* 5 (1973): 139–41.

38 For Mirabeau's conversion see Meek, *EP,* 16–18. On Quesnay's life see Jacqueline Hecht, "La vie de François Quesnay," in *François Quesnay et la physiocratie,* 2 vols. (Paris: Institut National d'Etudes Démographiques, 1958).

39 As quoted by Weulerrse, *Le Mouvement physiocratique*, 1: 159.
40 Robert V. Eagly, *The Structure of Classical Economic Theory* (New York: Oxford University Press, 1974), 10.
41 It is interesting that the largest collection of English translations from physiocratic writings, Meek's *EP*, does not include any excerpts from this article.
42 Quesnay, "Fermiers," *François Quesnay et la physiocratie*, 2: 427; my translation; emphasis in original.
43 Ibid., 455; my translation.
44 Ibid., 446, 452, 451.
45 Ibid., 428, 435, 431, 440; my translations.
46 Ibid., 452; my translation.
47 Meek, *EP*, 267.
48 Quesnay, "Grains," *François Quesnay et la physiocratie*, 495; as translated by Meek, *EP*, 76.
49 Quesnay, "Grains," 498; as translated by W. A. Eltis, "François Quesnay: A Reinterpretation, 1. The *Tableau économique*," *Oxford Economic Papers*, n. ser., 27 (1975): 170.
50 Quesnay, "Grains," 83; my translation. This does not mean that Quesnay consciously pursued a capitalist orientation, merely that the social arrangements he advocated were capitalist, whether he knew it or not.
51 Ibid., 480, 505; my translation. On Cantillon's influence on this work see Meek, *EP*, 268.
52 Quesnay, "Grains," 484; my translation.
53 Ibid., 496.
54 Ibid., 505, 505–6; as translated by Meek, *EP*, 82.
55 Quesnay, "Hommes," *François Quesnay et la physiocratie*, 527–28, 547, 560, 563; as translated by Meek, *EP*, 91, 95, 98, 100. The last passage clearly disproves Beer's thesis.
56 Ibid., 524, 548, 553–54, 568.
57 Ibid., 558; as translated by Meek, *EP*, 98.
58 Ibid., 553; as translated by Meek, *EP*, 97. On feudalism see "Hommes," 567.
59 Ibid., 540; my translation.
60 Quesnay, "Impôts," *François Quesnay et la physiocratie*, 2: 581; as translated by Meek, *EP*, 103.
61 Ibid., 582; my translation.
62 On the history of the various editions of the *Tableau* see the introduction to *Quesnay's Tableau Economique*, ed. and trans. Marguerite Kuczynski and Ronald Meek (London: Macmillan and Co., 1972). Quesnay's major elaborations of the *Tableau*—the famous "Analysis," the "First Problem," and the "Second Problem"—are reprinted in Meek, *EP*. The *Tableau* also figured centrally, in a revised form, in Mirabeau's *Philosophie rurale* and was succinctly explained in the abbé Baudeau's *Explication du tableau économique*. Mark Blaug's statement in *Economic Theory in Retrospect*, 3d ed. (Cambridge: Cambridge University Press, 1978), 26, that the *Tableau* "should not be regarded as

the centerpiece of the physiocratic system" shows a failure to grasp the crucial role of this work in the physiocratic schema.

63 Victor Riqueti, marquis de Mirabeau, *Philosophie rurale* (Amsterdam, 1763), 19; Marx, *Theories of Surplus Value*, 1: 344; see also Karl Marx and Frederick Engels, *Selected Correspondence*, 2d ed. (Moscow: Progress Publishers, 1965), 142–46; and Karl Marx, *Capital*, vol. 2, trans. David Fernbach (Harmondsworth: Penguin, 1978), esp. chaps. 18–20; Schumpeter, *Economic Doctrine and Method*, 52. For a review of positions on the *Tableau* see Almarin Phillips, "The *Tableau économique* as a Simple Leontief Model," *Quarterly Journal of Economics* 69 (1955): 137–38.

64 "Letter from Quesnay to Mirabeau," Meek, *EP,* 117.

65 Quesnay, "The Analysis of the Tableau économique," Meek, *EP,* 153; Mirabeau, *Philosophie rurale*, 31, 71, 118, 151–52, 163, 337.

66 Kuczynski and Meek, *Quesnay's Tableau*, 15.

67 For an argument which demonstrates that the *Tableau* does indeed constitute a workable model, see Eltis. Meek, *EP,* 278n2, argues convincingly that Quesnay wrote chap. 7 of *Philosophie rurale*.

68 "Letter from Quesnay to Mirabeau," 117.

69 Kuczynski and Meek, *Quesnay's Tableau*, 22.

70 Quesnay, "General Maxims for the Economic Government of an Agricultural Kingdom," Meek, *EP,* 237; Kuczynski and Meek, 13, Quesnay's emphasis; Quesnay, "General Maxims," 246.

71 Quesnay, "The Second Economic Problem," in Meek, *EP,* 202, 190.

72 Quesnay, "Analysis," ibid., 163n1.

73 Quesnay, "General Maxims," ibid., 231; emphasis in original.

74 Ibid.

75 Ibid., 260.

76 Fox-Genovese, *Origins of Physiocracy*, 292.

77 Quesnay, "The First Economic Problem," in Meek, *EP,* 180n1; see also "General Maxims," 238.

78 Kuczynski and Meek, 17, 11na.

79 Ibid., 12; Quesnay, "Analysis," 159; idem, "General Maxims," 231; idem, "Fermiers," 454–55; Mirabeau, *Philosophie rurale*, 34.

80 Quesnay, "General Maxims," in Meek, *EP,* 233.

81 Quesnay, "Fermiers," 453; Kuczynski and Meek, 14–15, 20na.

82 Weulerrse, *Le Mouvement physiocratique*, 1: 412; see also Kaplan, 1: 116.

83 As quoted by Fox-Genovese, *Origins of Physiocracy*, 243.

84 Quesnay, "General Maxims," 232.

85 Quesnay, "Analysis," 160; Kuczynski and Meek, 21.

86 Weulerrse, *Le Mouvement physiocratique*, 1: 85–86.

87 This point is made convincingly by Foley. However, certain Newtonian and Lockean influences have been detected by some commentators (e.g., Weulerrse, *Le Mouvement physiocratique*, 2: 118), although these must, in my view, be seen as influences adapted to a largely Cartesian framework.

88 Mirabeau, *Philosophie rurale*, 190; my translation.

89 Quesnay, "Despotisme de la Chine," in *François Quesnay et la physiocratie*, 2: 921; my translation.

90 Guillaume-François Le Trosne, *De l'ordre social* (Paris, 1777), 106; my translation.

91 Mirabeau, *Philosophie rurale;* as translated by Meek, *EP*, 70.

92 Le Trosne, 134; my translation. See also Georges Weulerrse, *Les Manuscrits économiques de François Quesnay et du marquis de Mirabeau aux Archives nationales* (Paris: Editions Mouton, 1910), 29, 53–54; and Quesnay, "Despotisme," 233.

93 Mirabeau, *Philosophie rurale;* as translated by Meek, *EP*, 58.

94 Quesnay, "Despotisme," 919; my translation.

95 Le Trosne, 120, 124; my translation.

96 As quoted by Weulerrse, *Le Mouvement physiocratique*, 1: 201.

97 Quesnay, "Hommes," 540; my translation.

98 Quesnay, "Despotisme," 918; Weulerrse, *Le Mouvement physiocratique*, 1: 8–31.

99 Mercier de la Rivière, *L'Ordre naturel et essentiel des sociétés politiques*, as quoted by Mario Einaudi, *The Physiocratic Doctrine of Judicial Control* (Cambridge, Mass.: Harvard University Press, 1938), 41; my translation.

100 For his views on the Physiocrats and the Paris *parlement* see Einaudi, 47; on the connection to the American doctrine of judicial control see 88. Einaudi recognizes (43) that Mercier did not believe in the priority of the judiciary.

101 Quesnay, "Hommes," 567; and "Despotisme," 933, 919; my translation.

102 Einaudi, 47.

103 Ibid., 34.

104 As quoted in ibid., 78; my translation.

105 Quesnay, "General Maxims," in Meek, *EP*, 231.

106 Weulerrse, *Manuscrits*, 66; Einaudi (34) sets out Le Trosne's support for a council of advisors to the king.

107 Weulerrse, *Manuscrits*, 32.

108 Kaplan, 1: 116.

109 See, for example, Kuczynski and Meek, 8; Quesnay, "Hommes," 550; idem, "The Analysis," 153; idem, "General Maxims," 237.

110 Kaplan, 1: 90–96.

111 Ibid., 2: 489, 498–515.

112 As quoted in ibid., 2: 476–81.

113 Ibid., 2: 594–601.

114 As quoted in ibid., 2: 609.

115 Ibid., 2: 610.

116 Indeed, Schumpeter believed that Turgot's capital theory was "distinctly superior" to that of Adam Smith (*History*, 248). See also Henry William Spiegel, *The Growth of Economic Thought* (Durham, N.C.: Duke University Press, 1971), 155.

117 Douglas Dakin, *Turgot and the Ancien Régime in France* (1939; reprint, New York: Octagon Books, 1965), 2.

118 Schumpeter, *History*, 243–44.

119 Turgot, "Plan for a Paper on Taxation," in *The Economics of A. R. J. Turgot*, ed. and trans. P. D. Groenewegen (The Hague: Nijhoff, 1977), 102–3.

120 Turgot, "Observations on a Paper by Saint-Peravy," ibid., 116.

121 Turgot, "Observations on a Paper by Graslin," ibid., 127; idem, "Observations on a Paper by Saint-Peravy," 110–11; idem, "Letters on the Grain Trade," ibid., 168.

122 Turgot, "In Praise of Gournay," ibid., 29.

123 Abbé Baudeau, *Première Introduction à la philosophie économique* (Paris, 1910) as quoted by Meek, *EP*, 309.

124 Turgot, "Plan for a Paper on Taxation," 103.

125 Mercier de la Rivière, *L'ordre naturel*, as quoted by J. J. Spengler, "The Physiocrats and Say's Law of Markets," pt. 2, *Journal of Political Economy* 53 (1945): 317.

126 As quoted by Warren J. Samuels, "The Physiocratic Theory of Property and the State," 103.

127 Turgot, "Observations on a Paper by Saint-Peravy," 115–16.

128 Turgot, "Reflections on the Formation and Distribution of Wealth," in *Turgot on Progress, Sociology, and Economics*, ed. Ronald Meek (Cambridge: Cambridge University Press, 1974), 147, 150; emphasis in original.

129 Ibid., 152, 153, 169.

130 Ibid., 181.

131 Ibid., 146.

132 Ibid., 172.

133 See James McLain, *The Economic Writings of Dupont de Nemours* (Newark: University of Delaware Press, 1977), 176–77.

134 Turgot, "Observations on a Paper by Graslin," 127, emphasis in original.

135 Turgot, "Letters on the Grain Trade," 178.

136 Turgot, "Observations on a Paper by Graslin," 132.

137 As quoted by W. Walker Stephens, ed., *The Life and Writings of Turgot* (New York: Longmans, Green and Co., 1895), 45.

138 Meek, *EP*, 312.

139 Marx, *Capital*, 2: 436.

140 The passage from Turgot is quoted by Marx, *Theories of Surplus Value*, 1: 56.

141 Quoted by Weulerrse, *Le Mouvement physiocratique*, 1: 147.

142 Marx, *Theories of Surplus Value*, 1: 66.

143 Ware, "The Physiocrats," 618.

144 Meek, *EP*, 393–94; Ware, "The Physiocrats," 608.

145 Isaac Ilyich Rubin, *A History of Economic Thought*, trans. Donald Filtzer (London: Ink Links, 1979), 106.

146 Ibid., 140.

147 Fox-Genovese, *Origins of Physiocracy*, 61.

148 Ibid., 31, 56–57.

149 On the aristocratic revolt see Albert Soboul, *The French Revolution*,

trans. Alan Forrest (London: New Left Books, 1974), vol. 1, chap. 3;
Georges Lefebvre, *The French Revolution from Its Origins to 1793,*
trans. Elizabeth Moss Evanson (New York: Columbia University
Press, 1962), vol. 1, chap. 6.

150 Schumpeter, *History,* 229n2.

151 Herbert Luthy, *From Calvin to Rousseau,* trans. Salvator Attanasio
(New York: Basic Books, 1970), 139.

152 Theda Skocpol, *States and Social Revolutions* (Cambridge: Cambridge
University Press, 1979), 21.

153 Kuczynski and Meek, 6na.

154 Tom Kemp, *Historical Patterns of Industrialization* (London: Longman
Group, 1978), 17.

155 John Bosher, *French Finance, 1770–1795: From Business to Bureaucracy*
(Cambridge: Cambridge University Press, 1970), 126.

156 Quesnay, "The First Economic Problem," 180n3; Mirabeau, *Philosophie rurale,* 61.

157 Quesnay, "General Maxims," 239.

158 Luthy, 148–49.

159 Turgot, "Plan for a Paper on Taxation," 107.

CHAPTER 4. COMMERCE, CORRUPTION, AND CIVIL
SOCIETY: THE SOCIAL AND PHILOSOPHICAL
FOUNDATIONS OF *THE WEALTH OF NATIONS*

1 Henry William Spiegel, *The Growth of Economic Thought* (Durham,
N.C.: Duke University Press, 1971), 234.

2 Joseph Cropsey, "Adam Smith and Political Philosophy," in *Essays on
Adam Smith,* ed. Andrew Skinner and Thomas Wilson (Oxford: Oxford University Press, 1975), 132.

3 Isaac Ilyich Rubin, *A History of Economic Thought,* trans. Donald
Filtzer (London: Ink Links, 1979), 166.

4 Eric Roll, *A History of Economic Thought,* 4th ed. (London: Faber and
Faber, 1973), 150.

5 Max Lerner, Introduction to *The Wealth of Nations,* by Adam Smith,
ed. Edwin Cannan (New York: Modern Library, 1937), ix. All further
references to *The Wealth of Nations* will be to the Glasgow edition of
1976 published by Oxford University Press.

6 C. B. Macpherson, Review of *Adam Smith's Politics: An Essay in Historiographic Revision,* by Donald Winch, *History of Political Economy* 11
(1979): 454. See also Hiroshi Mizuta, "Moral Philosophy and Civil
Society," in *Essays on Adam Smith,* 114.

7 Nathan Rosenburg, "Adam Smith and Laissez-Faire Revisited," in
*Adam Smith and Modern Political Economy: Bicentennial Essays on The
Wealth of Nations,* ed. Gerald P. O'Driscoll (Ames: Iowa State Press,
1979), 21.

8 Adam Smith, *The Wealth of Nations,* ed. R. H. Campbell and A. S.

Skinner (Oxford: Oxford University Press, 1976), 1: 265–67, 144 (hereafter cited as *WN*).

9 Ibid., 1: 144, 258, 2: 675.

10 Adam Smith, "Lectures on Jurisprudence, Report dated 1766," in *Lectures on Jurisprudence*, by Adam Smith, ed. R. L. Meek, D. D. Raphael, and A. S. Skinner (Oxford: Oxford University Press, 1978), 522. This work contains two sets of reports on Smith's lectures, one from the 1762–1763 session, another dated 1766 (believed to be based on the lectures of 1763–1764). I shall follow academic convention in referring to these reports as *LJ(A)* and *LJ(B)* respectively (hereafter cited in this form).

11 Ibid., 541.

12 R. H. Campbell, "An Economic History of Scotland in the Eighteenth Century," *Scottish Journal of Political Economy* 11 (1964): 20. On Scotland's economic takeoff in the 1760s see Henry Hamilton, *An Economic History of Scotland in the Eighteenth Century* (Oxford: Oxford University Press, 1963), 70; Bruce Lenman, *An Economic History of Modern Scotland* (London: B. T. Batsford, 1977), 71; and T. C. Smout, *A History of the Scottish People, 1560–1830* (Glasgow: William Collins Sons and Co., 1969), 226.

13 Smout, 227.

14 Adam Smith, *WN*, 1: 237–40; Hamilton, 56–57; Smout, 272–274; Tony Dickson, ed., *Scottish Capitalism: Class, State, and Nation from before the Union to the Present* (London: Lawrence and Wishart, 1980), 90.

15 Smout, 277; see also idem, "Scottish Landowners and Economic Growth, 1650–1850," *Scottish Journal of Political Economy* 11 (1964): 229.

16 Dickson et al., 107.

17 R. H. Campbell, "The Scottish Improvers and the Course of Agrarian Change in the Eighteenth Century," in *Comparative Aspects of Scottish and Irish Economic and Social History, 1600–1900*, ed. L. M. Cullen and T. C. Smout (Edinburgh: John Donald, 1977), 206.

18 Smout, *History*, 289; Hamilton, 86. See also T. M. Devine, *The Tobacco Lords* (Edinburgh: John Donald, 1975), 24.

19 Hamilton, 74; Lenman, 91–92; Devine, 22–25.

20 Smout, "Scottish Landowners," 228–30. See also Dickson, 95–98; and Smout, *History*, 275.

21 Campbell, "Economic History," 18; Smout, "Scottish Landowners," 220, 231; idem, *History*, 275. For the argument that the tobacco trade was not central to industrial growth see Devine, 48. See also R. H. Campbell, "The Industrial Revolution: A Revision Article," *Scottish Historical Review* 46 (1967): 45.

22 Nicholas Phillipson, "Scottish Public Opinion and the Union in the Age of Association," in *Scotland in the Age of Improvement*, ed. Nicholas Phillipson and Rosalind Mitchison (Edinburgh: Edinburgh University Press, 1970), 141.

23 Hamilton, 75; Lenman, 97.
24 George Davie, *The Scottish Enlightenment* (London: The Historical Association, 1981), 1, 7–8, 13. On Fletcher see *Andrew Fletcher of Saltoun: Selected Writings*, ed. David Daiches (Edinburgh: Scottish Academic Press, 1979); Nicholas Phillipson, "The Scottish Enlightenment," in *The Enlightenment in National Context*, ed. Ray Porter and Mikulas Teich (Cambridge: Cambridge University Press, 1981), 22–25; and John Robertson, "The Scottish Enlightenment at the Limits of the Civic Tradition," in *Wealth and Virtue: The Shaping of Political Economy in the Scottish Enlightenment*, ed. Istvan Hont and Michael Ignatieff (Cambridge: Cambridge University Press, 1983), 141–51. The Scottish debate over economic development is usefully surveyed by Istvan Hont, "The 'Rich Country–Poor Country' Debate in Scottish Classical Political Economy," in *Wealth and Virtue*, 271–315.
25 David Hume, "Of the Balance of Trade," in *Writings on Economics*, by David Hume, ed. Eugene Rotwein (Madison: University of Wisconsin Press, 1970), 62–63.
26 David Hume, "Of Money," ibid., 45.
27 Ibid., 37.
28 Ibid., 43.
29 Ibid., 44.
30 Oswald to Hume, October 1749, ibid., 190–96.
31 Josiah Tucker, "Four Tracts on Political and Commercial Subjects," in *Precursors of Adam Smith, 1750–1775*, ed. Ronald Meek (London: J. M. Dent and Sons, 1973), 193, 189.
32 Ibid., 177.
33 David Hume, "Of the Jealousy of Trade," in *Writings on Economics*, 81.
34 Hume to Kames, 4 March 1758, ibid., 201.
35 Hume, "Of the Jealousy of Trade," ibid., 79.
36 George Davie, "Berkeley, Hume, and the Central Problem of Scottish Philosophy," in *McGill Hume Studies*, ed. David Fate Norton, Nicholas Capaldi, and Wade L. Robinson (San Diego: Austin Hill Press, 1976), 44.
37 Bernard Mandeville, *The Fable of the Bees*, ed. F. B. Kaye (Oxford: Oxford University Press, 1924), 1: 369. For a useful introduction to Mandeville's thought see Thomas Horne, *The Social Thought of Bernard Mandeville: Virtue and Commerce in Early Eighteenth-Century England* (London: Macmillan and Co., 1978).
38 Gladys Bryson, *Man and Society: The Scottish Inquiry of the Eighteenth Century* (Princeton: Princeton University Press, 1945), 8.
39 From Shaftesbury's *Moralists*, as quoted by W. R. Scott, *Francis Hutcheson* (Cambridge: Cambridge University Press, 1900), 158–59; see also 165–74.
40 Francis Hutcheson, *Reflections upon Laughter and Remarks upon the Fable of the Bees* (Glasgow: R. and A. Fowles, 1750), 55–56, as quoted by W. L. Taylor, *Francis Hutcheson and David Hume as Predecessors of Adam Smith* (Durham, N.C.: Duke University Press, 1965), 104.

41 For an insightful summary of Hutcheson's views on these issues see Thomas Horne, "Moral and Economic Improvement: Francis Hutcheson on Property," *History of Political Thought* 7 (1986): 115–30.

42 As quoted by Bryson, 215.

43 As quoted by Gary Wills, "Benevolent Adam Smith," *New York Review of Books*, 9 February 1978, 42.

44 Francis Hutcheson, *An Inquiry Concerning Beauty, Order, Harmony, Design*, ed. Peter Kivy (The Hague: Nijhoff, 1973), 71.

45 Hume to Hutcheson, 17 September 1739, as quoted by Scott, 117.

46 Hume, "Of Refinement in the Arts," in *Writings on Economics*, 27, 22, 24.

47 David Hume, *A Treatise of Human Nature*, ed. L. A. Selby-Bigge (Oxford: Oxford University Press, 1888), 529.

48 Ibid., 499, 552. See also David Fate Norton, "Hume's Common Sense Morality," *Canadian Journal of Philosophy* 5 (1975): 523–43.

49 Hume, *Treatise*, 499–500; emphasis in original.

50 David Hume, "An Enquiry Concerning the Principles of Morals," in *Hume's Ethical Writings*, ed. Alasdair MacIntyre (London: Macmillan and Co., 1965), 66.

51 Robertson, 156.

52 David Hume, "Of Public Credit," in *Essays: Moral, Political, and Literary*, by David Hume, ed. Eugene F. Miller (Indianapolis: Liberty Classics, 1985), 357–58.

53 David Hume, "Of Parties in General" and "Of the Populousness of Ancient Nations," ibid., 60, 419–20.

54 See Robertson, 151–75; and Phillipson, "Scottish Enlightenment," 31.

55 Robertson, 159. My position is thus critical of the view of Istvan Hont and Michael Ignatieff, "Needs and Justice in *The Wealth of Nations*: An Introductory Essay" in *Wealth and Virtue*; they see Hume and Smith as rejecting the civic tradition in favour of that of natural jurisprudence. In my view, such an approach to intellectual history is excessively mechanical since it constitutes theoretical perspectives as discursive traditions whose internal logic and coherence exclude interaction with other distinct traditions of thought. It is my view that Hume and Smith addressed social issues—morality, justice, and economic development—within a framework constituted by varying analytic perspectives or discourses. In all the Scottish theorists we find unique combinations of such discursive approaches. The task for modern commentators is not to reduce Hume or Smith to one or another specific tradition but rather to explore the manner in which they drew upon different traditions, to address problems posed by the transformation of European society.

56 J. G. A. Pocock, *The Machiavellian Moment: Florentine Political Thought and the Atlantic Republican Tradition* (Princeton: Princeton University Press, 1975), 499. In my interpretation of Ferguson I have benefited from David Kettler, "History and Theory in Ferguson's *Essay on the History of Civil Society*: A Reconsideration," *Political Theory* 5 (1977): 437–60.

57 Adam Ferguson, *An Essay on the History of Civil Society*, ed. Duncan Forbes (Edinburgh: Edinburgh University Press, 1966), 180, 144, 105, 180.
58 Ibid., 19.
59 Ibid., 40.
60 Ibid., 56.
61 Ibid., 158. See also Kettler, 22, 24.
62 On the Commonwealth campaign for a citizens' militia see Pocock, 500.
63 John Rae, *Life of Adam Smith*, introduction by Jacob Viner (1895; reprint, New York: Augustus M. Kelley, 1965), 4; and Alexander Gray, *Adam Smith* (1948; reprint, London: Historical Association, 1968), 7.
64 Gray, 4.
65 W. R. Scott, *Adam Smith as Student and Professor* (1873; reprint, New York: Augustus M. Kelley, 1965), 27.
66 For a helpful discussion of the Select Society see Phillipson, "Scottish Enlightenment," 32–35; and idem, "Culture and Society in the Eighteenth-Century Province: The Case of Edinburgh and the Scottish Enlightenment," in *The University in Society*, ed. Lawrence Stone (Princeton: Princeton University Press, 1974), 444–46.
67 Rae, 107–15.
68 Davie, *Scottish Enlightenment*, 17.
69 Rae, 31.
70 Ibid., 245.
71 On the Political Economy Club see Scott, *Adam Smith*, 86–87.
72 Rae, 11.
73 Smith, *WN*, 2: 790.
74 J. Ralph Lindgren, ed., *The Early Writings of Adam Smith* (New York: Augustus M. Kelley, 1967).
75 My appreciation of this point is due especially to J. Ralph Lindgren, *The Social Philosophy of Adam Smith* (The Hague: Nijhoff, 1973), chap. 4.
76 Adam Smith, "Of the External Senses," in *Early Writings*, 210–11.
77 Adam Smith, "Logics," as quoted by Lindgren, *Social Philosophy*, 13.
78 Adam Smith, "Language," in *Early Writings*, 229 (this essay was appended to the third edition of Smith's *Theory of the Moral Sentiments* published in 1761).
79 Ibid., 241.
80 Lindgren, *Social Philosophy*, 12.
81 Adam Smith, "The Principles Which Lead and Direct Philosophical Enquiries: Illustrated by the History of Astronomy," in *Early Writings*, 45.
82 Smith, "Language," ibid., 248.
83 Ibid., 249, 251.
84 Adam Smith, *The Theory of the Moral Sentiments* (Indianapolis: Liberty Press, 1969), 167 (hereafter cited as *TMS*).
85 Adam Smith, *Lectures on Rhetoric and Belles Lettres*, ed. John M.

Lothian (Carbondale: Southern Illinois University Press, 1971), 22–23; emphasis in original.

86 Smith, *TMS*, 531.

87 Ibid., 501.

88 Ibid., 47.

89 T. D. Campbell, "Scientific Explanation and Ethical Justification in the *Moral Sentiments*," in *Essays on Adam Smith*, 71.

90 Smith, *TMS*, 162.

91 Ibid., 265–66.

92 This is the phrase employed with respect to Hume by David Fate Norton, "Hume's Common Sense Morality." This does not imply, however, that absolute values are foreign to Smith's system. On this point see Knud Haakonssen, *The Science of a Legislator: The Natural Jurisprudence of David Hume and Adam Smith* (Cambridge: Cambridge University Press, 1981).

93 Smith, *Rhetoric and Belles Lettres*, 51.

94 Smith, *TMS*, 126.

95 Ibid., 301, 127, 129.

96 Ibid., 302.

97 Ibid., 303.

98 Ibid., 304.

99 Ibid.

100 Ibid., 246, 128, 351–52, 286, 128.

101 Ibid., 166.

102 Ibid., 310.

103 Ibid., 305.

104 Ibid., 307.

105 Ibid., 380–81.

106 Smith, *WN*, 2: 781–82. See also the excellent discussion of this point by Louis Schneider, "Human Nature and Social Circumstance," in *Adam Smith and Modern Political Economy*, 62–63.

107 Lindgren, *Social Philosophy*, 74.

108 Smith, *TMS*, 63–65.

109 D. D. Raphael, "The Impartial Spectator," in *Essays on Adam Smith*, 92.

110 Smith, *TMS*, 127. Smith added this distinction between inferior and superior prudence to *TMS* in 1790. On this point see Ralph Anspach, "The Implications of *The Theory of the Moral Sentiments* for Adam Smith's Economic Thought," *History of Political Economy* 4 (1972): 176–206.

111 Smith, *TMS*, 127.

112 Ibid., 380.

113 Ibid., 167.

114 Smith, *WN*, 2: 771.

115 Smith, *TMS*, 357, 537.

116 See S. T. Bindhoff, *Tudor England* (Harmondsworth: Penguin, 1950), 129; G. R. Elton, *England Under the Tudors*, 2d ed. (London: Methuen

and Co., 1974), 185; and Zera S. Fink, *The Classical Republicans*, 2d ed. (Evanston: Northwestern University Press, 1962), chap. 2.

117 For a good discussion of this point see Quentin Skinner, *The Foundations of Modern Political Thought* (Cambridge: Cambridge University Press, 1978) vol. 1, *The Renaissance*, chap. 8.

118 See chap. 2 above, pp. 43–44.

119 This was the judgement of H. F. Russell Smith, *Harrington and His Oceana* (Cambridge: Cambridge University Press, 1914), 131.

120 John Locke, *Several Papers Relating to Money, Interest, and Trade* (1696; reprint, New York: Augustus M. Kelley, 1968) esp. 42, 100, 112. For a discussion of Shaftesbury as a "neo-Harringtonian" see Pocock, Introduction to *The Political Works of James Harrington* (Cambridge: Cambridge University Press, 1977), 129–33; and idem, *Politics, Language, and Time: Essays on Political Thought and History* (New York: Atheneum, 1971), chap. 4.

121 See K. H. D. Haley, *The First Earl of Shaftesbury* (Oxford: Clarendon Press, 1968), 350–51; Perez Zagorin, *The Court and the Country: The Beginning of the English Revolution of the Seventeenth Century* (New York: Atheneum, 1970), chap. 4; and J. B. Owen, "The Survival of Country Attitudes in the Eighteenth-Century House of Commons," in *Britain and the Netherlands*, ed. J. S. Bromley and E. H. Kossman (The Hague: Nijhoff, 1971), 43–44.

122 For Shaftesbury's modification of Harrington see Pocock, *Politics, Language, and Time*, chap. 4. For some important qualifications to Pocock's general interpretation see J. C. Davis, "Pocock's Harrington: Grace, Nature, and Art in the Classical Republicanism of James Harrington," *Historical Journal* 24 (1984): 683–97; Kathleen Toth, "Interpretation in Political Theory: The Case of Harrington," *Review of Politics* 37 (1975): 317–39; and Jesse Goodale, "J. G. A. Pocock's Neo-Harringtonians: A Reconsideration," *History of Political Thought* 1 (1980): 237–59; but see also Pocock's "A Reconsideration Impartially Considered," *History of Political Thought* 1 (1980): 541–45. On Sidney see Blair Warden, "The Commonwealth Kidney of Algernon Sidney," *Journal of British Studies* 24 (1985): 1–40.

123 On the Tory revival see J. P. Kenyon, *Revolution Principles: The Politics of Party, 1689–1720* (Cambridge: Cambridge University Press, 1977), chaps. 5 and 6; and J. A. W. Gunn, *Beyond Liberty and Property: The Process of Self-Recognition in Eighteenth-Century Political Thought* (Kingston: McGill-Queen's University Press, 1983), chap. 4.

124 H. T. Dickinson, *Liberty and Property: Political Ideology in Eighteenth-Century Britain* (London: Methuen and Co., 1977), 102–18.

125 On Shaftesbury and his followers see Caroline Robbins, *The Eighteenth-Century Commonwealthmen* (Cambridge, Mass.: Harvard University Press, 1959), chap. 4.

126 Pocock, *Machiavellian Moment*, 395, 414, 432. See also Donald Winch, *Adam Smith's Politics: An Essay in Historiographic Revision* (Cambridge: Cambridge University Press, 1978), chap. 2. As will become clearer, on

a number of major points I depart from Winch in interpretation of Smith's relationship to the English commonwealth tradition.

127 James Moore, "Locke and the Scottish Jurists," paper presented on John Locke and the political thought of the 1680s, Conference for the Study of Political Thought, Folger Shakespeare Library, Washington, D.C., 21–23 March 1980, 30.

128 On Hutcheson's political views see Robbins, 174–95; on his economic views see Taylor, passim.

129 Francis Hutcheson, *A System of Moral Philosophy* (London, 1755), 2: 113–14.

130 Horne, "Moral and Economic Improvement," 118–20.

131 Rae, 11.

132 See Hume, "Of the First Principles of Government," "Of the Origin of Government," "Of the Independency of Parliament," "Whether the British Government inclines more to Absolute Monarchy, or to a Republic," "Of the Parties of Great Britain," "Of the Original Contract," "Of Passive Obedience," "Of the Coalition of Parties," in *Essays: Moral, Political, and Literary.* For an important attempt to understand Hume as a sceptical Whig, although it underestimates the persistence of civic humanist concerns in his thought, see Duncan Forbes, *Hume's Philosophical Politics* (Cambridge: Cambridge University Press, 1975).

133 Smith, *LJ(A)*,207.

134 *LJ(B)*, 401.

135 *LJ(A)*, 208; see also *LJ(A)*, 404.

136 *LJ(B)*, 401; *LJ(A)*, 338.

137 *LJ(A)*, 264–74, 311; *LJ(B)*, 421–22.

138 *LJ(B)*, 433; see also *LJ(A)*, 325–27.

139 *WN*, 1: 426.

140 Ibid., 2: 848.

141 Ibid., 1: 461.

142 Ibid., 2: 706.

143 Ibid., 2: 622.

144 *LJ(A)*, 70.

145 Nicholas Phillipson, "Adam Smith as Civic Moralist," in *Wealth and Virtue*, 197.

146 Smith, *WN*, 1: 412.

147 Ibid., 1: 405.

148 Ibid., 1: 411–12.

149 Ibid., 1: 418–19, 420–21.

150 Ibid., 1: 422.

151 Ibid., 1: 343.

152 Ibid., 1: 541.

153 Ibid., 1: 111–12.

154 Ibid., 1: 345.

155 See Duncan Forbes, "Sceptical Whiggism, Commerce, and History," in *Essays on Adam Smith*, 184–86, 193.

156 Smith, *WN*, 2: 905.

157 Ibid., 1: 96.

158 In this respect I agree with much of the argument made by Istvan Hont and Michael Ignatieff, "Needs and Justice in *The Wealth of Nations:* An Introductory Essay," in *Wealth and Virtue*, 2–8, bearing in mind, however, the criticisms I raised in note 55 to this chapter.

159 Smith, *WN*, 1: 468, 428.

CHAPTER 5. AGRARIAN CAPITALISM AND *THE WEALTH OF NATIONS*

1 The most important attempt to establish the general philosophical principles which inform all of Smith's works, including *The Wealth of Nations*, is that of J. Ralph Lindgren, *The Social Philosophy of Adam Smith* (The Hague: Nijhoff, 1973).

2 Joseph Schumpeter, *History of Economic Analysis* (New York: Oxford University Press, 1954), 187. Schumpeter's statement is largely accurate with respect to Book 1 of *The Wealth of Nations* but, as we shall see, does not apply to the theory of accumulation developed in Book 2.

3 Adam Smith, *The Wealth of Nations*, ed. R. H. Campbell and A. S. Skinner (Oxford: Oxford University Press, 1976), 1: 25–26 (hereafter cited as *WN*).

4 Ibid., 1: 37. See also idem, *The Theory of the Moral Sentiments* (Indianapolis: Liberty Classics, 1969), 166.

5 Smith, *WN*, 1: 26–27.

6 Ibid., 2: 781.

7 Ibid., 2: 712, 612, 709, 608, 1: 295.

8 Ibid., 1: 341–2; my emphasis.

9 Ibid., 1: 343.

10 Ibid., 1: 467, 2: 555, 628.

11 Ibid., 2: 612.

12 Ibid., 2: 649; my emphasis.

13 Ibid., 2: 660, 1: 283.

14 Samuel Hollander, *The Economics of Adam Smith* (Toronto: University of Toronto Press, 1973), 146.

15 Smith, *WN*, 1: 96, 2: 748. For Smith's use of "sober and industrious poor" see ibid., 2: 872, 887.

16 This is the phrase used by Marian Bowley, *Studies in the History of Economic Theory Before 1870* (London: Macmillan and Co., 1973), 113.

17 Smith, *WN*, 1: 147, 50, 51.

18 Ibid., 1: 48.

19 Ibid., 1: 69.

20 Ibid., 1: 72.

21 Hollander, 121–24.

22 Smith, *WN*, 2: 864.

23 Ibid., 2: 869–70; my emphasis.

24 J. M. A. Gee, "The Origin of Rent in Adam Smith's *Wealth of Nations: An Anti-Neoclassical View,*" *History of Political Economy* 13 (1981): 1–18.

25 Smith, *WN*, Book 1, chap. 3. See also Nathan Rosenburg, "Some Institutional Aspects of the *Wealth of Nations,*" *Journal of Political Economy* 68 (1960): 557–70.

26 Smith, *WN*, 1: 105.

27 Ibid., 1: 113.

28 Adam Smith, *Lectures on Jurisprudence*, ed. R. L. Meek, D. D. Raphael, and P. G. Stein (Oxford: Oxford University Press, 1978), Report dated 1766, 497. Smith's *Lectures* consist of two "Reports," one from the session of 1762–1763, the other dated 1766 (hereafter cited as *LJ(A)* and *LJ(B)*).

29 Smith, *WN*, 1: 78–79.

30 Ibid., 1: 114, 115.

31 Hugh Blair to Adam Smith, 3 April 1776, and Adam Ferguson to Adam Smith, 18 April 1776, in Ernest Campbell Mossner and Ian Simpson Ross, eds., *The Correspondence of Adam Smith* (Oxford: Oxford University Press, 1977), 188, 193.

32 Smith, *WN*, 1: 267.

33 Ibid., 1: 493, 494.

34 Ibid., 1: 144.

35 Ibid., 1: 267, 2: 555, 1: 471, 493, 2: 613.

36 Ibid., 2: 660. On this aspect of natural liberty see ibid., 1: 470 and 2: 687.

37 Ibid., 1: 360–75.

38 Ibid., 2: 607.

39 Ibid., 2: 611.

40 Ibid., 2: 627.

41 Ibid., 2: 848–89.

42 Ibid., 1: 493.

43 Ibid., 1: 267.

44 Ibid., 2: 641.

45 Ibid., 2: 687.

46 Ibid., 1: 78–79.

47 Bowley, 127–29.

48 Smith, *WN*, 1: 146.

49 Ibid., 2: 612.

50 Nathan Rosenburg, "Adam Smith on Profits—Paradox Lost and Regained," in *Essays on Adam Smith*, ed. Andrew Skinner and Thomas Wilson (Oxford: Oxford University Press, 1975), 386.

51 Smith, *WN*, 1: 378.

52 Ibid., 1: 144.

53 Ibid., 1: 143, 144. For Smith's comments on the limits of the division of labour in agriculture see ibid., 1: 16.

54 Ibid., 2: 781–82.

55 Ibid., 2: 783.

56 Ibid., 2: 795.

57 Ibid., 1: 461–62.

58 Ibid., 1: 265.

59 Ibid., 1: 377, 180–82.

60 Ibid., 1: 363.

61 Ibid., 1: 364, 377, 2: 848, 1: 380.

62 Ibid., 1: 411–12.

63 Ibid., 1: 426.

64 Ibid., 2: 927.

65 Ibid., 1: 391–92, 2: 865, 1: 392.

66 Ibid., 2: 832. John Robertson has seriously misunderstood this discussion in *WN* of landlords in his article "Scottish Political Economy Beyond the Civic Tradition: Government and Economic Development in *The Wealth of Nations*," *History of Political Thought* 4 (1983): 462*n*. Smith is not writing off large landlords here or denying their potential as improvers; rather, he is favouring the new arrangement between landlords and capitalist tenant farmers over the older one based on the employment of bailiffs.

67 David Hume, *Writings on Economics*, ed. Eugene Rotwein (Madison: University of Wisconsin Press, 1970), 217.

68 Schumpeter, 184.

69 Edwin Cannan, Editor's Introduction to *The Wealth of Nations*, by Adam Smith (New York: Modern Library, 1937), xxxix.

70 Hollander, 316.

71 Smith, *LJ(A)*, 353.

72 John Rae, *Life of Adam Smith* (1895; reprint, New York: Augustus M. Kelley, 1965), 197–205.

73 Dugald Stewart, "Account of the Life and Writings of Adam Smith, LL.D.," in *Essays on Philosophical Subjects*, by Adam Smith, ed. W. L. D. Wightman (Oxford: Oxford University Press, 1980), 304.

74 Rae, 216; Rae quotes Dupont on 215.

75 P. D. Groenewegen, "Turgot and Adam Smith," *Scottish Journal of Political Economy* 16 (1969): 274; Viner, 128–38.

76 Smith, *WN*, 2: 663, 671–72, 678.

77 Ibid., 2: 673–74.

78 Edwin Cannan, *A History of the Theories of Production and Distribution from 1776 to 1848* (1893; reprint, New York: Augustus M. Kelley, 1967), 12.

79 Ibid., 144.

80 Ibid., 32.

81 See Smith, *LJ(A)*, 353–54; *LJ(B)*, 495–96; Early Draft in *Lectures on Jurisprudence;* Bowley, 362; Hollander, 114.

82 Ronald Meek, "Adam Smith and the Classical Theory of Profit," in *Economics and Ideology and Other Essays* (London: Chapman and Hall, 1967), 20.

83 Smith, *WN*, 1: 83; my emphasis.

84 Ibid., 1: 332.

85 Ibid., 1: 337–38.

86 Marian Bowley, "Some Aspects of the Treatment of Capital in *The Wealth of Nations*," in *Essays on Adam Smith*, 373.
87 Hollander, 105; see also 238–39.
88 Ibid., 155, 191–92, 189.
89 Ibid., 192.
90 Smith, *WN*, 1: 68.
91 Ibid., 1: 280, 363.
92 Hollander, 18.
93 Ibid., 19.
94 Smith, *WN*, 1: 53.
95 Ibid., 1: 206, 510.
96 John Hicks, *Capital and Growth* (New York: Oxford University Press, 1965), 16–18. See also Hla Myint, *Theories of Welfare Economics* (1948; reprint, New York: Augustus M. Kelley, 1965), 5.
97 Karl Marx, *Capital*, trans. Ben Fowkes (Harmondsworth: Penguin, 1976), 1: 736.
98 Cannan, *History*, 61.
99 Ibid., 53.
100 Ibid.
101 Smith, *WN*, 2: 823.
102 Myint, 8.
103 Groenewegen, 281; I. C. Lundberg, *Turgot's Unknown Translator* (The Hague: Nijhoff, 1964), 70–72.
104 Schumpeter, 324n2.
105 See especially Lundberg's interesting discussion of this correspondence of terms. Although Lundberg enormously overstates her general case, she is convincing on this point. In this connection see, for example, Viner, 134.
106 Sheldon S. Wolin, *Politics and Vision*, 290, as quoted by Andrew Skinner, *A System of Social Science: Papers Relating to Adam Smith* (Oxford: Oxford University Press, 1979), 209. See also George Stigler, "Smith's Travels on the Ship of State," in *Essays on Adam Smith*, 237.
107 Smith, *WN*, 1: 471, 472.
108 Ronald Meek, *Smith, Marx, and After* (London: Chapman and Hall, 1977), 14–16.
109 Smith, *WN*, 1: 540; my emphasis.
110 Ibid., 2: 910.
111 Ibid., 1: 428, 372.
112 Ibid., 1: 357.
113 Ibid., 1: 324.
114 Ibid., 1: 465, 522–23.
115 Ibid., 2: 687–88.
116 Ibid., 2: 724, 731.
117 Ibid., 2: 781, 782.
118 Ibid., 2: 785, 786.
119 Ibid., 2: 562, 606.
120 Ibid., 2: 833. My analysis thus departs from the often insightful dis-

cussion by Donald Winch, *Adam Smith's Politics: An Essay in Historiographic Revision* (Cambridge: Cambridge University Press, 1978), who draws attention (170–72) to Smith's advice to the legislator but who argues (140) that Smith's "agrarian bias cannot be regarded as having great political significance"—a position clearly at variance with the argument I have advanced.

121 Karl Marx, *Theories of Surplus Value*, trans. Emile Burns, ed. S. W. Ryazanskaya (Moscow: Progress Publishers, 1963), 1: 43.

CONCLUSION: POLITICAL ECONOMY AND CAPITALISM

1 Karl Marx, *Grundrisse*, trans. Martin Nicolaus (Harmondsworth: Penguin, 1973), 252–53.

2 Karl Marx, *Capital*, trans. Ben Fowkes (Harmondsworth: Penguin, 1976), 1: 876. See also Marx, *Grundrisse*, 507, 769.

3 Karl Marx, *Capital*, trans. David Fernbach (Harmondsworth: Penguin, 1981), 3: 919.

4 Smith's doctrine is, however, somewhat inconsistent. At times he follows Petty's view that rent is price-determining, not price-determined, especially when he is developing his theory of natural price. Elsewhere, he tends to treat rent as price-determined—and in such places (as in chap. 11, Book 1 of *The Wealth of Nations*, "Of the Rent of Land"), he clearly departs from the analysis set down by Petty.

5 Karl Marx, *The Poverty of Philosophy* (New York: International Publishers, 1963), 121.

6 J. Ralph Lindgren, *The Social Philosophy of Adam Smith* (The Hague: Nijhoff, 1973), xiv.

7 This shift in the conceptual structure of classical economics is clearest in the case of Ricardo and Say. On Ricardo see note 5 to the introduction. Say's narrowing of the focus of political economy was a source of concern to the Physiocrat Dupont who wrote the former that "you have narrowed the scope of economics too much in treating it only as the science of wealth. It is *la science du droit naturel* applied, as it should be, to civilized society." This letter of 22 April 1815 is quoted by Thomas P. Neill, "Quesnay and Physiocracy," *Journal of the History of Ideas* 9 (1948): 108. The case of Bentham is somewhat different given the breadth of his intellectual concerns. Nevertheless, he reconstructed Smithian economics in a manner quite foreign to Smith's outlook (and one which decisively influenced James Mill and John Stuart Mill). This issue is perceptively discussed by Robert Denoon Cumming, "Giving Back Words: Things, Money, Persons," *Social Research* 68 (1981): 227–59.

8 Marx, *Grundrisse*, 452–70, esp. 462.

9 Marx, *Capital*, 1: 928, 929.

Bibliography

PRIMARY SOURCES

Armstrong, Clement. "Howe to Reforme the Realme in Setting Them to Werke and to store Tillage." In *Tudor Economic Documents,* ed. R. H. Tawney and Eileen Powers, 3: 115–29. 1924. Reprint, New York: Barnes and Noble, 1963.

———. "A Treatise Concerninge the Staple and the Commodities of this Realme." In *Tudor Economic Documents,* ed. R. H. Tawney and Eileen Powers, 3: 90–114. 1924. Reprint, New York: Barnes and Noble, 1963.

Bacon, Francis. *The New Organon.* Ed. Fulton H. Anderson. Indianapolis: Bobbs-Merrill Co., 1960.

Barbon, Nicholas. *A Discourse of Trade.* Ed. Jacob Hollander. 1690. Reprint, Baltimore: Johns Hopkins University Press, 1905.

Baudeau, Abbé. *Explication du tableau économique.* Paris: Editions d'Histoire Sociale, 1967.

Boisguilbert, Pierre. "Le Détail de la France." In *Pierre de Boisguilbert ou la naissance de l'économie politique.* 2 vols. Paris: Institut National d'Etudes Démographiques, 1966.

———. "Dissertation de la nature des richesses, de l'argent et des tributs. . . ." In *Pierre de Boisguilbert ou la naissance de l'économie politique.* 2 vols. Paris: Institut National d'Etudes Démographiques, 1966.

———. "Traité de la nature, culture, commerce, et intérêt de l'argent." In *Pierre de Boisguilbert ou la naissance de l'économie politique.* 2 vols. Paris: Institut National d'Etudes Démographiques, 1966.

Cantillon, Richard. *Essai sur la nature du commerce en général/Essay on the Nature of Commerce in General.* Trans. and ed. Henry Higgs. New York: Augustus M. Kelley, 1964.

Child, Josiah. "Brief Observations Concerning Trade and Interest of Money." In *Selected Works of Josiah Child, 1668–1697.* 2 vols. Farnborough Honts, England: Gregg Press, 1968.

———. "A Discourse on the Nature, Use, and Advantages of Trade." In

Selected Works of Josiah Child, 1668–1697. 2 vols. Farnborough Honts, England: Gregg Press, 1968.

———. "A New Discourse of Trade." In *Selected Works of Josiah Child, 1668–1697.* 2 vols. Farnborough Honts, England: Gregg Press, 1968.

———. *Selected Works of Josiah Child, 1668–1697.* 2 vols. Farnborough Honts, England: Gregg Press, 1968.

Culpepper, Thomas. "A Tract Against Usurie." In *Selected Works of Josiah Child, 1668–1697.* 2 vols. Farnborough Honts, England: Gregg Press, 1968.

Ferguson, Adam. *An Essay on the History of Civil Society.* Ed. Duncan Forbes. Edinburgh: Edinburgh University Press, 1966.

Fletcher, Andrew. *Andrew Fletcher of Saltoun: Selected Writings.* Ed. David Daiches. Edinburgh: Scottish Academic Press, 1979.

Groenewegen, P. D., ed. and trans. *The Economics of A. R. J. Turgot.* The Hague: Nijhoff, 1977.

Harrington, James. "Aphorisms Political." In *The Political Works of James Harrington,* ed. J. G. A. Pocock. Cambridge: Cambridge University Press, 1977.

———. "The Art of Lawgiving in Three Books." In *The Political Works of James Harrington,* ed. J. G. A. Pocock. Cambridge: Cambridge University Press, 1977.

———. "The Commonwealth of Oceana." In *The Political Works of James Harrington,* ed. J. G. A. Pocock. Cambridge: Cambridge University Press, 1977.

———. "The Model at Large of a Free State." In *The Political Works of James Harrington,* ed. J. G. A. Pocock. Cambridge: Cambridge University Press, 1977.

———. "The Prerogative of Popular Government." In *The Political Works of James Harrington,* ed. J. G. A. Pocock. Cambridge: Cambridge University Press, 1977.

———. "A System of Politics." In *The Political Works of James Harrington,* ed. J. G. A. Pocock. Cambridge: Cambridge University Press, 1977.

Hill, Henry Bertram, ed. and trans. *The Political Testament of Cardinal Richelieu.* Madison: University of Wisconsin Press, 1961.

Hull, Charles Henry, ed. *Economic Writings of Sir William Petty.* 2 vols. New York: Augustus M. Kelley, 1963.

Hume, David. "Of the Balance of Trade." In *Writings on Economics,* by David Hume, ed. Eugene Rotwein. Madison: University of Wisconsin Press, 1970.

———. "Of the Coalition of Parties." In *Essays: Moral, Political, and Literary,* by David Hume, ed. Eugene F. Miller. Indianapolis: Liberty Classics, 1985.

———. "An Enquiry Concerning the Principles of Morals." In *Hume's Ethical Writings,* ed. Alasdair MacIntyre. London: Macmillan and Co., 1965.

———. *Essays: Moral, Political, and Literary.* Ed. Eugene F. Miller. Indianapolis: Liberty Classics, 1985.

———. "Of the First Principles of Government." In *Essays: Moral, Politi-*

cal, and Literary, by David Hume, ed. Eugene F. Miller. Indianapolis: Liberty Classics, 1985.

————. "Idea of a Perfect Commonwealth." In *Essays: Moral, Political, and Literary*, by David Hume, ed. Eugene F. Miller. Indianapolis: Liberty Classics, 1985.

————. "Of the Independency of Parliament." In *Essays: Moral, Political, and Literary*, by David Hume, ed. Eugene F. Miller. Indianapolis: Liberty Classics, 1985.

————. "Of the Jealousy of Trade." In *Writings on Economics*, by David Hume, ed. Eugene Rotwein. Madison: University of Wisconsin Press, 1970.

————. "Of Money." In *Writings on Economics*, by David Hume, ed. Eugene Rotwein. Madison: University of Wisconsin Press, 1970.

————. "Of the Original Contract." In *Essays: Moral, Political, and Literary*, by David Hume, ed. Eugene F. Miller. Indianapolis: Liberty Classics, 1985.

————. "Of the Origin of Government." In *Essays: Moral, Political, and Literary*, by David Hume, ed. Eugene F. Miller. Indianapolis: Liberty Classics, 1985.

————. "Of Parties in General." In *Essays: Moral, Political, and Literary*, by David Hume, ed. Eugene F. Miller. Indianapolis: Liberty Classics, 1985.

————. "Of the Parties of Great Britain." In *Essays: Moral, Political, and Literary*, by David Hume, ed. Eugene F. Miller. Indianapolis: Liberty Classics, 1985.

————. "Of Passive Obedience." In *Essays: Moral, Political, and Literary*, by David Hume, ed. Eugene F. Miller. Indianapolis: Liberty Classics, 1985.

————. "That Politics may be reduced to a Science." In *Essays: Moral, Political, and Literary*, by David Hume, ed. Eugene F. Miller. Indianapolis: Liberty Classics, 1985.

————. "Of the Populousness of Ancient Nations." In *Essays: Moral, Political, and Literary*, by David Hume, ed. Eugene F. Miller. Indianapolis: Liberty Classics, 1985.

————. "Of Public Credit." In *Essays: Moral, Political, and Literary*, by David Hume, ed. Eugene F. Miller. Indianapolis: Liberty Classics, 1985.

————. "Of Refinement in the Arts." In *Writings on Economics*, by David Hume, ed. Eugene Rotwein. Madison: University of Wisconsin Press, 1970.

————. *A Treatise of Human Nature*. Ed. L. A. Selby-Bigge. Oxford: Oxford University Press, 1888.

————. "Whether the British Government inclines more to Absolute Monarchy, or to a Republic." In *Essays: Moral, Political, and Literary*, by David Hume, ed. Eugene F. Miller. Indianapolis: Liberty Classics, 1985.

————. *Writings on Economics*. Ed. Eugene Rotwein. Madison: University of Wisconsin Press, 1970.

Hutcheson, Francis. *An Inquiry Concerning Beauty, Order, Harmony, Design*. Ed. Peter Kivy. The Hague: Nijhoff, 1973.

———. *A System of Moral Philosophy.* 2 vols. London, 1755.

Kuczynski, Marguerite, and Meek, Ronald, eds. and trans. *Quesnay's Tableau Economique.* London: Macmillan and Co., 1972.

Lansdowne, Marquis of, ed. *The Petty Papers: Some Unpublished Papers of Sir William Petty.* 2 vols. London: Constable and Co., 1927.

Le Trosne, Guillaume-François. *De l'ordre social.* Paris, 1777.

Lindgren, J. Ralph, ed. *The Early Writings of Adam Smith.* New York: Augustus M. Kelley, 1967.

Locke, John. "The Second Treatise of Government." In *Two Treatises of Government,* ed. Peter Laslett. Rev. ed. New York: New American Library, 1965.

———. *Several Papers Relating to Money, Interest, and Trade.* 1696. Reprint, New York: Augustus M. Kelley, 1968.

———. "Short Observations on a Printed Paper." In *Several Papers Relating to Money, Interest, and Trade,* by John Locke. 1696. Reprint, New York: Augustus M. Kelley, 1968.

———. "Some Considerations of the Consequences of the Lowering of Interest, and Raising the Value of Money." In *Several Papers Relating to Money, Interest, and Trade,* by John Locke. 1696. Reprint, New York: Augustus M. Kelley, 1968.

MacIntyre, Alasdair, ed. *Hume's Ethical Writings.* London: Macmillan and Co., 1965.

Malynes, Gerrard. "A treatise of the Canker of England's Common Weal." In *Tudor Economic Documents,* ed. R. H. Tawney and Eileen Powers, 3: 386–404. 1924. Reprint, New York: Barnes and Noble, 1963.

Mandeville, Bernard. *The Fable of the Bees.* Ed. F. B. Kaye. 2 vols. Oxford: Oxford University Press, 1924.

Marx, Karl. *Capital.* Vol. 1. Trans. Ben Fowkes. Harmondsworth: Penguin, 1976.

———. *Capital.* Vol. 2. Trans. David Fernbach. Harmondsworth: Penguin, 1978.

———. *Capital.* Vol. 3. Trans. David Fernbach. Harmondsworth: Penguin, 1981.

———. *A Contribution to the Critique of Political Economy.* Trans. S. W. Ryazanskaya. Moscow: Progress Publishers, 1970.

———. *Grundrisse.* Trans. Martin Nicolaus. Harmondsworth: Penguin, 1973.

———. *The Poverty of Philosophy.* New York: International Publishers, 1963.

———. *Theories of Surplus Value.* Trans. Emile Burns, ed. S. W. Ryazanskaya. 3 vols. Moscow: Progress Publishers, 1963, 1968, 1971.

Marx, Karl, and Engels, Frederick. *Selected Correspondence.* Second Edition. Moscow: Progress Publishers, 1965.

Meek, Ronald, ed. and trans. *The Economics of Physiocracy: Essays and Translations.* Cambridge, Mass: Harvard University Press, 1963.

———. ed. *Precursors of Adam Smith, 1750–1775.* London: J. M. Dent and Sons, 1973.

———. ed. *Turgot on Progress, Sociology and Economics*. Cambridge: Cambridge University Press, 1974.

Mirabeau, Victor Riqueti, marquis de. *Philosophie rurale*. Amsterdam, 1763.

Misselden, Edward. *The Circle of Commerce*. 1623. Reprint, Amsterdam: Theatrum Orbis Terrarum, 1969.

Montchrétien, Antoyne de. *Traicté de l'oéconomie politique dédié en 1615 au roy et la reyne mère du roy*. Ed. Théodor Funck-Brentano. Paris: Librairie Plon, 1889.

Montesquieu, Baron de. *The Spirit of the Laws*. Trans. Thomas Nugent. New York: Hafner Press, 1949.

Mossner, Ernest Campbell, and Ross, Ian Simpson, eds. *The Correspondence of Adam Smith*. Oxford: Oxford University Press, 1977.

Mun, Thomas. *England's Treasure by Forraign Trade*. 1664. Reprint, Oxford: Basil Blackwell, 1928.

North, Dudley. *Discourses Upon Trade*. Ed. Jacob Hollander. 1691. Reprint, Baltimore: Johns Hopkins University Press, 1907.

North, Roger. Introduction to *Discourses Upon Trade*, by Dudley North, ed. Jacob Hollander. 1691. Reprint, Baltimore: Johns Hopkins Press, 1907.

Petty, William. "Inclosing Commons." In *The Petty Papers*, ed. Marquis of Lansdowne. 2 vols. London: Constable and Co., 1927.

———. "Irish Land Registry." In *The Petty Papers*, ed. Marquis of Lansdowne. 2 vols. London: Constable and Co., 1927.

———. "Observations of England." In *The Petty Papers*, ed. Marquis of Lansdowne. 2 vols. London: Constable and Co., 1927.

———. "Political Anatomy of Ireland." In *Economic Writings of Sir William Petty*, ed. Charles Henry Hull. 2 vols. 1889. Reprint, New York: Augustus M. Kelley, 1963.

———. "Political Arithmetick." In *Economic Writings of Sir William Petty*, ed. Charles Henry Hull. 2 vols. 1889. Reprint, New York: Augustus M. Kelley, 1963.

———. "A Treatise of Taxes and Contributions." In *Economic Writings of Sir William Petty*, ed. Charles Henry Hull. 2 vols. 1889. Reprint, New York: Augustus M. Kelley, 1963.

———. "The Wealth of England." In *The Petty Papers*, ed. Marquis of Lansdowne. 2 vols. London: Constable and Co., 1927.

Pocock, J. G. A., ed. *The Political Writings of James Harrington*. Cambridge: Cambridge University Press, 1977.

"Policies to Reduce this Realme of England Unto a Prosperous Wealthe and Estate." In *Tudor Economic Documents*, ed. R. H. Tawney and Eileen Powers, 3: 311–45. 1924. Reprint, New York: Barnes and Noble, 1963.

Quesnay, François. "The Analysis of the Tableau économique." In *The Economics of Physiocracy: Essays and Translations*, ed. and trans. Ronald Meek. Cambridge, Mass.: Harvard University Press, 1963.

———. "Despotisme de la Chine." In *François Quesnay et la physiocratie*. 2 vols. Paris: Institut National d'Etudes Démographiques, 1958.

———. "Fermiers." In *François Quesnay et la physiocratie*. 2 vols. Paris: Institut National d'Etudes Démographiques, 1958.

———. "The First Economic Problem." In *The Economics of Physiocracy: Essays and Translations*, ed. and trans. Ronald Meek. Cambridge, Mass.: Harvard University Press, 1963.

———. "General Maxims for the Economic Government of an Agricultural Kingdom." In *The Economics of Physiocracy: Essays and Translations*, ed. and trans. Ronald Meek. Cambridge, Mass.: Harvard University Press, 1963.

———. "Grains." In *François Quesnay et la physiocratie*. 2 vols. Paris: Institut National d'Etudes Démographiques, 1958.

———. "Hommes." In *François Quesnay et la physiocratie*. 2 vols. Paris: Institut National d'Etudes Démographiques, 1958.

———. "Impôts." In *François Quesnay et la physiocratie*. 2 vols. Paris: Institut National d'Etudes Démographiques, 1958.

———. "Natural Right." In *The Economics of Physiocracy: Essays and Translations*, ed. and trans. Ronald Meek. Cambridge, Mass.: Harvard University Press, 1963.

———. "The Second Economic Problem." In *The Economics of Physiocracy: Essays and Translations*, ed. and trans. Ronald Meek. Cambridge, Mass.: Harvard University Press, 1963.

Ricardo, David. "Essay on Profits." In *The Works and Correspondence of David Ricardo*, ed. Piero Sraffa. Vol. 4. Cambridge: Cambridge University Press, 1962.

Smith, Adam. "Of the External Senses." In *The Early Writings of Adam Smith*, ed. J. Ralph Lindgren. New York: Augustus M. Kelley, 1967.

———. "Language." In *The Early Writings of Adam Smith*, ed. J. Ralph Lindgren. New York: Augustus M. Kelley, 1967.

———. *Lectures on Jurisprudence*. Ed. R. L. Meek, D. D. Raphael, and P. G. Stein. Oxford: Oxford University Press, 1978.

———. *Lectures on Rhetoric and Belles Lettres*. Ed. John M. Lothian. Carbondale: Southern Illinois University Press, 1971.

———. "The Principles Which Lead and Direct Philosophical Enquiries: Illustrated by the History of Astronomy." In *The Early Writings of Adam Smith*, ed. J. Ralph Lindgren. New York: Augustus M. Kelley, 1967.

———. *The Theory of the Moral Sentiments*. Indianapolis: Liberty Classics, 1969.

———. *The Wealth of Nations*. Ed. R. H. Campbell and A. S. Skinner. 2 vols. Oxford: Oxford University Press, 1976.

Smith, Thomas. *A Discourse of the Commonweal of This Realm of England*. Ed. Mary Dewar. Charlottesville: University Press of Virginia, 1969.

Sraffa, Piero, ed. *The Works and Correspondence of David Ricardo*. Vol. 4. Cambridge: Cambridge University Press, 1962.

Stephens, W. Walker, ed. *The Life and Writings of Turgot*. New York: Longmans, Green, and Co., 1895.

Stewart, Dugald. "Account of the Life and Writings of Adam Smith." In *Essays on Philosophical Subjects*, by Adam Smith, ed. W. L. D. Wightman. Oxford: Oxford University Press, 1980.

Tucker, Josiah. "Four Tracts on Political and Commercial Subjects." In

Precursors of Adam Smith, 1750–1775, ed. Ronald Meek. London: J. M. Dent and Sons, 1973.

Turgot, Anne Robert Jacques. "Letters on the Grain Trade." In *The Economics of A. R. J. Turgot*, ed. and trans. P. D. Groenewegen. The Hague: Nijhoff, 1977.

———. "Observations on a Paper by Graslin." In *The Economics of A. R. J. Turgot*, ed. and trans. P. D. Groenewegen. The Hague: Nijhoff, 1977.

———. "Observations on a Paper by Saint-Peravy." In *The Economics of A. R. J. Turgot*, ed. and trans. P. D. Groenewegen. The Hague: Nijhoff, 1977.

———. "Plan for a Paper on Taxation." In *The Economics of A. R. J. Turgot*, ed. and trans. P. D. Groenewegen. The Hague: Nijhoff, 1977.

———. "In Praise of Gournay." In *The Economics of A. R. J. Turgot*, ed. and trans. P. D. Groenewegen. The Hague: Nijhoff, 1977.

———. "Reflections on the Formation and Distribution of Wealth." In *Turgot on Progress, Sociology, and Economics*, ed. Ronald Meek. Cambridge: Cambridge University Press, 1974.

Vauban, Sébastien Le Prestre de. *La Dîme royale*. Paris: Bibliothèque Nationale, 1872.

Weulerrse, Georges, ed. *Les Manuscrits économiques de François Quesnay et du marquis de Mirabeau aux Archives nationales*. Paris: Editions Mouton, 1910.

SECONDARY SOURCES

Amati, Frank, and Aspromourgos, Tony. "Petty *contra* Hobbes: A Previously Untranslated Manuscript." *Journal of the History of Ideas* 66, 1985: 127–32.

Anderson, Perry. *Lineages of the Absolutist State*. London: New Left Books, 1974.

Anspach, Ralph. "The Implications of the *Theory of the Moral Sentiments* for Adam Smith's Economic Thought." *History of Political Economy* 4, 1972: 176–206.

Appleby, Joyce Oldham. *Economic Thought and Ideology in Seventeenth-Century England*. Princeton: Princeton University Press, 1978.

———. "Ideology and Theory: The Tension between Political and Economic Liberalism in Seventeenth-Century England." *American Historical Review* 81, 1976: 499–515.

Ashcraft, Richard. *Revolutionary Politics and Locke's Two Treatises of Government*. Princeton: Princeton University Press, 1986.

Aston, Trevor, ed. *Crisis in Europe 1560–1660*. London: Routledge and Kegan Paul, 1965.

Beer, Max. *Early British Economics*. 1938. Reprint, London: Frank Cass and Co., 1967.

———. *An Inquiry into Physiocracy*. 1939. Reprint, New York: Russell and Russell, 1966.

Beloff, Max. *The Age of Absolutism, 1660–1815*. London: Hutchinson and Co., 1954.

Bindhoff, S. T. "Clement Armstrong and His Treatises of the Commonweal." *Economic History Review* 17, 1944: 64–73.

———. *Tudor England*. Harmondsworth: Penguin, 1950.

Blaug, Mark. *Economic Theory in Retrospect*. 3d ed. Cambridge: Cambridge University Press, 1978.

Bleaney, Michael. *Underconsumption Theories: A History and Critical Analysis*. New York: International Publishers, 1976.

Bloch, Marc. *Feudal Society*. Trans. L. A. Manyon. 2 vols. Chicago: University of Chicago Press, 1961.

———. *French Rural History: An Essay on Its Basic Characteristics*. Trans. Janet Sondheimer. Berkeley: University of California Press, 1966.

———. "La lutte pour l'individualisme agraire dans la France du XVIIIe siècle, 2e partie." *Annales d'histoire économique et sociale* 2, 1930: 511–58.

Bois, Guy. *Crise du féodalisme*. Paris: Presses de la Fondation Nationale des Sciences Politiques, 1976.

Bosher, John. *French Finance, 1770–1795: From Business to Bureaucracy*. Cambridge: Cambridge University Press, 1970.

Bourde, André. *The Influence of England on the French Agronomes*. Cambridge: Cambridge University Press, 1953.

Bowley, Marian. "Some Aspects of the Treatment of Capital in *The Wealth of Nations*." In *Essays on Adam Smith*, ed. Andrew Skinner and Thomas Wilson, 361–76. Oxford: Oxford University Press, 1975.

———. *Studies in the History of Economic Theory Before 1870*. London: Macmillan and Co., 1973.

Brailsford, H. N. *The Levellers and the English Revolution*. Ed. Christopher Hill. 1961. Reprint, London: Spokesman, 1976.

Brenner, Robert. "Agrarian Class Structure and Economic Development in Pre-Industrial Europe." *Past and Present* 70, 1976: 30–75.

———. "The Agrarian Roots of European Capitalism." *Past and Present* 97, 1982: 16–113.

Briggs, Robin. *Early Modern France, 1560–1715*. Oxford: Oxford University Press, 1977.

Bryson, Gladys. *Man and Society: The Scottish Inquiry of the Eighteenth Century*. Princeton: Princeton University Press, 1945.

Campbell, Mildred. *The English Yeoman Under Elizabeth and the Early Stuarts*. New Haven: Yale University Press, 1942.

Campbell, R. H. "An Economic History of Scotland in the Eighteenth Century." *Scottish Journal of Political Economy* 11, 1964: 17–24.

———. "The Industrial Revolution: A Revision Article." *Scottish Historical Review* 46, 1967: 37–55.

———. "The Scottish Improvers and the Course of Agrarian Change in the Eighteenth Century." In *Comparative Aspects of Scottish and Irish Economic and Social History, 1600–1900*, ed. L. M. Cullen and T. C. Smout, 204–15. Edinburgh: John Donald, 1977.

Campbell, T. D. "Scientific Explanation and Ethical Justification in the *Moral Sentiments*." In *Essays on Adam Smith*, ed. Andrew Skinner and Thomas Wilson, 68–82. Oxford: Oxford University Press, 1975.

Cannan, Edwin. Editor's Introduction to *The Wealth of Nations*, by Adam Smith. New York: Modern Library, 1937.

———. *A History of the Theories of Production and Distribution from 1776 to 1848*. 1893. Reprint, New York: Augustus M. Kelley, 1967.

Chambers, J. D., and Mingay, Gordon E. *The Agricultural Revolution, 1750–1850*. London: B. T. Batsford, 1966.

Church, William F., ed. and trans. *The Impact of Absolutism in France*. New York: John Wiley and Sons, 1969.

Cobban, Alfred. *The Social Interpretation of the French Revolution*. Cambridge: Cambridge University Press, 1964.

Cole, Charles Woolsey. *Colbert and a Century of French Mercantilism*. 2 vols. 1939. Reprint, Hamden, Conn.: Archon Books, 1964.

———. *French Mercantilism, 1683–1700*. 1943. Reprint, New York: Octagon Books, 1965.

Coleman, D. C. "Eli Heckscher and the Idea of Mercantilism." In *Revisions in Mercantilism*, ed. D. C. Coleman, 92–117. London: Methuen and Co., 1969.

———, ed. *Revisions in Mercantilism*. London: Methuen and Co., 1969.

Court, W. H. B. *The Rise of Midland Industries, 1600–1838*. 1938. Reprint, London: Oxford University Press, 1953.

Cropsey, Joseph. "Adam Smith and Political Philosophy." In *Essays on Adam Smith*, ed. Andrew Skinner and Thomas Wilson, 132–53. Oxford: Oxford University Press, 1975.

———. *Polity and Economy: An Interpretation of the Principles of Adam Smith*. The Hague: Nijhoff, 1957.

Cumming, Robert Denoon. "Giving Back Words: Things, Money, Persons." *Social Research* 68, 1981: 227–59.

Dakin, Douglas. *Turgot and the Ancien Regime in France*. 1939. Reprint, New York: Octagon Books, 1965.

Davie, George. "Berkeley, Hume, and the Central Problem of Scottish Philosophy." In *McGill Hume Studies*, ed. David Fate Norton, Nicholas Capaldi, and Wade L. Robinson, 43–62. San Diego: Austin Hill Press, 1976.

———. *The Scottish Enlightenment*. London: The Historical Association, 1981.

Davis, J. C. "Pocock's Harrington: Grace, Nature, and Art in the Classical Republicanism of James Harrington." *Historical Journal* 24, 1984: 683–97.

Day, Christopher. "A Redistribution of Incomes in Fifteenth-Century England?" In *Peasants, Knights, and Heretics*, ed. Rodney Hilton, 192–215. Cambridge: Cambridge University Press, 1976.

Dent, Julian. *Crisis in Finance: Crown, Financiers, and Society in Seventeenth-Century France*. Newton Abbot, England: David and Charles, 1973.

Devine, T. M. *The Tobacco Lords*. Edinburgh: John Donald, 1975.

Dewar, Mary. Introduction to *A Discourse of the Commonweal of This Realm of England*, by Thomas Smith. Charlottesville: University Press of Virginia, 1969.

Dickinson, H. T. *Liberty and Property: Political Ideology in Eighteenth-Century Britain.* London: Methuen and Co., 1977.

Dickson, Tony, ed. *Scottish Capitalism: Class, State, and Nation from Before the Union to the Present.* London: Lawrence and Wishart, 1980.

Dobb, Maurice. *Studies in the Development of Capitalism.* Rev. ed. New York: International Publishers, 1963.

Duby, Georges. *Rural Economy and Country Life in the Medieval West.* Trans. Cynthia Postan. Columbia: University of South Carolina Press, 1968.

Dumont, Louis. *From Mandeville to Marx: The Genesis and Triumph of Economic Ideology.* Chicago: University of Chicago Press, 1977.

Eagly, Robert V. *The Structure of Classical Economic Theory.* New York: Oxford University Press, 1974.

————, ed. *Events, Ideology, and Economic Theory.* Detroit, Mich.: Wayne State University Press, 1968.

Einaudi, Mario. *The Physiocratic Doctrine of Judicial Control.* Cambridge, Mass.: Harvard University Press, 1938.

Elitis, W. A. "François Quesnay: A Reinterpretation, 1. The *Tableau économique.*" *Oxford Economic Papers,* n. ser., 27, 1975: 167–201.

Elton, G. R. *England Under the Tudors.* 2d ed. London: Methuen and Co., 1974.

Fink, Zera S. *The Classical Republicans.* 2d ed. Evanston: Northwestern University Press, 1962.

Foley, Vernon. "An Origin of the *Tableau économique.*" *History of Political Economy* 5, 1973: 121–50.

————. *The Social Physics of Adam Smith.* West Lafayette: Purdue University Press, 1976.

Forbes, Duncan. *Hume's Philosophical Politics.* Cambridge: Cambridge University Press, 1975.

————. "Sceptical Whiggism, Commerce, and History." In *Essays on Adam Smith,* ed. Andrew Skinner and Thomas Wilson, 179–201. Oxford: Oxford University Press, 1975.

Forster, Robert. *The Nobility of Toulouse in the Eighteenth Century: A Social and Economic Study.* Baltimore: Johns Hopkins University Press, 1960.

Fox-Genovese, Elizabeth. *The Origins of Physiocracy: Economic Revolution and Social Order in Eighteenth-Century France.* Ithaca: Cornell University Press, 1976.

Fussell, George Edwin. *The Old English Farming Books From Fitzherbert to Tull, 1523–1730.* London: Lockwood and Son, 1947.

Gee, J. M. A. "The Origin of Rent in Adam Smith's *Wealth of Nations:* An Anti-Neoclassical View." *History of Political Economy* 13, 1981: 1–18.

Goodale, Jesse. "J. G. A. Pocock's Neo-Harringtonians: A Reconsideration." *History of Political Thought* 1, 1980: 237–59.

Goubert, Pierre. *Louis XIV and Twenty Million Frenchmen.* Trans. Anne Carter. New York: Vintage, 1970.

Gray, Alexander. *Adam Smith.* 1948. Reprint, London: Historical Association, 1968.

Groenewegen, P. D. "Turgot and Adam Smith." *Scottish Journal of Political Economy* 16, 1969: 271–87.

Gunn, J. A. W. *Beyond Liberty and Property: The Process of Self-Recognition in Eighteenth-Century Political Thought.* Kingston: McGill-Queen's University Press, 1983.

———. *Politics and the Public Interest in the Seventeenth Century.* London: Routledge and Kegan Paul, 1969.

Haakonssen, Knud. *The Science of a Legislator: The Natural Jurisprudence of David Hume and Adam Smith.* Cambridge: Cambridge University Press, 1981.

Habakkuk, H. J. "English Landownership, 1680–1740." *Economic History Review* 9, 1940: 2–17.

Haley, K. H. D. *The First Earl of Shaftesbury.* Oxford: Clarendon Press, 1968.

Hamilton, Henry. *An Economic History of Scotland in the Eighteenth Century.* Oxford: Oxford University Press, 1963.

Hecht, Jacqueline. "La Vie de François Quesnay." In *François Quesnay et la physiocratie.* 2 vols. Paris: Institut National d'Etudes Démographiques, 1958.

Heckscher, Eli. *Mercantilism.* Trans. Mendel Shapiro. 2d ed. 2 vols. London: George Allen and Unwin, 1955.

Hicks, John. *Capital and Growth.* New York: Oxford University Press, 1965.

Higgins, J. P. P., and Pollard, Sydney. *Aspects of Capital Investment in Great Britain, 1750–1850.* London: Methuen and Co., 1971.

Higgs, Henry. "Cantillon's Place in Economics." *Quarterly Journal of Economics* 6, 1892: 436–56.

———. "Richard Cantillon." *Economic Journal* 1, 1891: 262–91.

Hill, Christopher. *The Century of Revolution, 1603–1714.* 1961. Reprint, London: Cardinal-Sphere Books, 1974.

———. *The Experience of Defeat.* New York: Viking Penguin, 1984.

———. *The Intellectual Origins of the English Revolution.* 1965. Reprint, London: Granada Publishing, 1972.

———. *The World Turned Upside Down.* 1972. Reprint, Harmondsworth: Penguin, 1975.

Hilton, Rodney. *Bond Men Made Free: Medieval Peasant Movements and the English Rising of 1381.* London: Methuen and Co., 1973.

———. "A Crisis of Feudalism." *Past and Present* 80, 1978: 3–19.

———. *The Decline of Feudalism in Medieval England.* London: Macmillan and Co., 1969.

———. *The Economic Development of Some Leicestershire Estates in the Fourteenth and Fifteenth Centuries.* Oxford: Oxford University Press, 1947.

———. *The English Peasantry in the Later Middle Ages.* Oxford: Oxford University Press, 1975.

———. "Y eut-il une crise générale de la féodalité?" *Annales. Economies, Sociétés, Civilisations* 6, 1951: 25–30.

———, ed. *Peasants, Knights, and Heretics.* Cambridge: Cambridge University Press, 1976.

Hirschman, Albert. *The Passions and the Interests: Political Arguments for Capitalism before its Triumph.* Princeton: Princeton University Press, 1977.

Hobsbawm, Eric, and Rudé, George. *Captain Swing: A Social History of the Great English Agricultural Rising of 1830.* New York: W. W. Norton, 1975.

Holderness, Barry. "Capital Formation in Agriculture." In *Aspects of Capital Investment in Great Britain, 1750–1850,* ed. J. P. P. Higgins and Sidney Pollard, 159–83. London: Methuen and Co., 1971.

Hollander, Samuel. *The Economics of Adam Smith.* Toronto: University of Toronto Press, 1973.

Hone, Joseph. "Richard Cantillon, Economist—Biographical Note." *Economic Journal* 65, 1944: 96–100.

Hont, Istvan. "The 'Rich Country–Poor Country' Debate in Scottish Classical Political Economy." In *Wealth and Virtue: The Shaping of Political Economy in the Scottish Enlightenment,* eds. Istvan Hont and Michael Ignatieff, 271–316. Cambridge: Cambridge University Press, 1983.

Hont, Istvan, and Ignatieff, Michael. "Needs and Justice in *The Wealth of Nations:* An Introductory Essay." In *Wealth and Virtue: The Shaping of Political Economy in the Scottish Enlightenment,* ed. Istvan Hont and Michael Ignatieff, 1–44. Cambridge: Cambridge University Press, 1983.

————, eds. *Wealth and Virtue: The Shaping of Political Economy in the Scottish Enlightenment.* Cambridge: Cambridge University Press, 1983.

Horne, Thomas. "Moral and Economic Improvement: Francis Hutcheson on Property." *History of Political Thought* 7, 1986: 115–30.

————. *The Social Thought of Bernard Mandeville: Virtue and Commerce in Early Eighteenth-Century England.* London: Macmillan and Co., 1978.

Hoselitz, Bert. "Agrarian Capitalism, the Natural Order of Things: François Quesnay." *Kyklos* 21, 1968: 637–63.

Hoskins, William George. *The Midland Peasant: The Economic and Social History of a Leicestershire Village.* London: Macmillan and Co., 1957.

Howell, Wilbur Smith. "Adam Smith's Lectures on Rhetoric: An Historical Assessment." In *Essays on Adam Smith,* ed. Andrew Skinner and Thomas Wilson, 11–43. Oxford: Oxford University Press, 1975.

Jevons, W. Stanley. "Richard Cantillon and the Nationality of Political Economy." In *Essai sur la nature du commerce en général,* by Richard Cantillon, trans. and ed. Henry Higgs. New York: Augustus M. Kelley, 1964.

John, A. H. "Agricultural Productivity and Economic Growth in England, 1700–1760." *Journal of Economic History* 25, 1965: 19–34.

————. "Aspects of English Economic Growth in the First Half of the Eighteenth Century." *Economica* 28, 1961: 176–90.

Jones, E. L. "Agricultural Origins of Industry." *Past and Present* 40, 1968: 58–71.

————. ed. *Agriculture and Economic Growth in England, 1650–1815.* London: Methuen and Co., 1967.

Jones, J. R. *The First Whigs: The Politics of the Exclusion Crisis, 1678–1683.* London: Oxford University Press, 1968.

Jones, Whitney R. D. *The Tudor Commonwealth, 1529–1559.* London: Athlone Press, 1970.

Kaplan, Stephen L. *Bread, Politics, and Political Economy in the Reign of Louis XV.* 2 vols. The Hague: Nijhoff, 1976.

Kemp, Tom. *Historical Patterns of Industrialization.* London: Longman Group, 1978.

Kenyon, J. P. *Revolution Principles: The Politics of Party, 1689–1720.* Cambridge: Cambridge University Press, 1977.

Keohane, Nannerl O. *Philosophy and the State in France.* Princeton: Princeton University Press, 1980.

Kerridge, Eric. *The Agricultural Revolution.* London: George Allen and Unwin, 1967.

———. "The Movement of Rent, 1540–1640." *Economic History Review,* 2d ser., 6, 1953: 16–34.

Kettler, David. "History and Theory in Ferguson's *Essay on the History of Civil Society:* A Reconsideration." *Political Theory* 5, 1977, 437–60.

Kula, Witold. *An Economic Theory of the Feudal System.* Trans. Lawrence Garner. London: New Left Books, 1976.

Laski, Harold. *The Rise of European Liberalism.* London: George Allen and Unwin, 1936.

Lazonick, William. "Karl Marx and Enclosures in England." *Review of Radical Political Economics* 6, 1974: 1–58.

Lefebvre, Georges. *The French Revolution from its Origins to 1793.* Trans. Elizabeth Moss Evanson. 2 vols. New York: Columbia University Press, 1962.

Lenman, Bruce. *An Economic History of Modern Scotland.* London: B. T. Batsford, 1977.

Lerner, Max. Introduction to *The Wealth of Nations,* by Adam Smith, ed. Edwin Cannan. New York: Modern Library, 1937.

Le Roy Ladurie, Emmanuel. *The Peasants of Languedoc.* Trans. John Day. Urbana: University of Illinois Press, 1974.

———. "A Reply to Professor Brenner." *Past and Present* 79, 1978: 55–59.

Letwin, William. *The Origins of Scientific Economics.* London: Methuen and Co., 1963.

Lindgren, J. Ralph. *The Social Philosophy of Adam Smith.* The Hague: Nijhoff, 1973.

Lublinskaya, A. D. *French Absolutism: The Crucial Phase, 1620–1629.* Trans. Brian Pearce. Cambridge: Cambridge University Press, 1968.

Lundberg, I. C. *Turgot's Unknown Translator.* The Hague: Nijhoff, 1964.

Luthy, Herbert. *From Calvin to Rousseau.* Trans. Salvator Attanasio. New York: Basic Books, 1970.

McLain, James. *The Economic Writings of Dupont de Nemours.* Newark: University of Delaware Press, 1977.

McNally, David. "Locke, Levellers, and Liberty: Property and Democracy in the Thought of the First Whigs." *History of Political Thought.* Forthcoming.

Macpherson, C. B. *The Political Theory of Possessive Individualism.* London: Oxford University Press, 1962.

———. Review of *Adam Smith's Politics: An Essay in Historiographic Revision,* by Donald Winch. *History of Political Economy* 11, 1979: 450–54.

Manning, Brian. *The English People and the English Revolution.* 1976. Reprint, Harmondsworth: Penguin, 1978.

Marczewski, Jan. "Some Aspects of the Economic Growth of France." *Economic Development and Cultural Change* 9, 1961: 369–86.

Meek, Ronald. "Adam Smith and the Classical Theory of Profit." In *Economics and Ideology and Other Essays.* London: Chapman and Hall, 1967.

———. "The Case of the French Physiocrats." In *Events, Ideology, and Economic Theory,* ed. Robert V. Eagly. Detroit, Mich.: Wayne State University Press, 1968.

———. *Economics and Ideology and Other Essays.* London: Chapman and Hall, 1967.

———. *Smith, Marx, and After.* London: Chapman and Hall, 1977.

———. *Studies in the Labour Theory of Value.* 2d ed. London: Lawrence and Wishart, 1973.

Methivier, Hubert. "A Century of Conflict: The Economic and Social Disorder of the 'Grand Siècle.'" In *France in Crisis, 1620–1675,* ed. and trans. P. J. Coveney, 64–77. London: Macmillan and Co., 1977.

Mingay, Gordon E. *English Landed Society in the Eighteenth Century.* London: Routledge and Kegan Paul, 1963.

———. *The Gentry: The Rise and Fall of a Ruling Class.* London: Longman Group, 1976.

———. "The Size of Farms in the Eighteenth Century." *Economic History Review,* 2d ser., 14, 1961–62: 469–88.

Miskimin, Harry. *The Economy of Early Renaissance Europe: 1300–1460.* Englewood Cliffs, N.J.: Prentice-Hall, 1969.

Mizuta, Hiroshi. "Moral Philosophy and Civil Society." In *Essays on Adam Smith,* ed. Andrew Skinner and Thomas Wilson, 114–31. Oxford: Oxford University Press, 1975.

Molinier, Jean. "L'Analyse globale de Boisguilbert ou l'ébauche de 'Tableau économique.'" In *Pierre de Boisguilbert ou la naissance de l'économie politique.* Paris: Institut National d'Etudes Démographiques, 1966.

Moore, Barrington, Jr. *Social Origins of Dictatorship and Democracy.* Boston: Beacon Press, 1966.

Moore, James. "The Social Background of Hume's Science of Nature." In *McGill Hume Studies,* ed. David Fate Norton, Nicholas Capaldi, and Wade L. Robinson, 23–41. San Diego: Austin Hill Press, 1976.

Moore, James. "Locke and the Scottish Jurists." Paper presented on John Locke and the political thought of the 1680s, Conference for the Study of Political Thought. Folger Shakespeare Library, Washington, D.C., 21–23 March, 1980.

Mousnier, Roland. "The Financial *Officiers* during the Fronde." In *France in Crisis, 1620–1675,* ed. and trans. P. J. Coveney, 136–68. London: Macmillan and Co., 1977.

Myint, Hla. *Theories of Welfare Economics.* New York: Augustus M. Kelley, 1965.

Neill, Thomas P. "Quesnay and Physiocracy." *Journal of the History of Ideas* 9, 1948: 153–72.

Norton, David Fate. *David Hume: Common-Sense Moralist, Sceptical Meta-physician*. Princeton: Princeton University Press, 1982.

————. "Hume's Common Sense Morality." *Canadian Journal of Philosophy* 5, 1975: 523–43.

Norton, David Fate, Capaldi, Nicholas, and Robinson, Wade L., eds. *Mc-Gill Hume Studies*. San Diego: Austin Hill Press, 1976.

O'Brien, Marie, and O'Brien, Conor Cruise. *A Concise History of Ireland*. 2d ed. London: Thames and Hudson, 1973.

O'Driscoll, Gerald P., ed. *Adam Smith and Modern Political Economy: Bicentennial Essays on The Wealth of Nations*. Ames: Iowa State University Press, 1979.

Outhwaite, R. B. *Inflation in Tudor and Early Stuart England*. London: Macmillan and Co., 1969.

Owen, J. B. "The Survival of Country Attitudes in the Eighteenth-Century House of Commons." In *Britain and the Netherlands*, ed. J. S. Bromley and E. H. Kossman. The Hague: Nijhoff, 1971.

Palm, Franklin Charles. *The Economic Policies of Richelieu*. 1922. Reprint, New York: Johnson Reprint Co., 1970.

Pauling, N. G. "The Employment Problem in Pre-Classical English Economic Thought." *Economic Record* 27, 1951, pp. 52–65.

Perroy, Edouard. "A l'origine d'une économie contractée: les crises du XIVe siècle." *Annales. Economies, Sociétés, Civilisations* 4, 1949: 167–82.

Phillips, Almarin. "The Tableau Economique as a Simple Leontief Model." *Quarterly Journal of Economics* 69, 1955: 137–44.

Phillipson, Nicholas. "Culture and Society in the Eighteenth-Century Province: The Case of Edinburgh and the Scottish Enlightenment." In *The University in Society*, ed. Lawrence Stone, 2: 407–48. Princeton: Princeton University Press, 1974.

————. "Scottish Public Opinion and the Union in the Age of Association." In *Scotland in the Age of Improvement*, ed. Nicholas Phillipson and Rosalind Mitchison, 125–47. Edinburgh: Edinburgh University Press, 1970.

————. "The Scottish Enlightenment." In *The Enlightenment in National Context*, ed. Ray Porter and Mikulas Teich, 19–40. Cambridge: Cambridge University Press, 1981.

Phillipson, Nicholas, and Mitchison, Rosalind, eds. *Scotland in the Age of Improvement*. Edinburgh: Edinburgh University Press, 1970.

Pocock, J. G. A. *The Machiavellian Moment: Florentine Political Thought and the Atlantic Republican Tradition*. Princeton: Princeton University Press, 1975.

————. *Politics, Language, and Time: Essays on Political Thought and History*. New York: Atheneum, 1971.

————. "A Reconsideration Impartially Considered." *History of Political Thought* 1, 1980: 541–45.

————, ed. The Political Works of James Harrington. Cambridge: Cambridge University Press, 1977.

————, ed. *Three British Revolutions: 1641, 1681, 1776*. Princeton: Princeton University Press, 1980.

Porshnev, Boris. "The Bourgeoisie and Feudal Absolutism in Seventeenth-Century France." In *France in Crisis, 1620–1675*, ed. and trans. P. J. Coveney, 103–35. London: Macmillan and Co., 1977.

———. "Popular Uprisings in France before the Fronde, 1623–1648." In *France in Crisis, 1620–1675*, ed. and trans. P. J. Coveney, 78–102. London: Macmillan and Co., 1977.

Postan, Michael. *Essays on Medieval Agriculture and General Problems of the Medieval Economy*. Cambridge: Cambridge University Press, 1973.

———. *The Medieval Economy and Society*. Harmondsworth: Penguin, 1975.

Rae, John. *Life of Adam Smith*. Introduction by Jacob Viner. 1895. Reprint, New York: Augustus M. Kelley, 1965.

Raphael, D. D. "The Impartial Spectator." In *Essays on Adam Smith*, ed. Andrew Skinner and Thomas Wilson, 83–99. Oxford: Oxford University Press, 1975.

Robbins, Caroline. *The Eighteenth-Century Commonwealthmen*. Cambridge, Mass.: Harvard University Press, 1959.

Roberts, Hazel Van Dyke. *Boisguilbert: Economist of the Reign of Louis XIV*. New York: Columbia University Press, 1935.

Robertson, John. "The Scottish Enlightenment at the Limits of the Civic Tradition." In *Wealth and Virtue: The Shaping of Political Economy in the Scottish Enlightenment*, ed. Istvan Hont and Michael Ignatieff. Cambridge: Cambridge University Press, 1983.

———. "Scottish Political Economy Beyond the Civic Tradition: Government and Economic Development in *The Wealth of Nations*." *History of Political Thought* 4, 1983: 45–82.

Robinson, Joan. "Prelude to a Critique of Economic Theory." *Oxford Economic Papers*, n. ser., 13, 1961: 53–58.

Roll, Eric. *A History of Economic Thought*. 4th ed. London: Faber and Faber, 1973.

Rosenburg, Nathan. "Adam Smith and Laissez-Faire Revisited." In *Adam Smith and Modern Political Economy: Bicentennial Essays on The Wealth of Nations*, ed. Gerald P. O'Driscoll, 19–34. Ames: Iowa State University Press, 1979.

———. "Adam Smith on Profits—Paradox Lost and Regained." In *Essays on Adam Smith*, ed. Andrew Skinner and Thomas Wilson, 377–89. Oxford: Oxford University Press, 1975.

———. "Some Institutional Aspects of the *Wealth of Nations*." *Journal of Political Economy* 68, 1960: 557–70.

Rothkrug, Lionel. *Opposition to Louis XIV: The Political and Social Origins of the French Enlightenment*. Princeton: Princeton University Press, 1965.

Routh, Guy. *The Origin of Economic Ideas*. London: Macmillan and Co., 1975.

Rubin, Isaac Ilyich. *A History of Economic Thought*. Trans. Donald Filtzer. London: Ink Links, 1979.

Salleron, Louis. "Boisguilbert, précurseur des physiocrates." In *Pierre de Boisguilbert ou la naissance de l'économie politique*. Paris: Institut National d'Etudes Démographiques, 1966.

Salmon, J. H. M. *Society in Crisis: France in the Sixteenth Century.* 1975. Reprint, London: Methuen and Co., 1979.

Samuels, Warren J. "The Physiocratic Theory of Economic Policy." *Quarterly Journal of Economics* 76, 1962: 145–62.

———. "The Physiocratic Theory of Property and the State." *Quarterly Journal of Economics* 75, 1961: 96–111.

Saville, John. "Primitive Accumulation and Early Industrialization in Britain." *Socialist Register,* 1969: 247–71.

Schneider, Louis. "Human Nature and Social Circumstance." In *Adam Smith and Modern Political Economy: Bicentennial Essays on The Wealth of Nations,* ed. Gerald P. O'Driscoll, 44–67. Ames: Iowa State Press, 1979.

Schumpeter, Joseph. *Economic Doctrine and Method.* Trans. R. Aris. London: George Allen and Unwin, 1954.

———. *History of Economic Analysis.* New York: Oxford University Press, 1954.

Schwoerer, Lois G. "The Bill of Rights: Epitome of the Revolution of 1688–89." In *Three British Revolutions: 1641, 1688, 1776,* ed. J. G. A. Pocock. Princeton: Princeton University Press, 1980.

Scott, W. R. *Adam Smith as Student and Professor.* 1873. Reprint, New York: Augustus M. Kelley, 1965.

———. *Francis Hutcheson.* Cambridge: Cambridge University Press, 1900.

Skinner, Andrew. *A System of Social Science: Papers Relating to Adam Smith.* Oxford: Oxford University Press, 1979.

Skinner, Andrew, and Wilson, Thomas, eds. *Essays on Adam Smith.* Oxford: Oxford University Press, 1975.

Skinner, Quentin. *The Foundations of Modern Political Thought.* Vol. 1, *The Renaissance.* Vol. 2, *The Age of Reformation.* Cambridge: Cambridge University Press, 1978.

Skocpol, Theda. *States and Social Revolutions.* Cambridge: Cambridge University Press, 1979.

Smith, H. F. Russell. *Harrington and his Oceana.* Cambridge: Cambridge University Press, 1914.

Smout, T. C. *A History of the Scottish People, 1560–1830.* Glasgow: William Collins Sons and Co., 1969.

———. "Scottish Landowners and Economic Growth, 1650–1850." *Scottish Journal of Political Economy* 11, 1964: 218–34.

Soboul, Albert. *The French Revolution.* Trans. Alan Forrest. 2 vols. London: New Left Books, 1974.

Speck, W. A. *Stability and Strife: England, 1714–1760.* London: Edward Arnold, 1977.

Spengler, J. J. "The Physiocrats and Say's Law of Markets." Part 2. *Journal of Political Economy* 53, 1945: 317–47.

———. "Richard Cantillon: First of the Moderns." Parts 1, 2. *Journal of Political Economy* 62, 1954: 281–95, 406–24.

Spiegel, Henry William. *The Growth of Economic Thought.* Durham, N.C.: Duke University Press, 1971.

Stigler, George. "Smith's Travels on the Ship of State." In *Essays on Adam Smith,* ed. Andrew Skinner and Thomas Wilson, 237–46. Oxford: Oxford University Press, 1975.

Stone, Lawrence. *The Causes of the English Revolution, 1529–1642.* London: Routledge and Kegan Paul, 1972.

———. *The Crisis of the Aristocracy, 1558–1641.* Abridged ed. Oxford: Oxford University Press, 1967.

———. "State Control in Sixteenth-Century England." *Economic History Review,* 14, 1947: 103–20.

Strauss, E. *Sir William Petty: Portrait of a Genius.* London: Bodley Head, 1954.

Supple, Barry. *Commercial Crisis and Change in England.* Cambridge: Cambridge University Press, 1959.

Tawney, R. H. *The Agrarian Problem in the Sixteenth Century.* 1912. Reprint, New York: Harper and Row, 1967.

Tawney, R. H., and Powers, Eileen, eds. *Tudor Economic Documents.* New York: Barnes and Noble, 1963.

Taylor, George V. "The Paris Bourse on the Eve of the Revolution, 1781–1789." *American Historical Review* 67, 1962: 951–77.

———. "Types of Capitalism in Eighteenth-Century France." *English Historical Review* 79, 1964: 478–97.

Taylor, W. L. *Francis Hutcheson and David Hume as Predecessors of Adam Smith.* Durham, N.C.: Duke University Press, 1965.

Thirsk, Joan. *Economic Policy and Projects.* Oxford: Oxford University Press, 1978.

Thompson, E. P. "The Moral Economy of the English Crowd in the Eighteenth Century." *Past and Present* 50, 1971: 76–136.

———. "The Peculiarities of the English." In *The Poverty of Theory and Other Essays,* 35–91. London: Merlin Press, 1978.

———. *The Poverty of Theory and Other Essays.* London: Merlin Press, 1978.

———. *Whigs and Hunters: The Origin of the Black Act.* New York: Pantheon, 1975.

Thompson, F. M. L. "Comments." In *Aspects of Capital Investment in Great Britain 1750–1850,* ed. J. P. P. Higgins and Sidney Pollard, 184–88. London: Methuen and Co., 1971.

———. "The Social Distribution of Landed Property in England Since the Sixteenth Century." *Economic History Review,* 2d ser., 19, 1966: 505–17.

Toth, Kathleen. "Interpretation in Political Theory: The Case of Harrington." *Review of Politics* 37, 1975: 317–39.

Tribe, Keith. *Land, Labour, and Economic Discourse.* London: Routledge and Kegan Paul, 1978.

Trimmer, Peter. "The Turnip, the New Husbandry, and the English Agricultural Revolution." *Quarterly Journal of Economics* 83, 1969: 375–95.

Underdown, David. *Revel, Riot, and Rebellion: Popular Politics and Culture in England, 1603–1660.* Oxford: Oxford University Press, 1985.

Vaughn, Karen Iversen. *John Locke: Economist and Social Scientist.* Chicago: University of Chicago Press, 1980.

Viner, Jacob. "Guide to John Rae's *Life of Adam Smith.*" In *Life of Adam Smith,* by John Rae. New York: Augustus M. Kelley, 1965.

Walter, John, and Wrightson, Keith. "Dearth and the Social Order in Early Modern England." *Past and Present* 71, 1976: 22–42.

Warden, Blair. "The Commonwealth Kidney of Algernon Sidney." *Journal of British Studies* 24, 1985: 1–40.

Ware, Norman J. "The Physiocrats: A Study in Economic Rationalization." *American Economic Review* 21, 1931: 607–19.

Webster, Charles. *The Great Instauration: Science, Medicine, and Reform, 1626–1660.* London: Duckworth and Co., 1975.

Weeks, John. *Capital and Exploitation.* Princeton: Princeton University Press, 1981.

Weulerrse, Georges. *Le Mouvement physiocratique en France (de 1756 à 1770).* 2 vols. 1910. Reprint, Paris: Editions Mouton, 1968.

Wills, Gary. "Benevolent Adam Smith." *New York Review of Books,* 9 February 1978, 40–43.

Wilson, Charles, and Parker, Geoffrey, eds. *An Introduction to the Sources of European Economic History, 1500–1800.* Vol. 1. London: Methuen and Co., 1977.

Winch, Donald. *Adam Smith's Politics: An Essay in Historiographic Revision.* Cambridge: Cambridge University Press, 1978.

Wood, Neal. *John Locke and Agrarian Capitalism.* Berkeley: University of California Press, 1984.

———. *The Politics of Locke's Philosophy.* Berkeley: University of California Press, 1983.

Zagorin, Perez. *The Court and the Country: The Beginning of the English Revolution of the Seventeenth Century.* New York: Atheneum, 1970.

Index

321

Compositor: G & S Typesetters
Text: 10/12 Plantin
Display: Plantin
Printer: Braun-Brumfield, Inc.
Binder: Braun-Brumfield, Inc.